Romantic Empiricism

Romantic Empiricism

*Nature, Art, and Ecology from
Herder to Humboldt*

DALIA NASSAR

Oxford University Press is a department of the University of Oxford. It furthers
the University's objective of excellence in research, scholarship, and education
by publishing worldwide. Oxford is a registered trade mark of Oxford University
Press in the UK and certain other countries.

Published in the United States of America by Oxford University Press
198 Madison Avenue, New York, NY 10016, United States of America.

© Oxford University Press 2022

All rights reserved. No part of this publication may be reproduced, stored in
a retrieval system, or transmitted, in any form or by any means, without the
prior permission in writing of Oxford University Press, or as expressly permitted
by law, by license, or under terms agreed with the appropriate reproduction
rights organization. Inquiries concerning reproduction outside the scope of the
above should be sent to the Rights Department, Oxford University Press, at the
address above.

You must not circulate this work in any other form
and you must impose this same condition on any acquirer.

Library of Congress Control Number: 2022934456
ISBN 978-0-19-009543-7

DOI: 10.1093/oso/9780190095437.001.0001

For Clara

No one is prepared to grasp that, both in nature and in art,
the sole and supreme process is the creation of form.
J. W. von Goethe

Contents

Acknowledgments — xi
Abbreviations — xiii
Note on Referencing — xvii

Introduction: Finding Romantic Empiricism — 1
  I.1 The Idea of Romantic Empiricism — 1
  I.2 Mapping the Terrain: Romantic Empiricism in Context — 2
  I.3 Romantic Empiricism: Methodology and Goals — 5
  I.4 Kant and Romantic Empiricism — 6
  I.5 Herder, Goethe, and Humboldt — 9

1. Setting the Stage: Kant and the *Critique of the Power of Judgment* — 13
  1.1 Reflecting Judgment: A First Look — 15
  1.2 The Analogical Structure of Teleological Judgment — 22
  1.3 The Place of Analogy in the Eighteenth Century — 28
  1.4 Kant's Critique of Analogy — 33
  1.5 The Inexplicability of Organization — 36
  1.6 The Antinomy of Teleological Judgment — 43
  1.7 Teleological Judgment, Intuitive Understanding, and the Goals of Science — 49

2. The Hermeneutics of Nature: Herder on Animal and Human Worlds — 53
  2.1 The Problem with "Nature" — 55
  2.2 Nature's Many Directions — 57
  2.3 Herder's Hermeneutics — 60
  2.4 Human and Animal Languages — 67
  2.5 The Analogical Structure of Cognition — 77
  2.6 Herder's Naturalism — 82
  2.7 A Dynamic Conception of Nature — 84

3. The Science of Describing: Herder, Goethe, and the *Hauptform* — 86
  3.1 Force versus Form: Historical Perspectives — 89
  3.2 Herder and the *Hauptform* — 91
  3.3 Goethe and the Intermaxillary Bone — 96
  3.4 Description, Explanation, and Necessity — 102

4. Aesthetic Education and the Transformation of the Scientist — 104
   4.1 Problems of Knowledge: A First Look — 107
   4.2 Goethe's Aesthetic Education — 110
   4.3 *Naturegemäße Darstellung* — 116
   4.4 The Structure and Aims of *The Metamorphosis of Plants* — 119
   4.5 The Question of "Seeing" — 127
   4.6 Mediating Elements — 131
   4.7 The Poetic Metamorphosis of the Plant — 137

5. Intuitive Judgment and Goethe's Ethics of Knowledge — 146
   5.1 Intuitive Judgment — 149
   5.2 The *Urphänomen* — 154
   5.3 Schiller on the *Urphänomen* and Rational Empiricism — 163
   5.4 Goethe's Environmental Ethics and the Source of Responsibility — 166

6. Organism and Environment: The Aesthetic Foundations of Humboldt's Ecological Insight — 176
   6.1 Thinking Observation: Goethe and the Origins of Humboldt's Methodology — 179
   6.2 External Teleology: Kant's Either/Or — 185
   6.3 Conditions Rather Than Causes: Goethe's Critique of External Teleology — 187
   6.4 The *Urformen* of Plants: Capturing the Trees *and* the Forest — 192
   6.5 Plant Forms and Contexts — 197
   6.6 The Physiognomy of Plants: The Physiognomy of Nature — 206
   6.7 Humboldt's Ecological Insight — 210

7. Embodied Cognition: Humboldt and the Art of Science — 212
   7.1 "Truth to Nature": Humboldt's Understanding of Truth in Art — 217
   7.2 Poetry versus Painting: Lessing, Schiller, and Humboldt — 223
   7.3 Embodied Landscapes: Schiller's "Walk" and Humboldt's *Views* — 228
   7.4 Steppes, Deserts, Jungles, and Waterfalls: Humboldt's Embodied Aesthetics — 232
   7.5 The Ecological Significance of Embodied Aesthetics — 237
   7.6 The Moral Significance of Embodied Aesthetics — 241

Conclusion: The Relevance of Romantic Empiricism — 245

Notes — 249
Works Cited — 287
Index — 299

Acknowledgments

There are many people and organizations who have played a crucial role in the development of this book. I want first to acknowledge the Australian Research Council, Discovery Project DP160103769 (2016–2018), the Humboldt Foundation grant for experienced researchers (2019–2020), and the Sydney Social Sciences and Humanities Advanced Research Council, Ultimate Peer Review grant (2018).

I also want to acknowledge a number of highly innovative and research initiatives at the University of Sydney, which have allowed me to deepen and expand my work in unexpected and exciting ways: Sydney Intellectual History Network, Theories and Conceptions of Life from the 19th Century to the Present, and the Multi-Species Justice research initiative. In this regard, I especially want to thank Danielle Celermajer, Stephen Gaukroger, Daniela Helbig, Jennifer Milam, Cat Moir, David Schlosberg, Michelle St. Anne, Dinesh Wadiwel, Thom van Dooren, Anik Waldow, Christine Winter, and Genevieve Wright. There is no doubt that this book has been shaped by the workshops, reading groups, and conversations that I have had with them over the years.

I also wish to thank the many wonderful thinkers from whose work I've learned and whose penetrating feedback has nudged me in new directions: Iain McCalman, Monica Gagliano, Sebastian Gardner, Moira Gatens, Craig Holdrege, Nigel Hoffmann, Simon Lumsden, Jennifer Mensch, Lydia Moland, Paul Redding, Ulrich Schlösser, Niels Weidtmann, and my friend and coeditor on other projects, Kristin Gjesdal. I want to thank Eric Watkins and Clinton Tolley and the PhD students in the history of philosophy colloquium at the University of California, San Diego. Their generous comments on an early version of the manuscript were immense, and I am grateful for their continued support. And, last—but not least—I want to thank Margaret Barbour, whose openness and interest have allowed us to undertake exciting new research together.

I am also grateful to many friends, with whom I've had some of the best conversations over the past years, especially Enite Giovanelli, Tanja Rall, Stefan Rall, and Kristin Funke. I want to thank Anselma Murswiek for permission to use her wonderful painting, and my parents, Rosette and Talal Nassar. I especially want to thank Luke Fischer, my favorite conversation partner and most incisive editor.

Abbreviations

Johann Wolfgang von Goethe

FA   *Sämtliche Werke. Briefe, Tagebücher und Gespräche* (Frankfurter Ausgabe). Edited by H. Birus et al. Frankfurt am Main: Deutscher Klassiker Verlag, 1985–2003.

HA   *Werke* (Hamburger Ausgabe). Edited by E. Trunz et al. Hamburg: Christian Wegner Verlag, 1949–1971.

LA   *Die Schriften zur Naturwissenschaft* (Leopoldina Ausgabe). Edited by D. Kuhn et al. Weimar: Hermann Böhlaus Nachfolger, 1947–.

MA   *Sämtliche Werke nach Epochen seines Schaffens* (Münchner Ausgabe). Edited by K. Richter et al. Munich: Carl Hanser, 1985–1998.

TAG   *Tagebücher*. Edited by W. Albrecht and E. Zehm. Stuttgart: Metzler, 2000.

WA   *Goethes Werke* (Weimarer Ausgabe). Edited by P. Raabe et al. Weimar: Hermann Böhlau, 1887–1919.

Johann Gottfried Herder

FHA   *Werke in zehn Bänden* (Frankfurter Ausgabe). Edited by Jürgen Brummack and Martin Bollacher. Frankfurt am Main: Deutscher Klassiker Verlag, 1985–2000.

HPW   *Philosophical Writings*. Edited and translated by Michael Forster. Cambridge: Cambridge University Press, 2002.

SW   *Sämtliche Werke*. Edited by Bernard Suphan. Berlin: Weidmann, 1877–1913.

SWA   *Selected Writings on Aesthetics*. Edited and translated by Gregory Moore. Princeton: Princeton University Press, 2006.

Alexander von Humboldt

CE 1   *Cosmos: A Sketch of a Physical Description of the Universe*. Volume 1. Edited and translated by E. C. Otté, with an introduction by Nicolaas Rupke. Baltimore: Johns Hopkins University Press, 1997. [Original: London: Bohn, 1849–1851.]

CE 2   *Cosmos: A Sketch of a Physical Description of the Universe.* Volume 2. Edited and translated by E. C. Otté, with an introduction by Michael Dettelbach. Baltimore: Johns Hopkins University Press, 1997. [Original: London: Bohn, 1850].

CE 3   *Cosmos: A Sketch of a Physical Description of the Universe.* Volume 3. Edited and translated by E. C. Otté. London: Bohn, 1851.

CE 5   *Cosmos: A Sketch of a Physical Description of the Universe.* Volume 5. Edited and translated by E. C. Otté and W. S. Dallas. London: Bohn, 1858.

DA   *Darmstädter Ausgabe.* Edited with commentary by Hanno Beck. Darmstadt: Wissenschaftliche Buchgesellschaft, 2018.

JB   *Die Jugendbriefe Alexander von Humboldts 1787–1799.* Edited by Ilse Jahn and Fritz Lange. Berlin: Akademie Verlag, 1973.

KNS   *Essay on the Kingdom of New Spain.* Volume 1: *A Critical Edition.* Edited with an introduction by Vera M. Kutzinski and Ottmar Ette. Chicago: University of Chicago Press, 2019.

Kosmos   *Kosmos. Entwurf einer physischen Weltbeschreibung.* Edited by Ottmar Ette and Oliver Lubrich. Frankfurt am Main: Eichhorn Verlag, 2004.

VN   *Views of Nature.* Edited by Stephen T. Jackson and Laura Dassow Walls. Translated by Mark W. Person. Chicago: University of Chicago Press, 2014.

Alexander von Humboldt and Aimé Bonpland

EGP   *Essay on the Geography of Plants.* Edited with an introduction by Stephen T. Jackson. Translated (from French) by Sylvie Romanowski. Chicago: University of Chicago Press, 2009.

PNR   *Personal Narrative of Travels to the Equinoctial Regions of America, During the Years 1799–1804.* Edited and translated by Thomasina Ross. 3 volumes. London: Bohm, 1852–1853.

PNW   *Personal Narrative of Travels to the Equinoctial Regions of America, During the Years 1799–1804.* Edited and translated by Helen Maria Williams. 7 volumes. London: Longman, Hurst, Rees, Orme, and Brown, 1814–1829.

Immanuel Kant

AA   *Gesammelte Schriften.* Edited by Preußische Akademie der Wissenschaft. Berlin: de Gruyter, 1902–.

Friedrich Schiller

NA   *Schillers Werke. Nationalausgabe.* Edited by Julius Petersen et al. Weimar: Hermann Böhlaus Nachfolger, 1943–2010.

Friedrich von Schlegel

KFSA   *Kritische Friedrich-Schlegel-Ausgabe.* Edited by E. Behler, J. J. Anstett, and H. Eichner. Paderborn: Schöningh, 1958–2006.

Note on Referencing

I have mostly used the FA edition of Goethe's work, as it is more easily accessible than the other editions. However, references to Goethe's *On Morphology* (*Zur Morphologie*) are to MA, because in this edition the works appear chronologically, according to their date of publication, and not (as is the case in FA), according to the date on which they were written. I have also referenced LA or WA in instances where a work does not appear in FA.

With regard to titles of works, I provide the English and German titles in my first reference, while in all following references I provide only the English title. In the case of Humboldt, however, I do the opposite: I refer to the German title (with an English translation in parentheses at the first mention), and only use the German title thereafter, unless I am specifically citing an English translation of Humboldt's works. This has to do with the fact that Humboldt played a role in translating his work—whether from French to German, or from German to English—such that some of the translations often include passages not in the original, use terms that were not employed in the original, or offer interpretations that further elucidate ideas expressed in the original.

Introduction

Finding Romantic Empiricism

I.1. The Idea of Romantic Empiricism

Romantic empiricism: two words that are not usually placed side by side, and that seem to suggest opposing philosophical views and tendencies. Romanticism is often associated with idealism and taken to imply a turn to the subject and a focus on the subjective conditions of knowledge. The romantic approach to nature thus tends to be regarded as a form of subjective constructivism. Furthermore, romanticism is identified with a strong interest in the arts and aesthetic experience. Empiricism, by contrast, is outwardly focused and bottom-up, in its view that all knowledge must begin with what is seen or experienced. In addition, some forms of empiricism appear from an idealist perspective to be naive: they underestimate the subject's creative role in knowledge, or they do not adequately differentiate between what is given to the senses and what is known through the understanding. Finally, contrary to romanticism, empiricism rarely pays attention to the arts and their epistemic significance. In short: romanticism and empiricism hardly resemble one another, and to place them side by side is to offer a paradox of sorts.

The thesis of this book is that romantic empiricism is not an oxymoron but refers to a philosophical tradition that deserves renewed attention today. While the roots of romantic empiricism can be traced back to mid-eighteenth-century France, the tradition achieved its greatest philosophical sophistication and rigor in Germany in the late eighteenth and early nineteenth centuries. Inspired by the questions and concerns articulated by Georges-Louis Leclerc de Buffon (1707–1788) and elaborated by Denis Diderot (1713–1784), thinkers from Johann Gottfried Herder to Alexander von Humboldt developed a distinctive methodological approach to the study of nature—an approach that drew significantly on the arts and aesthetic experience. Through this aesthetic science, the romantic empiricists were able to deepen and expand their understanding of nature and, as I will show, contribute to the emergence of ecology and ecological thinking more generally.

These thinkers are *romantic* not only because they were contemporaries of the Jena romantics, but also, and more significantly, because they developed an approach to the study of nature in which the arts and aesthetic experience play a crucial role. They are romantic, in other words, because they recognized that artistic capacities and devices can transform the way in which we *perceive* and *think* about the world and ourselves within it. They are *empiricist* because they emphasize observation and seek to remain with the phenomena. They are critical of systematic approaches to nature that begin with an abstract idea or postulate. Instead, they begin with what is seen and sensed. But they depart from mainstream empiricism in two crucial ways. On the one hand, like the rationalists, their aim is to arrive at the necessary, the idea, within the phenomenon. On the other hand, and like the idealists, they recognize the creative role of the knower.

However, it is important to emphasize that this group of thinkers was not simply synthesizing various aspects from different philosophical schools or methodologies. Rather, they developed a coherent approach to the study of nature, one which does not simply map onto more well-known approaches. Furthermore, their approach was not only theoretically articulated, but was also developed through their practice. In fact, their practice often influenced and transformed their theory. By practice I mean both the study of nature and their practice as literary critics, artists, appreciators of art, travelers, and explorers. It would be no exaggeration to describe the romantic empiricists as thinkers for whom theory and practice were intertwined and deeply aligned: the one realized in and shaped by the other. Who, then, were the romantic empiricists?

I.2. Mapping the Terrain: Romantic Empiricism in Context

Although the nineteenth century is often identified with the exploitation and destruction of nature and culture (Indigenous cultures in particular), it also involved what Sankar Muthu has described as a "historically anomalous and understudied episode" in social thought, a moment in which philosophers, artists, and scientists turned a critical eye on the dominant views of nature and sought to offer alternative accounts of the natural world and the human place within it.[1] This period of critical engagement, which reached its apex in Germany, remains singular in both its breadth and its philosophical rigor. It was a time when philosophers, scientists, and artists worked together to investigate the metaphysical and epistemological dimensions of the human relation to the natural world and determine their ethical implications.

While this focus on the study of nature, and the human place within it, was defining for German philosophies at the turn of the nineteenth century, the methodologies they employed were not always aligned and, in some instances, radically differed. Friedrich Schelling, for instance, sought to "construct" nature on the basis of a priori principles, arguing (on systematic grounds) that human culture develops out of nature.[2] This contrasts with philosophies that questioned the goal of systematicity and the methodology of construction, which are perhaps epitomized in Friedrich Schlegel's statement that "it is equally deadly for the spirit to have a system and not to have one" (KFSA 2, 173, no. 53). And it also contrasts with nonspeculative approaches to nature and mind (culture), which emphasize experience and observation and seek to understand both nature and culture in light of a larger (historical) context—as in the work of Herder.

The romantic empiricists, as the name suggests, belonged to the latter group, and the four figures that this book investigates are Kant (1724–1804), especially his *Critique of the Power of Judgment* (1790), Goethe (1749–1832), Herder (1744–1803), and Alexander von Humboldt (1769–1859). The central claim of *Romantic Empiricism: Nature, Art, and Ecology from Herder to Humboldt* is that these thinkers developed a philosophically sophisticated empiricist approach to the natural world by working together—sometimes as rivals, but more often than not as teachers and collaborators. While Herder, Goethe, and Humboldt clearly belong to the romantic empiricist tradition, Kant's place within it is more ambivalent, as I will discuss shortly.

Kant, Herder, Goethe, and Humboldt are widely regarded as major figures of the late Enlightenment, Weimar classicism, and romanticism.[3] While Kant continues to be considered the most important philosopher of the modern period, over the last few years Herder has received ample attention, leading Marion Heinz to describe the current interest as a "Herder Renaissance."[4] Similarly, Goethe's philosophical significance has been recently highlighted—especially by Eckart Förster[5]—while Andrea Wulf's 2015 book on Humboldt is just one example of the works that have drawn attention to his important philosophical legacy.[6]

However, these figures are rarely studied side by side and seldom considered as participating in one philosophical project.[7] In fact, the opposite is usually the case: Kant and Herder are often depicted as rivals,[8] while Kant and Goethe are interpreted as contemporaries who misunderstood one another's work.[9] Even in the case of Herder and Goethe, who cofounded the Sturm und Drang movement in the late 1760s, little attention has been paid to connections in their later writings or the similarities in their approaches to the natural world.[10] In turn, while Humboldt's link to the others is always acknowledged, it is seldom comprehensively discussed.[11]

Why might this be the case? For one, the idea that an empiricist tradition emerged in the midst of the era of German idealism sounds, at least at first hearing, odd. Furthermore, although there has been a significant rise of interest in the philosophies of nature that emerged in Germany around 1800, little work has focused on the *methodologies* that underpin these philosophies. Precisely because we assume that all philosophies in Germany at the turn of the nineteenth century were idealist *in some way*, we do not make the effort to examine their methodologies or consider how their methodologies may have varied.[12]

Furthermore, in the history of philosophy, as well as in German studies, romanticism is typically identified with the Jena romantics—the Schlegel brothers, their journal, the *Athenäum*, as well as the regular contributors to their journal, Friedrich Schleiermacher, Friedrich von Hardenberg (Novalis), Ludwig Tieck, and (sometimes also) Schelling. Thinkers such as Herder and Goethe—who certainly *influenced* the romantics[13]—are usually regarded as participating in different, sometimes opposed, traditions. This is above all the case with Goethe, the great representative of Weimar classicism.[14] Accordingly, the idea that Goethe—not to mention Kant, Herder, and Humboldt—was a *romantic* simply sounds wrong.[15]

While from one perspective, the identification of romanticism with Jena romanticism is perfectly acceptable, from another, it is limiting and unnecessary. For it implies, first, that romanticism is a historical moment that is long past and, second, that the ideas that motivated romanticism were *only embodied* by these few thinkers. Neither claim can withstand scrutiny.

Let us consider Friedrich Schlegel's famous definition of "the romantic imperative," as articulated in *Athenäums-Fragment* 586. Schlegel writes: "All nature and science should become art—[and all] art should become nature and science" (KFSA 16, 134, no. 586). In formulating the romantic imperative, Schlegel was clearly inspired by Herder and Goethe (and perhaps also

Kant) and can in some sense be regarded as a member of this tradition.[16] However, while Herder, Goethe, and Humboldt sought to *realize* the "romantic imperative"—before Schlegel had articulated it—through a sustained engagement with the natural world and the natural sciences, Schlegel's interest in the study of nature was sporadic. Put differently, while Schlegel is famous for formulating the romantic imperative, he was neither the first to establish it as a goal nor the one to bring it to fruition. Rather, and as I hope to show in the following chapters, "the romantic imperative" was widespread before Schlegel gave it a name, *and* it was practiced by Herder, Goethe, and Humboldt. This is not to say that Herder, Goethe, and Humboldt were the *only* romantic empiricists; rather, they are the most exemplary representatives of this tradition.

I.3. Romantic Empiricism: Methodology and Goals

Kant's, Herder's, Goethe's, and Humboldt's search for a new methodology was motivated, on the one hand, by the desire to acknowledge nature's diversity and the utter uniqueness of natural phenomena and, on the other, by the sense that these phenomena are closely interconnected and transform over time, such that they can only be understood in their (historical and geographical) relatedness. Thus, their project emerged in response to the perennial philosophical problem of the relation between the one and the many, unity and diversity, but it had the advantage of hindsight: they agreed that the two rival schools of philosophy, rationalism and empiricism, had failed to respond to this problem, and only an approach that could wed these two methodologies (i.e., rationalism and empiricism) would have any hope of success.

As I have already noted, their methodological considerations were not (always) purely theoretical. Goethe and Humboldt were practicing scientists, who developed their approaches through sustained empirical research and aesthetic experience and education. Herder was a literary critic, a historian, and perhaps the first anthropologist, whose approach to nature emerged through his work in hermeneutics. Accordingly, their philosophical perspectives were not developed in a purely theoretical way, but through practice and application. They were, moreover, familiar with advances in the empirical sciences and contributed, theoretically or practically, to methodological questions underlying empirical research. All four were innovators in various empirical fields: Herder and Kant contributed to natural history, geography, and anthropology, Goethe developed comparative morphology, and Humboldt founded plant geography. And, as I will argue, they all played a crucial role in the emergence of ecology, broadly construed.

Specifically, the romantic empiricists' distinctive approach allowed them to develop a capacious understanding of nature and natural relations—one in which natural beings appear as dialogical, sensitive, and responsive, and in which nature as a whole appears as a dynamic context of ongoing development and collaboration. It is this expansive approach to science, which can be traced back to Herder's notion of animal "worlds" and Humboldt's "physiognomy of nature," that enabled the emergence of the discipline of ecology. What they saw—and what their predecessors had not seen—was that living beings both inhabit their world and are inhabited by their world. In other words, there is a deeply dynamic and reciprocal relationship between a living being and its environment, one which some two hundred years after the romantic empiricists we continue to find difficult to understand and convey. As I will show, the romantic empiricists arrived at these crucial insights through *aesthetic means and methods*. In short, the foundations of an ecological understanding of nature are aesthetic.

Furthermore, the romantic empiricists developed an ecological understanding of the enterprise of knowledge. That is, their conceptualization and practice of knowledge were founded on an ecological model. Knowledge is dialogical, responsive, context-sensitive, and collaborative. It demands continuous practice and education and places the knower under significant obligations. By conceiving of the process of knowledge itself as ecological, the romantic empiricists challenge us to rethink our ideals and practices of knowing and to reexamine the relationship between epistemology, ontology, and ethics. It is here that the contemporary relevance of romantic empiricism lies.

I.4. Kant and Romantic Empiricism

As I indicated previously, Kant can only be regarded as a romantic empiricist with significant qualification. After all, he is the philosopher of the a priori, and to describe him as an "empiricist" of any kind would certainly have irked him. In what sense, then, does he contribute to this tradition?

To begin with, it is important to highlight that it is specifically Kant's *Critique of the Power of Judgment* that can be regarded as part of this tradition.

However, even in that work, Kant makes statements that appear to challenge the view—which I have identified with romantic empiricism—that art has the power to transform and enrich knowledge. After all, Kant agrees with Edmund Burke's distinction between aesthetic pleasure and cognition. Both argue (for different reasons) that aesthetic pleasure is noncognitive, and thus cannot contribute to our understanding of nature. To this end, they contend that as soon as we have cognitive insight into nature (as a botanist does in relation to a plant), the experience of aesthetic pleasure disappears.

Despite Kant's ambivalence toward romantic empiricism, in the third *Critique* he takes a significant step in that direction. In so doing, he explicates the reasons behind this step as well as the challenges of taking it. He articulates these challenges in both methodological and epistemological terms, homing in on a problem that Buffon had formulated some two decades earlier.

In 1766, Buffon explained that a key problem facing the student of nature lies in a dissonance between our cognitive faculties and the processes of nature. While our intellect proceeds linearly—we apprehend one object, then another, then another, and so on—nature does not. Rather, Buffon writes, nature "does not take a single step except to go in all directions; in marching forward, she extends to the sides and above."[17] We see objects as separate and grasp relations along a linear causal nexus: one thing moves and causes another to move. In nature, however, objects are interrelated, and relations are manifold and multidirectional. How are we to overcome this epistemological incommensurability?

Kant rearticulated this difficulty in the third *Critique*, arguing that the reason we fail to understand living beings has to do with the character of our cognitive faculties. The fact that we proceed from one object to the next means that we can only grasp a *certain kind* of whole, a whole that is made up of separate, preexisting parts. A clock is one such whole: the bits and pieces that make up the clock are produced separately. When they are put together, we have a clock.

Living beings are not wholes of this sort. Their various parts—the heart, lungs, veins, and so on—do not emerge separately from one another. Rather, they emerge in relation to one another and as parts of a living body. This reveals a certain circularity in the structure of living beings: the parts exist only through the whole and the whole exists only through the parts. And this circularity, Kant concludes, makes it impossible for us to properly grasp them.

In this way Kant (and Buffon before him) explicated how and why our cognitive tendencies lead us to apprehend the world as composed of separate objects, whose relations are exclusively linear. He also explicated the *kind* of unity that we appear to be incapable of grasping. In so doing, Kant laid out the epistemological and methodological challenges facing any attempt to grasp nature as an integrated unity—challenges that the romantic empiricists sought to overcome.

But Kant did more than simply point to challenges. By placing "beauty and biology" side by side in the third *Critique*, he drew a connection between aesthetic experience and the study of nature, locating this connection in the reflecting form of judgment.[18] The implication is that the same form of judging that we employ in our aesthetic encounter with nature is also at work in our cognitive encounter with nature. When reflecting judgment turns to understanding the natural world, however, it does not result in pleasure (as it does in aesthetic experience). Still, like the noncognitive (i.e., aesthetic) form of reflecting judgment, it does not proceed from the a priori concept or principle to the observed object. Rather, as Kant puts it, reflecting judgment seeks to "find the universal for the particular" (AA 20, 211). Its procedure, then, embodies the bottom-up approach to the study of nature that underlies romantic empiricism.

Importantly, when applied to the study of nature, reflecting judgment becomes analogical. This is because it proceeds on the assumption that nature is a work of art, or, as Kant famously puts it, it proceeds by regarding nature *as if* it were a work of art. In other words, reflecting judgment (in this mode) compares nature with art, and in so doing, sees the one *in and through* the other, sees nature *as* art. Only in this way, Kant contends, can we begin to order the natural world (arrive at a "system" of nature) *and* grasp the structure of organized beings.

Underlying Kant's turn to the analogy between nature and art is the view that we can discern organization in nature only if we conceive of nature in terms of *forms*. After all, the work of comparing requires forms to compare, forms through which we can discern similarities and distinctions, and thereby draw connections. Furthermore, by regarding organized beings as forms in the way that artworks are forms (expressions of a coherent unity), we are able to see them not as *outcomes* of contingently connected parts, but as integrated unities, which—like a piece of music—are inseparable from their various parts (tone, rhythm, tempo, etc.) but which are also irreducible to these parts (a piece of music is not reducible to any of its tones, for instance).

The different parts, in turn, are only meaningful within this unity—as parts of this whole. Accordingly, the analogy with art enables a new way of seeing nature—a way that aims to overcome the challenges that Kant (and Buffon) had outlined.

While Kant's move to develop a methodology based on analogy and form was hesitant and one that he did not clearly embrace,[19] his contemporaries—schooled in the works of Buffon and others in the French tradition—had already for some time been concerned with the questions that prompted Kant's introduction of reflective judgment: how can we develop a natural history that takes account of nature's diversity without overlooking the significant relations between various beings? And how can we grasp organization within nature?

I.5. Herder, Goethe, and Humboldt

In the 1770s, Herder came to the same conclusions that Kant would later reach: it is only via analogy that we can discern unity in diversity, because it is only by seeing one thing through another that we can see how it is both like and unlike the other. Herder, however, took his argument on the role of analogy further, claiming that *cognition* itself is analogical. Specifically, he contends that the relationship between our various cognitive faculties (sensibility, imagination, and understanding) is analogical: they not only *work* together, but *also* intimate, anticipate, and approximate one another. His claim is that it is only if what is given to sensibility *implicitly* contains the image of the imagination, and it is only if the image similarly *implicitly* contains the concept of the understanding, that we can properly grasp what is before us and develop a concept that is not separate from the image or the phenomenon—a concrete concept as opposed to an empty universal.

Herder designated this concrete concept *Hauptform* (main form) and argued that it is only through the *Hauptform* that we can discern relations within nature across vast geographical and historical distances. Importantly, Herder did not regard the *Hauptform* as a Kantian regulative ideal, because it is realized in the world—even if never completely—and it is through its material expressions that we can grasp it. The question then is, how do we grasp the *Hauptform*? Herder's answer, as we will see, was both illuminating and surprising—and, like Kant's turn to art and analogy, points to the significance of artistic capacities and devices in the study of the natural world.

Like Herder and Kant, Goethe sought to discern unity in nature through a comparative approach—one that takes account of both similarities and differences, and that aims to grasp the form of living beings in relation to their larger context. Underlying Goethe's interest in the notion of form was the view that form is neither a static object nor something that can be simply seen with the physical eyes. Rather, as Goethe came to formulate it, it must be discerned with the mind's eye, or what he called "intuitive judgment [*anschauende Urteilskraft*]."

Goethe first articulated the idea of intuitive judgment in response to Kant's claim in the third *Critique* that our discursive form of understanding cannot proceed intuitively. In contrast, Goethe remarked that he had practiced intuitive judgment throughout his work, both in his comparative anatomy and in his study of plant metamorphosis. It is through intuitive judgment that he was able to discover the intermaxillary bone, and it is through intuitive judgment that he grasped the internal coherence of the plant. What makes a judgment intuitive, Goethe explains, is its ability to discern how the sequences within nature are part of *one* process of formation. In other words, unlike our usual procedures of knowing, intuitive judgment can see how what appears as a merely sequential relation is *not only* sequential, but is also an expression of other, nonsequential relations. A plant, for instance, does not develop only sequentially, from seed to fruit (and finally to seed), but also simultaneously, and in two senses: its various parts grow *at the same time* (as the stem grows, so do the leaves), and the parts emerge *in relation* to one another. Thus although the fruit is the last stage of development, all preceding stages are working toward achieving it. Accordingly, one can say that the fruit is "already" in the seed, in the flower, in the root, and that the relation between fruit and flower, fruit and seed, or fruit and root is not purely sequential, but also nonsequential and nonlinear.

This nonsequential unity can be discerned, Goethe contends, by observing the forms of the plant's different parts—the way in which each of the plant's parts *expresses* its place within the whole and thus its relation to what precedes and what follows it. This is particularly evident in transitional stages of development, where aspects of the preceding stage are "carried forward" into the following stage, or vice versa, where aspects of the following stages are anticipated by what preceded them. For instance, the first petals that appear might be green—recalling the green of the stem leaves—or leaves can become increasingly complex on some trees, approaching the shape of a branch. By assuming the form of what precedes or follows them, these parts offer clues to the observer, clues for *how* to look and *what* to look for.

While in his early works Goethe had simply spoken of observation, following his encounter with philosophy—in particular his reading of Kant and friendship with Schiller—he developed a nuanced epistemology and methodology, which was based on his distinction between, as he put it, "seeing and seeing"—that is, the difference between seeing with the physical eye alone, and seeing with the physical eye and the mind's eye simultaneously. To achieve this second form of seeing, however, requires education. More specifically, and as I will argue, it requires an aesthetic education in both senses of the term: an education of our aesthetic or perceptual capacities and an education in the arts. Intuitive judgment can only be achieved through this education.

This means that we are not born with intuitive judgment. After all, as Buffon and Kant had noted, our natural tendency is to judge things in a non-intuitive way—to regard parts or objects as separate and static, and to see their relations in purely linear terms. Intuitive judgment is thus a *task* that stands before us, and it is our *responsibility* as knowers to educate our cognitive capacities so that they become intuitive. This responsibility, as I argue, is not only epistemic, but also ethical, in that *how* we know—the capacities and devices we invoke in our attempt to investigate a phenomenon—determines how the phenomenon will *appear* to us. In turn, the manner in which the phenomenon appears—whether it is appears as a machine or as a sentient being—will inform our behaviors and actions toward it.

Among the four figures, Humboldt is the thinker who is most clearly identifiable as a "scientist."[20] He is perhaps also the thinker who most vehemently argued for the significance of art and aesthetic experience. He contended, for instance, that in order to grasp living beings in their context, the student of nature must learn to regard nature as a landscape painter. Furthermore, Humboldt devoted part of the second volume of his five-volume *Kosmos* (*Cosmos*) (1845–62) to tracing the development of science in relation to the arts. In this way, he both preceded recent efforts in the history of science to demonstrate the significance of the arts (widely construed) for the development of natural-scientific disciplines and practices and offered one of the first integrated histories of knowledge.[21] In turn, although among the four Goethe is the only figure recognized as an artist, Humboldt was, in a significant sense, also an artist.

Humboldt composed essays which he called *Naturgemälde* (nature paintings), and which might best be described as *scientific works of art*—as contradictory as that term might sound. These essays, which draw on feeling, impression, and mood to give the reader an embodied sense of what a particular place is *like*, challenge distinctions between art and science, and between feeling and understanding. In them, Humboldt not only develops a new genre, but also shows how in order to know nature we must invoke feeling, sensibility, and imagination, and anchor knowledge in lived experience. Only in this way can we cultivate knowledge that moves and motivates us, that inspires ethical action. Only in this way can knowledge be transformative.

Just as Goethe's understanding of intuitive judgment as a task requires us to think differently about the ideals and practices of knowing, so Humboldt's realization of knowledge as embodied demands that we rethink our usual oppositions between subjective and objective, between feeling and knowing. Both offer important challenges—as well as clues—for how to think about our obligations as knowers, and what is involved in knowing *well*. These challenges and clues, I believe, remain relevant today, giving us excellent reasons for turning to study the romantic empiricists.

1
Setting the Stage

Kant and the *Critique of the Power of Judgment*

It might seem peculiar to begin a book about an understudied philosophical tradition, distinguished as romantic and empiricist, with Kant. Kant is by no means understudied, and his thought is rarely regarded as either empiricist or romantic. Rather, Kant is most well-known as the philosopher of the a priori, the philosopher who identifies the empirical with the merely contingent, and who seeks to construct nature through the "legislative" power of the understanding. As he puts it in the *Critique of Pure Reason* (1781; 1781), "without understanding there would not be any nature at all" (A125–26). And while he grants a significant role to sensibility, he insists that knowledge in general and knowledge of nature in particular must always be based on the a priori rules provided by the pure concepts of the understanding.

In turn, Kant's connections to romantic empiricism are not entirely straightforward. While his *Critiques* impacted the questions the romantic empiricists posed, and the ways in which they sought to answer them, Kant's conclusions often appear to stand at the opposite end of the spectrum to those of Herder, Goethe, and Humboldt. The most relevant example for our discussion is the view elaborated in the first part of the *Critique of the Power of Judgment* that aesthetic judgments are noncognitive, i.e., that they cannot yield insight into an object, and only pertain to the feelings that emerge within the subject.

But this is precisely where the understudied part of the story comes in. Kant was not only a philosopher of the a priori, and in the third *Critique* he turns his attention to those aspects that he had neglected in his earlier work: the contingent, empirical, and underdetermined. Furthermore, the book's dual focus—aesthetic judgment in the first part, organization in nature in the second part—suggests a connection between the two, which becomes increasingly evident in the second part, i.e., the Critique of Teleological Judgment.

Still, the third *Critique* might seem like a strange first station in our story. It was published some five years after the appearance of the first two volumes of Herder's *Ideas for a Philosophy of History of Humanity* [*Ideen zur Philosophie der Geschichte der Menschheit*] (1784–1791), and in the same year as Goethe's essay *Metamorphosis of Plants* [*Versuch die Metamorphose der Pflanzen zu erklären*]. Furthermore, it is a hesitant text. This wavering is perhaps most evident in Kant's claims regarding the scientific status of teleological judgment. On the one hand, he claims that the reality of organized beings demands that we "subordinate" all mechanism to teleology, and that teleological judgment is "indispensable" for scientific inquiry (AA 5, 379; 398). On the other hand, he describes teleological judgment as "problematic," and (just after emphasizing its indispensability) concludes that that we are under an "obligation" to subordinate teleological judging to judging according to mechanical principles (AA 5, 370; 415).

However, it is precisely in this hesitation, in Kant's small steps forward, followed by sudden retreats, that both the significance and the radicality of romantic empiricism becomes evident. For Kant's hesitation evinces the challenges facing any attempt to develop a bottom-up account of nature, which aims to arrive at more than the mere collection of unrelated data. In the third *Critique* Kant's goal was to achieve "interconnected empirical laws," "interconnected experience," and an "empirical system of nature" (AA 20, 204; 217; 215; see also AA 5, 183). Thus, in contrast to his earlier writings, where the aim was to legislate necessity onto nature, the third *Critique* seeks to "find" necessity in nature: discern unity *in* the multiplicity, integrity *in* diversity, coherence *in* empirical phenomena (AA 5, 179).

Kant's hesitations, then, should not throw us off but provide us with illuminating insights into the challenges facing the project, and into how it can potentially succeed. While Kant makes some important headway in this direction, he refuses to take the final step. In his wavering, he stops short of developing a clear stance regarding the place of organization in nature, and perhaps more poignantly, of articulating the scientific status of teleological judging. His contemporaries, by contrast, do take the crucial step of developing a science inspired and underpinned by the methodologies and insights of aesthetic forms of judgment. Accordingly, in considering Kant's relationship to and differences from Herder, Goethe, and Humboldt, we will be better able to understand how and why they took that final step—and assess their success in taking it.

1.1. Reflecting Judgment: A First Look

Kant begins the *Critique of the Power of Judgment* by pointing to a deficiency on the part of the understanding. "The understanding," he writes in the Introduction, "is of course in possession of *a priori* universal laws of nature, without which nature could not be an object of experience at all; but still it requires in addition a certain order of nature in its particular rules, which can only be known to it empirically and which from its point of view are contingent" (AA 5, 184). This means that the laws of the understanding cannot legislate the "infinite multiplicity of empirical laws" and the "great heterogeneity of forms of nature." In fact, Kant writes in the First (unpublished) Introduction, these empirical laws are "entirely alien to the understanding" (AA 20, 203). The pure concepts of the understanding are simply too general, too underdetermining, to construct experience and nature in all their empirical distinctiveness. Or, as Kant puts it in the first *Critique*, the understanding can only give us "*nature in general*" (B165). This is because, Kant explains in 1790, the objects of nature are "determinable in so many ways apart from ... what they have in common as belonging to nature in general" (AA 5, 183). Accordingly, if we are to capture the great heterogeneity of the forms of nature, "experience must be added" (B165).

The implication is that in the third *Critique* Kant is approaching nature in a new way—a way that seeks to account for, rather than overlook, empirical diversity; a way that aims to make intelligible, rather than set aside, the contingent; a way that regards nature not as something to be legislated or determined by the understanding, but as "free from all restrictions of our law-giving faculty of cognition" (AA 20, 210).

But how is this aim to be achieved? How can we move from *legislating* an abstract, "general" nature, to *experiencing* nature in its full diversity? And more specifically, how can we achieve a rich, heterogeneous, *ordered* experience of nature? The goal, after all, is not simply to amass random, disconnected images and arbitrary concepts. Rather, the goal is to achieve "interconnected empirical laws" and "interconnected experience" (AA 20, 204; 217; see also AA 5, 183). How can we arrive at a coherent picture of nature, "a system of experience" and "an empirical system of nature" (AA 5, 181; AA 20, 215)?

Kant's answer is reflecting judgment. Unlike determining judgment, which is the familiar mode of judgment elaborated in the first *Critique*, reflecting judgment does not determine experience in accordance with the a priori rules provided by the understanding. Rather, reflecting judgment "ascends from the particular in nature to the universal." Thus, instead of applying rules given by a priori concepts, it "finds" them (AA 20, 210; AA 5, 179). Reflecting judgment is a mode of discovery, which proceeds through comparing and holding together. As Kant explains, "to reflect is to compare and hold together given representations either with others or with one's faculty of cognition, in relation to a concept thereby made possible" (AA 20, 211).

However, reflecting judgment does not only compare and behold. For, again, Kant notes, it could run the risk of failing to discern connections in experience and between forms of nature. Simply comparing, in other words, could end up with unrelated images and concepts. In order to achieve an interconnected experience, reflecting judgment must proceed in accordance with a crucial assumption: that there is unity in nature's diversity (AA 20, 203), or as he puts it in the (published) Introduction, that nature is "purposive" (AA 5, 180).

In the First Introduction Kant is clear about what this involves: to regard nature as a unity is to regard "nature as art" (AA 20, 204). In other words, in comparing natural phenomena, in regarding empirical representations as belonging together, reflecting judgment proceeds on the assumption that nature is a work of art. On the basis of this assumption, reflecting judgment begins to discern forms and relations among these forms, which it would otherwise overlook. Through the analogy with art, then, reflecting judgment *sees* nature differently: with greater specificity and concreteness, but also with greater focus on forms and the relations between them.

While this analogy with art is central to the First Introduction, it is pushed to the side in the published Introduction, where Kant's mentions of nature in relation to art appear largely negative—*distinguishing* nature from art, rather than asking his readers to regard nature as art. Thus speaking of the concept of purpose in nature, he writes, "This concept is also entirely distinct from that of practical purposiveness (of human art [*menschliche Kunst*] as well as of morals), although it is certainly conceived of in terms of an analogy with that" (AA 5, 181).[1] In turn, instead of claiming that reflecting judgment is driven by the analogy between nature and art, that is, that this analogy provides reflecting judgment with its fundamental principle, Kant places greater emphasis on understanding. Accordingly, when he explains the origins of the assumption (that nature is a unity), Kant writes that it is given to judgment by "an understanding (even if not ours)," "in order to make possible a system of experience in accordance with particular laws of nature" (AA 5, 180).

It is important to take note of these differences because they point to the diverging ways in which Kant conceptualizes reflecting judgment and its procedure. On the one hand, the First Introduction's emphasis on art, on seeing nature *as* art, suggests not an analogy between nature and *any* form of end-oriented productivity (artistic or moral). Rather, it suggests that the analogy is specific to art, inclining us to think carefully about the distinctive character of both artistic productivity *and* the work of art. On the other hand, the published Introduction connects unity and purpose in nature with practical purposiveness (as end-oriented activity) and the idea of "an understanding (even if not ours)." Kant is here alluding to his later discussion (in Sections 76 and 77) of "intuitive understanding," which contrasts with our discursive understanding. The implication is that the idea of an intuitive understanding, introduced late in Kant's writing of the third *Critique, replaces* the analogy with art.[2]

My interest in pointing out these differences is not historical—I do not aim to add to the work done by scholars to determine the genesis of the third *Critique*. Rather, what I find most significant is the fact that Kant replaces the analogy between nature and art with intuitive understanding. Whatever his reasons were for doing so, Kant's replacement gives us important clues concerning the nature of intuitive cognition, and, as we shall see, its connection to art, symbol, and analogy—all of which are crucial for the activity and procedure of reflecting judgment in its cognitive mode (i.e., teleological judgment).

Before turning to these points, let us consider the analogy between nature and art that Kant invokes in the First Introduction. As noted, he uses this analogy to explicate the assumption according to which reflecting judgment must proceed. If reflecting judgment is to proceed in a directed and coherent way, it must assume unity in nature. Only on this assumption, Kant contends, are we able to "*classify* the whole of nature according to empirical differences." However, he importantly adds, "classification is not a common experiential cognition, but an artistic one." This is because it discerns similarities and draws connections between forms. Thus, if we are to assume that nature can be classified, then we must also assume that nature's forms share common features—i.e., that there is a formal unity within nature. In other words, we must assume that nature is a *composition*, whose various parts (forms) relate to one another. Or, as Kant puts it, we must assume that nature "specifies" itself—brings its products forth—"as *art*" (AA 20, 215).

What does the analogy with art imply? It implies, first, intention, purpose, or idea. A work of art is brought forth with a purpose or idea in mind. This idea grants it unity. Thus to ask readers to conceive of nature as art is to ask them to regard nature as if it were unified through an idea or intention.

But this is not all, and, as I will argue, it is not the crucial element in the analogy between nature and art. For a work of art is a composition. This means, first, that each of its parts is essential to the whole. We cannot take a chord out of a symphony and expect that it will be the same symphony. Each part, in other words, is necessary. And its necessity is connected to its distinctiveness. We cannot replace one chord with another. Accordingly, each chord—in its singularity—plays an essential role. This shows that a work of art involves a certain kind of togetherness of its parts: each, in its distinctive way, works with all the other parts to bring about the whole.

The work of art is thus the outcome of its distinctive, conjoined, and necessary parts. But the reverse is also true. For although the parts make up the whole, they do not exist outside of or prior to the whole. A chord in a symphony assumes a distinctive meaning *in relation* to the (idea of the) whole, as part of the whole. The same holds for colors or shapes in a painting. Just as the painting depends on its specific colors, lines, shapes, so also these colors, lines, and shapes depend on the whole painting. This dependence is both metaphysical and epistemological: the parts assume a specific meaning in light of (the idea of) the whole; and they can only be understood in relation to the whole.

Following his claim that nature should be regarded as art, Kant goes on to say that this idea gives us a "maxim by which to observe nature and to hold its forms together [*die Formen der Natur damit zusammen zu halten*]" (AA 20, 205). The implication is that by regarding nature as art, the crucial aim is not so much to see nature as the realization of an intention or purpose, but rather to hold the forms of nature *together*. This, after all, is what is required for grasping a work of art.

When we view a painting, we do not consider the different parts that make up the whole in isolation (the colors, shapes, lines, brushstrokes, etc.). Rather, we see them in their relation to one another; we hold them together, and thereby discern how each part—in its distinctive way—works with the other parts and contributes to the whole. Similarly, when we listen to a piece of music, we do not hear one sound, irrespective of what precedes or follows it. Rather, again, we hold the parts together. The listener hears every part *as* part of the whole. Each phrase is heard both in its distinctiveness *and* in its relation to the whole. Otherwise, the phrase would be mere noise. Accordingly, the listener must hear every phrase as an *expression* of the whole, which means that in listening to the particular, one is *also* listening to the whole—beholding the whole. Put differently, the listener must hear the whole *in every one of the piece's phrases*. The whole thus emerges in and through the parts, even though it underpins the parts and their relations. It does not exist beyond or outside of them, but only in them and their relations.

The same, Kant suggests, is necessary for grasping nature as a unity. To discern nature's unity requires us to consider the different parts of nature not only as individuals, but also as members of an integrated whole to which they contribute in distinctive but related ways. It also requires us to see how the whole (nature) emerges in and through the parts. In other words, it demands that we regard the different parts of nature as *expressions* of nature's unity.

By invoking an analogy between nature and art, then, Kant is asking his readers to *see* nature differently—to see nature's parts as expressions of unity, and to see this unity as emerging in and expressed through the various parts. In viewing nature as art, we seek to discern the ways that different beings exhibit a structural similarity, and how this similarity points to an integrity in nature. This implies that what we are looking for are not *mere parts*, so to speak, but *expressions* or *forms*—parts that manifest the whole *through* their distinctive *form*, in the same way that a phrase in a piece of music expresses and points to the whole work.

This, I suggest, is the crucial element of the analogy between nature and art in the First Introduction. And while this analogy is not prominent in the published Introduction, the emphasis on form and structure remains throughout the Critique of Teleological Judgment. In the opening section (Section 61), for instance, Kant invokes the "structure [*Bau*] of a bird" in order to introduce the reader to teleological judgment. For, he explains, it is the bird's structure that cannot be grasped through efficient causality and mechanical principles. He writes:

> if one adduces, e.g., the structure of a bird, the hollowness of its bones, the placement of its wings for movement and of its tail for steering, etc., one says that given the mere *nexus effectivus* in nature, without the help of a special kind of causality, namely that of ends (*nexus finalis*), this is all in the highest degree contingent [*zufällig*]: i.e., that nature, considered as mere mechanism, could have formed itself in a thousand different ways without hitting precisely upon the unity in accordance with such a rule, and that it is therefore only *outside* the concept of nature, not within it,

that one would have even the least ground *a priori* for hoping to find such a principle. (AA 5, 360)

Kant's claim is that from the perspective of efficient causality and mechanical physics, the structure of the bird appears "contingent." In other words, from that perspective there is nothing necessary about the different parts that make up the bird. In the Introduction, Kant had articulated the problem that the third *Critique* aims to address in terms of contingency in nature, and the need to make the contingent appear lawful—i.e., necessary (AA 5, 176). While there he did not mention efficient causality and mechanism, but focused on the a priori laws of the understanding, here he is pointing to "certain things" that appear contingent from the perspective of mechanical physics and efficient causality.[3] Furthermore, while in the Introduction, Kant identifies contingency with the fact that the a priori laws of the understanding cannot legislate for every empirical law, here he is specifically speaking of mechanism and efficient causality. The question is: what is the precise relationship between the a priori laws of the understanding and mechanism and efficient causality?

This question has been hotly debated in the literature, and for good reason. On the one hand, Kant identifies efficient causality and mechanism with the a priori laws of the understanding at various points in the text. In Section 70, for instance, he notes that the mechanical principle "is provided ... by the mere understanding *a priori*." In Section 71, he states that mechanism follows the order of the "sensible world," which is furnished by the transcendental structures of experience (AA 5, 389).[4] On the other hand, mechanism and efficient causality appear to be far more determining, far more concrete, than the a priori laws of the understanding.[5] While this may be the case, Kant's claims imply that mechanism and efficient causality go hand in hand with the a priori laws of the understanding, such that even if they *do* tell us a lot more about empirical nature, their foundation is—ultimately—a priori.

Nevertheless, even if a priori and empirical laws (i.e., the laws of the understanding and mechanism and efficient causality, respectively) work hand in hand, they remain insufficient to explain all aspects of nature, in that they leave certain parts of nature underdetermined or contingent. This brings us back to Kant's claim that the bird's structure has been left underdetermined, not simply by the laws of the understanding, but also by efficient causality and the mechanical laws of motion. What does this tell us about the meaning of contingency?

It tells us that it is the *structure* of the bird that is contingent. In other words, it points us to the unity between the various parts of the bird—its tail, the placement of its wings, the hollowness of its bones, and so on—and claims that, from the perspective of efficient causality and mechanism, this unity is highly unlikely. From that perspective, the specific parts of the bird and their relations appear entirely accidental. There is nothing *necessary* about these particular parts, or about their relationship. In the place of the specific bone structure, or the tail, or the wings, something else—entirely different—could have emerged. Ultimately, then, Kant's claim is that if we consider the bird's structure according to efficient causality and the laws of mechanics, we find nothing necessary in either these parts, or in their relation and specific combination, i.e., in the whole. *They could have been otherwise.*

However, to simply state that this combination is highly unlikely does not tell us much about the bird—its structure, its parts, their various functions and relations, its health and well-being, its connection to other beings, its connection to its context, and so on. Thus, while regarding it as "contingent" may be appropriate from one perspective (that of general mechanics), it is inappropriate from another perspective: the perspective that seeks to order and classify nature. If our goal, in other words, is to discern relations between nature's parts, see connections between forms, then efficient causality and mechanism are of no use.

This is precisely where reflecting judgment becomes crucial. By seeing the bird as a work of art, reflecting judgment considers the bird's various parts as expressions of an integrated unity. From this perspective, they appear interconnected, with each part playing a distinctive role in the bird as a whole. The hollowness of the bird's bones, the specific placement of its wings, its feathers, its size and overall structure, all appear to be variations on a theme, parts of one whole. In other words, when considered in light of the whole, the hollowness of the bird's bones appears to be essential, just like its wings—both of which clearly go hand in hand. As such, the various parts, and their placement, no longer appear contingent or arbitrary. Rather, they appear to be working together to enable the bird to achieve flight. In this way, reflecting judgment begins to discern a necessity in the parts, to regard them not as accidental, but as essential, to the bird. (It is *as if* the bird has been *purposively constructed* to achieve the *end* of flight.)

There are, of course, significant differences between a work of art and a bird—differences which Kant notes, and which lead him to emphasize the analogical structure of reflecting judgment. For, as he says in the Introduction, reflecting judgment proceeds "in terms of analogy" with art and morals. Or, as he puts it later, organized products in nature are an "analogue of art" (AA 5, 374). Accordingly, when reflecting judgment turns its attention to nature, and to certain entities within nature, it regards them *as* something else: *as* art. In so doing, it also recognizes that they *are not* art. This is the essence of analogy.

This provides us with an important clue. When reflecting judgment turns its attention to nature and its products, it *proceeds* analogically. Now not all teleological judging proceeds analogically. The judgment that a cup is *for* drinking is teleological insofar as it tells me the end or purpose of a cup. But it is not analogical, insofar as it *determines* the nature of its object (the cup). By contrast, teleological judgment in its reflective (i.e., nondeterminative) mode follows the *as-if* structure of reflecting judgment, and is for this reason analogical. It regards nature *as if* it were a work of art. It does not thereby tell us that nature *is* a work of art. Rather, it tells us to reflect on nature in the way that one reflects on a work of art. This means that teleological judgment is not only *motivated* by the assumption that nature is like art, but also that teleological judgment—in its reflecting mode—is *itself* a form of seeing-as: of seeing nature, or specific entities within nature, *as* something else. In other words, teleological judgment (in this reflective mode) does not schematize but *analogizes*. Or, to use the language Kant introduces in Section 59, it is a "symbolic" mode of knowing, a knowing of something *as* or *through* something else.

1.2. The Analogical Structure of Teleological Judgment

In his first iteration of teleological judgment, Kant speaks of it in terms of analogy. He writes:

> teleological judgment is rightly drawn into our research into nature, at least problematically, but only in order to bring it under principles of observation and research in *analogy* with causality according to ends, without presuming thereby to *explain* it. (AA 5, 360)

Immediately several crucial aspects of teleological judgment become evident: it is both justified *and* problematic. It is problematic because it proceeds via analogy. This means, Kant continues, that it is nonexplanatory. Instead of "explaining" its object, teleological judgment brings it under principles of "observation." Or, as Kant puts it in the First Introduction, reflecting judgment provides us with "a maxim by which to observe nature and to hold its forms together" (AA 20, 205). In other words, reflecting judgment—in its teleological mode—concerns observation, discernment, holding together, but not explanation.

In Section 59 of the Critique of Aesthetic Judgment Kant describes cognition achieved through analogy as "symbolic." A symbol, he writes, is "a presentation [*Darstellung*] in accordance with mere analogy," and analogy is a presentation "in which the power of judgment performs a double act." This double act involves, first, the application of "the concept to the object of a sensible intuition," and then the application of "the mere rule of reflection on that intuition to an entirely different object, of which the first is only the symbol" (AA 5, 352). In other words, the work of analogy involves applying the rule of one object onto a second object. Through this application, the first object becomes a "symbol" or an "analogue" for the second object.

In the context of Section 59, Kant's claim is that beauty is a symbol of morality. Beauty, in other words, is an analogical presentation of morality. To justify this claim, Kant must demonstrate an analogy between beauty and morality, which he locates not in beauty and morality as *objects* (i.e., not by determining the properties or attributes of beauty and morality and recognizing a significant similarity between their attributes) but in the way in which we *reflect* on beauty and the way we *reflect* on morality.[6]

To explain what he means, Kant offers two examples: a constitutional monarchy governed by the rule of law, which is symbolized by an animate body, and a monarchy governed by an individual will, which is symbolized by a hand mill. The constitutional monarchy requires complex collaboration—like the animate body. A monarchy, by contrast, is ruled by a single will—like the hand mill. The animate body and the hand mill are symbols, Kant contends, not because they share common properties with the monarchies they respectively symbolize, but because of the way in which we reflect on them.

This might be surprising; after all, one might ask, why would we see the two as in any way alike if they do not have anything in common? Mustn't there be some common ground in order for us to regard the one as a symbol of the other? Kant's answer is yes, but his aim is to draw out a form of symbolic representation that has—thus far—been largely ignored. For, as he explains, "between a despotic state and a handmill there is . . . no similarity" (AA 5, 352). What he means is that there are no shared *material properties* between the two: there is nothing in their *material makeup* that should lead us to see the one (the hand mill) as a symbol of the other (the despotic state).

This property-based use of analogy is, of course, the more widely known form of analogical reflection, and the one that Kant had discussed in his lectures on logic. In that context, he describes analogy as a form of a posteriori knowledge not unlike induction. Induction proceeds by determining universal characteristics and categorizing particulars under these universal concepts. Analogical inference, by contrast, proceeds from particular to total similarity between two things. While inductive inference is based on the principle of universalization such that what belongs to many things of the genus also belongs to the remaining ones, analogical inference is based on the principle of specification: it concerns the attributes or properties of two *different* entities. In the "Dohnau Logic" (1780s), he puts it in the following way:

> I infer according to analogy thus: when two or more things from a genus agree with one another in as many marks as we have been able to discover, I infer that they will also agree with one another in the remaining marks that I have not been able to discover. . . . I infer, then, from some marks to all the other ones, that they will also agree in these. (AA 24, 772)

In the "Hechsel Logic," he provides the example of the earth and moon to explicate this kind of analogy. They are the same kind of entity (i.e., celestial bodies), and they share several features (e.g., they have valleys and mountains). On this basis, we can go on to infer that they share additional features, e.g., the earth has water, so the moon may also have water. Of course, this analogy turned out to be wrong—and this is why analogical inference must always stand to be corrected.[7]

As presented in the lectures on logic, then, analogy involves comparing the attributes or properties of different entities and, on the basis of shared properties, making an inference to unknown properties. It is this conception of analogy that Kant wants to depart from in the third *Critique* when he claims that there is "no similarity" between the despotic state and the hand mill. The question then is: on what basis can we draw an analogy?

Kant's claim is that the similarity has to do with the way we *reflect* on them. When we reflect on a constitutional monarchy, we proceed from the whole to the part, and this permits us to appeal to the symbol of an organized being. In the case of an individually governed monarchy, by contrast, we proceed from part to whole, and thereby appeal to the mechanical metaphor of a hand mill. The symbolic relation, then, is connected to our mode of reflection.

This, Kant contends, is also the case for the relation between beauty and morality. The symbolic relation between them does not rest on shared properties; rather, it has to do with our manner of reflecting on them. While our experience of beauty involves harmony between understanding and imagination, our experience of morality involves harmony between reason and will. On the basis of the harmony *in our experience* of the two, Kant argues, we discern a symbolic relation between beauty and morality—such that beauty is a symbol of morality.[8]

While this makes some sense, it does not fully account for why we should *reflect* on the objects in the same way. After all, there is a reason behind my proceeding in a particular way, a reason that has to do with a *structural similarity* between the despotic state and the hand mill, on the one hand, and the constitutional monarchy and the animate body, on the other. Accordingly, although they do not share *material* properties (as the earth and the moon do), they do share a crucial structural similarity, and it is this similarity that permits us to reflect on them in a particular way—and thereby draw an analogy.

What this means is that symbolic presentation must be connected to the objects and their respective *structures*—if not to their material properties.[9] On this basis, Kant goes on to write that analogy is a "carrying over [*Übertragung*] of reflection on one object of intuition to another, quite different concept, to which perhaps no intuition can ever directly correspond" (AA 5, 352–53). In other words, analogy involves "carrying over" the rules of (reflecting on) one object onto another (perhaps nonpresentable) object, with the goal of presenting the second object. The analogy is thus based on the rules of reflecting. However, these rules are connected to the (structure of the) objects. By applying the rules of reflecting on one object onto another (lesser known, or perhaps nonpresentable) object, we gain (further) insight into the second object.

In some ways, this use of analogy approximates the attributive conception of analogy described in the logic lectures. Like attributive analogy, it illuminates one object through another. However, it differs from it in two crucial ways. First, it does not concern specific (material) properties. Second, in this case, the second object might have no adequate intuition and is thus no "object" at all. In other words, the second object can be an idea of reason. Accordingly, the work of analogy here does not specifically involve gaining insight by comparing two *objects*. Rather, it involves "carrying over" the rules of (reflecting on) one object onto a second, perhaps otherwise unpresentable, object, and in this way *bringing the second object to (some form of) presentation*.

Ideas for which there is no adequate intuition include God, immortality, and the soul, i.e., ideas which cannot be schematized because they are thought outside of temporal conditions. However, it is not only supersensible ideas that fail to be fully schematized. There are also ideas that are not supersensible, that fall within the purview of experience, but which cannot be articulated through schematic presentation. These ideas might thus be designated as imminent or sensible ideas, to distinguish them from supersensible ideas.[10]

Kant in fact points to these two different kinds of ideas in Section 49. He writes, "the poet ventures to make sensible [*versinnlichen*] rational ideas of invisible beings, the kingdom of the blessed, the kingdom of hell, eternity, creation, etc., as well as make that of which *there are examples in experience* [*in der Erfahrung*], e.g., death, envy, and all sorts of vices, as well as love, fame, etc., sensible *beyond the limits of experience* [*über die Schranken der Erfahrung hinaus*]" (AA 5, 314; emphasis added). In other words, not only the supersensible ideas of God and immortality (which cannot be schematized at all) but also those ideas which cannot be *fully* schematized (i.e., which are left underdetermined by the schematizing of the concepts of the understanding) require symbolic presentation. As Kant puts it, we have "examples in experience" of ideas such as death, envy, love, and fame, but the goal of the poet is to make them sensible "beyond the limits of experience," i.e., portray them in a way that the concepts of the understanding cannot. Although Kant does not explicitly draw the connection here, the poet's work involves symbolic presentation. For what the poet is doing is nothing other than "carrying over" the rules governing reflecting on one object onto another object, and in this way enabling us to gain (greater) clarity into the second object. Let us consider some examples.

The relata in an analogy can be supersensible and sensible *or* sensible and sensible. An example of the first instance would be the idea of God and the symbol of the clockmaker, while an example of the second would be "All the world's a stage, / And all men and women merely players," where "stage" is used to clarify the idea of the human world, and "players" aims to illuminate the structure of human life. In the first instance, the goal is to offer an intimation, via the symbol of the clockmaker, of how to understand the relationship between something supersensible (God) and something sensible (the world). In the second, the goal is to grant a deeper sense of something that is already part of our experience ("the world"), but which can never be fully schematized.

It is this second form of analogy (between two sensible relata) that is relevant for the analogy between artworks and organized beings. On the one hand, organized beings cannot be fully schematized. On the other hand, they clearly differ from ideas such as God or heaven, insofar as they appear in experience. However, their very appearance, their very coming into presentation, *depends on* the analogy with art. For, Kant writes, we must judge these objects "as intentionally formed... in order to obtain even an experiential *cognition* [*Erfahrungserkenntniß*] *of their internal constitution*." In other words, we cannot experience them without invoking the analogy with art. Kant goes further still, adding that "*even the thought* [*Gedanke*] *of them* as organized things is impossible without associating the thought of a generation with an intention" (AA 5, 398; emphasis added).

Kant's claim is that the very possibility of both "thinking" and "experiencing" organization in nature depends on the double act of judgment—i.e., of seeing something *as* something else. It is only by "carrying over" the rules of reflecting on one object (e.g., art) onto another, otherwise unpresentable object, that this second object comes to presentation—that it becomes part of our "experiential cognition."[11] In other words, we can experience and think organization in nature *only through* symbolic presentation.

In this instance, the work of analogy appears at the most basic level of cognition. It is not simply that we cannot *investigate* organized beings without analogy (a claim Kant explicitly makes) but also that our *experiential cognition* and *thought* of them depends on analogy. What are we to make of this claim, and its implication: that the analogical structure of teleological judgment enables us to undertake basic cognitive acts?

A first response to this question must involve historical considerations, insofar as Kant's understanding of analogy in the third *Critique* approximates views expressed by his predecessors and contemporaries, including those of Buffon and his former student Herder. However, while Kant was generally sympathetic to Buffon, he was deeply critical of Herder.[12] Just five years prior to the publication of the *Critique of the Power of Judgment* Kant authored two scathing reviews of Herder's *Ideas*, in which he challenged Herder's use—or misuse—of analogy. By 1790, however, Kant appears to be far more sympathetic to analogy than in the two reviews—and his perspective appears close to Herder's. Accordingly, the first question to consider concerns Kant's apparently changing attitudes to analogy, and how they map onto the larger historical-intellectual context of the eighteenth century.

The second, more systematic response to the question turns on the fact that Kant's use of analogical reflection and symbolic cognition plays a crucial role in the emergence of a new methodology and approach to nature. The focus on the empirical and contingent that we find in the third *Critique*, and the interest in discovering, rather than legislating, nature go hand in hand with (and indeed depend on) the success of analogical reflection and symbolic cognition. However, it is not clear where this new methodology, and the knowledge which it furnishes, fit into Kant's larger system. In other words, it is not evident how the fruits of analogical reflection can be brought to bear on what Kant designates as "objective knowledge."

But first let us turn to the larger context in which Kant was writing, and the competing evaluations of analogy and its use in natural history. This will help us to assess Kant's critical reviews of Herder's use of analogy and to better appreciate the development of Kant's position on analogy. For, as will become evident, one of Kant's central aims in the third *Critique* concerns understanding the place of analogy in natural science—and this means both assessing *and* limiting its significance.

1.3. The Place of Analogy in the Eighteenth Century

When considered in its historical context, Kant's turn to analogy in the third *Critique* is not surprising. By 1790, analogy had become a key methodological tool for natural history and the emerging science of biology.[13] In his widely read and influential *Natural History* [*Histoire naturelle*] (1749–1804), Buffon noted that it is only "by the force of analogy [*par la force de l'analogie*]," that we can advance natural history.[14] Similarly, and under the influence of

Buffon, Herder argued in his *Ideas* that it is only by digging deeper into the "*analogy of nature* [Analogie der Natur]," that we can "begin to gather hope" (FHA 6, 165).

The hope to which Herder alludes coincides with Buffon's aims: both agreed that classifications of nature had, thus far, failed to provide an adequate depiction of the relations within nature. Not only did these classifications misrepresent the place of the human being in nature but they also failed to consider natural beings in their structural wholeness and context. Through analogy, through seeing one object *as* another, they argued, deeper insight into *both* the objects *and* their relations will be achieved.

In 1735 Linnaeus created the class "quadruped," and under it the anthropomorphic order, in which he included human beings, monkeys, lizards, and sloths.[15] The reasoning for this was that they all shared the same arrangement of teeth. Buffon, among others, considered this to be arbitrary and far too narrow a way by which to draw classifications. Linnaeus's classification, Buffon argues in *Natural History*, is based on "a metaphysical error." He writes,

> it is easy to see that the great fault in all of this is a metaphysical error ... in wanting to judge a whole by only one of its parts: a very obvious error, and one that is surprisingly found everywhere; for almost all of the classifiers have employed only one part, such as teeth, claws, or talons, to classify animals, and leaves or flowers to categorize plants, instead of using all of the parts, looking for the differences and similarities in the entire individual thing.[16]

By confusing the part for the whole, by narrowly focusing on one aspect of an animal's or plant's structure without taking account of the "entire individual thing," Linnaeus's system imposed abstract categories on nature, which had little or nothing to do with the order of nature itself. Thus Buffon contends, "that way of knowing is not a science, it is only a convention, an arbitrary language."[17]

To address this problem, Buffon introduced a distinction between "real" or "physical" and "abstract" truths.[18] Abstract truths are precisely those truths that result in convention; for they are invented by the human mind. Physical truths, by contrast, are real; they exist in the natural world and are the proper object of inquiry. Buffon's claim is that the natural researcher must be concerned with physical truths.

Buffon's distinction between abstract and physical truths, and his prioritization of physical truths over abstract ones, strongly distinguishes him from the prevalent views in Germany at the time, especially those espoused by Christian Wolff (1679–1754) and his followers. According to Wolff, analogy (which he termed *Witz*)[19] is useful because it allows us to recognize similarities between different things or systems, and thereby make a discovery.[20] Thus, an analogy between arithmetic and counting money will help a child, who knows only one but not the other, to discover that the rules of one obtain for the other, and thereby apply the rules of arithmetic when counting money.[21] However, precisely because analogy is based on inductive inference, it can never achieve the apodictic certainty of axiomatic demonstration and must therefore be supplanted by other methods when these become available. Thus, the Wolffian Johann August Eberhard (1739–1809) argues that while analogy is useful for guiding the investigator of nature, its use is limited, precisely because it cannot achieve certainty. In fact, Eberhard notes, inferences achieved through analogy are often contradicted by experience. For instance, he reports that until recently, natural historians had argued on the basis of analogy that moss—like other plants—reproduces through seeds. Experience has, however, shown this to be incorrect. For this reason, Eberhard concludes that "analogy is only an aid, with which we must dispense as soon as we have other means."[22]

For Wolff and the Wolffians, analogy is a heuristic tool, necessary to commence investigation, to "guide" the investigator, but it provides no certainty, or constitutive knowledge (to use Kant's language), and must be superseded by more secure methods. However, it was not clear whether other methods—axiomatic demonstration based on first principles—can be used for empirical inquiry. This was, at least, Buffon's wager. In contrast to Wolff and his followers, Buffon argued that mathematics and mathematical certainty should not serve as ideals for philosophical knowledge and do not obtain for empirical inquiry into nature. This is because they are merely "abstract," inventions of the human mind and have nothing to do with reality: they do not furnish physical truths.

The differences in their views are most evident in their estimation of historical knowledge. While Wolff and his followers argued that historical knowledge lacks the certainty that can be achieved in mathematics and that ought to be achieved in philosophy, Buffon argued that historical knowledge is the highest form of knowledge. In fact, Buffon goes so far as to claim that history should serve as the ideal for research into nature. He writes in the First Discourse of his *Epochs of Nature* [*Époques de la Nature*] (1778):

> In civil history, we refer to titles, we search for ancient coins, and we make out antique inscriptions to determine the course of human revolutions and record the dates of changes of customs; it is the same in natural history; it is necessary to mine the archives of the world, to pull old monuments from the entrails of the earth, to collect their ruins, and put together in one body of evidence all the signs of the physical changes that can let us go back to the different ages of nature. This is the only way to establish a few points in the immensity of space, and to place a certain number of milestones on the eternal road of time.[23]

Buffon's claim, then, is that history (and not mathematics) is the highest form of knowledge because it is through history—and in turn, the historical study of nature—that we are able to study and discern "real" (as opposed to abstract) relations. As he puts it in *Natural History*,

> [N]atural history must follow description, and must solely center around the relations which natural things have among themselves and with us: the history of an animal must not be the history of the individual, but that of the whole species; it must treat their generation . . . the number of their young, the care of their parents . . . , their place of habitation, their food . . . , and finally the services they can render us.[24]

In other words, in order to overcome the abstract systems of taxonomy, it is necessary to reconceive natural history, to make it *historical*—in the modern sense of the term. This involves (a) considering a species in its context and (b) regarding a species not as a static (eternal) entity, but as the continuation of a group of individuals (in time) through reproduction.[25] Natural history, then, is not classification based on apparently eternal (and apparently arbitrary) markers, but the study of the history of a species—of its generation and transformation in time and place.

Buffon's emphasis on physical facts and history challenged the domination of mathematics in empirical areas of inquiry. And the popularity of Buffon's challenge is evident in a number of works that appeared immediately after the publication of *Natural History*. Thus, in his *Thoughts on the Interpretation of Nature* [*Pensées sur l'Interprétation de la Nature*] (1753/

1754),[26] Diderot exclaims that "the domain of mathematicians is a world purely of the intellect, where what are taken for absolute truths cease entirely to be so when applied to the world we live in."[27] To this he adds that "so long as something exists only in the mind, it remains there as an opinion, or a notion which may be either true or false, and which can be accepted or contradicted. It becomes meaningful only when linked to things which are external to it."[28]

Without mathematics or a priori foundations, however, it is not clear how natural history is to proceed: how can it discern "real" links or relations between species or individuals within a species? Diderot voices precisely this concern. For, he writes, the infinitude of nature seems to imply that there is no way to achieve systematic unity, such that "[e]ven if experimental science continued to work for century after century, the materials which it accumulated would eventually have become too great to fit into any system, and the inventory of them would still be far from complete."[29]

Buffon too was aware of this difficulty, although he expresses the challenge in slightly different terms. The trouble, he explains, has to do with the difference between the way in which our intellect operates and the way in which nature operates. Our intellect proceeds linearly, taking only single steps in one direction. Nature, by contrast, "does not take a single step except to go in all directions; in marching forward, she extends to the sides and above."[30] With this apparent incongruity between mind and nature, the question of how the natural historian is to discern real relations (connections, unity) in nature's infinite multiplicity becomes all the more difficult. Lacking a priori theoretical foundations, it is not at all evident how natural history can capture nature's diversity in a coherent or meaningful way. A new approach, a new method, was needed, and this new approach required a new conception of unity, one that contrasted with the subsumption of the particular under an a priori universal, and which was able to account for individuality and historicity.

For Buffon this alternative methodology must be based on analogy and comparative analysis.[31] Thus he writes in *Natural History*,

> This goal is the most important one . . . to combine observations, to generalize about facts, to tie them together by the force of analogy and to try to arrive at this high degree of knowledge where we can judge that particular effects depend on more general effects, where we can compare nature with

herself in her great operations, and from where we can finally open up the paths that will permit us to perfect the different parts of physics.[32]

Natural history requires analogy because it is only through comparing various structures that we can begin to discern similarities without overlooking differences between and within species. Thus in his account of anatomy, Buffon notes that it was not until anatomists began to compare human and animal bodies that any knowledge was achieved. For, he explains,

> What real knowledge can be derived from a single object? Is not every science founded on the comparison of similar and different objects, of their analogous or opposite properties, and of all their relative qualities? Absolute knowledge, if it has an existence, exceeds the powers of man: we can only judge by the relations of things.[33]

By discerning similarities and differences, analogy provides a means by which to grasp continuity—real relations—in nature that are not based on just one structural similarity, or an abstract principle. Such an analogically based account of nature differs significantly from a systematic account founded on mathematical construction or axiomatic demonstration. For one, it remains open to being corrected—analogical inference may be wrong. Furthermore, it cannot establish certainty—analogical inference achieves probability only. For these reasons, Diderot came to the conclusion that the study of nature is an activity of *interpretation*: an ongoing dialogue, a continuous question posed to nature, whose answer might illuminate in one instance, but, in another, cast dark shadows, result in unforeseen questions, demand an entirely new analogy, or even unhinge the question itself. For Buffon and Diderot, this interpretive mode is the only mode that can arrive at genuine insights into nature—anything else would be a misunderstanding of the task at hand.

1.4. Kant's Critique of Analogy

In light of these claims, Herder's claim in the *Ideas* that it is only via analogy that we can gather hope for natural history seems hardly far-fetched. In fact, it not only approximates Buffon's use of analogy, but also Kant's own earlier understanding of the significance of analogy. In *Universal Natural History and*

Theory of the Heavens [*Allgemeine Naturgeschichte und Theorie des Himmels*] (1755), for instance, Kant speaks of the "analogies of nature" (AA 1, 349) as necessary for the "expansion" of cognition (AA 1, 351). This claim accords with statements Kant makes in his logic lectures. In the "Hechsel Logic," he contends that it is only through analogy that we can achieve "extended cognition [*ausgebreitete Erkenntnis*],"[34] while in the "Jäsche Logic," Kant argues that analogical inference is capable of "extending our cognition by experience" (AA 9, 133). In turn, Herder's specific use of analogy in the *Ideas* mirrors Kant's account of attributive analogy as developed in these lectures—i.e., inferring from some shared attributes to additional shared attributes.

Yet, in his reviews of Herder's work, Kant's critique centers on Herder's use of analogy. Specifically, Kant contends that Herder's analogical inferences result in a "monstrous" conclusion. The monstrous conclusion is that all living beings have their origin in "a single original species, or from a single procreative maternal womb"—a claim from which, Kant writes, reason must recoil (AA 8, 54).

The problem with Herder's approach, it appears, has to do with the fact that it overlooks significant differences—between humans and animals, primarily. For by seeing similarities and underemphasizing differences, Herder—Kant contends—goes on to draw unfounded connections.[35] More specifically Kant argues that Herder's claim that human beings and animals exhibit similar *structural* features leads him to draw inferences regarding the *origins* of humans and animals. Thus by discerning *some* similarities of *form* between humans and animals, Herder goes on to infer *additional* similarities that have to do with the *origin* of these similar forms. In this way, he arrives at conclusions that cannot be verified.

At first sight Kant's critique of Herder appears to be aimed at Herder's *specific use* of analogy—which results in the purported claim that humans and animals share the same origin—and not at analogy per se. In fact, Kant's statement preceding his critique seems to affirm this interpretation. Kant writes, "The reviewer must admit that he does not understand this inference from the analogy of nature, even if he were to concede that continuous gradation of its creatures, together with the rule governing it, namely, the approximation of the human being. For," he importantly adds, "they are *different* beings that occupy the many stages of the ever more perfect organization" (AA 8, 52–53).

Accordingly, Kant appears to concede similarity of forms in nature ("the continuous gradation of its [i.e., nature's] creatures"), and implicitly acknowledges the importance of analogy for discerning this similarity. But he also challenges the conclusion that is drawn from this similarity. Kant's critique, then, seems to be not a critique of analogy per se but of the results of Herder's *particular* use of analogy. The implication is that there is an *appropriate* use of analogy, and an *inappropriate* one. Accordingly, the question that emerges is: what is the difference between them?

In the review, Kant does not broach this question. In fact, at no point in the review does he clearly articulate the reasons why Herder's use of analogy is distinctively problematic—other than its apparently monstrous conclusion. The fact that Kant provides no clear enunciation of the problematic use of analogy, or an account of its proper use, becomes even more troubling when we realize that what Kant describes as Herder's use of analogy aligns with his own understanding of analogy at the time. As noted above, in various lectures on logic, Kant indicates that analogy involves an inference on the basis of shared attributes. This is precisely the kind of inference that Kant takes Herder to be making: from shared attributes between various species, we can go on to infer further shared attributes. (Whether Herder is *in fact* using analogy in this way will be discussed in the following chapters.)

However, it is precisely with these questions in mind that Kant turns to analogy in the third *Critique*, with the aim of providing an account of the appropriate use of analogy. In this way he determines both its scope and its limits, establishing what analogy *can* and *cannot* deliver. Thus, even if Kant does not clearly say it in the review, his ultimate critique of Herder rests on what he takes to be Herder's (mis)understanding of the scope and limit of analogy, and in particular his misunderstanding of the methodology and aims of science.

This interpretation seems to be confirmed in Kant's 1788 essay, "On the Use of Teleological Principles in Philosophy [*Über den Gebrauch teleologischer Prinzipien in der Philosophie*]." His claim is that the real problem with the study of nature has to do with the blurring of boundaries, where, in the hope of discerning similarity, difference is repeatedly overlooked or denied. As he puts it,

> I have become totally convinced that through the mere separation of what is heterogeneous and what previously had been left in a mixed state, often a new light is cast upon the science . . . which opens up many authentic sources of cognition where one would not at all have expected them. (AA 8, 162)

The aim of the scientist, Kant goes on, must be to challenge "the carelessness of letting the boundaries of the sciences run into each other," a challenge which, in light of the two reviews, seems to be directed at his former student's use of analogy—and perhaps even at his *own* former estimation of analogy.

1.5. The Inexplicability of Organization

Kant introduces teleological judgment in Section 61 of the third *Critique* because efficient causality and mechanism fail to make intelligible the structure of a living being, as in the example of the bird. On the basis of "mere mechanism" and efficient causality, the structure of a bird appears to be contingent. While this may be an appropriate conclusion from one perspective, from the perspective that aims to classify and order nature, it is hardly appropriate. For if the goal is to understand the relations between beings in nature, it is necessary to grasp the structures of these beings—their forms—and discern similarities between and within their forms. By introducing teleological judgment at this juncture, Kant is claiming that teleological judgment should help us to grasp the structures of these beings. But how exactly does it achieve this task?

To answer this question, we have first to consider why it is the case that mere mechanism and efficient causality *cannot* do this. In other words, we have to consider why it is the case that from the perspective of mechanical physics the structure of a bird appears contingent, and, as Kant puts it, "inexplicable." This, however, requires understanding what Kant means by mechanism, efficient causality, and their relation.

Kant most clearly articulates his account of mechanism in his 1786 *Metaphysical Foundations of Natural Science* [*Metaphysische Anfangsgründe der Naturwissenschaft*]. In contrast to the first *Critique*, where Kant's goal was to establish the transcendental principles of experience and thereby provide the a priori foundations for objects of experience in general, in the *Metaphysical Foundations* Kant is concerned with what he calls the "special metaphysical" part of science, which determines the a priori laws of nature as instantiated in corporeal substances, i.e., matter. Thus while in the first *Critique* his goal is to determine "the laws that make the concept of nature in general possible, without relation to any determinate object of experience," in the *Metaphysical Foundations*, his aim is to explicate how the a priori laws of nature are realized in *matter* (AA 4, 469–70). This involves, as Kant puts it in the Preface to the *Metaphysical Foundations*, the rational "construction" of matter, which is achieved through "mathematics."[36] Through this construction, Kant aims to articulate an account of what he calls "proper science [*eigentliche Wissenschaft*]," which uniquely achieves "apodictic certainty" (AA 4, 468).

On the basis of mathematical construction, Kant arrives at crucial conclusions regarding the nature of matter and its capacity for change. Most significantly, he argues that transformation in matter can only occur externally. This is because matter, as "mere object of outer senses, has no other determinations except those of external relations in space, and therefore undergoes no change except by motion" (AA 4, 543). In other words, matter—rationally constructed—transforms only in accordance with the mechanical laws of motion.

This has significant implications for the *kind* of entity that we can expect to find in space. For it implies, first, that this entity is composed of parts that are externally drawn together or repelled from one another. In other words, the *relations* between the entity's parts are determined entirely by the laws of motion. Second, it implies that the *parts themselves* are entirely externally determined: *what* they are, *how* they behave, depends on their location in space and the laws of motion. Put differently, what they are has nothing to do with their internal structure, but only with their external relations. Together, these two points imply that the relations between the entity's parts are wholly external, dependent on their location and motion in space, and have nothing to do with their specific capacities or qualities.

This implies, third, that the kind of unity we can expect to encounter is composed of parts whose internal structure and composition are irrelevant, i.e., as a spatial entity it can be construed as entirely homogeneous.[37] In other words, it is not an internally differentiated unity, i.e., a unity that emerges through and depends on the differences of its parts. Fourth, this entity is an *outcome* of the (spatial) coming together of its parts. As such, it is entirely dependent on and determined by its (homogeneous) parts and their place in space. This means that it lacks what Kant calls "internal activity," which he identifies with spontaneity and life (AA 29, 913). Transformations within it are thus dependent on transformations in its parts, which are themselves determined by the laws of motion. This unity, in other words, is not *self*-moving; its movement and all change within it depend on the laws of motion. For this reason, Kant concludes in the *Metaphysical Foundations*, matter must be "lifeless" [*leblos*] (AA 4, 544).

Now, in contrast to the *Critique of Pure Reason* and the *Metaphysical Foundations*, the third *Critique* aims to establish the possibility of explaining "*particular* material objects of experience."[38] Because this is a task that necessarily involves empirical research as opposed to a priori determination, it follows that its results—unlike those of the earlier works—can only be regulative. This does not mean, however, that Kant's conception of mechanism in the third *Critique* differs from the account he provides in the earlier work, as some have argued.[39] Rather, in the third *Critique* Kant largely assumes his articulation of mechanism, as outlined in the *Metaphysical Foundations*.

First, along the lines of his conceptualization of matter in terms of the laws of motion in the *Metaphysical Foundations*, in the third *Critique* Kant speaks of mechanism as "the capacity for movement" (AA 5, 374) "in accordance with the mere laws of motion" (AA 5, 390). Furthermore, in the third *Critique* Kant identifies mechanical causality with efficient causality, wherein an external force is the only possible cause of change. Efficient causality, he writes, is "a connection that constitutes a series (of causes and effects) that is always descending," such that every effect presupposes a cause that is necessarily external and antecedent to it (AA 5, 372).

On the basis of these two characteristics, Kant distinguishes two *kinds* of entities in the third *Critique*: entities that are based on the laws of motion and efficient causality, and which result in a "physical-mechanical connection," and entities that are not based on these laws, and result in a "connection to ends" (AA 5, 388).[40] The first kind is what Kant calls a "material whole," which he describes as "a product of the parts and of their forces and their capacity to combine by themselves" (AA 5, 408). Entities that are based on the laws of motion and efficient causality are outcomes of the mechanical relations of their parts in space. Accordingly, their parts precede them, and the relations between their parts are explicable according to the laws of mechanics and efficient causality. The implication, then, is that entities that result in a "connection to ends" are not the outcome of their parts, and their parts are not (merely) determined by the laws of motion and efficient causality.

If we return momentarily to the example of the bird and consider it in light of Kant's conceptualization of mechanism, efficient causality and material wholes, it appears that Kant's claim is that mechanical physics cannot make intelligible the *kind* of whole that a bird is. In other words, if we conceive of the bird as a "material whole," as an outcome of homogeneous parts, which come together on the basis of the laws of motion, then we cannot make sense of the parts of the bird or their relations. This is because, from the perspective of mechanical physics, which does not concern their distinctive capacities or internal relations, but only focuses on their external relations and place in space, they appear to be entirely contingent. Put differently, mechanical physics does not tell us why these parts in particular are relevant for the bird.

Insofar as mechanics and efficient causality are the source of necessity in nature, it follows that the bird's structure—its distinctive parts and their relations—appears non-necessary (i.e., contingent). Accordingly, if we want to discern necessity here—if we want to make the bird's structure intelligible—we must conceive of the bird as a *different kind of whole*. We must, in other words, assume a perspective other than that of mechanical physics. Teleological judgment enables us to conceive of the bird as this different kind of whole, a whole that Kant describes, at least to begin with, as a "cause and effect of itself" (AA 5, 370).

To explain what he means by "cause and effect of itself," Kant offers the example of a tree. The tree is a cause and effect of itself in three ways. First, it is a member of a species, and is thereby both an "effect" and a "cause" of its species. Second, it nourishes itself. This involves taking in external material and transforming it for its own goals. In this way it is "causing" itself—enabling its own growth and development. Finally, and most relevant for our purposes, the tree is a whole that cannot exist without its parts. For instance, the leaves on the tree are necessary for the tree, but they also cannot exist outside the tree. Accordingly, the tree both "causes" its parts and is "caused" by them. There is, in other words, a distinctive causal relationship between the parts and the whole: neither can exist without the other, such that neither precedes the other.

Immediately, it becomes evident why the unity of a tree or a bird is unlike that of a material whole: the material whole is a product of its parts and their coming together in space. This means that to explicate a material whole, we can reduce it to its parts, and their place and motion in space. The tree, by contrast, is not merely the outcome of its parts. It is also their cause. Accordingly, understanding the tree cannot involve reducing it to its parts, or their movement in space. Furthermore, the fact that they emerge *in* the whole rather than before it means that the parts and their relations are not (only) determined by the laws of motion. They are (also) determined by the whole in which they emerge.

To grasp these wholes, Kant contends, we must invoke the notion of purpose or final cause. For it will allow us to see how all the parts are acting *in concert* to bring about the whole (the purpose), and, in turn, to see how the whole (the purpose) enables the emergence of the parts. But what exactly does this involve? There are, at least, two ways by which to understand the whole as a "purpose," which means that there are at least two ways by which to try to understand the *kind* of purpose an organized being is.

First, we can conceive of purpose as something *external* to the whole: as an end or goal which the whole is working toward. This is what Kant describes as "external purposiveness" in Section 63, where he distinguishes two forms of external purposiveness. In the first instance, external purposiveness concerns the relationship between an organized being and other organized beings (e.g., humans) or an organized being and its context (i.e., its environment). On this view, an object is purposive because of its relation to other beings—a relation that is often identified as a service. A clock, for instance, is purposive because it can tell the time. A flower can be similarly considered purposive because of its significance for bees. In both cases, the object (clock, flower) is understood in relation to this external purpose. A clock is the kind of thing it is because it is for telling time. A flower is the kind of thing it is because of the services it renders to bees.

The second instance of external purposiveness is based on the artifact model. On this view, something is what it is because of the idea (the blueprint) upon which it is based. As in the first case, so here the purpose is external: the idea precedes and is outside the object. A cup, for example, is made according to an idea that originates in the mind of its maker. When this notion of purpose is applied to organized beings, organized beings are understood as created according to an external idea, which originates in the mind of a creator (God). This means that the structure, behavior, and actions of the object (whether the cup or the organized being) are understood in terms of an idea or intention that originated *outside* the object. As in the first case of external purposiveness, so also here, the objects are explicable through something beyond themselves (the services they render, their relations to other beings, or the blueprint according to which they are constructed).

Both forms of external purposiveness contrast with what Kant calls "internal purposiveness." In this instance, the whole is not serving a goal outside of itself. Rather, its goal is internal: itself. Furthermore, an internally purposive object is not constructed according to an idea that originates outside of the object (the mind of its maker). Rather, the "idea," the "blueprint," is *in* the object—and cannot be located elsewhere. But if the "blueprint" is wholly internal, then the object cannot be constructed by something outside it. As such, it is *self*-constructing.

This is the conception of purpose or final causality that Kant invokes to explicate organization in nature. Like Aristotle's conception of final cause, it approximates the notion of formal cause.[41] A formal cause concerns the design or structure of an object. When it comes to artifacts, this design is, to begin with, external—in the mind of the maker, or in the blueprint. Once the object is made, the design or structure is realized in the object, and thus becomes (in some sense) internal. In living beings, by contrast, the design or structure is always internal. This is because the structure of a living being is deeply connected to its purpose: the structure is *realized* through the purpose (self-construction; self-maintenance), and the purpose is realized in and through the structure. Put differently, in the case of internally purposive beings, the purpose is *nothing other than* the maintenance of the structure. The final cause, in other words, is the ongoing realization of the formal cause. In a clock, by contrast, the final cause—telling the time—requires the structure but does not aim to realize it. It has a different aim, and the formal cause is only a means for achieving this aim. Accordingly, in the case of artifacts, the final and formal causes are ultimately separable.

Interestingly, Kant claims that there can only be *two* kinds of causes: efficient and final (AA 5, 373). While this might suggest that Kant does not take formal causality seriously, in light of his understanding of internal purposiveness, a more appropriate interpretation would be that internal purposiveness *includes* both final and formal cause, and it is for this reason that Kant claims that there are only two causes. My suggestion then is that when Kant speaks of internal purposiveness, he is invoking both formal and final cause: a cause that *actively* maintains its *structure* or *form* as its end.[42]

This helps us to better understand the structure of organized beings and how they differ from machines. For, machines are—as we have seen—also purposive.[43] They are made *with a purpose* in mind, such that to understand the clock *as a clock* we must invoke its purpose (consider what it is *for*). However, understanding the *function* of a clock—the way its parts relate to one another, the way that these parts emerge, and so on—does not require us to conceive of the clock in terms of a purpose. Its function is explicable through the mechanical laws of motion. This is not the kind of purpose that Kant locates in organized beings, which is internal and concerns the relations between its parts. These relations—unlike in the case of the clock—are inexplicable through the laws of motion and efficient causality. Why is this the case?

First, in an organized being, the parts do not preexist the whole *and* do not preexist one another. Rather, they exist *in and through* one another and the whole. As Kant explains, the parts must "be combined into a whole by being reciprocally the cause and effect of their form" (AA 5, 373). In other words, the parts are reciprocal cause and effect. They are *formed* in and through their relations with one another, *and* they *inform* one another. Or, as he puts it later, an organized being "must be thought of as an organ that *produces* the other parts (consequently each produces the others reciprocally)," and is therefore rightly described as "self-organizing" (AA 5, 374).

What distinguishes clocks from organized beings, then, are the distinctive relations between the parts and between the parts and the whole. It is *these* relations that cannot be explicated by either the mechanical laws of motion or external purposiveness (i.e., what it is *for*). For the relationship between the parts of an organized being is not simply a relationship of cooperation aimed to achieve an end (e.g., telling the time or flight), but also—and more fundamentally—a relation of absolute dependence, such that no part exists independently of the other, and every part is at once cause and effect. It is in light of this distinctive structure that Kant describes an organized being as having a "formative power," in contrast to the "motive power" of a machine (AA 5, 374).

Now the fact that in an organized being the parts are reciprocally self-forming, that they are formed in and through their relations with one another, carries with it important structural and epistemological implications. First, it implies that in organized beings there is not only a successive temporal structure, but also a recursive one.[44] In other words, once we start to conceive of all the parts as causes and effects of one another, it becomes evident that the parts that emerge at the *end* of development cannot only be conceived as "effects," but must also be understood as "causes." That is to say, it is not only the beginning that determines the end, but the end also determines the beginning, and indeed the entire developmental process. In the same way that the formation of the fruit presupposes the formation of the flower, so also the *possibility* of the fruit is *implied* in the *development* of the flower. The flower *anticipates* and *makes possible* the fruit. Accordingly, in an organized being, the past, present, and future are internally related to one another, such that the end (future) is inscribed at the beginning and at every moment of development.

This means that all are equally cause and effect, such that cause and effect cannot be easily or fully distinguished. Rather, and in close alignment with formal causality, what we find is an identity between the "cause" and the "effect"—between the structure of the house and the house itself, or the structure of the bird and the bird itself. This suggests that the language of cause and effect might not be useful in this context, and it is perhaps the reason why Kant describes the notion of "cause and effect of itself" as "provisional." It is a first step, and our goal is to develop a better conceptual apparatus—which is achieved in the idea of "self-organization" (AA 5, 374).

It is precisely because organized beings exhibit these characteristics that, as Kant writes, they "cannot be *explained* [*erklärt*] through the capacity of movement alone (that is, mechanism)" (AA 5, 374; emphasis added). However, it is not clear that they can be "explained" at all. For, as Kant notes some pages later, "to explain is to derive from an a priori principle [*denn erklären heißt von einem Prinzip ableiten*]" (AA 5, 411). Given that organized beings cannot be derived from the a priori laws of the understanding, or the mechanical laws of nature, the question is: from which principle are they to be derived?

This is, in a crucial sense, the question that is being posed in the Antinomy of Teleological Judgment. For, as we shall see, the goal of the antinomy is to determine the scientific status of teleological judgments—that is, determine their ability to "explain." If they cannot explain—"derive from a principle"—then their scientific status is, at best, questionable.

1.6. The Antinomy of Teleological Judgment

In the Antinomy of Teleological Judgment Kant turns his attention to the competing claims of mechanical physics, on the one hand, and teleology, on the other. In so doing, he addresses the *scientific status* of teleological judgment over against judgments based on mechanical principles. That is, in pitting mechanical principles against teleological ones, Kant's aim is to determine the role of teleological judgment in scientific research. Given that teleological judgment is based on analogy and proceeds analogically, in considering the status of teleological judgment in science, Kant is also assessing the significance of analogical reflection and symbolic cognition in our understanding of nature. In short, he is determining the place *and* the limits of analogy in knowledge.

That the Antinomy of Teleological Judgment offers the most direct engagement with these central questions is not surprising, given the significance of antinomies in Kant's overall project.[45] This particular antinomy, however, is riddled with difficulties and differs in form from Kant's other antinomies: it contains two different antinomies, it proceeds in a way that leads the reader to assume a resolution has been reached when in fact, the reader soon realizes, the resolution remains to be developed, and finally, this resolution—if and when it does arrive—is not clearly justified.[46]

The difficulties that the antinomy and its structure pose have not gone unnoticed, and many attempts to determine its resolution have been provided.[47] That these difficulties concern the relationship between explanation and nonexplanation in science, and the place of analogy and analogical reflection in scientific research, has not, however, been widely noted. As I will argue, the Antinomy of Teleological Judgment is concerned with the role of nonexplanatory modes of knowledge in science, and thus offers an important response to the question concerning the status of analogy.

As aforementioned, when applied to the natural world, teleological judgment is analogical. It is motivated by an analogy between nature and art, and it proceeds analogically. That is, it applies the rules of reflecting on art onto organized beings, and in this way makes them intelligible. As noted, the "thought" of such beings, as well as "experiential cognition" of them, is impossible without this analogy (AA 5, 398). Accordingly, when Kant considers the place of teleological judgment in scientific research, he is also considering the role of analogical reflection—of seeing something *as* something else—in science.

Now, the antinomy contains two different antinomies—the first thesis and antithesis are concerned with regulative principles, while the second set is concerned with constitutive ones, i.e., with whether there are in fact beings that are mechanically inexplicable. In the first set, the conflict is on the level of judgment, while in the second it is on the level of ontology. Given that the *Critique of the Power of Judgment* is concerned with judging, it is (now) generally agreed that the first antinomy (on the level of judgment) is the true antinomy.[48] I will follow this interpretation, which means that the conflict is between the two following maxims:

Thesis: "All generation of material things and their forms must be judged as possible in accordance with merely mechanical laws."

Antithesis: "some products of material nature cannot be judged as possible according to merely mechanical laws," such that, "judging them requires an entirely different law of causality, namely that of final causes." (AA 5, 387)

The two maxims are (purportedly) reflective and thus do not determine objects a priori. Rather, they obtain only for empirical study, which means that the conflict pertains to the directive for undertaking empirical research. The aim is to offer a resolution to these conflicting directives—should we judge nature *only* according to mechanical laws (thesis)? Or should we allow that certain objects require us to judge nature according to teleological principles (antithesis)?

A crucial question concerns the justifications of the two claims. In Section 70, Kant claims that when it comes to the reflecting power of judgment, its two maxims (i.e., the thesis and the antithesis) are derived from, on the one hand, "the mere understanding a priori" (thesis), and, on the other hand, "particular experiences" (antithesis) (AA 5, 386). The justifications of the two claims are thus, respectively, the a priori laws of the understanding and empirical experience. This seems to be confirmed by Kant's statement that judgment according to mechanical principles "never strays from the sensible world" (AA 5, 389). In other words, judgments according to mechanical principles are justified because they structure experience. Judgments according to teleology, by contrast, are justified through particular experiences.

The different sources of justification seem to imply a hierarchy. Given that the thesis is justified on the basis of the a priori laws of the understanding, there is good reason to prefer it. And, indeed, this seems to be Kant's ultimate "resolution."[49] For although he claims that teleological judgment is "indispensable" and mechanical principles "must always remain inadequate for things that we have once recognized to be natural ends," such that "we must always subordinate all such mechanical grounds to a teleological principle," he goes on to add that we have an "authorization [*Befugniß*]" and indeed an "obligation [*Beruf*]" "to give a mechanical *explanation* of all the products and events in nature, *even the most purposive*" (AA 5, 415; emphasis added). The implication is that we *ought* to give a mechanical explanation, even in cases where such an explanation would not be illuminating. And the reason for this appears to be simply that *as scientists* we *must* seek to uphold the basic premises of science. In other words, there is an imperative here—an obligation and an authorization—to uphold the a priori categories of the understanding.[50]

If this is the "resolution" to the antinomy—and I am not suggesting that it is, only that it might appear so given Kant's statements—then it leaves many questions unanswered. For one, the two conflicting maxims remain side by side. On the very same page we are told to proceed in opposing ways, without explicit justification for the one or the other. Furthermore, and from a practical perspective, Kant does not offer the scientist a clear directive. On what occasions, in which contexts, are we permitted to invoke teleological principles—if at all? What do we do in a situation where we *are* confronted with an organized being: are we still under the obligation to explain it according to mechanical principles? Or is this an occasion where we must subordinate mechanical principles to teleological ones?

Without completely leaving these questions behind, I want to return to the question concerning explanation broached above, as a way to think beyond the conflict. Kant identifies mechanism with science at various junctures in the third *Critique*: without "the principle of mechanism," he writes, "there can be no science of nature at all" (AA 5, 418). Or, as he puts it some pages earlier, lacking mechanical principles "no insight into the nature of things can be attained" (AA 5, 410). The claim is that mechanism is scientific because it can offer explanations—it can derive its objects from (a priori) principles.

The antithesis, by contrast, cannot offer an explanation, because, as Kant puts it, the ground for such an explanation (i.e., teleological principles) lies beyond the boundaries of science (AA 5, 412). Accordingly, the antithesis does not possess the same scientific status as the thesis. Nonetheless, Kant grants it a special capacity, which he describes as "elucidation [*Erörterung*]" and "description [*Beschreibung*]" (AA 5, 412; 417). To elucidate is not to explain, to derive from a principle, to determine *where* something comes from or *why* it is the way it is. To elucidate, rather, is to describe, hold together, and compare. It is to see things in relation to one another, *without* drawing inferences about their cause. Thus, Kant writes that although teleological judgment "does not make the way in which these products *have originated more comprehensible*, it is still a heuristic principle for researching the particular laws of nature" (AA 5, 411; emphasis added). As a principle of elucidation, teleological judgment does not tell us anything about how organized beings come about; it does not illuminate their a priori conditions of possibility. This recalls Kant's description of teleological judgment in Section 61: it is "problematic," we are told, because it proceeds via analogy. Accordingly it can bring nature "under principles of observation ... without presuming thereby to explain it" (AA 5, 360).

In Section 61, Kant does not tell us the exact meaning or import of the terms *explanation* and *observation*. Nonetheless, he is signaling two different tasks, to which he will turn in his discussion of the antinomy. For, as we have just seen, judgments according to mechanical principles (i.e., the thesis) are explanatory. We have an obligation "to give a mechanical explanation of all products in nature." And it is presumably their explanatory capacity that leads Kant to prioritize them. By contrast, teleological judgments are nonexplanatory and become *problematic* as soon as they presume to explain.

What then do teleological judgments achieve, if not explanations? What, in other words, does it mean to "elucidate," "describe," "bring under principles of observation," while refraining from explanation as derivation? To answer these questions, it is crucial to consider what teleological judgment *can do* in contrast to mechanical principles. As we have seen, teleological judgment can grasp a distinctive *kind* of whole or unity: one that is not the outcome of its parts, and one that is not merely for an external purpose or end. Rather, the kind of unity that teleological judgment is able to grasp is a whole that is irreducible to its parts, where each of the parts is necessary, and where the parts are informed by one another. To enable us to grasp this distinctive whole, teleological judgment directs us to draw an analogy with art, i.e., to see these entities *as* works of art.

The analogy with art is often understood in terms of purpose or intentionality, given Kant's claims that the concept of purpose in nature is "conceived in terms of an analogy" with "that of practical purposiveness (of human art as well as of morals)" (AA 5, 181). In other words, the analogy between nature and art appears to focus on the intentional character of art, with the implication being that if we consider certain beings *as* intentional, then we begin to grasp their distinctive structure.

This, however, does not cohere with Kant's distinction between machines and organized beings, between external purpose and inner purpose. As we have seen, what differentiates "purposive" machines from "purposive" organized beings is that the former are to be understood in terms of an *external purpose or end*—what they are *for*. Organized beings, by contrast, should not be regarded in this way. In fact, to conceive of them in this way amounts to offering an explanation, insofar as explanation involves deriving from an external principle. To claim that an organized being is *for* something is one way of *deriving* it—for example from some external purpose or idea in the mind of its creator.

However, as Kant emphasizes, the purposive character of organized beings has nothing to do with an external intention, but with the formative relations between the parts and between the parts and the whole. In other words, when one considers an organized being, the crucial question is not *what is it for*—as would be the case with a machine—but *how does it appear*. Put differently, the crucial question is not *why does it act in this way* (where the answer would be: for some external end that determines its activity and development), but rather, *how does it act* (where the answer would be: on account of its distinctive part-whole structure, and the relations between its parts).

This is the reason why Kant repeatedly directs his readers to consider the *structure* or *form* of the organized being. It is, after all, not any individual part of the bird that is inexplicable by mechanical principles, but its *structure* and the *relations* between its parts. And, as he puts it in Section 64, in order for us to determine something as a natural end, we must consider how its "form" is not "possible according to mere natural laws" (AA 5, 370). The implication then is that there is something *about the form* itself that is inexplicable and requires teleological judgment.

If we consider the structure of the bird, we attend to the shape of its wings and their placement in the body as a whole, take note of the tail and its placement, recognize its hollow bones, and so on. In so doing, we begin to discern a relationship *between* the parts: that the hollowness of the bird's bones *goes hand in hand* with its wings and feathers; that the shape of its wings *goes hand in hand* with their place on the bird's body. In other words, as soon as we focus on the structure of the whole, and consider the parts in relation to one another, we begin to see that the parts are fundamentally connected, that each is a part *of* the whole and is playing a crucial role within it, that the whole is "inscribed" on every part, and each part is expressing and contributing to the whole in its distinctive way. Ultimately, once we regard the parts as part of a whole, and see them in their relations to one another, they no longer appear random or contingent. We see that there is a continuity between them—each part *works with and in relation to* the other parts.

This is what teleological judgment conveys: it is elucidation, description, and observation that does not involve derivation from a principle. Rather, it makes intelligible a structure and relations that had previously appeared unintelligible or contingent—without "explaining" them. As such, teleological judgment *remains with* the phenomenon. But if this is the case, then the *analogy with art* is not so much an analogy with art *as intentional activity* but rather with art *as composition*: with an artwork as an integrated unity, whose parts are related to one another, and are expressions of the whole. This, I submit, is the meaning and significance of *internal* purposiveness.

1.7. Teleological Judgment, Intuitive Understanding, and the Goals of Science

An important interpretation of the resolution of the antinomy of teleological judgment invokes the final sections in which Kant introduces the notion of "intuitive understanding." Put forward by Eckart Förster, this interpretation claims that the resolution of the conflict between the two principles (mechanism and teleology) is only possible for an intuitive understanding.[51]

Kant introduces the idea of an intuitive understanding in Sections 76 and 77 of the third *Critique*, where he distinguishes discursive and intuitive forms of understanding by way of three examples. The third example, which concerns the difference between mechanical and teleological judgments, is the most relevant for our purposes and so I will focus on it.

In this context, Kant claims that while for us (as discursive beings) there is a conflict between the two principles (mechanical and teleological), for an intuitive understanding no such conflict arises (AA 5, 404–5). A discursive understanding proceeds from the "analytically universal" to the particular. That is, it begins with the pure concepts of the understanding, and goes on to apply them to the particular. This results in knowledge. In cases where there are no adequate concepts, however, knowledge cannot be achieved, and instead we have contingency.

An intuitive understanding, by contrast, begins with the "synthetically universal," which Kant identifies with "the intuition of the whole as such." From this "intuition of the whole as such," intuitive understanding goes on to grasp the particular. Unlike the pure concepts of the understanding, the intuition of the whole as such—the synthetically universal—is not a concept that fails to grasp the particular in all its necessity. Rather, Kant continues, the intuitive understanding proceeds "from the whole to the parts, in which, therefore, and in whose representation of the whole, there is no *contingency* in the combination of the parts" (AA 5, 407).

Immediately, several questions emerge. First, what does Kant mean by "the whole as such"? Second, how does intuitive understanding differ from teleological judgment? And finally, if intuitive understanding offers a resolution to the antinomy of teleological judgment, then does it also offer an "explanation"?

Kant's description of *the whole as such* appears to closely approximate the kind of unity that teleological judgment aims to grasp. This is because *the whole as such* is a unity in which the parts appear necessary. This necessity is not located outside the whole, but is internal to it, having to do with its distinctive parts and their relations. As Kant puts it, there is no contingency *in the combination* of the parts, such that we could not say, *they could have been otherwise*. Accordingly, *the whole as such* differs from a *material whole*, where necessity is located outside the parts and their relations, i.e., in the laws of motion. It also differs from the unity we find in a machine. For there too, necessity is not internal. What joins the parts, what puts them in their particular place and activates them, is either an external goal—a goal beyond the individual parts and indeed the whole itself (the goal of a clock is not the clock itself, but telling the time)—or an idea that originates in the mind of the creator. It thus appears that *the whole as such* is the self-organizing unity that Kant has been describing all along.

At this point it is important to recall that Kant first speaks of intuitive understanding in the (published) Introduction to the third *Critique*. By contrast, Kant makes no mention of intuitive understanding in the First Introduction. Instead, he emphasizes the analogy between nature and art and claims that teleological judgment must proceed analogically. By regarding nature as art, teleological judgment discerns unity and necessity in nature's forms. Thus, through the analogy with art, teleological judgment is able to grasp the *whole as such* of intuitive understanding. The close connection between the two modes of knowing is confirmed by the fact that the analogy with art disappears in precisely that part of the (published) Introduction where Kant introduces intuitive understanding. It appears that Kant *replaces* the analogy with art, and the analogical procedure of teleological judgment, with intuitive understanding. Accordingly, rather than describing teleological judgment as a mode of seeing nature as art—seeing nature as a whole that is composed of interrelated and necessary parts—Kant invokes the idea of an intuitive understanding, which, unsurprisingly, also sees nature as this kind of whole. What then distinguishes the two forms of cognition?

A clear difference has to do with the fact that teleological judgment when it turns to consider nature, relies on analogy. Intuitive understanding does not. After all, teleological judgment arrives at its insights into nature by *way of the analogy with art*, i.e., by seeing one thing (organization in nature) *through* or *as* another (the work of art). We can therefore say that while intuitive understanding has no need for analogy, teleological judgment (of nature) depends on it. It thus appears that we invoke teleological judgment in order to overcome our cognitive tendency to see the whole as a mere outcome of preexisting parts. Through the analogy with art, then, teleological judgment enables us to see relations in nature that would otherwise remain inaccessible to us (AA 5, 408).

This includes relations of internal purpose, which, as we have seen, differ significantly from relations in externally purposive objects. In an internally purposive being, the parts are parts of the whole and are—in a significant sense—also the whole. The leaves are parts of the tree, but they are *also* the tree. This is because the whole that they realize is not outside of them (the "tree" does not exist somewhere beyond the leaves). In turn, they cannot emerge outside the whole. Furthermore, the parts emerge in relation to one another. Accordingly, their "goal" is not an external end—a service they render to an external party. Rather, they serve one another. The leaves of a tree depend on the tree's branches, just as much as the branches depend on the leaves. Neither part is external to the tree, or to the other part. These internally purposive relations, ultimately, have to do with the fact that the whole (as the "end") is nothing other than the parts and their ongoing relations (the structure). The tree, in other words, is both the final cause *and* the formal cause.

This implies that teleological judgment is best understood as a means of arriving at insight into *the whole as such*. If this is the case, then the insight *achieved* through teleological judgment is the insight with which intuitive understanding *begins*. In short, teleological judgment's goal is *the whole as such* of intuitive understanding.

This leaves us with many questions. For one, if *the whole as such* is the goal of teleological judgment, then can we, through teleological judgment, achieve intuitive understanding? This question can be understood in two ways. On the one hand, we are asking whether, through teleological judgment, we might become privy (despite our discursive intellect) to the insights of intuitive understanding. That is to say: can we somehow grasp *the whole as such* of the intuitive understanding—via teleological judgment? And if so, what is the (scientific and cognitive) status of this insight? Does it amount to scientific knowledge? Or does it remain *problematic*—because it is the outcome of analogical reflection?

On the other hand, and more radically, we are asking whether, through the *practice* of teleological judging, we might actually *achieve* intuitive understanding—and not simply its insights. In other words, can we, through a concerted practice of seeing nature as art, *transform* our cognitive capacities so that they *become* intuitive?

The fact that Kant did not consider these questions is, perhaps, the reason why the resolution to the antinomy of teleological judgment is so elusive. For if, with Förster, we regard intuitive understanding as the resolution to the antinomy, it remains unclear how this can function as a genuine solution—unless, of course, we were to *become* intuitive. After all, the antinomy concerns scientific practice, and unless we become intuitive, it is not clear how intuitive understanding offers a way beyond the conflict between opposing directives in scientific research.

Ultimately, Kant's resolution needs to respond to crucial methodological and epistemological questions concerning when, and how, teleological judgment (or intuitive understanding) is appropriate (and justified) and when it is not; questions concerning the *kinds* of contributions teleological judgment (or intuitive understanding) can make to scientific research, and the *status* of these contributions; questions, in other words, that make sense of Kant's claim that teleological judgment is "indispensable" even though it is nonexplanatory. What would a nonexplanatory scientific research program look like and how would it fit with an explanatory one? Or, put differently, how can *elucidation* and *description* expand and deepen our understanding of nature—without offering explanations?

Lacking answers to these questions, the methodology that Kant articulates in the *Critique of the Power of Judgment* remains ambiguous. Yet it was precisely these questions that motivated the romantic empiricists and inspired them to develop a new approach to the natural world. And while Kant provided no final answers on the role of analogical reflection and intuitive understanding in scientific knowledge and practice, Herder, Goethe, and Humboldt were convinced of their significance for deepening and expanding our understanding of nature. In fact, they came to the conclusion that the model of science and scientific explanation that Kant had assumed, and which led him to prioritize mechanical explanation, is problematic and undesirable. For, they argued, the goal of science is not derivation from a priori principles, but observation, description, elucidation, and understanding—all of which *serve and enable* genuine explanation.

2

The Hermeneutics of Nature

Herder on Animal and Human Worlds

If there is one lesson to be taken from Kant's *Critique of the Power of Judgment*, it is that nature *appears* differently, depending on the tools, assumptions, and methods deployed. While from the perspective of mechanical physics, the structure of a bird appears entirely contingent, from the perspective of teleology, each of the bird's parts appears necessary, a member of an integrated unity. Seeing, in other words, is not neutral, and what appears—or disappears—depends on *how* one observes. Through the lens of mechanical physics, the whole organism disappears. Through the analogy with art, it appears.

In the Antinomy of Teleological Judgment, Kant sought to overcome the opposition between the two positions, the two *appearances*. However, it is not self-evident that this reconciliation is possible, or even necessary. As Goethe will argue, there are different levels of inquiry, and the phenomenon appears differently depending on the level at which the inquiry is undertaken—on the questions asked, the devices used, and the skills that are applied. Accordingly, rather than seeking to reconcile the two appearances, Goethe contends, it is important to acknowledge that there are *different* appearances and the aim is to arrive at the *richest* perspective: the one that reveals the phenomenon most fully.

The lens of analogical reflection—of seeing nature *as* art—offers a richer perspective, in that it can account for both the distinctive structure of organized beings *and* the mechanical relations between their parts. As Kant notes, while teleology can accommodate simple (mechanical) growth (there is, for instance, nothing paradoxical about the growth of hair or nails within a living being) mechanical principles cannot accommodate ("explicate") organized relations. This means that teleology, precisely because it offers the richer account, should be prioritized. This does not imply, however, that mechanical relations do not exist or that certain phenomena are not explicable entirely mechanically. Rather, it implies that different approaches, invoking different methodologies, are apt for different levels of inquiry, and the real question is not how to overcome the opposition between them, but rather, how to work with *both* approaches in a coherent way. In other words, the crucial question is an *interpretive* one: given the various modes of inquiry, it is necessary to consider which mode is apt in a given context.

This interpretive understanding of scientific inquiry is at the heart of Herder's project. Like Buffon and Diderot before him, Herder was convinced that genuine knowledge must remain *with* the phenomenon, rather than look beyond it for explanations. Accordingly, if the goal is to discern order and understand relations within nature, then we must aim to discern unity *in*, rather than impose it *upon*, the natural world. The question then is, how and where are we to find this unity? This was the question that Diderot posed in *Thoughts on the Interpretation of Nature*, and the question with which Kant introduced the *Critique of the Power of Judgment*.[1] And, interestingly, both invoked literary modes of knowledge: analogy, "interpretation," and reflecting judgment.[2] However, while Diderot—and Buffon before him—embraced these modes, Kant, as we have seen, remained ambivalent, inviting his readers to find in his writings two (radically) different approaches to the study of nature.[3]

The question of course remains as to how exactly the use of analogy and "interpretation" play a role in the development, expansion, and deepening of our understanding of the natural world. Does knowing nature via analogy lead us to think of nature (and our place within it) differently?

This question, in fact, contains two questions, each of which takes a different (though related) angle on the place of analogy in knowledge. On the one hand, there is the question concerning the use of analogy—as a (literary) tool—for the expansion of knowledge. Through the analogy between nature and art, for instance, objects and relations that had been previously hidden are made visible. On the other hand, there is the question concerning the significance of analogy *as such* in cognition. For instance, the claim that our experience of organized beings in nature depends on analogy suggests that analogical reflection is a basic cognitive process. In other words, analogy is not simply a heuristic device, but underpins cognitive activity.

This dual significance of analogy was evident to Herder, and his project can be understood as an attempt to explicate both aspects of analogy. Like Buffon and Diderot, Herder was convinced that knowledge of the "real relations" within nature depends on the use of analogy—that is, analogy as a (literary) tool for the expansion of knowledge. As he puts it 1778, "Newton became a poet contrary to his wishes," and, like Buffon, "gave birth to the greatest and boldest theories" through "*a single* new image [*Bild*], *a single* analogy [*Analogie*], *a single* striking metaphor [*auffallendes Gleichnis*]" (FHA 4, 330; HPW 188). Analogy, in other words, is a crucial means by which to expand and deepen our understanding of the natural world. Furthermore, Herder agreed with Diderot that the use of analogy involves interpretation, because analogical reflection invites revisitation and thus reinterpretation of the phenomena. For Herder, analogical reflection facilitates a new hermeneutic, interpretive approach to the study of nature—an approach that he carried out far more extensively than either Buffon or Diderot.[4] In so doing, as I hope to show in the following, Herder delivered a novel—ecological—understanding of nature.[5]

However, Herder did not regard analogy simply as a tool for the expansion of knowledge. Rather, he came to the conclusion that knowledge itself is analogical. As he writes in "On Cognition and Sensation of the Human Soul [*Vom Erkennen und Empfinden der menschlichen Seele*], (1778)" "What we know, we only know through analogy" (FHA 4, 330; HPW 188). That is to say, the as-structure of analogy—seeing one thing as or through another—underlies the cognitive process *as such*. This is because, as Herder contends in the 1772 "Treatise on the Origin of Language [*Abhandlung über den Ursprung der Sprache*]," we are essentially *interpretive* beings: beings who encounter a meaningful, expressive world, a world that speaks to us, and that calls upon us to "read" its signs. This does not mean, however, that we do not need the tool of analogy for interpreting these signs aptly or appropriately. We do. What it does mean is that human beings posses the ability to read the world, to discern its sounds and signs, and to reflect upon them. And with this ability, as Herder suggests and Goethe and Humboldt go on to elaborate, comes a particular responsibility.

2.1. The Problem with "Nature"

Any consideration of Herder's understanding of analogy must begin with his critique of philosophical methodology and abstraction, including his critique of the concept of nature. The problem with "nature," as Herder sees it, is that it is an abstract concept that is used to convey and refer to concrete realities and specific processes and activities. Or, as he puts it in a 1769 letter to Moses Mendelssohn,

> Nothing in the world has produced more opinions and perhaps also more errors than that one has considered and hypostatized [*realisiert*] abstract concepts as individual existences. Thus do we hypostatize the word Nature, Virtue, *Reality, Perfection*. Originally these concepts were nothing but abstractions, relations of this to that, so-to-speak shadows and colors of things; we make them into things themselves, and hence imagine finished objects [*Fertigkeiten*].[6]

The problem with certain concepts—such as nature—is not that they are abstract, but that they are "hypostatized." That is, they are taken to refer to concrete realities when in fact they cannot. After all, "nature" does not refer to any one object, and its meaningfulness ultimately rests on conceptual opposition (with "culture"). In other words, "nature" only makes sense in its difference from another (equally abstract) concept. Accordingly, any attempt to describe something as "natural" assumes this (largely implicit) opposition. This hypostatized character of the concept of nature leads to two mistakes.

On the one hand, we believe that when we call something "natural" we are offering a concrete description. The opposite, however, is the case. For one, the concept of nature is too general to be able to tell us anything concrete or to adequately account for the diversity of objects that sit under its conceptual umbrella. Furthermore, given that its meaningfulness appears to arise via conceptual opposition (with culture), in employing the term we are implicitly employing that opposition. This means, as Herder argues, that the only way we can productively use terms like nature is when we contextualize them—understand how the particular phenomenon realizes "nature."

On the other hand, hypostatized concepts are taken to apply to "finished objects." In the case of nature, this means that we take *nature* to refer to *some object*—a tree, a waterfall, a kangaroo. Thus we end up identifying nature with objects, things. But, as Herder will later argue (drawing on Spinoza to do so), nature is not a finished product (*natura naturata*), but productivity (*natura naturans*), an ongoing process.[7] Accordingly, if we are to use the concept *nature*, we must find a way by which to grasp and convey nature as process, as productivity. This means that we must not attend to objects, but to the relations between objects. Only in this way can we grasp nature as process.

This is important, not only for understanding Herder, but also for assessing his "naturalism." Herder has been traditionally interpreted as a "naturalist"—an interpretation that goes back to Kant's critical reviews of *Ideas*.[8] However, if Herder is a critic of the common use of the concept of nature, it follows that any interpretation of his "naturalism" must take account of both his critique and his alternative. This means taking account of his methodology. For, as Herder explains in the same letter to Mendelssohn, the only way to overcome hypostatization is by "going back to the origin of these words [*Ursprünge dieser Worte zurückzugehen*]." Only in this way, he continues, can begin to "see in them the substantive phenomena [*phenomena substantia*]." Accordingly, crucial questions concerning Herder's understanding of "nature" and his "naturalism" require grasping what Herder means by "going back" to the origin of concepts, and how this going back permits us to see the substantive phenomena "in them." The question thus is: how does this "going back" allow us to avoid hypostatization, and enable us to develop a non-abstract account of nature—of nature as it manifests itself concretely in and through processes, situations, and relations?

To answer these questions, we too will have to "go back," even if only briefly, to Buffon, and in particular to Buffon's articulation of the crucial problem facing any attempt to grasp the natural world and its manifold relations.

2.2. Nature's Many Directions

As we have seen, Buffon articulates the epistemological problem in terms of direction: our intellect proceeds linearly, takes one step at a time, and in one direction. We consider one part of a living being, then move to consider another part, and then another, and so on. Nature, however, does not. Rather, "in marching forward, she extends to the sides and above."[9] This is because nature does not consist of isolated parts emerging in a purely sequential order, but of manifold relations among many different beings, relations that can be historical, geographic, genetic, and so on. Nature is not unidirectional, but multidirectional and multivalent. Grasping this multiplicity and finding unity therein is the crucial aim of the scientist. Or in Buffon's words: "one can say that the love and study of nature presuppose in the spirit of the investigator two qualities that are opposed: the grand view of an ardent genius, who embraces everything in one glance [*embrasse tout d'un coup d'oeil*], and the detailed attention of a laborious instinct that does not attach itself to any one point."[10] The student of nature, in other words, must find a way by which to unify two conflicting gestures: an all-embracing "one glance" and careful, detailed description. This is no easy task.

For one, the task faces an epistemological hurdle—a point that Kant highlights in the third *Critique*. As he puts it in the Introduction, "for us" nature appears "so confused." To this Kant adds that nature's "infinitely manifold . . . is not fitted for *our power of comprehension*" (AA 5, 185; emphasis added). The epistemological incongruence necessarily results in methodological difficulties and the need for a methodological solution, as suggested by Buffon's statement. For the goal must be to overcome this incongruity between our cognitive faculties and the natural world; otherwise, as Herder puts it, we cannot "gather hope" (FHA 6, 165). What, then, are the methods needed in order to achieve this goal? What concepts, approaches, and skills must be developed to overcome this epistemological incongruence?

Buffon's articulation of the problem, and his solution to it, were crucial for Herder's own understanding of the problem. Buffon's *Natural History* was an unparalleled success in the eighteenth century. It was translated into almost every European language, and by 1780, it was the third most read book in France. Herder may have first learned about Buffon through Hamann, but it is certain that by the time he arrived in Paris in November 1769 and met with Diderot, Herder was familiar with the *Natural History*.[11] He mentions Buffon in a number of his works from the period—first in his 1768 essay on the philosopher and writer Thomas Abbt, "On Thomas Abbt's Writing [*Ueber Thomas Abbts Schriften*]," and then again in the essay on the origin of language. However, Herder's attitude toward Buffon is mixed. On the one hand, he prizes Buffon's critique of abstraction, and regards it as necessary to combat all those systematizers who fail to observe nature. As he puts it in the essay on Abbt, "when our systematic philosopher becomes *Linnaeus* in the study of the mind, classifying according to their own principles [*eigensinnig*], an unsystematic mind, like *Buffon*, must be placed alongside them . . . in order to analyze the individuals" (FHA 2, 572). On the other hand, however, he worries about Buffon's tendency to dissect and analyze without finding a way by which to synthesize.

Herder expresses this worry clearly in the essay on the origin of language, where he places Buffon alongside Condillac and Bonnet, and criticizes all three for their failure to unify what they have dissected. He writes: "All dissections of sensation in the case of *Buffon's*, *Condillac's*, and *Bonnet's* sensing human being are abstractions; the philosopher has to neglect one thread of sensation in pursuing the other, but in nature all these threads are a single web!" (FHA 1, 745; HPW 107). Although Herder is here specifically concerned with their respective accounts of human psychology and physiology, his critique obtains for what he sees as a general tendency in Buffon's approach. Though Buffon *intends* to offer an integrated account of the natural world, his efforts are not fully realized.

This difference between Buffon and Herder is most evident in their respective responses to the problem of nature's many directions. To address this problem, Buffon introduces the notion of "climate," alongside nourishment.[12] By climate, he means primarily temperature, but also geography.[13] Speaking of horses, for instance, Buffon remarks that "studs kept in dry light soils produce active, nimble, and vigorous horses, with nervous limbs and strong hoofs; while those kept in moist ground, and in too rich pasturage, have generally large heavy heads, gross bodies, thick legs, bad hoofs, and broad feet. It is easy to perceive," he concludes, "that these differences proceed from the varieties in climate and food."[14] Similarly, when speaking of variation in human skin color, Buffon contends that it is due, on the one hand, to the climatic zone a human inhabits, and, on the other, to the influence of food.[15] By focusing on the particular situation, the context in which something emerges and develops, the concept of climate allows Buffon to follow nature's various directions: to discern the relations between the horse's overall structure and activity, on the one hand, and the soil, on the other.

While Buffon's notion of climate, and his focus on nourishment, make some headway in following nature's many directions, they are also limited. After all, they are only two factors, among many more. They follow *some* of nature's directions, but not *all* of them. As such, they do not achieve Buffon's goal of "embracing everything in one glance."

Though Herder does not specifically mention Buffon when he takes up this problem, his statements suggest that Buffon did not fully address the matter. Thus in contrast to Buffon's two categories (climate and nourishment), Herder contends that "it is much more the case that a large storehouse of other forces, both disadvantageous and advantageous, are connected to us" (FHA 6, 265). The implication is that Buffon—despite his efforts—was unable to follow nature's many directions, along a nonlinear path, and find unity therein. By homing in on just two categories, Buffon, Herder suggests, remains one-sided in his analysis; he does not account for the complexity and multidirectionality of nature's (many) "forces."

60 ROMANTIC EMPIRICISM

To properly account for this complexity, Herder sought to develop better concepts than climate and nourishment: concepts that are more encompassing, but that remain concrete; concepts that capture nature's many directions, without leading us away from the phenomenon. While Herder's understanding of nature as relational and dynamic has been recognized, the crucial concept that he developed in response to Buffon's difficulty has not been.[16] My claim is that the crucial concept is the idea of a "circle" or "world."

Throughout his writings on nature, Herder invokes the notion of an animal's "circle" or "world" to explicate the reality that the animal inhabits and that also inhabits the animal—i.e., the way in which the animal is both a reflection of its reality *and* an active presence within this reality. Through the idea of a world, Herder aims to develop a more encompassing account of the animal's relation to its context—and thereby move beyond Buffon's limited one-to-one comparisons. For his goal is not simply to compare the structure of one species or variety to another in light of a specific natural phenomenon, such as heat. Rather, his goal is to take account of a multiplicity of factors—a "chaos of causes and effects" (FHA 6, 266)—and their nonlinear codetermination. The notion of a circle or world achieves precisely that.

The question is: how did Herder arrive at this idea of circle or world, and how successful was it in resolving Buffon's (and Kant's) dilemma of finding unity in nature's vast diversity? The answer, I believe, is to be found in Herder's hermeneutics.

2.3. Herder's Hermeneutics

Herder's hermeneutics, like Buffon's methodology, is critical of a priori theories of interpretation. In their place Herder develops a theory of interpretation that seeks to grasp the particularity of a culture, and understand it from within (FHA 1, 97). As he puts it in *This Too a Philosophy of the History of the Formation of Humanity* [*Auch eine Philosophie der Geschichte zur Bildung der Menschheit*] (1774), "every nation has its own center of well-being with itself, just as every globe has its center of gravity" and the task of the interpreter is to grasp this center (FHA 4, 39). How can an interpreter find the "center" of a culture long gone, or discern the "center" of a text or work of art?

Well before his writings on the philosophy of history, Herder had begun to consider these questions in relation to biography and the interpretation of works of art. In the essay on Abbt, Herder's concern is with how he—as the biographer of Abbt—is to approach his subject in the appropriate way. For Herder this involves recognizing both Abbt's individuality *and* his indebtedness to his time and culture. As Herder puts it,

> most of all it is necessary to distill [*abzieht*] what belongs to *the author's time* or to the *past world*, and what he leaves over for *the world of posterity*. He bears the chains of his age, to which he offers his book as a gift; he stands in his century like a tree in the realm of earth into which it has driven its roots, from which it draws nourishing juices, with which it covers its originating members. (FHA 2, 579; HPW 172; translation modified)

The natural imagery serves to elaborate Herder's point: an author is not born isolated; rather, the author is dependent on their surroundings, the climate, geography, but also language, history, and the culture into which they are born. They become what they are in relation to this larger context. The aim of the interpreter (like the aim of the natural historian) must therefore be to discern *the individuality* or *distinctness* of an author (of a species) *in relation to this larger context* and not outside or beyond it. Only in this way, Herder contends, can we discern what is truly unique or individual about the work—how the author creatively adapts, transforms, or challenges their context. Thus, Herder continues, whoever wishes to rob the author of the "birthmarks of his time," risks "taking from him the traits of his individuality [*Eigenheiten*]" (FHA 2, 579; HPW 172). An author neither exists nor can be understood outside of their cultural framework; it is not something artificially imposed, nor is it a hindrance to understanding. Rather, it is only by taking this framework into account that we can properly assess the author's distinctive contribution or individuality.[17]

This means that the interpreter must, first, avoid any a priori generalizations about the author or the author's work: given that the author is born in a specific time and place, one cannot make any presumptions about her work or aims without investigating the particularities into which she is born. The interpreter must, however, also avoid getting lost in particulars and thereby fail to find a "center," a meaningful and coherent unity in light of which the author's work can be interpreted. Thus, just like the historian of nature, the interpreter must avoid both abstraction and the mere accumulation of data; the interpreter must find a way to grasp the particular and find significance, coherence, *therein*. As such, Herder's conception of context is not of an undifferentiated or homogenous whole, but of an internally differentiated one, composed of the individual contributions of its various members, which are themselves dependent on this unity, this context. There is, in other words, a reciprocity at work here, such that neither the whole nor the parts can exist without the other.

In the essay on Abbt, Herder explains that the means by which to achieve this goal is by explaining "one in terms of the other [*eins aus dem andern erkläret*]," i.e., by seeing how the context is reflected in the individual author's work, and how the individual author's work adds to, or challenges aspects of, this context (FHA 2, 575; HPW 171). It is only by seeing one (the author) through the other (their context) that we see how each reflects but also differs from the other. Herder undertakes this hermeneutic practice in his essay on Shakespeare (1773; draft 1771) in order to assess Shakespeare's genius.

A key aim of the essay is to challenge French views of theater, which take Aristotle's understanding of tragedy as foundational for aesthetic judgment. The trouble with the French approach, Herder notes, is that it fails to recognize that the world out of which Greek tragedy emerged fundamentally differs from Shakespeare's world. Thus, Aristotle's rules regarding tragedy (i.e., the rules determining the genre) no longer obtain and in fact hinder us from appreciating Shakespeare and recognizing his genius. "In Greece," Herder contends, "drama developed in a way that it could not in the north. In Greece it was what it can never be in the north. In the north it is not and cannot be what it was in Greece" (FHA 2, 499; SWA 292). After all, he continues, "as everything in the world changes, so nature, the true creator of Greek drama, was bound to change also. *The Greek worldview, manners, the state of the republics, the tradition of the heroic age, religion,* even *music, expression*, and *the degrees of illusion* [*Illusion*] changed" (FHA 2, 503; SWA 294). Thus, to judge Shakespeare according to the rules of Greek drama is not only problematic, but also absurd. A work of art is of its time, such that its appropriateness, its "genius," can only be measured and determined in relation to its time. The French could not grasp Shakespeare's genius so long as they failed to recognize this.

Herder begins his interpretation of Shakespeare by noting general differences between ancient Greek drama and Shakespeare's, differences that are connected to their respective worlds. Accordingly, Herder attempts to draw a picture of the two worlds, a picture that is founded on their *sense* of their world. A world, after all, is not an abstract backdrop, but an inhabited reality that constantly changes in relation to its inhabitants.

In ancient Greece, Herder notes, there was an overarching sense of unity of time and place, as well as a sense of simplicity among the Greek people and their polity. One can say that the Greeks lacked a modern sense of history and of cultural differences. This was, Herder contends, reflected in their dramatic works (most, though not all, of Greek drama was set in one place, for instance). By contrast, Shakespeare's world is composed of "a rich variety of different estates, ways of life, convictions, peoples and idioms—any nostalgia for the simplicity of former times would have been in vain" (FHA 2, 508; SWA 298). Shakespeare's works reflect this different world: they do not occur in one place, but move from one location to the next, and involve people from a variety of backgrounds. It is also for this reason, Herder continues, that for Shakespeare plot no longer held the meaning the Greeks had bestowed upon it (i.e., a single action), but came to mean "event" or "great occurrence." In other words, in Shakespeare's works we witness transitions and movements that are simply not present in Greek drama, and this is a reflection of the world that Shakespeare inhabits.

In addition, Herder remarks that ancient Greek drama was a public institution *and* a religious event, while Shakespearean drama did not have religious motivations (FHA 2, 516; SWA 304; see also SW 16, 101). This means that the *aim* of a Greek drama differed from that of a Shakespearean drama, and it is only in light of this difference that either can be properly appreciated and understood. Shakespeare's tragedies, for instance, include comedy, a fact that challenges the distinction between tragedy and comedy that had been upheld since Aristotle (FHA 2, 525; SW1 306). However, given that the aims of Shakespeare's drama differ from those of Greek tragedy, there is no reason to abide by the Aristotelian understanding of tragedy in order to appraise Shakespeare's work.

A further important difference between Greek tragedy and Shakespearean drama concerns the origin of their dramatic form, the source from which they drew their inspiration. While the Greeks drew on mythico-historical events, history—as the instantiation of change over time—did not play a clear role in their self-understanding. Nor did they have a conception of history as a solely human affair (gods were involved). This is not the case for the moderns for whom Shakespeare was writing, who regard human life as essentially historical, and history as essentially human. For this reason, Herder contends, it makes perfect sense for Shakespeare's plays to be a presentation of history. He writes, "in Othello," we have before us a *"living history of the genesis, development, eruption, and sad end to the passion of this noble and unfortunate man!"* (FHA 2, 511; SWA 300). The Greek tragedian was, by contrast, no historian, and his genius did not lie in his ability to draw on and convey historical events. For this reason, Herder argues that the origin or inspiration of a work of art must be taken into account when we judge its value. In other words, genius must be measured differently.[18]

What then is the genius of Shakespeare? According to Herder, it is not unlike the genius of a historian or a natural historian—or indeed the genius of the interpreter. For it has to do with Shakespeare's ability to assemble the various characters, estates, and ways of life into a meaningful whole. Shakespeare "embraces a hundred scenes of a world event in his arms, orders them with a gaze, and breathes into them the one soul that suffuses and animates everything," Herder writes (FHA 2, 511; SWA 300). This means, he elaborates, that every scene, every character, not only meaningfully contributes to the whole, but is also an expression of the whole. Speaking of *Macbeth*, Herder notes that every scene and character—from the opening with the three witches on the heath, the thunder and lightning, to the slaying of Macduff's children, Lady Macbeth's sleepwalking, and the fulfillment of the prophecy—presents us with "a single, dreadful indivisible whole" (FHA 2, 514; SWA 302).

In the essay on Shakespeare, Herder shows us how the work of the interpreter is also based on this twofold ability. As noted above, the interpreter seeks to "explain the one through the other," which is to say, grasp the text or the author through his or her context, and vice versa. In the case of Shakespeare, Herder begins with detailed comparisons of the ancient Greek worldview and the modern, Elizabethan worldview; he then draws connections between these worldviews and the works of art that emerged out of them. Finally, Herder considers the distinguishing feature, the genius, of Shakespeare. While Shakespeare's contemporaries may have been similarly inspired by the emerging historical consciousness and the increasingly differentiated world they inhabited, Shakespeare was able to *present* this multivalent world on stage in a *coherent* way. Thus despite the highly differentiated set of characters, locations, and events, Shakespeare's dramas display unity. This unity grants the works coherence, but also tragic purpose: it allows the audience members to imaginatively enter a world—the world of "fate, regicide, and magic," as Herder puts it speaking of *Macbeth*—and in so doing, to become emotionally engaged with this world.

For this reason, Herder describes Shakespeare as "Sophocles' brother" (FHA 2, 515; SW 303). Both achieve "tragic purpose," by enabling their audience to enter into the world they are presenting and become involved with it. They arrive at tragic purpose, however, through significantly different means. Shakespeare's genius lies in his ability to create a coherent, meaningful world out of the diverse elements that he presents—features that Sophocles did not share.

In this way, Herder locates Shakespeare's genius in relation to his time and place, to what he was able to achieve within his context, and how he was able to realize tragic purpose in and through this context. Shakespeare's genius is not to be found in an a priori criterion (for instance, one that accords with Aristotle's account of tragedy), nor in isolated descriptions of Shakespeare's dramas and their characters. The first approach (assumed by the French) moves from the universal or a priori to the particular. In so doing, it overlooks or denies the particularity of the particular. The second approach, by contrast, focuses entirely on the particular, and thus fails to grasp its broader significance. Though the two approaches seem opposed, they share one important feature: neither is able to mediate between the universal and the particular—neither is able to "embrace a hundred scenes" and "order them with a gaze."[19]

How can this mediation between the particular and universal take place? The interpreter of a work of literature must at all times behold two things at once: the work itself, and the world in which this work was created. In considering the work, the interpreter reads one part after the other (i.e., sequentially). The work, however, extends in many directions: each of its parts (its characters, its acts, etc.) is in dialogue not only with the part that preceded it or the one that comes after it, but also with other parts (the first scene of *Macbeth*, for instance, portends what is to come, while the relations among characters are not limited to the characters with whom they appear on stage). Every scene, every character, is in dialogue with every other scene and character. Accordingly, although the work usually proceeds (and is read) sequentially—following a narrative from beginning, to middle, to end—its *meaning* is nonsequential.[20] Thus to properly grasp the text, the reader must always move forward and backward, enriching her understanding of what preceded in light of what follows, allowing what comes later to shed new light on, modify, or challenge what came before.

The activity of understanding is ongoing, and involves a back-and-forth movement, a mediation between what is presented at the beginning, and what is presented later. This is possible only because the reader retains the past and grasps it in light of the present and the future. This means that although reading must proceed sequentially, understanding cannot be solely sequential. The interpreter must grasp the parts, which are apprehended sequentially, as partaking in and contributing to a multi-directional and meaningful whole. The interpreter must, in other words, find a nonsequential unity in the sequence; she must find a unity that is not determined by the sequential order in which the work is presented and apprehended, but which nonetheless determines each part of the sequence. Of course, the work of interpretation is never completed. The reader must continue to move back and forth between the parts and revisit her interpretation in light of new insights and new connections.

The work of interpretation must, of course, go hand in hand with understanding the world of the author. For it is only by taking account of Shakespeare's world, by connecting him to his language and culture, to his place and time, that we can properly discern his distinctiveness: see how he is both like and unlike his world, how he emerges from it, reiterates its mores and ideas, but also contributes something new to it, challenges it, or expands it (consider, for instance, Shakespeare's expansion and transformation of the English language). This too, however, is a task that is never completed: new insights into the author's world emerge, which can shed new light on the author, and the work, and vice versa.

From this we can see that there are three "circles" at work in the activity of interpretation. First, we have the circle that is the work itself—a circle that proceeds (usually) in a linear way, from beginning to end, but which is in fact multidirectional, where every part is in dialogue with every other part, whether portending what is to come, or looking back on what has been. Second, we have the hermeneutic circle—the circle that requires the interpreter to read the work not only from beginning to end, but also from the end and middle back to the beginning. For the middle and end are anticipated in the beginning and also shed new light on the beginning. Third is the circle that is the world of the author—the circle without which we would not be able to discern the author's genius; the world that the author inhabits and that also inhabits the author.

These circles are, I believe, the basis for Herder's parallel notion of "circle" or "world," which he introduces in his essay on language. In that context, his aim is to explicate the differences between animals and between animals and humans, in order to arrive at an answer to the question concerning the origin of human language. He invokes the notion of a circle or world to explicate similarities and differences among animals and between humans and other animals. And this gives him the crucial clue—both to understanding the "origin" of human language and, as we shall see, to understanding living beings more generally.

2.4. Human and Animal Languages

Herder's "Treatise on the Origin of Language," which was written as a response to the Berlin Academy's question concerning the origin of language, is perhaps the most well-known of his writings.[21] In it, Herder attempts to chart a path different from the ones taken in the mid-eighteenth century: the Epicurean-naturalist path,[22] which regarded human language as a transformation of animal sounds; and the divine-origin path, which argued that human language could not have emerged naturally, but was implanted in the human mind by God.

The Epicurean-naturalist perspective, espoused by French philosophes, contends that human language differs only in degree, and not in kind, from animal sounds. Thus the origin of human language can be traced back to animal groans, and is for this reason wholly natural. There is nothing supernatural about the invention of human language. Though Rousseau was a proponent of this view, he was also the first to articulate the difficulties that it faced. In his *Discourse on the Origin of Inequality* [*Discours sur l'origine et les fondements de l'inégalité parmi les hommes*] (1755), Rousseau asks how it happened that human (i.e., artificial) language came to differ from animal (i.e., natural) language.[23] The difference, he notes, has to do with the fact that human languages involve a certain amount of arbitrariness and convention, while natural language does not. Rousseau identifies three main challenges with the naturalistic account of language, two of which were particularly troubling.[24] The first is the problem of how convention can be achieved without consent, i.e., without speech. As Avi Lifschitz explains, "The substitution of arbitrary sounds for natural interjections could have hardly occurred accidentally or as an unforeseen response to needs."[25] This is because in order for convention to have been possible in the first place, humans needed to have language; without language, it would have been impossible to achieve consent. We thus end up with the paradoxical claim that human language, which is based on convention, must precede convention. Or as Rousseau puts it, "speech seems to be highly necessary to establish the use of speech."[26] The second problem has to do with abstraction. The source of abstraction,

Rousseau notes, may be thinking or reason itself. Abstract thought, however, depends on signs. This means that language, as the medium of artificial signs, could not be the *result* of thought. Abstraction (thought) requires artificial signs (language), yet artificial signs could not have been invented without abstraction.

Ultimately, the problem, as Rousseau saw it, was that the naturalistic account of language failed to provide an explanation for the transition from natural to artificial language. How did this leap take place, and how was it even possible? Lacking any such explanation, it was not evident how a naturalistic account could be maintained.[27] Johann Peter Süßmilch's account offered a way out of this dilemma, by claiming that the origin of human language is not natural but divine.

Herder was not satisfied with either the naturalistic or the divine-origin theory of language. His aim in the Prize Essay is to offer an account of human language that does not rely on divine origin, but that also does not suffer from the difficulty faced by the Epicurean-naturalistic position, i.e., the difficulty of a transition from natural to artificial language.

In the opening remarks of his essay, Herder appears to be developing an account that mirrors, or is at least closely aligned with, the Epicurean-naturalist position. He directs his readers to a characteristic that unifies all sentient beings, identifies it with the experience of pain and pleasure, and explains that the expression of these experiences—the cries, groans, and screams—is "an immediate law of nature" (FHA 1, 699; HPW 66). What unifies us with animals, in other words, is our impetus to share our experience, to let others know of our passions, our suffering, and our joy. However, Herder adds that although the "language of sensation," the language of the "nerve structure," binds all animals together, and thus binds humans to other animals, it does not follow that it is the basis for human language *or* the sole criterion or essence of animal language (FHA 1, 699; HPW 67). Thus, Herder not only disagrees with the Epicurean-naturalist identification of cries and groans with *human* language; he also disagrees with their identification of these cries and groans with *animal* languages. As we shall see, Herder contends that animal languages involve communicative skills developed in line with and for the specific contexts that the animals inhabit. This means that for Herder, it is not only human languages, but also animal languages, which cannot be reduced to the "language of sensation." It is not for nothing that Herder speaks of animal *languages* as opposed to *one* animal language (FHA 1, 732; HPW 96).

Herder explains that in order to answer a question about the "origin" of language, he will have to do what other philosophers have not yet properly done—they have not "gone back" far enough (FHA 1, 711; HPW 77).[28] Echoing his critique of abstraction in the letter to Mendelssohn, Herder's claim is that Condillac and Rousseau are also working with abstractions, and the only way to overcome these abstractions is to "go back" to the phenomenon itself, i.e., to language. The trouble, as he sees it, is that both Condillac and Rousseau conjectured a state in which humanity existed prior to its acquisition of language, and on that basis sought to determine how language was acquired. Condillac imagined two children living in a desert after the flood, while Rousseau posited a "state of nature" prior to the emergence of society. In both cases, then, the attempt to trace the origin of language is based on an imagined prelinguistic state, and on speculations regarding the transition from it to the linguistic state. In the place of such speculations, Herder chooses to pursue a different path.

First, he does not begin by imagining a prelinguistic human condition, a condition which cannot be empirically observed and verified. This has an important implication. For if the attempt to understand the origin of human language cannot be based on a conjecture, then it also cannot proceed diachronically. In other words, by challenging Rousseau's and Condillac's starting point, Herder cannot then go on to assume, as they had done, that the only way to determine the origin of language is through a (conjectural) diachronic perspective on the matter. But, if a (conjectural) diachronic account of the origin of language is no longer valid, then how is one to go about answering the question? In other words, how is Herder to provide a response to a question concerning the *origin* of language without a diachronic account?

Herder's response to this question both challenges diachronic perspectives (and methodologies) and offers an important alternative to these perspectives—the only one that he considers to be empirically valid. As such, Herder's response to the Berlin Academy's question regarding the origin of language turns the question on its head: in the place of a diachronic account, he offers a synchronic one, arguing that only such an account is valid.[29]

Herder explains that to go back far enough is not to go back to a conjectured prelinguistic state; rather, it is to go back to the *phenomena*, to regard them carefully, to grasp what is at the heart of the difference between humans and animals that led to the emergence of (artificial) language. This means that instead of beginning by making a leap to an imagined past and attempting to derive language from a speculative cause or trigger, Herder begins by observing and describing the human being and the animal in their environments. As Herder explains, in contrast to his predecessors, who have sought but failed to offer a causal explanation of various human and animal capacities, his aim is to offer "observations [*Bemerkungen*]" which can "throw much light on the doctrine of the human soul" (FHA 1, 712; HPW 78). The goal of these observations is to answer the question: what is it like to be human, and what might it be like to be various animals?

The first striking characteristic of the human being, Herder notes, is the fact that the human is "far inferior to the animals in strength and sureness of instinct, indeed ... he ... lacks what in the case of so many animal species we call innate abilities and drives" (FHA 1, 711; HPW 77–78). In contrast to humans, animals are born with specific strengths and capacities, which reflect and are reflected in their natural environment. There is an intimate relation between the animal and its environment, such that its abilities fit or map onto what Herder calls the animal's "circle" or "world." He writes: "*Each animal has its circle* to which it belongs from birth, into which it immediately enters, in which it remains all its life and in which it dies." Importantly, this circle corresponds to the animal's inborn capacities: "the sharper the animals' senses are, and the more marvelous the products of their art, then the smaller their circle is, the more limited in kind the product of their art" (FHA 1, 712; HPW 78).[30] There is, Herder continues, an inverse proportionality between the animal's capacities (its "drives and arts") and its circle or world: the larger the circle, the less focused (specialized) its capacities; the smaller the circle, the more focused. This is evident in the case of bees, for instance, whose world centers around the beehive; within the beehive, the bee's "drives and arts" are a display of precision and efficiency. Once bees exit the beehive, however, their distinctive capacities, which are perfectly suited to the beehive, place them in a precarious position. Their capacities, so well fitted to the beehive, are inversely unfit for the non-beehive environment. The same is the case for other insects, such as the spider, whose "world" centers around its web, and whose capacities are perfectly attuned to this world—but hardly beyond it.

When considering those beings whose "circle" is much wider, the opposite appears to be the case. In contrast to bees and spiders, the capacities of animals that roam, for instance, are less specialized, and not as clearly determined for or by a specific context. This leads to a general decrease in the power and efficiency of their senses in relation to their surroundings. As Herder puts it,

> *the more numerous the functions and the destiny of the animals are, the more dispersed their attention is over several objects, the less constant their manner of life is, in short, the larger and more diverse their sphere is, then the more we see their sensuousness distribute itself and weaken.* (FHA 1, 712; HPW 78)

This dispersion of attention and weakening of the senses is most acute in the case of the human being, who lacks a world altogether. The human being does not live in any one environment but can inhabit a multitude of geographic contexts. Human capacities are, accordingly, not aligned with any particular context. They are not shaped or molded by the needs of a specific world. As Herder puts it: "The human being has no such uniform and narrow sphere where only a single sort of work awaits him; a world of occupations and destinies surrounds him." For this reason, he elaborates, "His senses and organization are not sharpened for a single thing; he has senses for everything and hence naturally for each particular thing weaker and duller senses" (FHA 1, 713; HPW 79).

The difference between humans and other animals, then, is connected to the different way in which human beings inhabit their world—a difference that is evident in the human lack of specific skills and capacities that would align with a particular world. Humans lack "direction," as Herder puts it, which means that the human being has *"no drive to art, no skill for art—* and, one thing which is more especially relevant here, *no animal language."* In contrast to other animals, the human being is not born with capacities that fit a particular context; the human being, one can say, is born worldless, and this worldlessness goes hand in hand with a lack of innate skills, one of which is an innate language.

It is here that Herder locates the difference between human and animal languages. While language is one of the innate skills that animals possess, human language is not. An animal's language, like its other capacities, matches its needs in relation to its world. Humans, who are not born into any world and who therefore have no specific capacities that align with this world, do not possess an innate language. Humans, then, are born neither into a world or into language. Rather, they must "invent" both (FHA 1, 722; HPW 87). *This* is the difference between human and animal languages, and it has nothing to do with whether human language originates in the groans and cries which we share with animals.

Before proceeding to consider the implications of Herder's claims, I want to consider his methodology—how he seeks to "go back" and provide an account (an explanation) of the difference between humans and animals. As already mentioned, unlike Rousseau and Condillac, he does not attempt to imagine a prelinguistic human state, and then go on to make a speculative jump from this state to a linguistic one. Herder does not offer a diachronic account of the emergence of human language. Instead, he offers a nuanced description of various animals in relation to their contexts, and seeks to demonstrate the significance of this relationship for the various animals and the human being. The aim of this *description* is to provide an *explanation* of the difference between humans and other animals, between human and animal languages—and to respond to the challenge facing naturalistic accounts of language which fail to provide precisely this explanation. This means that for Herder there is no difference—as there is in Kant—between what description and explanation offer. In fact, it is only via description that explanation is possible. We will return to this point in the following chapters. For now, I'd like to look more carefully at what Herder's description involves.

Herder begins with sameness, assuming that humans, *like* other animals, are inextricably connected to their context. He then moves to consider the significance of the relation between an animal and its context through comparative analysis. What he realizes is that the more enclosed an animal's context, the narrower its "circle" or "world," the more attuned its features and capacities are to this context, such that it appears as if made for the particular circle which it inhabits. There is a deep reciprocity between the animal and its context; its form and function mirror its context and vice versa: its context is suited for its form and function. Importantly Herder does not move from here to make a conceptual leap and claim that the context is the *cause* of the animal's specific features—such an account would seek to derive the one (the features and functions) from the other (the environment). In fact, Herder would argue, the two are so intimately intertwined that the one *could not exist* without the other. As such, the one could not precede and cause the other. For instance, the bee and the hive form a unity, such that it is deeply problematic to derive the bee's characteristics from the hive (as if the hive preexisted the bee).[31]

It is through comparative descriptions of different animals in relation to their contexts that Herder arrives at the conclusion that the less enclosed an animal is by its context, the less aligned are its features to this context. This provides an important clue, and ultimately an *explanation* for differences among animals: differences in morphology have to do with the animal's relation to its environment. This explanation is not, however, a form of causal derivation (i.e., the environment is not understood as the *cause* of morphological differences). For the goal is precisely not to divide what is fundamentally united (animal and circle), and not to abstract from the observed phenomenon to an unobserved or unobservable cause. Rather, the explanation that Herder offers remains with the phenomenon, locating the "law [*Gesetz*]" that underlies the differences *in* the unified character of the observed phenomenon.[32] By recognizing a connection between an animal's capacities, its morphology, and its circle, Herder's account makes intelligible the differences between animal capacities. He does this without deriving these differences from something other than themselves (whether an a priori principle, an efficient cause, or a *causa occulta*).

In the place of derivation, then, Herder offers description. This description, however, is not of isolated elements; it does not simply enumerate or list random details. Rather, it is a description of the *animal whole in its world*. After all, it is only the animal *as a whole* that can act in, be influenced by, and influence its context.[33] This goes hand in hand with Herder's view that the animal and its world are interdependent. The animal is not passive in relation to its world—it is not an "outcome" of its world, a passive being that is simply "caused" by its world. Rather, it is actively involved in this world. This means that the two (animal and world) cannot be separated. Precisely because they reciprocally form and inform one another—recall the beehive and the bee—they are essentially one. To separate them is to fail to understand the phenomenon.

Along these same lines, Herder does not seek to "explain" the distinctive character of the human being (language and rationality) by deriving it from any one thing—whether from the brain, or the erect posture, as Kant had argued in his reviews, or from a moment in a conjectured history, where suddenly (and for no apparent reason) humans develop a conventional and arbitrary system of signs. By contrast, Herder's goal is to provide a nonreductive account of the differences between human and animal capacities, including differences in their linguistic capacities. This means an account that considers the *whole* human being in its relation to its world.

The conclusion he draws from his observations and descriptions of the human being's relation to its world is that its distinguishing feature is a lack—a lack of inborn capacities that match any particular environment. This lack is also a lack of an innate language. Humans are not born with any one language. Rather, they appear to "invent" languages. Similarly, and as Herder will argue in the *Ideas*, humans are not born with reason. Rather, reason is "learned" (FHA 6, 144). How is this possible? How is it possible to go from a "lack" to a positive reality—to language and reason?

To answer this question, Herder explains that we need to find the missing link, the "middle term," that unites the disparate characteristics of the human being, that brings coherence to the various aspects of being human: the human's "senses and needs, forces and the circle of efficiency that awaits him, his organs and his language" (FHA 1, 176; HPW 81). This requires seeing the whole human being in relation to the whole of nature, or, more specifically, it requires seeing how the human being fits into the "whole analogy of nature [*aller Analogie der Natur*]" (FHA 1, 176; HPW 81). In other words, by thinking about the human in comparative terms to animals—by seeing how the human is both like and unlike other animals—the goal is to locate the aspect of the human being that *makes up for* all that humans lack. This, Herder maintains, will provide us with the "genetic proof" of "'*the true orientation of humanity*,'" that is to say, with what distinguishes humans from animals "*in kind*" and not simply in degree (FHA 1, 176; HPW 81).

Precisely because the human being finds herself without any determination, without any clear goals imprinted on her body and instincts, what she needs is, as Herder puts it, "*more clarity [mehrere Helle]*" (FHA 1, 717; HPW 82). Language—and with it reason—provide the clarity that the human requires if she is not to "fall blindly on one point and remain lying there blindly." In other words, in light of the lack of fitness between human capacities and any one context, it is *intelligible* that human beings find some other way of making sense of their world—a way that is not fit for any one context, but that can serve in a number of highly differentiated contexts. Furthermore, the human lack of innate capacities makes way for a more open relation to the world, one that is not ruled by impulse or instinct, and thus allows for what Herder calls *Besonnenheit*, "taking awareness."[34] *Besonnenheit*, which contains the word *Sonne* (sun), alludes to Herder's claim that the human being requires more "clarity [*Helle*]," which can also be translated as "light." Accordingly, to make up for the various lacks, the human being has the positive attribute of clarifying or shedding light—an attribute that is not attuned to any one context but is applicable to and useful in any context.

To give his readers a concrete sense of what he means, Herder offers the example of a human being encountering a sheep. While a wolf or a lion regards the sheep as food, and the ram regards the sheep as an object of sexual pleasure, the human being may be wholly indifferent to the sheep. (Though of course the human being *can* also be interested in the sheep as food. Herder's point is that this *need not* be the case.) This indifference toward the sheep is a manifestation of the human lack of innate capacities. Precisely because the human being lacks specificity, the human being *must not* regard the sheep in a particular way. The relationship between human being and sheep, in other words, is not already determined. This openness allows the human being to direct her attention to the sheep as something to discover, to take account of. As Herder puts it,

> As soon as he develops a need to become acquainted with the sheep, no instinct disturbs him, no sense tears him too close to the sheep or away from it; it stands there exactly as it expresses itself to his senses. White, soft, woolly—his soul, operating with awareness, seeks a characteristic mark—*the sheep bleats!*—his soul has found a characteristic mark. The inner sense takes effect. This bleating, which makes the strongest impression on the soul, which tore itself away from all the other properties of viewing and feeling, jumped forth, penetrated most deeply, remains for the soul. The sheep comes again. White, soft, woolly—the soul sees, feels, takes awareness, seeks a characteristic mark—it bleats, and now the soul recognizes it again! Aha! You are the bleating one! The soul feels inwardly. The soul has recognized it in a human way, for it recognizes it and names it distinctly, that is, with a characteristic mark. (FHA 1, 723; HPW 88)

Herder's claim, then, is that the "origin" of human language is to be found in taking awareness, or *Besonnenheit*. A human being take awareness, becomes interested in the phenomenon as a phenomenon, because she is not determined to see the phenomenon in a particular way. Language, in turn, emerges through taking awareness. It is important to emphasize that Herder's account is not *causal*. He is not saying that language is *caused* by taking awareness, which is itself *caused* by our lack of determination. Rather, his account is descriptive. It shows that human language is *intelligible*, it *makes sense*, given that human beings do not belong to a particular world and lack specific capacities. This freedom from specificity—from being determined to regard the sheep in a particular way—both requires and makes space for *Besonnenheit*, for taking account of what stands before us. Through *Besonnenheit*, the human being is able to consider the sheep as a phenomenon, discern a characteristic mark, bleating, and, when this same phenomenon is encountered again, recall this characteristic mark. Once it is recalled, the phenomenon becomes a "grasped sign," that is, a word (FHA 1, 724; HPW 89).

Precisely because human languages are the outcome of an encounter with the world, they are not something with which we are born, but require our attentiveness and creativity. In other words, and as Herder puts it, language is "invented" (FHA 1, 724; HPW 89). This is evident in the fact that languages have a history: they change over time. They can degenerate if not widely practiced and disappear altogether. What was once a rich spoken language can become a dead language, or one that is spoken in only its most rudimentary form. Animal languages, by contrast, do not change over time. They only die when the species becomes extinct. Furthermore, human languages are connected to the place—the world—in which they emerge. They can be more or less sophisticated when it comes to describing certain phenomena, for instance, and this has to do with *where* they were invented.

By creating languages, then, human beings also create their world—a linguistic, expressive world, a world of artificial signs and symbols. It is through this world that the human being comes to know himself and, as Herder puts it, "becomes his own end and goal of refinement" (FHA 1, 717; HPW 82). This is the source of so-called culture, or what Herder describes as human "self-mirroring." Now this can be taken to imply that with language the human being shuts herself off to the more-than-human world, becomes enclosed in her uniquely linguistic sphere. This, however, is not how Herder sees it. For although the human world is a world of conventional signs and symbols, the human encounters the world in a linguistic, interpretive way. In other words, to the human, the world is expressive and meaningful—it speaks and signs itself.

Herder's image of the "origin" of human language revolves around an encounter with a sounding animal. By calling the human being to attention, the sheep at once expresses itself and inspires human expression. In turn, in hearing the sound of bleating, the human being does not experience a brute sensation, but grasps it *as* a sound belonging to someone. This allows the human listener to draw out the characteristic mark, "the bleating one." As such, the human encounter with the world is an essentially linguistic, indeed analogical, encounter, insofar as it is determined by an *as*-structure. The world appears *as* meaningful. The sound is taken *as* belonging to a sounding being. It is precisely because the world appears to human beings in this way that we go on to develop signs ("marks") by which to represent it. And in so doing, we "create" our world: a world of signs that aims to draw connections between the sounds, smells, and sights we encounter. This insight, which Herder intimates in the essay on the origin of language, becomes crucial for his understanding of human cognition—and his claim that human cognition is essentially analogical.

2.5. The Analogical Structure of Cognition

In essays composed some five years after the origin of language essay, Herder turns to a question that emerged from his earlier discussion. For, he came to realize, if we are to understand the linguistic character of the human being and the human world, then it is necessary to grasp *how* this world emerged. In other words, it is necessary to understand the cognitive processes that underpin the encounter between human being and sheep, and which allow the sheep to *become* "the bleating one."

Herder begins "On Cognition and Sensation in the Human Soul" by noting that philosophers have for far too long neglected the most basic level of cognition, i.e., the "deep abyss of obscure sensations [*Abgrund dunkler Empfindungen*]" (FHA 4, 340; HPW 189; translation modified).[35] Bodily irritations and sensations, he contends, are the entry point of external impressions into the mind. Without sensation, "we [would] know nothing beyond ourselves" (FHA 4, 348; HPW 203).

He proceeds to examine irritation, sensation, cognition, and volition in that order. Though in every instance his aim is to consider each capacity of the soul on its own—recognizing its distinctive function, and noting its physiological underpinnings (e.g., the nerve structure)—he also emphasizes that the various capacities are neither isolated from one another, nor heterogeneous (i.e., resulting in unconnected products). Rather, he contends that each of these cognitive capacities (irritation, sensation, imagination, and reason) participates in one connected, even if differentiated, process. This process is cognition itself, which is both a unifying *and* a transforming activity. In the first instance, cognition unifies (it unifies various sensations, for example), and then it transforms (sensations into images, images into words or concepts). This twofold character of cognition as unifying and transforming will become clearer if we examine one of the capacities more carefully, namely sensation.

To begin with, Herder emphasizes that the senses do not work separately or in opposition to one another.[36] Rather, they must collaborate in order to present the external world to us—hearing, sight, smell, and touch must work in tandem to give us what Herder calls the "world-structure [*Weltstruktur*]" (FHA 4, 348; HPW 203).[37] This is because no individual sense can achieve on its own what it achieves in collaboration. Consider sight. Herder notes that sight as an isolated sense can only give us the superficial aspects of visible objects (i.e., surfaces, colors, planes, figures). On its own, it cannot perceive three-dimensional bodies (i.e., volume, form). However, sight "borrows" from touch (feeling), which is the sense that does grant us insight into three-dimensionality, and in this way, we are able to see more than just surfaces. Through the collaboration of sight and touch, we come to *see* three-dimensional bodies in space (FHA 4, 349; HPW 204).

Herder articulates this point in greater detail in the "Fourth Critical Forest [*Viertes kritische Wäldchen*]" (1769), where he invokes research on blind persons who were, following surgery, able to see. At first, however, they were not able to connect what they see with their eyes (the superficial phenomena) to the three-dimensional space they had known through touch. It was only after they learned to connect touch and sight, to see via touch, Herder notes, that their vision *became* three-dimensional (FHA 2, 294–95). Their sight was thus *transformed* via touch. This shows that the senses *work together* and it is only through this cooperation between the senses that the world appears to us as it does. There is, accordingly, a unifying and transforming capacity already at work at the most basic level of cognition.

For this reason, Herder maintains that the senses are never "neutral," which is to say that there is no such thing as "brute" or "mere" sensation. As he puts it in "On Image, Poetry, and Fable [*Über Bild, Dichtung und Fabel*]" (1787), the senses are "separating objects from each other," "giving them outline, dimension and form" in the midst of the "chaos" of the "forests of sensible objects" (FHA 4, 635). The senses are working together to give shape to the world we encounter. For this reason, he continues,

> we do not see, rather we create images for ourselves [*Wir sehen nicht, sondern wir erschaffen uns Bilder*] ... for the image that is projected on the retina of your eyes is not the idea that you derive from its object; it is merely a product [*Werk*] of your inner sense, a work of art created by your soul's

faculty of perception [*ein Kunstgemälde der Bemerkungskraft deiner Seele*]. (FHA 4, 635)

In other words, mere "seeing" (i.e., seeing regarded as separate from the larger unity to which it contributes) is not what gives us the world; rather, it is seeing as a member of a unified sensing organism that gives us this world.

But how exactly does sensing (and, more specifically, seeing) contribute to the activity of knowing? In other words, how do the various capacities of the human organism join so as to give us a "world"? In posing this question, Herder is following the insight he came to in the essay on the origin of language: the human being is a linguistic being, and the human world is a linguistic world. But how exactly does this world emerge? In other words, how does the encounter with the sheep become an encounter with the "bleating one"?

To answer this question, Herder writes in these later essays, it is necessary to investigate the ways in which sensations become meaningful. That is, how sensation *becomes* image, and how image *becomes* concept—how the *sound* of the bleating sheep *becomes* "the bleating one." The difficulty, as Herder articulates it in "On Image," has to do with the fact that there appears to be very little similarity between sensation, image, and concept, such that it is not clear how one can *become* or *lead to* the other. As he puts it, "the object has so little in common with the image, the image with the thought, the thought with the expression, the visual perception with the name," such that it seems impossible to connect them in any way (FHA 4, 636).

Yet we do connect them. Otherwise, we would not be able to see three-dimensional surfaces, or recognize the bleating one. Accordingly, despite their apparent differences, our various cognitive capacities must join or work together in some way. Or, as Herder explains, there must be a fundamental "communicability" between them: it is "only the *communicability* [*Mitteilbarkeit*] among our several senses and the *harmony prevailing between them*, whereupon this communication rests," that makes cognition possible (FHA 4, 636). In other words, the various senses must be both parts and expressions of the unifying and transforming process of cognition. Only in this way can sensation be unified and transformed into an image, just as it is also only in this way that an image can be transformed into a concept.

This implies that what is sensed must always already be "stamped" by the cognitive process of unification and transformation. Herder writes: "When the soul sees objects *as images* or rather when it *transforms* [*verwandelt*] them into mental images [*Gedankenbilder*] according to rules, what does it do other than translate, *metaschematize*?" (FHA 4, 635; emphasis added). In turn, he goes on, "if the soul aims to illuminate [*aufzuhellen*] these images, which are its work, through signs and express them to others, what does it do other than translating, *allocating* [*alläosieren*]?" (FHA 4, 636).[38] In each instance, the soul is seeing one thing *as* another—a seeing that involves "metaschematizing," and "translating," or "allocating." The Greek term "schema" means to form or shape, such that the process of metaschematization is a process of formation. This shaping, however, also involves translating or allocating.

What the mind is doing, then, is *forming* an object through an analogical process. By seeing the sensation *as* an image, it *forms* the image; by seeing the image *as* a concept, it *forms* the concept. The activity of knowing is an activity of giving shape or forming *by* translating or allocating. One thing *becomes* another.

Herder describes this as a "pairing of images and thoughts [*Bilder und Gedanken paaren*]." This pairing is dependent on the ability to recognize similarity or affinity between the image and the concept (or between the sensation and the image). For this reason, he continues, this pairing is based on analogy (FHA 4, 645). This is because, in every instance, cognition must move back and forth between the two elements—between sensation and image, between image and concept. Through analogy, through seeing one *as* the other, cognition learns to *see* or *discern* the image *in* the sensation, *discern* the concept *in* the image, and in this way *draw out* or *distill* the image implicit in the sensation, the concept implicit in the image.

Here, then, we see the analogical structure of cognition. For it is by moving forward and backward between two elements (sensation and image, image and concept), by seeing the one in light of the other, that cognitive objects emerge. Accordingly, cognition proceeds analogically precisely because it beholds two elements and sees them *in* or *as* one another. It is by beholding the two elements and seeing their relation that the mind discerns the *conceptual* content that is *implicit* in the image, and similarly, the *imagistic* content that is *implicit* in the sensation.

It is for this reason that Herder identifies cognition as both a unifying process (bringing various elements together by discerning their similarities) *and* a transformative one (it translates the one element into the other, through discerning similarities and differences, drawing out what is implicit in each element). Sensation proceeds analogically by unifying the various senses, as in the case of the sense of sight with the sense of touch, so that sight is transformed via touch. Sight comes to perceive the surface object *in and through* the felt object, and in this way, gives us a three-dimensional, embodied visual landscape. The product of sensation is thus the product of seeing one thing *as* or *in light of* another (the visible surfaces are seen *through* or *as* the touched surfaces). Thus one can say that sensation itself is an analogizing capacity, and its product is born out of the seeing-as of analogy.

The implication is that reason cannot be separated from imagination or sensation. After all, the product of reason, the concept, emerges in dialogue with what preceded it (the image and the sensation). The concept is implicit in the image, which is drawn out, made explicit, in the act of cognition—by seeing the image *as* a concept. Thus the tools of reason—concepts—are not independent of either the products of the imagination or those of sensation, such that reason itself is also not independent of imagination or sensation.

Such a view of reason would have certainly irked Kant. Indeed, it is highly likely that Kant's critical reviews of the *Ideas* were not only inspired by Herder's use of analogy, but also by Herder's claim that "reason is a perceiving, a learned property and direction of ideas and powers [*etwas Vernommenes, eine gelernte Proportion und Richtung der Ideen und Kräften*]" (FHA 6, 144).[39] Reason is a "perceiving" insofar as it is inseparable from imagination and sensation. The three work together, although each brings with it increasing clarity (*mehrere Helle*). What distinguishes them is the fact that each level of cognition involves a transformation of what preceded—a making explicit of what had been previously implicit.

Accordingly, although each of the capacities has a different object (sensation, image, concept), they also depend on one another, such that it would be a mistake to regard them as isolated or independent. Rather, as Herder writes in "On Cognition and Sensation," "our cognition is therefore, although admittedly it *is* the deepest self *in us*, not as autonomous, voluntarily choosing, and unbound as is believed" (FHA 4, 358; HPW 212). For, he continues, reason depends on "the support of the staffs that were reached in our earliest childhood," i.e., sensation and imagination.

Reason is thus "learned" insofar as it is a higher (clearer) manifestation of the same creative capacities that underlie sensation and imagination. But this also means that reason is something that we must *achieve*. For if reason is a higher form of perceiving and imagining, then reasoning *well* requires us to discern the concept *in* the image, and discern the image *in* the sensation. This is because there is the possibility that the concept that we develop has little to do with either the image or the sensation—that it is only tangentially connected to them. There is, in other words, the possibility that the transformations from one stage of cognition to the next are not apt. Knowing well, however, requires achieving aptness: arriving at a concept that is not divorced from the image or sensation, but implicit within them.

In this way, Herder carves out a distinctive position on the relationship between sensation, imagination, and reason—one that allows him to maintain, with the empiricists, the significance of sensations for the articulation of concepts, and with the rationalists, that sensations, images, and concepts are outcomes of one unifying process, which he recognizes as analogical.[40] His most significant insight, which distinguishes him from the dualist, is that the products of reason and imagination are *already implicit* in the products of the capacities that preceded them (concepts are implicit in images; images in sensations).[41] Thus despite their differences, sensation, imagination, and reason are not only working together, but also imply and anticipate one another.

Through observing and describing the human being in her context, Herder furnishes an image of the distinctive form of human cognition. What he realizes is that the as-structure of analogy is not only a special cognitive tool or operation—as Kant had argued in the third *Critique*—but also the basis for human cognition. For just as it is only through seeing the organized being *as* a work of art that it (organization in nature) becomes thinkable for us, so Herder contends, it is only by seeing the various sensations *through* or *as* one another, by seeing sensations *as* an image, by seeing the image *as* a word or concept, that we have objects in the first place. In short, we are essentially interpretive beings: beings who encounter a meaningful world, a world that appears *as*, and we seek to reflect these meanings through signs of our making.

2.6. Herder's Naturalism

In light of these conclusions, the question arises as to how Herder can maintain a naturalist position. In what sense is human language (and with it human reason) "natural"? And does Herder offer a resolution to the dilemma faced by other naturalist accounts of language?

Herder's quick answer to the first question would be that human language and reason are natural *for humans*. In other words, given the structure and organization of the human being—including the fact that the human being lacks an orientation toward a specific environment—developing language and rationality is necessary. Seen in light of the whole human, in light of the human situation, language is not something "artificial" that needed to emerge *after* some kind of break with "natural" language. Rather, human language is, from the start, the (only) language that the human being can possess. In this way, Herder challenges the meaning of the terms "natural" and "nature": what is *natural* is not synonymous with what is animal (as opposed to human). To claim that a certain form of language is "natural" because it is identified with animal groans and cries (as Condillac and Rousseau had done) is nonsensical, an abstraction based on an illusory "animal essence." After all, different animals have different capacities, which means that they possess different means of communication or different languages. A bee is a very different being from a lion. It expresses itself in its distinctive bee manner, just as a lion does. For the bee to achieve certain ends is natural, while these ends would be completely unnatural for the lion. The same holds for the human. For the human to invent language is natural, while human language would be unnatural for the bee and the lion.[42]

This means that to speak of something as "natural" and to develop a "naturalist" account do not entail identifying the human with an illusory abstraction (whether it be an abstract concept of "nature" or an abstract "animal essence" or "animal language"). Rather, what is natural can only be understood in light of the structure and organization of the being before us—i.e., in light of its various capacities, context, and development. Thus in the place of an overarching definition of the term "nature," Herder offers a concrete conception of what is "natural," i.e., a conception based on careful description of the phenomenon and the world of which it is part. Herder, then, is a naturalist, but in a very specific sense. For he does not rely on an abstract notion of nature, opposed to culture, to justify his claims. Rather, he offers concrete elaborations of the phenomenon in question, in order to discern its structure, circumstance, and way of life.[43]

In this way, Herder does offer a resolution to the dilemma faced by the Epicurean-naturalist position. For there is, on Herder's account, no transition from an originally nonhuman language to an artificial, human language. Human language is an aspect of being human. There is no jump from an animal being to a human being. And this means that there is no need to search for a "cause" of language that precedes and makes human language possible.

Thus, in contrast to both the Epicurean-naturalist approach and the divine-origin theory, which seek to locate the origin of language in something outside language (animal groans and God, respectively), Herder recognizes that language is an expression of the whole human being and the human situation. Accordingly, the "origin" of language is found *in* the structure and function of the human whole—not in a conjectured history or a divine cause. In turn, the various aspects of the human being are not efficient causes along a causal chain—language does not *cause* the upright gait, nor does the upright gait *cause* language. Rather, and as Herder argues in the *Ideas*, they are all expressions of the human form and its relation to its world.

2.7. A Dynamic Conception of Nature

In his early writings—from his work on hermeneutics and the language essay to the essays on cognition—Herder offers two crucial insights that have not been adequately recognized in the literature. First, he transforms the very project of understanding. Rather than seeking to "explain" something by deriving it from something else—outside of itself—he aims to explain through concrete description, comparative analysis, and analogy. This does not mean, however, the limited one-to-one analogy we find in Buffon (e.g., seeing the shape of the horse in light of its climate). Rather, by invoking the notion of a "world," or "circle," Herder extends the use and significance of analogical thinking, such that what is being compared is not one object to another, but a phenomenon to its world. This approach was based on Herder's hermeneutics, where he came to the conclusion that the only way by which to understand a work is through its "world," i.e., by seeing how this world is reflected in the work and how the work reflects the world—how it expands or challenges aspects of its world. By taking up this hermeneutic model and applying it to the study of nature, Herder extends analogical reflection beyond the one-to-one comparison in Buffon, to encompass the world in which living beings emerge, the world that they inhabit and that inhabits them. And in this way, he moves from comparing structural similarities and differences, to seeing a dynamic relationship between a living being and its world, a relationship of mutual and ongoing influence.

Second, by transforming Buffon's largely superficial notion of climate into a *world*, Herder transforms the way we think about and perceive nature. In the place of an abstract concept under which we subsume certain things and from which we separate others (e.g., mind or culture), Herder developed a picture of an inhabited and inhabiting reality, a community of individuals that form and are informed by their context (and by one another), and which can only exist in and through this context and one another.

Herder thus displaces the abstract idea of nature with a notion of nature as an effected and effecting reality: a context of reciprocal and ongoing influence among its inhabitants. In so doing, he offers a dynamic conception of nature, the legacy of which remains with us today.[44] From this perspective, Herder can be regarded as first in a long line of ecological thinkers.[45] And the *origins* of this dynamic conception of nature are Herder's hermeneutics and his expanded use of analogy. By seeing one thing through or as another, by seeing the animal *through* its world and vice versa, Herder was able to recognize an interconnectedness between the organism and its context, to see how the one can exist only in relation to the other. It was this approach that allowed him to see nature as a dynamic relation, a collaboration of beings. For this reason, it is not far-fetched to claim that the origins of our modern idea of nature as an ecological community are to be found in Herder's application of literary tools and methods to the study of nature.

Herder's significance, however, should not be limited to giving us this important clue. Rather, the dynamic conception of nature that Herder articulated, and that Goethe and Humboldt developed and applied, has been lost in contemporary conversations about "nature"—and should be rehabilitated. This is because Herder's conception of nature challenges any view that places nature "outside" of human culture, that sees nature in opposition to culture. And it also challenges abstraction and hypostatization: what is *natural* is not based on an abstract idea or essence but has to do with the *whole* being *in* its world.

If nature is a dynamic living community, it follows that the human mind and its creations (culture) cannot be regarded as outside of or distinct from the natural world. And yet, as the conscious reflection of nature (*Besonnenheit*), it is also the case that human beings have a special relation to the natural world. More specifically, as interpreters of nature, we bear a certain responsibility concerning our interpretations—how apt, or inapt they are. Knowing is not, as Herder put it, neutral. Or, as Goethe will write some twenty years later, there is a difference between "seeing and seeing," such that it is our responsibility to see *well*. The question then is: what demands does this conception of knowledge place on the knower? How, in other words, can the knower meet her obligations *as* a knower? Herder's notion of a *Hauptform*—and Goethe's adoption and adaption of it—offers a first answer.

3
The Science of Describing

Herder, Goethe, and the *Hauptform*

In the "Treatise on the Origin of Language," Herder provided a first articulation of a distinctive methodology: a methodology based on careful observation and description, which refuses to depart from the phenomena, but aims to find meaning—necessity—within them. This methodology was, in large part, closely aligned with the methodology he had developed for interpreting literary texts. It was also closely aligned with the methodology that Buffon had intimated, but not fully realized, in his *Natural History*: a methodology which sought develop a "real" system or order of nature, by using analogy and comparison, i.e., by seeing one thing *as* or *through* another. Herder's expansion of Buffon's singular comparisons and analogies—by seeing the whole organism in relation to its world—allowed him to move beyond Buffon's superficial conception of climate to the complex and rich notion of a "world."

Similarly, Herder affirms the importance of analogy in the *Ideas*, where he writes that if we want to do more than "play with sweet words," then we must dig deeper into the "*analogy of nature* [*Analogie der Natur*]." Only by examining "nature's totally reigning similarity," he continues, can we begin "to gather *hope*" (FHA 6, 165). The hope to which he is alluding is the same hope that motivated Buffon and Kant: the hope of establishing a coherent and meaningful account of natural order and diversity. Herder's contention is that this can only be achieved if we study one object "in the other," such that "the one explains the other" (FHA 6, 73–74). Accordingly, if we want to discern *necessity* in nature—if we want to discern order and relation within the natural world—then we must (consciously) invoke analogy.

In the *Ideas* Herder emphasizes that this analogical seeing-as specifically refers to the comparison of *forms* as opposed to *forces*, i.e., those hidden powers that purportedly grant various beings specific capacities (e.g., "life force" is what makes living beings alive). Herder's focus on form is methodologically motivated. For, he explains, it is impossible for us to actually *perceive* nature's forces—the physical force of gravity, the chemical force of affinity, and the various newly posited forces attached to living beings. What we perceive are the *effects* of these forces. It is for this reason that Newton described gravity as an "occult quality [*qualitas occulta*]," and Johann Friedrich Blumenbach (1752–1840) adopted this Newtonian vocabulary to speak of his version of the life force, the "formative drive," or *Bildungstrieb*. For in both instances, as Newton put it in his response to Leibniz, we are speaking of a "power whose cause is unknown."[1] Or, as Blumenbach put it in his 1788 essay on the *Bildungstrieb*:

> I hope it will be superfluous to remind most readers that the word *Bildungstrieb*, like the words attraction, gravity, etc. should serve, no more and no less, to signify a power whose constant effect is recognized from experience and whose cause, like the causes of the aforementioned and the commonly recognized natural powers, is for us a *qualitas occulta*.[2]

Although Herder invokes the notion of force in a variety of ways, he also expresses caution about using it.[3] In the essay on the origin of language, for instance, he describes the divine-origin theory of language as another version of Newton's *hypotheses non fingo*.[4] By claiming that language originates in God, Herder contends, this account of language claims that the answer to the question lies in a realm beyond human understanding—in a *qualitas occulta*—and as such offers no answer. Herder is clear that his approach will not require such a conclusion: "I shall make no leap. I shall not straightaway suddenly give the human being new forces [*Kräfte*], 'no language-creating ability,' like an arbitrary *qualitas occulta*. I shall merely search further among the previously noted gaps and shortcomings" (FHA 1, 715; HPW 81).

In contrast to those who posit an unknowable force as a means of "explanation," Herder emphasizes careful observation of the phenomena. Through observing the phenomenon—through seeing various animals in their world, comparing them to one another and comparing their relations to their world—he was able to discern what is distinctive about the human being: not only the "lack" of a world, but also what this lack implies, the positive need for "more clarity," for *Besonnenheit*.

The same critical attitude toward such forms of "explanation" remains in the *Ideas*, where Herder writes that "we cannot perceive in the inner realm of nature's forces; it is thus in vain and unnecessary to desire internal, essential inference, no matter what circumstance it concerns. But the effects and forms [*Wirkungen und Formen*] of her power lie before us" (FHA 6, 165). In other words, when it comes to nature's forces, all we can do is *presume* that they exist on the basis of what appears before us—their effects and forms. Accordingly, our research program should not regard these forces as having explanatory value. For the forces are mere presumptions or placeholders, such that we cannot expect to offer an explanation of a phenomenon through them. This means that we cannot use them to draw inferences about similar objects. In other words, we cannot compare two (similar) objects, and infer, on the basis of their similarity, that the (hidden) cause of the one object must be the same as the (hidden) cause of the other. Rather, Herder emphasizes, the goal must be to *remain* with what is before us, with the phenomenon. Analogical reflection, for Herder, does not move to infer (hidden) causes.

It is for this reason, I think, that Herder repeatedly distinguishes analogical reflection from the purported goal of explanation by positing a force: "I do not say that I hereby *explain* [erkläre] anything; I have not yet known any philosophy that explains what *force is*, whether force stirs in a single being or two beings. What philosophy does is *observe* [bemerken], *order* [ordnen] together, *elucidate* [erläutern]" (FHA 4, 338–39). These remarks reveal that Kant's critique of Herder's methodology in the *Ideas* was misplaced—Herder clearly did not presume to be offering an *explanation* (i.e., an inference to causes) by way of analogy. They also reveal a surprising proximity between Kant and Herder. For Herder's statement prefigures Kant's distinction, in the third *Critique*, between the work of analogical reflection, which he identifies with elucidation and description, and the work of explanation, which involves a priori derivation. Herder's claim differs from Kant's, however, in its appreciation of the value of elucidation and description. In contrast to Kant, Herder regards observation, ordering, and elucidating as the only valid methods of scientific research. Explanation, understood as derivation of an object through an a priori principle, is, by contrast, an impossible goal.

If explanation involves either a priori derivation (from an established principle) or causal inference (from a hidden force), then what exactly does it mean to refuse to engage in explanation? What does it mean, in other words, to refuse to determine or uncover the hidden causes of a phenomenon or the a priori principles from which it can be derived? In turn, what is the outcome of this form of knowledge? What is the goal of knowledge if not derivation or inference?

The answers to these questions will illuminate the second sense in which reason is, according to Herder, "learned" (i.e., something that must be achieved), and will also lead us form Herder to Goethe. Before we turn to these considerations, however, it is important to contextualize (even if very briefly) Herder's (and Goethe's) choice to focus on form, as opposed to force. This will enable a deeper understanding not only of their conceptions of form, but also of their methodologies, and of the ways in which their methodologies enabled them to understand forms—and their significance—in a new way.

3.1. Force versus Form: Historical Perspectives

While the notion of force played an important role in the establishment of biology, Herder and Goethe had good reason to regard *form*, rather than force, as the starting point of their investigation.[5] Forces are, as Herder notes, beyond our ability to perceive them, such that a science focused primarily on forces or that regards forces as its starting point is, ultimately, speculative (all we can see are the effects of the forces). This, however, is not the only problem with a science focused on forces. Another, more significant, problem has to do with the fact that it is impossible to derive a *particular form* from the *general forces* of nature. While useful in articulating the universal laws of nature, forces are far too general to explain the specificity of natural forms.

The problem with force is thus twofold: it requires us to look *behind* the phenomenon in order to explain it (via some hidden cause or intention); and it demands that we reduce the particularity of the phenomenon to something general, divesting the various objects of precisely that which grants them their integrity and unity. These problems go back to mechanical philosophy's attempt to explain "animal generation" through the laws of motion.[6]

The aims of mechanical philosophy were to determine the fundamental nature of reality by reducing it to one homogeneous stuff, matter, and to explicate its actions according to a set of laws concerning motion in space. Newton introduced the notion of force in order to explain the relations between nonimpact objects, but maintained the view that matter, efficient causality as realized in the laws of motion, and various forces are the fundamental principles according to which reality can be understood. This perspective ran into difficulties in the mid-eighteenth century, when repeated attempts to explain animal generation according to mechanical principles failed. What became apparent was that matter, efficient causality, and various (active and passive) forces simply could not account for the active character of the material bodies of living beings: nourishment and growth, generation and reproduction demanded a different set of explanatory principles. The fact that, as Abraham Trembley (1710–1784) demonstrated in 1741, the freshwater polyp could be cut in half and grow its missing parts anew, so that out of one polyp two emerged, led to the question of how a material body could spontaneously generate *new* parts.[7] Where did these parts come from, if they had not previously existed in the body? How could new parts emerge at all? Some (nonblind) force or drive, it appeared, must exist that is internal to matter and that makes this generation possible.

Thus in contrast to the previously widespread view that generation did not involve the formation of new parts, but simply concerned the mechanical growth (enlargement) of very small ones—the view called "preformation" or "evolution"—a number of thinkers began to adopt the perspective that new parts did in fact emerge—the view called "epigenesis." This implied that matter could not be merely passive (moving according to the laws of motion), or blind (acting without any direction), but active and capable of *internal* transformation. In other words, its laws of transformation were not reducible to the (external) laws of mechanical physics.

To justify epigenesis, however, it was necessary to invoke a new force or law according to which matter operated. What would such a force be? Is it some kind of active (but blind) Newtonian force—as Caspar Wolff (1733–1794) had argued, calling it *Bildungskraft* (formative force)? If this force were blind, how is it the case that a human being always generates a human being, a chicken always a chicken? In other words, how can a blind force produce the same results every time? Or, as Albrecht von Haller (1708–1777) put it, how is it that the eyes are always in the right place, and never on the knee?[8] Ultimately, the question that Haller posed, and which could not be easily answered was: how can you explain (derive) *form* by means of the notion of *force*?

One response was to grant force some form of intelligence—force is not blind; rather it is oriented or driven by a goal, an end. While Kant argued that ascribing intelligence to matter is impossible (and had described matter as "lifeless"), Blumenbach regarded it as necessary.[9] Thus, contra Wolff, Blumenbach argued that the force that underpins living beings cannot be blind, and for this reason must be described as a *drive* as opposed to force. He called it *Bildungstrieb* (formative drive).

Even if Blumenbach was onto something, the question remained: how can we derive particular forms from the (very general) notion of drive? Can we actually *explain* the *distinctive forms* of living beings (the forms of animals and plants, not to mention the forms of the various beings within these kingdoms, e.g., the form of mammal or the form of reptile) through the notion of force or drive? The answer can only be negative. Form implies specificity and distinctness as well as a certain continuity over space and time: if we consider form, we can, for instance, discern a connection between plants across continents. By contrast, force (or drive) implies generality and nondistinctness and thus cannot function as a means by which to explain continuity within and between species across geographic and temporal distances.

The trouble, however, does not simply have to do with an incongruity between the general and the particular, but also with an implicit methodological assumption on the part of those seeking to explain phenomena via the notion of force: the assumption that the only way by which to *understand* natural phenomena is by looking for *something behind or beyond them*, looking for a force that can somehow "explain" them. On this view, understanding requires *deriving* an object from a (hidden) principle (a force, a drive, or a cause).

But what if there is an alternative to this methodology and its assumptions? What if we do not need to look behind or beyond the phenomena in order to understand them? What if, in other words, we do not need to derive these phenomena from (hidden) forces or drives that are *behind* the phenomena, but grasp them in terms of laws which are *themselves* the phenomena? This question guided the romantic empiricists to their key insight—an insight that led Herder, Goethe, and Humboldt to pay more attention to form as opposed to force or drive. While Herder did not completely disavow the notion of force, and it certainly plays an important role in his metaphysics, his emphasis on what *appears*—on the phenomenon and the form—challenges any reading of Herder that places force, as opposed to form, at the heart of his methodology and philosophy of science.[10] In turn, and as we shall see in the chapters to come, Goethe and Humboldt were far less equivocal about the usefulness of the notion of force—they both rejected it.[11]

3.2. Herder and the *Hauptform*

At first sight Herder's claim that we can only know the "effects and forms" of nature might imply that analogical reflection concerns only superficial or surface phenomena and does not allow for serious investigation of the internal makeup of an object. Furthermore, it is not clear how Herder's use of analogical reflection can furnish a resolution to the problems outlined above, i.e., to overcoming the explanatory gap between the unformed (the general force or drive) and the formed. In turn, if analogical reflection is merely description or elucidation, then in what sense can it achieve scientific insight? The three points are related. For the question ultimately is: what is the *outcome* of analogical reflection—does it grant us insight beyond contingent, superficial knowledge, and how does it deliver something other than a generalizing concept that is divorced from the phenomenon?

To answer these questions, we must consider Herder's understanding of analogy more carefully. For the claim is that we must "explain the one through the other" (FHA 6, 73). Accordingly, in analogy there is no subsumption of one element under the other. While the connector "is" implies identity and some form of subsumption (of particular under general, for instance), the analogical connector "as" does not. Rather, the "as" contains both the difference and similarity of the two elements, beholding the like and unlike simultaneously, without collapsing them into a relation of identity. There is thus no move to an abstract concept, no transition from empirically grounded observation and comparison to a concept that is divested of difference and particularity. Rather, by referring to both elements at once, by regarding them in and through one another, analogical reflection maintains a tension that obstructs any such transition. What emerges out of this tension is not an abstract concept that precludes difference, but insight into the *relation* between the two elements; insight that maintains the likeness and unlikeness of the two elements. For it is only by seeing the two elements *in and through* one another that they emerge as objects of knowledge.

In the *Ideas* Herder elaborates this insight by providing examples from nature and drawing on the idea of world or circle. To begin with, he explains that it is only by seeing fish, for instance, in relation to birds, by seeing the form of a fish in and through that of a bird, that we gain insight into their similarities and differences, discern the ways in which their structures mirror their worlds, and begin to grasp the significance of their structures. In turn, if we consider their respective forms in relation to their worlds, observe fish and birds in their elements (water and air, respectively), we gain further insight into their differing (and also similar) structures. Thus, Herder writes, "The bird flies in the air," such that "every divergence of its form from the build of land animals can be explicated through its element. . . . The fish swims in water; its feet and hands are grown into fin and tail: it has only little articulation of its members" (FHA 6, 75–76). By comparing the two organisms, and considering their structures in relation to the world that they inhabit, we begin to see how they are both like and unlike one another: we see the differences in their members, and how these differences map onto their contexts, and we see their similarities—similarities that also evidence their diverging environments, e.g., how what is wing in bird appears as fin in fish. (Or, to put it via an analogy: wings are to birds what fins are to fish.)

As noted in the preceding chapter, Herder's aim is to see how the organism is in dialogue with its environment—how the structure of the fish reflects the water, in the same way that the structure of the bird reflects the air, such that the two can only exist *as they are* in their respective elements. The deep relationship between fish and water mirrors the deep relationship between birds and air. This is not to "explain" the fish via its environment, by deriving its particular structure from something *other than* the fish (i.e., the water). For that would imply moving beyond the fish (looking to understand the fish through something else). Rather, Herder locates the fish in its environment, and regards it as *intelligible* only through this environment.

Herder suggests that in comparing the structure of birds and fish, humans and other animals, we begin to understand their relationships, discern their distinctive yet related characters, and thus glean a continuity in nature that does not imply identity. In turn, by seeing living beings within the worlds they inhabit and by comparing, for example, fish to terrestrial animals, we discern the extent to which their respective structures are in dialogue with their contexts, and thereby arrive at an insight into the ways in which the structure of a fish or a bird both differs from and *reiterates* the structure of other animals.

But what exactly does it mean to regard living beings as *reiterations* of one another? This notion of reiteration—and the ability to discern it—are, I believe, the key reason why Herder considers analogical reflection to be essential. For to regard various beings as *reiterations* implies, first, seeing continuity *in* the differences between the various beings. It also implies discerning similarity without reducing it to identity. And, finally, it implies finding meaning (lawfulness) in what at first sight appears meaningless or chaotic. In these three ways, the notion of reiteration—of seeing similarity that is irreducible to identity—implies discerning a principle of continuity *in the phenomena themselves* (rather than in a principle above or beyond them) and thereby discerning the "real" system of nature rather than constructing an abstract one.

But it means more. For it points to an underlying structure or prototype—what Herder calls a *Hauptform*. As he puts it, the notion that natural forms reiterate one another reveals a "certain uniformity of structure and a *Hauptform*" in the most diverse beings (FHA 6, 73). This uniformity is evident, for example, in the "similar skeletal structure of land animals . . . the head, the back, the hands, the feet are the main parts in all of them. Even their finest members," Herder adds "are formed according to one prototype and at the same time only infinitely varied [*nach einem Prototyp gebildet und gleichsam nur unendlich variieret*]" (FHA 6, 73).

Herder does not offer a detailed explication of the *Hauptform*; nonetheless, on the basis of his remarks, we can conclude the following: as "one prototype" that is "at the same time only infinitely varied," the *Hauptform* is like a musical theme that appears only in variation. Just as a musical theme is at once one and many, so also the prototype is both *one* and *many*. In fact, and again like a musical theme in variation, the *Hauptform* only appears *in* its variations, even if it is just *one* theme—one prototype.

The *Hauptform* then is not a concept that subsumes the observed particulars under an abstract unity; rather, it is a unity that emerges out of, or, better, that *resides in*, the particulars. It is not separable from its particular manifestations, for it only appears in variation—in reiteration. This means that the *Hauptform* is not an object in the world, something that can be *seen* immediately with the eyes. Because the *Hauptform* is expressed *only in variation*, more is required for it to be seen. This is where analogical reflection becomes necessary: analogy allows us to see how this one form re-emerges (variously) in different beings.

What analogical reflection brings forth, then, is not a static or abstract concept, nor is it something that is merely empirically perceived. Rather, through analogical reflection we gain insight into *how* something appears, i.e., *how* the structure of a living being differs from or reflects its context, *how* its specific form anticipates similar yet different forms in other beings, or *how* what is implicit in one living being becomes explicit in another. Precisely because it grants insight into the *how,* and discloses a being in and through its similarities, differences and relations, the *Hauptform*—the result of analogical reflection—might be best described as a dynamic idea, as opposed to a static idea.

While a static idea is clearly determined (through subsumption, for instance) and can perhaps be pointed to (as an object in the world), a dynamic idea can only be discerned through analogical reflection because it resists being subsumed by a more general concept and does not appear in any one object. It can only be "seen" in its various manifestations, and, more specifically, when these manifestations are regarded "in and through" one another. This means that it requires the constant and active engagement of the knower.

By emphasizing the *how* rather than the *why*, by focusing on how something appears (the conditions in which it appears, the forms of its appearance) rather than why it appears (the causes of its appearance), analogical reflection moves from empirical observation to intelligible insight (the *Hauptform*) without recourse to abstraction. In other words, it arrives at the idea of a *Hauptform* without invoking an external cause or hidden intention, and also without applying a general principle in order to make the particular object intelligible.

Herder's hermeneutic methodology is evident both in his emphasis on analogy and in the idea of the *Hauptform*. Like the meaning of a literary text, the *Hauptform* is expressed in each one of its parts. In turn, just as this meaning is neither purely intelligible (an a priori idea, or a Platonic form), nor merely empirical (i.e., a particular object or accumulated data), but hovers between the two, so the *Hauptform* is neither purely ideal nor purely empirical. And, in the same way that the interpreter will continually come to new thoughts that enrich her understanding of the text's meaning, so also the student of nature will deepen her understanding of the *Hauptform* through ongoing observation and comparison. Furthermore, just as the goal of reading a text is to grasp not only the meaning and significance of each of its parts, but also their relations, so also the *Hauptform* aims to grasp the meaningfulness of natural forms in and through their relations. And, finally, both require the ongoing engagement of the reader/observer.

Given the peculiar status of the *Hauptform*, and its connection to literary interpretation, it is difficult to determine its significance: is it real? Or, more to the point, is it necessary? After all, necessity is, for Kant at least, the mark of science: only necessary knowledge is designated as "proper science." Accordingly, the scientific significance of the *Hauptform* should be considered in relation to its necessity. Herder makes suggestions regarding the necessity of analogical reflection and the *Hauptform*. His suggestions remain theoretical, in that he does not actually employ the idea of the *Hauptform* to undertake empirical research. Goethe, however, propelled by Herder's ideas and his method, undertook precisely this research. In so doing, he offered the most compelling evidence of the *necessity* of the *Hauptform*.

3.3. Goethe and the Intermaxillary Bone

Herder arrived in Strasbourg on September 4, 1770, and a week later met Goethe, who at the time was an unhappy student of law. Goethe was excited about meeting Herder, who was five years his senior, and the author of some acclaimed works. Despite their age difference, Goethe quickly gained Herder's trust and friendship, and benefited from his guidance.

The influence, however, was not one-sided. The eight months that the two lived in the same city proved to be momentous for both. It was during this time that they formulated their Sturm und Drang project. It was also during this time that Herder worked on his essay on Shakespeare and his treatise on the origin of language—both of which, as we have seen, bore significant fruit for Herder's understanding of the natural world and his methodology. Goethe's greatest impact on Herder can be found, however, in his support for the *Ideas*. As Herder puts it in a letter to Hamann, "if my wife, the author of the author of my writings, and Goethe, who happened to see the book first, had not encouraged and driven me, everything would have remained in the Hades of the unborn."[12]

Thus, although it is fair to claim, as Nicholas Boyle put it, that by 1770 Herder "had a purpose," while Goethe did not, such a statement overlooks the sense of a shared project that emerged out of their friendship.[13] Although this project has its seeds in Herder's thought, it was enthusiastically embraced, and brought to further realization, by Goethe. More specifically, and more pertinently for our purposes, it was in the hands of Goethe that the notion of a *Hauptform* became a key scientific tool, a guiding idea by which to go about examining and understanding natural phenomena. This can be most clearly seen in Goethe's discovery of the intermaxillary bone.

In the winter of 1783–84, while Herder was working on the *Ideas*, Goethe became interested in the question of the existence of the intermaxillary bone. The intermaxillary bone—now known as the premaxilla or premaxillary bone—which is located in the upper jaw and holds the incisor teeth, had been found in the majority of mammals, including apes. It is most obvious in animals with long faces, such as horses, though it is also visible in animals with shorter skulls, such as monkeys. A number of prominent anatomists, among them Blumenbach, Petrus Camper (1722–1789), and Samuel Thomas Sömmering (1755–1830), had claimed that the bone cannot be found in human beings, and they saw this lack as a distinguishing mark of the human—the mark that made the human *not* animal.[14] By the early 1780s, as Goethe remarks, the *os intermaxillare* had become *the* bone separating the human from the animal, such that its discovery implied precisely the kind of connection between the human and animal that theologically minded scientists worried about. This is how he puts it in his reflections back on this moment in the history of science:

> The distinction between man and animal long eluded discovery. Ultimately it was believed that the definitive difference between ape and man lay in the placement of the ape's four incisors in a bone clearly and physically separate from other bones. Thus the whole science, in jest or in earnest, vacillated between attempts to prove what was half true and attempts to lend the semblance of truth to what was false—but all with the purpose of keeping itself occupied and sustaining itself through whimsical and willful activity. (MA 12, 19)

Despite the controversy around this supposed key piece of evidence, Goethe set himself the task of finding it. And in 1784 he did precisely that. Thus, he joyfully reports to Herder on March 27, 1784:

> I have found it—neither gold nor silver, but something that makes me unspeakably happy—the *os intermaxillare* in the human! With Loder I compared human and animal skulls, came upon its trace, and saw that it is. Now please do not mention this to anyone, since it must be kept secret. It should also make you glad since the capstone for man is not lacking, it's there. Indeed, I have thought about it in relation to your whole [book], how wonderful it will be. (WA 4/6, 258)

The intensity and enthusiasm with which Goethe reports to Herder evinces the extent to which they understood themselves as collaborators—working together to find this link between humans and other animals. Although Goethe asks Herder to keep this discovery to himself, he recognizes its significance for Herder's forthcoming publication, the *Ideas*. Herder too sees its importance and makes use of Goethe's discovery to support his notion of the *Hauptform* in the *Ideas*. Following his description of the similarities and differences between humans and apes, Herder adds that further similarity can be found in the intermaxillary bone: it is "the final feature of the human countenance" shared with animals (FHA 6, 119).

How did Goethe find what other—far more experienced—anatomists had not found?[15] How was Goethe able to "see" the intermaxillary bone, given that the others had not seen it? The answer to this question is at the heart of the romantic empiricist project. For what the romantic empiricists realized is that there is a difference between seeing and seeing—between seeing well and seeling badly, and seeing and knowing well involve work, practice and constant engagement.

To begin with, it is important to note that what Goethe saw was not an exact replica of the bone as it appears in other animals; rather, it was a variation or a transformation, a *reiteration*, of the bone in the human. This reiteration made sense in light of the whole human form, or the human *Hauptform*. As Goethe puts it years later, his study of osteology, which drove him to surround himself "with a collection of older and more recent remains," also led him to posit the idea of a *Typus* or prototype:

> In the process I soon felt the need to posit a type [*Typus*], from which all mammals could be tested to find points of agreement or divergence. . . . I now aspired to find the archetypal animal [*Urtier*]; in essence, the concept or idea of the animal [*die Idee des Tiers*]. (MA 12, 19)

With the idea of *Hauptform* or *Typus* in mind, Goethe knew what to look for, what *not* to look for, and, most importantly, *how* to look for it. Thus, on the basis of this idea, he knew not to look for an exact replica of the bone as it appears in any other animal. He knew that to find the bone in the human, he must take account of the human organism as a whole and compare it to the structure of other animals in their wholeness and in their context. (Recall that the same bone appears differently in a horse than it does in an ape.) As Goethe puts it in a letter to Karl Ludwig von Knebel: "Unity of the whole makes every creature into that which it is. The human being is a human being as much through the form and nature of his upper jaw as through the form and nature of the tip of his little toe."[16] In other words, what Goethe looked for was the bone *within its larger context*—the human body—and this means taking into account the whole human body, and regarding every part as a member *of* this whole, as *expressive* of it. Following Herder, Goethe noted that the human frame is distinctively upright, such that the intermaxillary bone must also reflect the feature of uprightness.[17]

Goethe knew that the human intermaxillary bone may not—indeed, *cannot—appear* like the bone in an ape or a horse. He knew, furthermore, that over time it may have undergone vast alterations so that it no longer bears any perceptible similarity to the bone in the ape or the horse. That turned out to be the case. While the human embryo shows a separate intermaxillary bone, in the adult human skull, as Robert Richards writes, there are only "vague outlines but no true sutures."[18] The human intermaxillary bone, in other words, bears hardly any resemblance to the bone in other animals. The similarity then is not to be found in the appearance of this particular bone, but in the structural and formal integrity of the whole—i.e., in the relation between this bone and the whole context of which it is part. The bone in the human *reflects* the human form and as such cannot appear like the bone in any other animal. These considerations are all informed by Herder's idea of the *Hauptform*, or Goethe's *Typus*.

Importantly, Goethe was *certain* that he would find the intermaxillary bone; this certainty was founded on his view that the *Hauptform* or *Typus* is not an arbitrary or subjective invention, but possesses necessity, or reality. In turn, precisely because the *Typus* was confirmed in experience, because it revealed something *real* about the world, Goethe's view that it displays necessity was confirmed.

But what kind of necessity are we talking about? Clearly, the necessity that Goethe and Herder recognize in the *Hauptform* or *Typus* has nothing to do with a priori derivation or construction. Nor is it a necessity based on the laws of motion, or the more specific laws of causality, for it does not involve establishing that something is the necessary effect of an antecedent cause. Furthermore, the *Hauptform* or *Typus* cannot be propositionally proven, for it is not a formal principle that can be derived from some other principle; nor is it a general concept under which more particular concepts can be subsumed.

Although we will continue exploring Goethe's methodology in the following chapters, investigating how he was able to "see" the *Typus*, at this stage we can surmise the following: the *Hauptform* or *Typus* involves a standpoint, a way of regarding nature, which can be confirmed or denied by experience. What distinguished Goethe from Camper, Blumenbach, and Sömmering, then, was the *standpoint* from which he investigated the various animal skulls: the standpoint that enabled him to see living beings as reiterations and to regard their parts as expressions of an underlying structural integrity.

In his 1795 essay on comparative anatomy and osteology (published in 1820), Goethe speaks in precisely these terms. He begins by noting that over the past century science had become riddled by a number of difficulties—difficulties that brought the attempt to categorize and systematize nature to a halt. The chief difficulty had to do with, as Goethe puts it, the "accumulation of detail," which "made it increasingly difficult to attain some sort of overview [*Überblick*]" (MA 12, 122). On account of this profusion of data, scientists felt compelled to compare "every animal with every animal and every animal with all the animals," a task that is not only copious but potentially also intractable. This made it all but impossible to achieve any conclusive insight into the relations between animal species. To overcome this difficulty, Goethe continues, it is necessary to postulate an archetype (*Urtypus*): "Hence, an anatomical archetype [*anatomischen Typus*] will be suggested here, a general picture [*einem allgemeinen Bilde*] containing the forms of all animals as potential, one which will guide us to an orderly description of nature" (MA 12, 122).

In this moment of reflection, Goethe offers one of the most explicit accounts of his reasons for positing an archetype and its use in his research. The archetype, he states, is not to be found in the physical world; it cannot be identified with any particular animal, because "the particular can never serve as a measure for the whole" (MA 12, 122). Rather, the archetype allows us to do justice to the diversity of nature's forms and at the same time reveals or points to the coherence and unity of nature. As such it serves as a guide in our attempt to discern connections and moments of transformation in nature's changing manifoldness.

This conception of the archetype might seem like an approximation of Kant's notion of a regulative ideal, i.e., a guide by which to undertake empirical investigation, given to us through reason's desire for completion but never realized or realizable in experience. While there are certain resonances between the two, the differences are significant and highlight the ways in which Goethe (and Herder) differed from Kant. For one, the archetype is gained in and through experience: it is not a pure idea of reason, but an idea that is achieved through careful, considered, and repeated observation. Thus, it might best be described as an *empirical* idea. As Goethe goes on to emphasize in this essay, empirical observation is paramount to the development of the archetype: "empirical observation must first teach us what parts are common to all animals, and how these parts differ." Second, the archetype is *confirmed* in experience. Indeed, it is only through this confirmation that we can be sure that it is genuine, i.e., that we've hit upon genuine insight into nature. Thus, Goethe continues, "once such an archetype is established, even if only provisionally, we may test it quite adequately by applying the customary methods of comparison" (MA 12, 122–23).

In light of this, we can conclude that the necessity that accompanies the notion of the archetype or *Hauptform* concerns the structural integrity of the phenomenon before us, the ways in which the phenomenon's various members relate to one another and express the whole.[19] The *Hauptform* or *Typus* points to and illuminates this integrity. It also shows how this integrity is reiterated, albeit in variation, across a number of species.

Accordingly, the notion of necessity that Herder and Goethe came to recognize as fundamental in scientific knowledge demands rethinking the meaning of necessity, and with it understanding. To understand is not to derive from a principle, but to discern the essential relations between objects and to see how the various parts of an object manifest the whole—how the various parts of an ape, for instance, express the mammal archetype, or how the various parts of a fish express the vertebral archetype. Once this is achieved, once we perceive how the parts are related—how they are parts of an integrated structure and various expressions of this structure—there is no need for an additional "explanation." For this *is* the explanation. The explanation, in other words, is to be found *in* the phenomenon, rather than beyond it.

This means that what Herder and Goethe articulate is a different conceptualization of the task of knowledge and the ideal of explanation. Explanation does not involve external principles or causes. Rather, explanation involves grasping the relations that *are* the phenomenon, and which the phenomenon expresses. As Goethe puts it in the *Theory of Colors* [*Farbenlehre*] (1810):

> With any given phenomenon in nature—and especially if it is significant or striking—we should not stop and dwell on it, cling to it, and view it as existing in isolation. Rather, we should look about in the whole of nature to find where there is something similar, something related. For only when related elements are drawn together will a whole gradually emerge that *speaks for itself and requires no further explanation* [*die sich selbst ausspricht und keiner weitern Erklärung bedarf*]. (FA 23/1, 96, no. 228; emphasis added)

The *Hauptform* or *Typus* provide precisely the perspective from which we can discern how elements are related, how they form an integrated unity, and how various species are—in light of the *Hauptform*—connected. What the *Hauptform* furnishes, then, is a perspective from which this integrity, this lawfulness, becomes evident *in* the phenomena themselves, and thereby allows the phenomena to "speak for themselves." Once this is achieved, no further explanation is needed. For, as Goethe puts it, the goal is not to "look behind the phenomena because the phenomena are themselves the theory [*Man suche nur nichts hinter den Phänomenen; sie selbst sind die Lehre*]" (FA 13, 49).

3.4. Description, Explanation, and Necessity

At this point, it is helpful to pause and consider the implications of Herder's and Goethe's methodology. The claim is that the study of nature demands the study of forms, not in order to determine their origins through a causal explanation, but to arrive at insight into their integral unity, into the ways in which their parts are inherently related, in dialogue with one another and their environment. This approach does not aim to grasp the phenomenon through something else—through some efficient or final cause, through an animating and occult force, or through its parts in isolation from one another. Rather, it describes and elucidates the phenomenon and thereby remains on the level of phenomenological description. However, it would be mistaken to identify this description with something like a travel narrative, where the speaker is simply led by her encounters to take note of various features of the natural environment, without a systematic approach or an interest in understanding. For although what Herder and Goethe offer is not a *causal* explanation, their approach is not nonexplanatory or nonilluminating. Rather, it reveals nature in a different way, a way that makes natural forms and relations intelligible and meaningful. As such, their approach is best described as a hermeneutics of nature, and more specifically a hermeneutics of natural forms. It illuminates by discerning lawfulness within the phenomenon—within the relations and transformations that *are* the phenomenon—and is guided in this endeavor by the idea of *Hauptform* or *Typus*.

As a dynamic idea that guides research by offering a standpoint from which to regard the phenomenon, the *Hauptform* enables the researcher to see how the various parts are not contingent, but inherently related, and how their relations manifest a distinctive lawfulness—a lawfulness that can only be gleaned *in and through* their forms and the transformations of their forms, not beyond them.

This requires a shift in perspective—away from causal explanation to intelligibility and expressiveness; away from derivation to seeing *how* a phenomenon manifests a *particular and integrated* structure, and *how* this particularity carries within itself, within its very makeup, necessity (e.g., how its parts could not be otherwise). This means that discerning necessity requires recognizing how particular situations are in fact necessary—i.e., seeing how there is necessity in what appears at first sight to be contingent. Explanation does not demand departing from the appearances, but remaining with them and finding necessity therein: i.e., in their particular, diverse and manifold structures and relations.

It was this new understanding of necessity and explanation, coupled with the significant notion of *Hauptform* or *Typus*, that inspired Goethe's further study of nature, leading him to what might strike us as surprising conclusions. For, as we shall see, Goethe came to realize that the science of morphology and the idea of *Typus* demand an *education* in which the knower develops new "organs of perception." Accordingly, for Goethe knowledge—and scientific knowledge in particular—implies an obligation: to educate and transform one's self in order to know *well*.

4
Aesthetic Education and the Transformation of the Scientist

When through lively observation a person begins to confront nature, he will at first experience a tremendous compulsion to submit nature's objects to his will. Before long, however, these objects will thrust themselves upon him with such force that he will have to recognize their power and revere their effects. As soon as he is convinced of this mutual influence, he will become aware of a double infinite: in the objects with their manifold ways of being and becoming, and their living interwoven relations, and in himself the possibility of *infinite education* [*unendliche Ausbildung*], in which he can transform his sensibility as well as his judgment to accord with new forms of grasping and responding [*neue Formen des Aufnehmens und Gegenwirkens*]. (MA 12, 11; emphasis added)

It is with these words that Goethe opens the first volume of *On Morphology* [*Zur Morphologie*] (1817–24), his collected writings on plants, animals, and scientific methodology.[1] Though some of these writings had been composed several decades earlier, and often refer to work Goethe had undertaken in those preceding decades, the majority were first published in *On Morphology*—prompting Goethe to begin the collection with the essay "The Enterprise Justified [*Das Unternehmen wird Entschuldigt*]." As the title implies, the goal of the essay is to offer reasons why Goethe chose to publish under one rubric what at times may appear as disconnected writings. In this essay, then, Goethe offers an apology (*Entschuldigung*) of sorts for his publication, with the intention or at least the hope to win his readers' sympathy for his goals.

These goals are intimated in Goethe's opening sentences, which offer a summation of his most important methodological insight: the task of the scientist involves not only careful and consistent observation of the objects before her, but also *the transformation of the scientist herself*.[2] Specifically, it demands the *education* or *formation* (*Ausbildung*) of the scientist's sensibility and judgment.

This education, Goethe explains, begins once the scientist recognizes that natural objects cannot be subdued to her will—her constructions, systems, or designs—but that they exhibit a power of their own, and her task is to grasp this power, i.e., to understand "nature's manifold ways of being and becoming, and their living interwoven relations." However, precisely when this recognition occurs, another, equally important, insight forms. For what the scientist realizes is that she is ill-equipped to achieve her task and must therefore develop "new forms of grasping and responding," i.e., capacities of seeing and knowing that would enable her to properly attend to the phenomena.

On the first page of *On Morphology*, then, we find what might be described as Goethe's methodological manifesto and the methodological manifesto of romantic empiricism more generally. For Goethe's claim is that seeing and knowing are not neutral: *how* we approach a natural phenomenon matters, in that it impacts both how the phenomenon will appear and how we comport ourselves in relation to it. There are less and more apt approaches to nature—and depending on which approach we take, we will have poorer or richer insights into the phenomenon and our relation to it. Furthermore, the more apt approach involves a transformation on the part of the scientist. For, Goethe suggests, it is only by transforming her cognitive capacities that she will be able to live up to the task she has set before her, the task of knowledge. This means that in entering the relationship of knowledge, the knower is implicitly agreeing to educate or transform herself in order to know *well*.

Immediately several questions emerge. Why must the knower transform herself? Why, in other words, is she ill-equipped to begin with? What is involved in this self-transformation? And how does the "object" of knowledge *guide* this transformation? In other words, how do natural phenomena "open up new organs of perceptions" in us (MA 12, 306)? Finally, what does this tell us about the obligations of the scientist, and the enterprise and activity of science more generally? Put differently, might the scientist be obliged—in an ethical sense—to transform? Is there a crucial ethical layer in the relation between knower and known?

While these questions are at the heart of Goethe's epistemology, philosophical interpretations of Goethe have rarely considered them.[3] As I will argue over the next two chapters, however, education is a central element in Goethe's thought and practice and provides the key to understanding his notion of intuitive judgment, his conception of the *Urphänomen*, and the *kind* of scientific text that Goethe was interested in producing. Furthermore, I will show that the education of which Goethe speaks, and which he himself undertook, is an *aesthetic* education in both senses of the term. It alludes to Baumgarten's notion of aesthetics as having to do with "all things perceived," and is thus an education of our perceptual capacities.[4] But it is also an aesthetic education in the more well-known sense of the term "aesthetic," i.e., an education *in and through art*. Goethe came to the view that studying and composing works of art is crucial for deepening and enhancing our understanding of nature. This means—contra Kant—that aesthetic experience carries not only *aesthetic* value, but also *cognitive* value. It also means that the scientist is (in some significant sense) under an obligation to undertake an aesthetic education—not to become an artist, but rather (to use Goethe's term) to become an artistic "dilettante."

My claim is that once we recognize the significant role that aesthetics and aesthetic education play in Goethe's epistemology, we gain important perspectives on both his scientific methodology and the aims of his scientific writings. Specifically, we will better understand the structure of and motivation behind Goethe's 1790 essay, *The Metamorphosis of Plants*. For, as I will show, this text is by no means a scientific treatise in the usual sense of the term, in that it is conscious of its linguistic medium, uses the medium to its advantage—and also seeks to make up for the medium's disadvantages. In this way it approximates works of art that reflect on their own medium and the medium's capacities and limits. Furthermore, like a work of art, Goethe's essay places certain demands on its reader—demands that seek to enable the reader to develop "new forms of knowing and acting."

In turn, Goethe's "turn to the poetic sphere," as he puts it at the end of the essay "Doubt and Resignation [*Bedenken und Ergebung*]" (1818), might be read as a pessimistic or complacent response to unresolvable epistemological difficulties. However, in light of the significance of aesthetics and art for Goethe's methodology, the turn to poetry will no longer appear as a turn away from a genuine resolution, but as its very opposite: a substantive investigation of how poetry *can* and *does* play a crucial role in helping the knower achieve her task.[5]

Accordingly, and as I will argue, we cannot consider Goethe's epistemology or his methodology apart from his understanding of the significance of art and aesthetic education in the development of our cognitive capacities. The question of course is: what *kind* of knowledge does aesthetic education and artistic practice result in, and what kind of *concepts* does this form of knowledge deliver?

To answer this question, we will begin by looking at the key epistemological and methodological difficulties that Goethe identified and sought to resolve. For it is in his attempt to overcome these difficulties that Goethe became increasingly convinced of the fact that the knower must transform—and that aesthetic education plays a key role in this transformation.

4.1. Problems of Knowledge: A First Look

Although Goethe's turn to epistemology is usually credited to his friendship with Friedrich Schiller, the Kantian who questioned Goethe's claim that he could "see" the primal plant or *Urpflanze* with his eyes, Goethe had begun to think about epistemological questions well before their famous 1794 encounter. In fact, Goethe's critical reflections on scientific methodology and epistemology even precede his reading of Kant's *Critique of Pure Reason* in 1789.[6] For it was in the summer of 1788, while still in Rome, that Goethe first articulated the "greatest difficulty" of scientific research—a difficulty that is both methodological and epistemological. He writes,

> The greatest difficulty ... consists in the fact that one must treat as fixed and stationary that which in nature is always in motion, that one must reduce to a simple, visible and at the same time graspable law that which in nature is eternally changing. (FA 24, 97)

When he formulated this problem, Goethe had been living and traveling in Italy for almost two years, having (quietly) made his way to the southern peninsula in September 1786. During those two years, he did not only encounter a different natural landscape than the one he had known in Weimar but was also able to observe, growing in their natural habitat, plants that he had previously only seen in his greenhouse. From the first moment he set foot in Italy, Goethe was struck by what he saw: the different vegetation, differing growth patterns, and also the different forms that the same plant species can assume, depending on its location. This is how he puts it in the *Italian Journey* [*Italienische Reise*] (1816–17), where he describes what he saw a few days after crossing the Alps:

> if in the lower region [of the Alps] the branches and stems were thicker and stronger, the buds closer to each other and the leaves broad, then higher

in the mountains the branches and stems were more delicate, the buds separated by greater intervals from node to node, and the leaves shaped more lanceolately. I noticed this both in a willow and a gentian and have become convinced that it was not, as one might think, a question of different species of these plants. (FA 15/1, 22)

The fact that the very same plant appears differently depending on its altitude struck Goethe profoundly, redirecting his interest and attention—often away from the artistic works he had intended to compose, to the study of plants. These observations challenged him to think more carefully about the nature of plants and the relation between plants and their surroundings. For what he witnessed was an incredible plasticity, connected to the plant's geographic location.

As he relates in his 1817/1831 "History of My Botanical Studies [*Geschichte meines botanischen Studiums*]," in Italy he turned his "attention more strongly to climatic influence," and began to closely observe the transformations of the single part as it develops in the plant.[7] When he first encountered a date palm tree, for instance, Goethe was surprised by the vastly different forms of its leaves: the "old offspring" of the tree, he writes, looks so different from the "simple, lace-shaped first leaves near the ground," that he could not help but think that the two were "unrelated [*in keinem Verhältnis stehendes Erzeugnis*]." He could not help but wonder how these two very differently shaped leaves were *leaves of the same plant*.

With the help of a gardener, Goethe continues, he "cut off an entire sequence of modifications [*die Stufenfolge dieser Veränderungen*]" and placed the various leaves side by side, in their order of development. Looking at them in this way, he began to discern how the form of the one can also be seen in the form of the other, and vice versa. This was, in a sense, Goethe's first presentation of the dynamism of plant form: his first attempt to find unity in the variety of leaf forms by seeing them in relation to one another. Through this presentation, he came to an important insight:

> the plant forms around us are not predetermined and established [*determiniert und festgestellt*]; instead, we find allotted to them, along with their stubborn clinging to genera and species, a happy mobility and flexibility [*Möbilität und Biegsamkeit*], enabling them to adapt themselves to the many conditions throughout the world which influence them, and to

be formed and reformed [*bilden und umbilden*] in accordance with them. (LA 1/10, 333)

As he continued to immerse himself in the study of plants, Goethe became increasingly aware of both the dynamism of the plant kingdom and the impoverished character of botanical terminology. The highly artificial Latin nomenclature, he quickly realized, is largely divorced from the phenomena it seeks to illuminate and convey, and thus often hinders rather than benefits understanding. It is static and fixed, while plants are dynamic and plastic. Reiterating Buffon's critique of Linnaeus, but from a different angle, Goethe remarks that "on the selfsame plant I discovered first round, then notched, and finally almost pinnate leaves, which later contracted, were simplified, turned into scales, and at last disappeared entirely." For this reason, he continues, "The problem of designating the genera with certainty, and of arranging the species under them, seemed insoluble to me. Of course, I read the method prescribed, but how could I hope to find a suitable classification when even in Linnaeus' time genera had been shattered and separated, and classes themselves dissolved?" (WA 2/6, 117).

The attempt to classify the plant—or any living being—on the basis of one organ can only be pursued in vain. For if we were to take the shape of the leaf as a key to classifying a plant, for instance, we would not know *which* shape to regard as its essential shape. After all, the leaf's form differs depending on where it is on the plant. The leaf's transformations within the same plant elude Linnaean classification.

For this reason, Goethe concluded that botanical terminology and practices are of no help. What they result in, he writes in "History of My Botanical Studies," is a "mosaic," in which "one completed block is placed next to another, creating finally a single picture from the thousands of pieces" (LA 1/10, 330). Goethe's goal, however, was not to offer a completed puzzle, in which the various plants are fitted into ready-made categories. Rather, his goal was to grasp how the different parts of the plant form a unity. This means taking account of the ways in which their parts transform, in relation to one another and in relation to their location.

It was not only the puzzle-like nature and artificial language of botany that Goethe came to regard as limited in its ability to capture plant dynamism. Laguage—in general—appeared to him to be not up to the task. Upon witnessing a proliferous carnation in Angelika Kauffmann's garden in Rome, Goethe tells the reader that he had no means by which to "preserve this miracle form [*Wundergestalt*]." In the place of words, he turns to the visual arts: "I undertook to sketch it in detail, and, in the process began to gain deeper insight into the basic concept of metamorphosis [*den Grundbegriff der Metamorphose*]" (FA 15/1, 404; FA 24, 751).[8]

It was thus in Rome, while Goethe was surrounded not only by visual artists, but also by the visual arts, that he began to develop his idea of metamorphosis.[9] And, in turn, it was through the practice of visual art that he began to deepen his understanding of metamorphosis.[10] The epistemic significance of visual art is evident not only in the passage cited above, but also in the many letters composed during his years in Italy. In a letter to Knebel from August 18, 1787, Goethe emphasizes that it was through drawing the carnation that he was able to gain insight into it. He then goes on to add that "this autumn, I will go to the country to sketch landscapes in order to enrich my imagination and to expand, purify, and enlarge my style," with the hope that through this process "much more will be achieved" (FA 30, 318).

In Italy, where Goethe found himself in a new context, he was able to become more reflective, not only about the natural world, but also about the arts and his own capacities as an artist and a scientist. He began to see an important link between the three—i.e., scientific knowledge, artistic practice and technique, and self-knowledge. Though this link left many of his readers confused, as will be discussed below, for Goethe it was crucial. As he saw it, it was only by "unlearning" the mechanical processes by which botany proceeded, and learning to proceed differently, to "see" differently, and to aim for a different kind of understanding, that it was possible to depict, portray, and communicate the living character of the natural world.

While Goethe returned again and again to the methodological and epistemological problems facing the natural scientist—considering them from different angles, with increasing philosophical acumen—the practices that he developed in order to grasp and portray the natural world in Italy and the epistemological insights which these practices afforded, remained with him throughout and provided him with the seeds for overcoming these problems.

4.2. Goethe's Aesthetic Education

On his way to Italy, Goethe stopped in Munich and visited the art galleries. This was not an entirely pleasant experience, for, as Goethe recounts, "In the hall of classical sculpture I could soon tell that my eyes were not trained to appreciate such objects and so did not want to stay and waste time" (FA 15/1, 14). Through this encounter with sculptures, Goethe gained insight into himself. He realized that his perceptual capacities were not adequate to the task of appreciating the artworks. By attending to the artworks, then, he grasped something about himself, which he would have otherwise missed. As he elaborates, "I was making this remarkable journey not to deceive myself but to become acquainted with myself through objects" (FA 15/1, 49). Like Herder, Goethe was convinced that perception is "formed" by experience—a view borne out in the fact that artists from different regions see and depict the world differently. Or, as he puts it in a note from Venice, "the eye is formed by the objects it beholds from childhood on, and so the Venetian painter must see everything more clearly and brightly than other people" (FA 15/1, 93). By turning outward, Goethe had every intention also to turn inward—to critically reflect on his cognitive capacities, and their potential.

Although Goethe had begun his aesthetic education in Verona and Venice, it was in Rome that he "learned to see for the first time." Quoting Winckelmann's letter to Francke, Goethe describes Rome as the "world's university" (FA 15/1, 159). It was, importantly, Rome *as a whole* and not any particular work of art or gallery that provided Goethe with his aesthetic education and proved to be decisive for the transformation of his perception. For, he notes, although he had seen replicas of many of the sculptures, it was an altogether different experience to see the originals, and to see them "now standing together before me" (FA 15/1, 135). Through his seeing the artworks together, Goethe's senses were awakened.

In the same way that seeing natural objects in different contexts led Goethe to ask different questions—and arrive at deeper insights—so seeing artistic objects in a different context enabled him to arrive at deeper insights into visual art. For seeing previously "known" objects *together* (rather than apart) means seeing how the one anticipates or precedes the other, how it departs from but also maintains aspects of the other, and how these aspects are transformed through a new medium, a new context, a new goal. It means, ultimately, seeing them in historical context and relation. What Goethe thus witnesses in Rome is the history of art—a perspective that allows him to see the works in a new and more profound light. By seeing them together, he was able to discern how the individual works (which are themselves harmonious unities) build on, respond to, or challenge one another, how they are both like and unlike, how each work anticipates or reflects on the other works. This way of seeing proved to be so tremendous for Goethe that he describes it as the beginning not only of a new era, but a "new life."[11] By seeing the works in relation to one another, Goethe senses himself as transformed, or, as he puts it, as "remolded from within" (FA 15/1, 150).

In Rome, then, Goethe finds himself seeing things *together, in relation*, and this way of seeing impacted his observations of nature. Thus, a few weeks later, he notes the significance of seeing statues for his understanding of anatomy:

> I am fairly well trained in anatomy and, not without effort, have acquired a certain degree of knowledge about the human body. Here, as a result of endlessly contemplating statues, my attention is constantly drawn to it, but in a loftier manner [*höhere Weise*]. In our medical-surgical anatomy it is just a question of recognizing a part, and even a wretched muscle will serve. In Rome, however, parts mean nothing unless they go together to make a noble, beautiful form. (FA 15/1, 174)

Rome set a new standard for Goethe—one which echoed and confirmed his earlier observations on the relations between plants and their contexts. For both reveal the importance of seeing things in context, as related members of a larger community. Just as the artworks became more meaningful when observed in relation to one another, so also a plant's significance, its distinctive (plant) form, became evident when considered in light of its context. Not only are the differences in the form of a date palm leaf fundamentally connected to the place of the leaf on the tree (i.e., its context), but also the form of any plant is deeply influenced by its geographic context. This means that context is just as important in science as it is in art. But it also means that to understand this context and its significance requires taking account of form. For in both art and science, it is the *form* of the object that reveals and is illuminated by its context—it is by taking note of a sculpture's distinctive form that we begin to grasp how it relates to other sculptures, just as it is by studying the form of the leaf, or the form of the tree as a whole, that we discern its relation to its context.

This gave Goethe an important clue. If both science and art were ultimately concerned with seeing *in the same way*—with seeing forms (transforming) in relation to their contexts—might not the study of art bear on scientific research? Might the practice of looking at works of art—and the practice of composing works of art—be advantageous for the study of nature? This is what Goethe came to conclude through the assiduous study of both while in Italy. For, he writes, "our eye is gradually attuned by artistic works to become increasingly receptive to the presence of nature," and in contemplating works of art—in becoming sensitive to their structure and composition—we become sensitive to the structure and composition of natural phenomena as well (FA 15/1, 432). This is because in both we find "a concealed symmetry [*verheimlichte Symmetrie*]," which is "the most essential factor in composition." "For," he explains, "just as in the organism of nature, so also in art, life manifests itself to perfection within the narrowest limits" (FA 15/1, 488–89).

What Goethe is alluding to here, and what becomes explicit in the science of morphology, is the fact that artworks and living beings are compositions, in two senses. First, they both exhibit a distinctive part-whole structure: their parts are informed by one another, such that every part is, in a certain sense, a reflection of the whole. The form of a leaf on a particular plant, just like the form of a torso of an ancient statue, bears the marks of the whole of which it is part. *How* it appears is informed by *the context* in which it appears—the tree or the statue. Thus artworks and living beings provide the context for their parts—such that the parts cannot exist outside of them. But the reverse is also true: artworks and living beings cannot exist outside of their parts. A piece of music does not exist outside or beyond the various elements that make it up (the key, the tempo, the different instruments, their sounds and their varying parts, and so on). A living being, similarly, cannot exist outside of its parts—a tree is *in* its bark, leaves, flowers, roots. These parts are, in turn, heterogeneous, in that each plays a distinctive role within the whole. And it is precisely their heterogeneity (particularity) that makes them necessary. Thus each part is *both* necessary *and* particular. Particularity does not imply contingency.

The second sense in which the artwork and the organism are compositions has to do with the fact that both are the outcome of a creativity that is also bound by limits. A piece of music is a particular work, which assumes a particular form, using specific media, and so on. The same is the case for the organism—every plant is a particular plant, and it is within certain limitations (e.g., of genus and species) that the creativity of life manifests itself and acts. Thus every work of art and every plant is at once particular and a presentation of the universal, i.e., of art as such or of plant as such.

Goethe had begun to sense the significance of contexts and relations after he crossed the Alps. While in Padua, he reflected on this issue more deeply and came to the conclusion that—despite differences in plant variation—it was necessary to posit "one plant" from which "all plant forms can be derived." For, he writes, "only in this way would it be possible truly to determine genera and species, which, it seems to me, has thus far been done arbitrarily" (FA 15/1, 65). In other words—and along the same lines that Goethe articulates in his 1795 essay on comparative anatomy and osteology—to determine the relations between plants, it is necessary to develop a concept that unifies the different plants.[12] This concept must capture something essential about plants without, however, making plants into static and fixed objects. It must encompass all plants and thus illuminate their common character *and* reveal the particular relations and connections between and within plants. The concept must, in other words, find a way by which to present the particular (the particular plants, or the particular parts of a plant and their particular relations) *as* essential rather than as contingent.

However, while in Padua, Goethe writes that "in my botanical philosophy I remain stuck on this point," adding, "I do not see yet how to proceed [*entwirren*]" (FA 15/1, 65–66). It was not until he went to Rome that Goethe began to understand how to proceed. The clue came to him through the study and practice of visual art. Years later, Goethe reflects on the significance of his training in composition and its effects on his natural science. Speaking to Eckermann, he notes that it was "my early landscape drawings and my later research into nature that led me to a constant and precise perception of nature." Through immersing himself in the practice of drawing, Goethe continues, he was able to "learn nature by heart up to her smallest details" (FA 39, 211). Drawing, of course, does not only aim to capture detail, but also to convey an overall impression. As Goethe puts it in Italy, "the few lines which I draw on paper, often hurried, rarely correct, facilitate for me the presentation of sensible things. For it is by soaring to the general that one observes the objects more precisely and acutely" (FA 15/1, 185). The goal, then, is to enrich our understanding of the details *through* the overall impression *and* to deepen our sense of the overall impression *through* the details.

This movement between the particular and the general, between focusing on the specific elements and then seeing them in relation to and as parts of a larger composition, became a crucial tool for Goethe as he grappled with plants. For, as he put it in Padua, he did not know *how* to discern the connections between the plants and thereby arrive at the concept that unified all of them. Should he proceed from the top down, by formulating a hypothesis and then trying to demonstrate it in the various forms of the plants? Or should he proceed from the bottom up, by focusing on the manifold forms of plants and attempting to derive a concept or a schema therefrom? These were the two obvious options. However, through his training in the visual arts, Goethe developed a third option: moving back and forth from detailed observation to general schema, a schema that is continuously adjusted in light of newly gained details, and details which are more fully grasped and appreciated in light of the general schema.

Goethe articulates this methodology in the notes for an essay he and Schiller worked on in 1799. The essay (which they did not complete) was titled "On Dilettantism [*Über den Dilletantismus*]," and reflects on the meaning of an artistic dilettante in the visual arts. Though Goethe and Schiller negatively contrast the dilettante to the artist—writing for instance that while "art gives itself its own rules and commands its times, dilettantism follows the tendencies of the time"—they also recognize the significance of dilettantism, noting its "uses for the subject" (FA 18, 778). Among these uses is "learning to see [*sehen lernen*]" (FA 18, 744).

The process of learning to see, they claim, occurs in three steps. First, everyone begins with a "general impression [*Totaleindruck*]" which lacks differentiation or detail. The second step is differentiation, the move to detail. The final step is "the return from differentiation to the feeling of the whole, which," they emphasize, "is the aesthetic" (FA 18, 746). In this procedure we witness movement from general to particular followed by a return to the general. However, the second general is not the same as the first: it is a thoroughly differentiated general, and for this reason they call it "the aesthetic." It is aesthetic because—like a work of art—this third step is able to behold the general and particular *at once*, to see that the overall impression and the specific details do not stand in contrast to one another but enrich and enable one another. While the details deepen our understanding of the overall impression, the overall impression grants meaning to the details. It is this beholding of the two *at once* and seeing them as inseparable that distinguishes the dilettante and the artist, on the one hand, from the casual observer, on the other.

But this is not all. For in undertaking these steps, the artist or dilettante becomes aware of what is involved in seeing. Or, as Schiller and Goethe put it, one "learns the rules of seeing [*die Gesetze kennen lernen, wornach wir sehen*]" (FA 18, 744). Accordingly, learning to see also involves reflecting on one's cognitive capacities and laws of cognition more generally.

This third stage of seeing, which arrives at a thoroughly differentiated whole, was what Goethe sought to achieve, and for two reasons. First, he realized that educating his cognitive capacities requires his active participation in this education. While encountering new objects certainly has an impact on the perceptual organs, it is also necessary that the knower engage with these new objects, and actively seek to be transformed in light of them. Thus when he sought to understand the relations between plants and arrive at a unifying concept, Goethe was aware of the fact that what is needed, as he put it in the *Italian Journey*, is a "thorough training of the eye [*vieljährige entschiedene Übung des Auges*]" (FA 15/1, 179). The visual arts and creative practice provide precisely such a training.

The second reason has to do with the *kind of concept* that Goethe was after. As noted above, the concept must capture the overall impression *in* the details and the details *in light of* the overall impression. There is no separation between general and particular; rather each shines—becomes more evident—through the other. Or, one can say, they mutually deepen and enhance one another, such that the one can only be properly grasped *through* the other. Thus, the concept that Goethe sought was not a formal abstraction, where the concept functions as a general rule under which particular objects are subsumed, nor was it a category for ordering and classifying the natural world. As we have seen, Goethe was acutely aware of the tendency in both philosophy and science to move away from the dynamic phenomenon to fixed, simple, and abstract rules, and thereby reduce the phenomenon to something that hardly resembles it. The reason that philosophy and science tend in this direction has to do with their interest in necessity. For the particular does not appear to be necessary. Accordingly, necessity can only be found in the universal: in the abstract or formal concepts or categories that subsume the particular, and thereby grant it necessity. Goethe, by contrast, sought to develop a concept that did not need to move beyond the particular phenomenon in order to discern necessity. Thus, the concept he was looking for must—in some way—enable us to "see" the dynamic character of the phenomenon, and reveal necessity *in* this dynamism, i.e., present the unity of plants *in* the particular plant.

4.3. *Naturegemäße Darstellung*

Goethe's turn to drawing following his encounter with the proliferous carnation in Kauffmann's garden indicates a general concern with the limits of language. Words and concepts have a tendency to abstraction, to become mere signs divorced from the things they seek to present. They can end up "killing" that which they attempt to portray. As Goethe puts it in the *Theory of Colors*, "it is very difficult not to replace the sign [*Zeichen*] with the object, to behold the living being and not to kill it with the word [*durch das Wort zu töten*]" (FA 23/1, 444). The trouble, Goethe elaborates in his autobiography, *Poetry and Truth* [*Dichtung und Wahrheit*] (1811), has to do with the fact that in nature things appear to have a "contradictory" character that cannot be captured by the simplification that a concept implies. Speaking of himself in the third person, he writes,

> He believed that he perceived in both living and lifeless nature, in both the animate and the inanimate, something that manifested itself only in contradiction and therefore could not be expressed in any concept, much less any word. (FA 14, 839)

What these statements indicate is that however we understand and attempt to invoke concepts—including the concepts of metamorphosis, *Typus*, and *Urpflanze*—we must be aware of their limits. Accordingly, the question is: how can these concepts be used to *overcome* their limitations as concepts, and what kinds of demands does this use place on Goethe's readers?

According to Goethe, it was in *The Metamorphosis of Plants* essay that he achieved a "method conforming to nature [*eine naturgemäse Methode*]." The method "conforms to nature [*naturgemäß*]," he writes in "Influence of the New Philosophy [*Einwirkung der neueren Philosophie*]" (1817), because it follows the plant step by step, thereby mirroring its step-by-step development. Importantly, Goethe notes, this "naturgemäße" method *emerged* through the *presentation*, i.e., in and through the writing of *The Metamorphosis of Plants*. This is how he puts it:

> Furthermore, in the presentation [*Darstellung*] of the essay on plant metamorphosis a method conforming to nature had to emerge [*mußte sich eine natrugemäße Methode entwickeln*]; for as vegetation performed its processes before me step by step, I could not err. Rather, insofar as I let them be, I recognized the ways and means by which they proceed from the most concealed circumstance to completion. (MA 12, 94)

Goethe reiterates the expression "naturgemäß" in the essay "Intuitive Judgment [*Anschauende Urteilskraft*]" (1817). In this context, "naturgemäß" is employed to describe Goethe's methodology in contrast to Kant's. As Goethe notes, Kant had argued that the human intellect cannot proceed "intuitively," i.e., from the synthetic universal to the particular. But, Goethe continues, this makes no sense given that he (Goethe) had proceeded in precisely the way that Kant claims is impossible. For, he elaborates, "I had striven, at first unconsciously, and out of an inner drive toward the primal image [auf jenes Urbildliche] and prototype [Typische] and even succeeded in building up a presentation that conforms to nature [eine naturgemäße Darstellung aufzubauen]" (MA 12, 99). Though here he does not specifically mention *The Metamorphosis of Plants*, it is implied. The claim then is that Goethe developed a "naturgemäße Methode" or "natugemäße Darstellung" in this work, that this conformity with nature emerged in the presentation itself, and that Goethe was able to achieve what Kant had deemed impossible.

Structurally, *The Metamorphosis of Plants* proceeds in the manner that Goethe and Schiller describe as the procedure of the visual artist. It begins with a general schema—"ein Totaleindruck"—proceeds with ample examples, detailed descriptions, comparisons, and exceptions, and concludes with a reiteration of the general schema, coupled with reflections on the text's goal, and what the reader has "learned" through the text. Furthermore, the essay performatively traces the sequential development of the plant: it proceeds step by step, focusing on a different part of the plant in each step. This aspect of the essay's structure clearly conforms to plant development: plant parts emerge in a largely sequential order, from seed to embryonic leaf, to stem, to leaf, to flower, to fruit, etc.

Although the essay proceeds sequentially and thereby imitates the plant's development, it does not only do this. More profoundly, the essay also moves cyclically, forward *and* backward, between general and particular, and thereby invites the reader to proceed in this way as well. Accordingly, the essay engages the reader's imagination and judgment, prompting the reader to try to see *for herself* the different parts in relation to one another, and through this seeing to grasp how the different parts are related, are "modifications" of the one organ. Thus, Goethe writes in the final remarks of the essay, "for the present . . . we must be satisfied with learning to relate these manifestations [of the leaf form] both forward and backward," and in so doing, discern the unity in the multiplicity—i.e., see the plant form in and through its various parts and their relations (MA 12, 67, no. 120).

In light of this, a question arises as to whether a similar kind of presentation would be appropriate for animals, i.e., would it be "naturgemäß"? The first thing to consider is the fact that although sequential development is most vivid in plants, it is present throughout nature. The development of insects, for instance, clearly proceeds sequentially: from egg, to larva, to adult. In certain kinds of insects, we witness a fundamental transformation or metamorphosis, which signifies a sequential development. Mammals also develop sequentially, but only in their embryonic state. Upon birth, mammalian development is largely nonsequential: the hand does not emerge out of the arm; rather, both hand and arm grow simultaneously in size. Accordingly, a first answer is that sequential development is present throughout nature, but in different degrees, such that variations of it would be appropriate in presentations of nonvegetal development.

However, something else should be taken account of here, something that, I believe, helps us to better understand and appreciate Goethe's focus on plants. A crucial difference between the stages of plant development and those of insect metamorphosis has to do with the fact that in the plant, all the stages of development *remain* such that, as viewers, we can actually *see* the various stages *together* at the end. We witness the appearance of the plant through stages, and thus see that the plant whole is not separable from its stages of development. In an insect, by contrast, each of the stages is shed (left behind), and every new stage assumes a new form. My suggestion is that by focusing on plants, Goethe was interested in precisely this aspect of visibility, i.e., the fact that in the plant the stages *are present before us* and *appear* as both successively developed and simultaneously coexisting. This helps us (as observers of nature, as readers of Goethe's works) to *see* transformation in the whole, to grasp how the whole is a transforming form, and to discern the whole in and through these transformations. Plants, in other words, make more visibly evident processes and relations that are often hidden in other beings. The interest in plants is thus also an interest in visibility. With this in mind, let us turn to a more detailed explication of the structure of the essay.

4.4. The Structure and Aims of *The Metamorphosis of Plants*

As noted, Goethe begins the essay by outlining the general schema of plant metamorphosis. Thus, he writes in the third paragraph, the goal is to discern "the laws of transformation [*die Gesetze der Umwandlung*], by which nature produces one part through another, creating a great variety of forms through the modification of a single organ" (MA 12, 29, no. 3). In this way, the reader is provided with an overall impression of the work and what it seeks to achieve: insight into the "laws of transformation." *How* this is to be done is made explicit in the opening paragraph, where Goethe writes that "anyone who has to some extent observed plant growth will easily note that certain external parts of the plant undergo frequent change and take on the shape of the adjacent parts—sometimes fully, sometimes more, and sometimes less" (MA 12, 29, no. 1). In these opening statements, then, we have a sense of what the work aims to achieve and how it expects to achieve it.

However, despite their significance, these claims are schematic and broad, and do not give the reader much to go on. In the proceeding sections, which are detailed and based on concrete examples, the reader begins to gain a better sense of what Goethe is after, and what is intended in these first paragraphs.

The text's mimetic procedure means that each main section follows and depicts one stage of plant development. After the introduction Goethe turns to seeds. As he puts it in the first paragraph of this section: "Since we intend to observe the successive steps [*Stufenfolge*] in plant growth, we will begin by directing our attention to the plant as it develops from the seed" (MA 12, 31, no. 10). This is then followed by eleven more sections, each of which focuses on a different part of the plant or on a moment of transition.

In every case, the focus is not on the part in isolation from what precedes or what comes after it. Rather, by following the plant's development successively, Goethe's goal is to demonstrate how each of the parts is related to the others—how it responds to and transforms in relation to what comes before it, and anticipates what is to come after it. As such, each of the detailed examples is also a concrete reiteration of the text's opening remarks.

To achieve this, Goethe points both to the *similarity* of form between the different parts and to the ways in which the parts *differ* from one another. Showing similarity involves seeing how different stages of development resemble one another—for instance, how the form of the stem leaf resembles that of the sepal, or how the calyx resembles the corolla. Taking note of difference, in turn, involves discerning how exactly one stage takes up and transforms preceding stages. Close observation reveals, for example, that the stages of plant development appear to follow a pattern of expansion and contraction: the corolla is an "expansion" of the aggregating form that we find in the calyx, which is, by contrast, "contracted." It also reveals that the plant's parts become increasingly complex and specialized as the plant grows, a process Goethe calls intensification, or *Steigerung*.[13] This increasing complexity goes hand in hand with the goal of reproduction.

Thus, as we proceed to examine each of the plant's parts, we consider the parts both individually and in light of this larger context, seeking to discern how they reflect what precedes them, and what is to come after them, and how they are shaped by their particular place within the plant. This allows Goethe to show *how* each of the parts is a variation on the "one organ."

The focus, throughout, is on *form*—the form that each part assumes, and how this particular form is an expression of the whole plant form. By placing the parts in a continuum, relating them to one another, and seeing them as expressions of one organ, Goethe's goal is to present to the reader the *transforming form* of the plant, i.e., to demonstrate how the plant *itself* is a transforming form: the "one organ" (like a musical theme in variation) manifesting itself differently at different stages of development and in different contexts.

In his description of flower petals, for instance, Goethe notes that we often find that some petals are, in the transitional stage, partially green. This reveals their connection to the preceding stages of development—the stem leaves. But it also reveals the way in which they are moving beyond this earlier (less developed) stage. For, ultimately, the petals assume a different hue, which indicates greater differentiation, or as Goethe puts it, a "refinement [*Verfeinung*]" (MA 12, 42, no. 45).

This same tendency can be seen in the differences among stem leaves, which Goethe had vividly witnessed in the date palm tree, and which he considers more closely in the essay. At first, he writes, the leaf of the date palm is simple and fanlike and resembles the leaves of many other plants. This simplicity gives way, however, to a very different leaf—a leaf that is "torn apart, divided, and . . . highly complex," one which "rivals a branch" in its form (MA 12, 34, no. 20). The very same organ, the leaf, appears differently depending on its place on the tree—in the first instance, it has the form that we commonly associate with a leaf, while later on it comes to resemble a branch. The similarity in form between the young leaf and leaves of other trees reveals a connection between plants in general—despite vast variations, plants share a basic leaf form. In turn, the fact that the more mature leaf comes to resemble a branch points to a connection between leaf and branch and confirms Goethe's view that plant parts anticipate what is to come after them.[14]

What this shows is that the leaf form transforms in relation to its place on the tree. The tree is the context of the leaf, and, as such plays a significant role in the leaf's manifestations. The different forms that a leaf assumes—increasing or decreasing complexity—are in relation to its context, to its place on the tree, and to its age. The tree (as the leaf's context) is thus in some sense determining the form of the leaf. This means that the one (the leaf) cannot be understood without the other (the tree). Or, put differently, the transforming form (the leaf form) is transforming *in relation* to the whole plant.

Now if the context is playing a role in transforming the leaf form, then the context cannot be understood as *outside* the leaf. It is therefore more accurate to say that the context (i.e., the tree) is in some significant sense "*in* the leaf." If the tree is in the leaf, it follows that the leaf is a particular expression of the tree. By tracing the transformation of the leaf along the tree, then, we are invited to visualize how the tree (the whole, the context) manifests itself in each of the parts, and thereby develop an image of the tree as a dynamic whole—i.e., as a whole that transforms in and through its transforming leaves.

By focusing on two things at once—the individual part and its relation to the whole—Goethe is able to grasp both more deeply. Consider his examination of the calyx and the cotyledon. Both, Goethe notes, exhibit a congregation of leaves around an axis (MA 12, 38, no. 32). While the cotyledon emerges prior to the stem leaves (and is the first or embryonic leaf), the calyx emerges after. This means that both the stage that precedes and the one that follows the stem leaf involve leaf congregation. As moments of congregation, the two stages (calyx and cotyledon) are expressions of "contraction" in the plant's development, which contrast to the "expansion" that we find in the stem leaf.

A similar proximity of form can be found between the calyx leaves and the stem leaves. Thus Goethe writes,

> In several flowers we find unaltered stem leaves collected in a kind of calyx right under the flower. Since they retain their form clearly, we can rely on the mere appearance in this case, and on botanical terminology which calls them *folia floralia* (flower leaves). (MA 12, 39, no. 34)

In other words, in some cases, the calyx looks like a collection of stem leaves. This proximity is evident even in plants in which the calyx appears as one leaf (Goethe offers the example of a bell-shaped calyx, which can be found in carnivorous plants). But, Goethe adds, close observation reveals that these apparent one-leaf calyxes are in fact composed of many leaves, which—due to their extreme physical proximity—represent an extreme form of contraction.

In some plants, the calyx is often mistaken for the corolla, i.e., the collection of petals that make up the main part of the flower. Think of calyxes which take on the color of the petals, or of lilies, where calyx and corolla are almost indistinguishable. There is, however, a way by which to distinguish the two—the calyx is a stage of contraction, while the corolla is one of expansion. The sepals of the calyx are often smaller than the petals of the corolla. Or, to put it differently, the sepals resemble contracted petals, while the petals resemble expanded sepals.

In this way, Goethe seeks to show his readers how the various parts of a plant express one theme ("the leaf") in variation, and are manifestations of the "one organ." This is the case even in the reproductive parts of the plant, which are a moment of contraction. The iris offers a particularly striking example, in that its reproductive organs look either entirely or in part like a petal. But, Goethe continues, with the aid of a microscope we realize that the stigma of numerous flowers is nothing other than "full single-leaved or multi-leaved calyxes (e.g., the crocus; or *Zannichellia*)" (MA 12, 50, no. 71). Similarly, when considering the seed, Goethe directs the reader to its coverings, which in a number of cases betray its resemblance to the leaf: "we can see the traces of such incompletely adapted leaf forms in many winged seeds, for example, the maple, the elm, the ash and the birch" (MA 12, 54, no. 83).

Through these various examples, Goethe demonstrates *both* the continuity *and* the transformation of form in the clearest possible way. However, his goal is not simply to rest with cases of exceptional clarity but to recognize that what they depict is something that underpins all plant generation and development. These cases, in other words, furnish the reader with guidance so that she should be able to investigate less obvious instances. Goethe writes that "this similarity will not escape our attention if we know how to follow it carefully through all its transitions [*wenn wir ihr in allen Übergängen sorgfältig zu folgen wissen*]" (MA 12, 53, no. 79). Through careful description and related concrete examples, the text offers a standpoint, a perspective, from which to regard the rest of the plant kingdom. One can therefore say that the goal of *The Metamorphosis of Plants* is to offer the reader with tools by which to *transform* her way of seeing the world, and, in turn, to begin to undertake investigations herself. Through the text's guidance, the reader not only sees connections where she had previously only seen differences, but also and most importantly, she begins to know *how* to look for these connections on her own.

Of course, an important question is whether the text was successful in achieving this aim. This question can be answered in two ways, first by considering whether it was successful in its time, and second, by considering whether it has the potential to be successful in general. The answer to the first formulation is a clear no.

With a few significant exceptions, the majority of scientists whom Goethe wanted to influence did not comprehend what he was trying to do, and the text fell on deaf ears.[15] The fact that so few contemporaries understood his aims did, nonetheless, give Goethe an important clue.

After all, a significant aspect of Goethe's methodology relies on the reader's active engagement with the text. While Goethe can structure the text in as "naturgemäß" a manner as possible, employing various techniques from the visual arts, with the goal of following nature's own "steps," unless his readers are engaging with both the larger schematic statements and the concrete examples, and seeing how they bear on and illuminate one another—unless, that is, his readers imaginatively trace the way in which the "one organ" manifests itself in the various plant parts—they are unlikely to see how the schematic statements at the beginning of the work are realized in its detail and structure. Instead, the text will simply appear like a number of largely unrelated observations, attempting to justify a speculative premise.

The fact that Goethe does not make these points explicit in *The Metamorphosis of Plants*, that he does not, for instance, write a preface in which he distinguishes his methodology and explains what is involved in the process of knowing, might imply that he was not aware (or at least not entirely aware) of what he was demanding of his readers. Or, put differently, it might imply that Goethe was—in 1790—a largely naive thinker who began to reflect on his methodology, and grasp the creative character of knowledge, only after his encounter with Kant and eventually Schiller.[16] Such an interpretation is, in fact, sometimes suggested by Goethe himself, who writes in the first line of "Influence of the New Philosophy" that "for philosophy in its proper sense, I had no organ" (MA 12, 94).[17] This interpretation is, however, not entirely accurate—at least not when it comes to Goethe's understanding of the difficulty of properly grasping natural phenomena, and the necessity of transforming our usual ways of knowing in order to do so.

In 1789, at the same time that he was working on *The Metamorphosis of Plants*, Goethe published an essay titled "On Simple Imitation of Nature, Mannerism, and Style [*Über Einfache Nachahmung der Natur, Manier, Styl*]." In it, he draws an important distinction between three ways in which the arts (and artists) relate to and represent the natural world: "simple imitation," "mannerism" (or manner), and "style." Mannerism describes works of art that were created by the artist in order to express the artist's particular tastes and idiosyncrasies, and thus is of the least interest to Goethe (and to us). The other two, imitation and style, engage with the world and do not simply seek to present the artist's "spirit."

While simple imitation seeks to offer an exact representation of what is perceived, style attempts to do more, and is for this reason the highest achievement of art. This "more," Goethe writes, involves several components: "the creation of a general language," "painstaking and thorough studies of diverse subject matters," and "familiarity with the characteristics [*Eigenschaften*] of things and with the *how* of their existence [*die Art* wie *sie bestehen*]" (FA 18, 227). In other words, the artist must be both creative (through language) and thorough (through study), with the goal of arriving at "the essence of things [*das Wesen der Dinge*]." Importantly, to arrive at the essence of things does not only mean grasping their character, but also grasping the "how" of their existence, i.e., how they appear, how they relate, how they emerge.

This goal, Goethe emphasizes, differs from simple imitation, which does not involve finding "order in the multiplicity of appearances" or being able "to juxtapose and recreate distinct and characteristic forms." Only insight into the essence of things would allow for that. This is because grasping the essence of things is not a simple re-presenting of everything that one observes (as in a travel narrative, for instance). Rather, it involves homing in on what is essential, and eliminating what is not, i.e., the accidental, by discerning order (necessity, continuity) and understanding its significance (and thus also understanding how it can be reordered meaningfully). Simple imitation fails to do this.

In his explication of style, Goethe notes that an artist would have much to gain through the study of botany, because it would allow the artist "to recognize, from the root onward, the influence of the different parts of the plant on its flourishing and growth, its determination and reciprocal effectivity." In other words, the study of botany would enable the artist to observe relations among the parts, and discern *how* the developing parts are related to one another, i.e., the way in which one member anticipates what comes after it or reiterates (in a modified form) what preceded it. As Goethe puts it, through botany, the artist would learn to "see and grasp the successive development of leaves, flowers, pollination and fruit and the new seed." Through this training, he continues, the artist will be able "at once to posit [*setzen*] and teach a correct presentation [*richtige Darstellung*] of the characteristics in transformation." In other words, through botany the artist will achieve something that she might otherwise fail to achieve: an ability to see and present the dynamic relational character of the object. Thus, Goethe concludes, "style . . . rests on the most fundamental principle of cognition, on the essence of things—to the extent that it is granted us to perceive this essence in visible and tangible form" (FA 18, 227–28).

But this is not all that is involved in style. For the artist is also *presenting* what she has learned from botany. This presentation cannot be mere imitation, precisely because it aims to grasp the essence of the plant—the way in which its various parts are manifestations of the one organ—and thus convey necessity in and through the multiplicity. How the artist does this, and whether she succeeds, depend on her skills and schooling. Nonetheless, her goal is clear: to bring to manifestation, to make visible, the "laws of transformation." Her goal, in other words, is to *show* how a plant is a thoroughly differentiated unity. A successful artwork, accordingly, is the making visible of the lawfulness of nature.[18]

There is no doubt that in composing *The Metamorphosis of Plants* Goethe was invoking the notion of style as opposed to simple imitation. The text certainly follows an order and is thus imitative. But it is not imitative in the sense that it takes in all that can be seen. Rather, it homes in on the essential, and discards the accidental. In turn, in deploying a step-by-step structure, the text demonstrates an awareness of its linguistic medium and of the form of the essay in particular: proceeding from one paragraph to the next in a linear manner, where one idea builds on the other. And it attempts to make up for its disadvantages. For instance, although the essay proceeds sequentially, it seeks to draw its reader back to preceding stages of development, inviting the reader to compare and consider the various parts in nonsequential relations.

These points indicate that *The Metamorphosis of Plants* is no straightforward scientific treatise. Rather, as a text that aims to embody or perform the very laws it seeks to present, Goethe's essay sits somewhere between science and art. The text's conscious deployment of its medium, its acknowledgment of the reader, its statements concerning "education," and its emphasis on visibility and seeing point to one of its most important goals—a goal that might be missed in a cursory examination. For, by joining science and art, by applying artistic skills and aims onto the observation of nature, *The Metamorphosis of Plants* aims to transform its readers' organs of perception, and thereby to transform the way they regard nature—just as great paintings can transform the way we regard the ocean or the mountains.

By reading the essay, following it step by step, drawing connections between the different parts of the plant, readers are *called upon* to "see" plant metamorphosis for themselves—to see how the various parts are modifications of the "one organ." If this educational aspect of the essay was not clear when it was published in 1790, Goethe made a point of clarifying it when he republished the essay in *On Morphology*.[19] For, as he emphasizes in the opening lines of *On Morphology*, it is only through educating our cognitive capacities that we can know nature well.

4.5. The Question of "Seeing"

One of the reasons why *The Metamorphosis of Plants* did not fare well among Goethe's contemporaries must surely have to do with the implicit expectations that he places on his readers.[20] The reader must not only actively seek to transform her cognitive capacities, but also attempt to "see" metamorphosis—i.e., see something that cannot be directly perceived by the physical eye. For it is only through this seeing that the reader does not commit the mistake of reducing, simplifying, and rigidifying. And yet it is not self-evident what this seeing involves, or how it is possible to "see" if we require more than our physical eyes.

This is the question that Schiller posed to Goethe during their first conversation. As Goethe famously recounts, the two of them were attending a scientific lecture in Weimar in July 1794. They exited the lecture at the same time, leading them to start a conversation. Soon they realized that they were both dissatisfied by the lecture. Schiller criticizes the speaker's fragmentary approach to nature, while Goethe responds that a different approach is clearly needed, one that does not regard nature as composed of isolated parts, but which seeks to portray nature as active and alive, as a whole that manifests itself in the various, fundamentally related parts. Goethe offers Schiller examples from his own research. The two are suddenly standing outside of Schiller's house, but this does not hinder Goethe from elaborating his theory of the metamorphosis of plants, his view that there is a fundamental unity that underpins the plant form, that makes a plant *plant*. To make his point more evident, Goethe takes out a piece of paper, and draws for Schiller a "symbolic plant."[21] Schiller, however, is not convinced. For, he maintains, what Goethe has drawn is not an observation from experience, but an idea, which cannot be acquired through experience. At first Goethe is taken aback by Schiller's response. But he quickly regains his composure and tells Schiller that he can in fact *see* ideas with his own eyes: "it can be so dear to me that I have ideas without knowing it, and even see them with my eyes [*und sogar mit Augen sehe*]" (MA 12, 89; emphasis added).

These words would have been perplexing to Schiller, a Kantian, who regarded ideas as products of reason, and therefore not intuitable by the senses. Goethe himself may have not been entirely clear on the meaning of his response. But it is safe to say that his response was not disingenuous. He had, after all, discovered the fundamental form of the animal and the plant—the "idea" of the animal (or, more accurately, the mammal)[22] and the "idea" of the plant. It was on the basis of this idea that he was able to locate the intermaxillary bone in the human and to follow plant growth and development. Thus one can say that, in a certain sense, Goethe did *see* the idea. Accordingly, it is only a matter of articulating more clearly what he means by "seeing." Did he see it with his physical eyes, or did he mean an intellectual form of seeing—seeing with the mind's eye?

Though the essay reports of events that took place in 1794, it was published in the first volume of *On Morphology* in 1817 just after another essay in which Goethe probes the question of seeing. In that essay, titled "Discovery of a Worthy Forerunner [*Entdeckung eines trefflichen Vorarbeiters*]," Goethe discusses the work and methodology of Caspar Wolff, with whom he allies himself.

As we have seen, Wolff had been an early and important critic of the preformationist theory of biological development—a theory which Goethe had also, albeit more implicitly, criticized in *The Metamorphosis of Plants*.[23] The preformationists argued that biological development occurs through the mechanical expansion of preformed germs or seeds—minute entities that contain the complete form of the adult. As such, the basic structure of a living being is present from the moment of conception (placed there by God), and development is simply growth in size. Nothing new emerges, everything is already "implanted" from the get-go. Wolff's most important argument against preformationism revolves around the question of seeing: can we actually "see" these germs or seeds? Examining the embryos of chicks under the microscope, Wolff repeatedly noted that no such germs can be found. Accordingly, Wolff argued, development cannot be based on these germs and must therefore involve more than increase in size. For if not everything is "already there," then development involves the emergence of *new* forms.[24]

Wolff's contention was based on empirical evidence, a fact for which Goethe commends him. Thus, Goethe begins his essay with laudatory remarks: "the fundamental assumption of his method [is] that one must not accept, admit, or assert anything except what one has seen with one's own eyes, and what one is always in a position to show others" (MA 12, 84).

However, while seeing with one's physical eye is certainly the starting point of all empirical inquiry—and thus discredits the preformationists— it must not, Goethe contends, also be the conclusion. For, Goethe adds, "it never occurred to the splendid man that there is a difference between seeing and seeing [*Sehen und Sehen*], and that the eyes of the mind [*Augen des Geistes*] always have to work in a living union with the eyes of the body. Otherwise, one runs the risk of seeing yet at the same time not seeing" (MA 12, 85).

Like Goethe, Wolff had been interested in plant metamorphosis. And, as the title of Goethe's essay reveals, Wolff was a "worthy forerunner" of Goethe's own theory of plant metamorphosis. Wolff, Goethe writes, had (before him) recognized "the identity of plant parts in spite of their variability" (MA 12, 84). However, Goethe argues that Wolff failed to arrive at the law of plant metamorphosis, namely that "contraction alternates with expansion" (MA 12, 85). Wolff did not recognize that plant development occurs along an axis of expansion and contraction, and proceeds in a directed way: toward increasing complexity and reproduction. This is because, Goethe contends, Wolff failed to see *how* the different parts of the plant relate to one another, *how* they are both like and unlike one another, and thus *how* they are various manifestations of the same organ. By focusing only on what can be seen with the physical eyes, Wolff was unable to see how the parts are moments in a continuum of transformation or metamorphosis.

This means that it is impossible to *see* plant metamorphosis, to see the *transitions* between the parts, the *ways* in which each of the parts exhibits the whole and relates to what precedes and comes after it, with the physical eyes alone. The eye of the mind is required to see the transitions between the different parts of the plant and therefore grasp how the different parts are variations on one theme—with each part anticipating what comes after it and reflecting what precedes it. Goethe says precisely this when he writes in late notes that to "see in *One* all of [the plant's] different effects," i.e., to see the whole plant in and through the leaf (for instance), is to "know it [i.e., the plant] more intuitively [*anschaulicher kennen*]" (FA 24, 101). Or, as he puts it in the essay on osteology, it is only once "we learn to see with the eye of the mind [*Auge des Geistes*]" that scientific research properly begins. Without it, he emphasizes, "we would be groping in the dark" (LA 1/9, 138).

Although composed well after Schiller's death, Goethe's essay on Wolff may be read as an indirect response to Schiller's challenge. Still, it was well before he encountered Schiller that Goethe had begun to think through the premises of Kantian philosophy and its implications for his methodology. He read the *Critique of Pure Reason* soon after his return from Italy, and prior to the publication of *The Metamorphosis of Plants*. Goethe recounts that the book led him to reflect more carefully on the relation between seeing and knowing, and on how seeing can be translated *into* knowing—how experience or apprehension can become an idea. As he puts it, before encountering the *Critique of Pure Reason*, "I truly believed that I saw my thoughts before my eyes [*meine Meinungen vor Augen*]" (MA 12, 95). Nonetheless, Goethe was not convinced by Kant's epistemology. As he writes in an early note, "it appears to me to be above all *dangerous* that Kant at the same time calls *knowledge* that which our soul brings to knowledge."[25] In other words, Kant makes a category mistake by claiming that knowledge is founded on what our mind brings to the table—whether that be the pure forms of intuition, or the categories of the understanding. For knowledge, Goethe implies, is something far more collaborative than Kant allows, and is based on a dialogue between the knower and the known. This means, however, that the knower will have to realize that her basic tools (her pure forms of intuition, her categories of the understanding) are not up to the task of knowing, and she must be educated, transformed, if knowledge is to be achieved.

Nonetheless, Goethe's encounter with Kant furnished him with the opportunity to become a better philosopher. For Kant, and eventually Schiller, presented him with a philosophical challenge that he wanted to meet. As he puts it in "Fortunate Encounter," if it is indeed the case that experience and idea are two different things, then "surely some mediating element, some connecting element, must lie between the two!" (MA 12, 89). In other words, if we are not to be mere empiricists or mere idealists, then we must find a way by which to join the sensibly given with ideas—or, in the language of the essay on Wolff, join "seeing" with "seeing." Otherwise, Goethe argued, we cannot claim to "know" nature—or any phenomenon that is given to sensibility.

4.6. Mediating Elements

Goethe's essay "The Experiment as Mediator between Subject and Object [*Der Versuch als Vermittler zwischen Subjekt und Objekt*]" (1792; published 1793) offers a first insight into the "mediating element" that connects seeing and seeing. As the title implies, a crucial difficulty concerns the relation "between object and subject."[26] However, and also as the title implies, the experiment—or the essay (the term *Versuch* means both)—mediates between the two, such that whatever chasm exists between subject and object, it is not, as it is for Kant, unbridgeable. Furthermore, and as a number of scholars have remarked, the essay also reveals the influence of Spinoza.[27] In the same way that Spinoza begins the *Ethics* with anthropological considerations, so also Goethe begins by articulating the problem of knowledge in anthropological terms, noting that our first encounter with the natural world is determined by pleasure and displeasure, attraction and repulsion, by what appeals and does not appeal (presumably to our senses). This is, as Goethe puts it, a "natural way of seeing and judging things" (FA 25, 26).

What interests Goethe in this essay, however, is not the "natural way" of relating to the world, but the disposition of the knower, i.e., the person for whom the natural world is not only a habitat, but also a place of wonder and experiment.

Echoing the problems articulated by Buffon and Kant, Goethe notes that the challenges of experimental research have to do with its procedure: it proceeds from part to part or from one object to the next, and thus ends up regarding every part or every object in isolation. In reality, however, nothing is isolated. Rather—again recalling Buffon—Goethe contends that "nothing happens in living nature that does not stand in some relation to the whole" (FA 25, 33). Importantly, this claim is not simply hypothetical, but is the motivating insight of Goethe's research and the clue to his success. After all, his discovery of the intermaxillary bone depended on the insight that as a part of the human organism, the human bone cannot resemble the bone in any other animal. In turn, his observations in Italy allowed him to discern how plants are composed of interrelated parts that are in dialogue with one another and with their surroundings.

In this way, Goethe homes in on a fundamental dissonance between reality (ontology, nature) and our cognitive procedures, including the processes of empirical research (methodology, epistemology). The goal is to find a way to connect experience (epistemology) and reality (ontology), and thus to "see" how the various parts that are known through empirical observation are members of a whole. Thus, Goethe continues, the chief methodological question is this: "how can we find the connection between these phenomena, these events?" (FA 25, 33). Or, put in terms of "Fortunate Encounter," what are the "mediating elements" between experience and idea?

In these questions we find a new iteration of the difficulty that Goethe had broached in Rome in 1788. While in 1788 he articulated the problem in terms of our natural and scientific inclination to reduce, simplify, and regard as fixed what is inherently dynamic and complex, here he focuses on a dissonance between experience and idea, which is connected to our inclination to see the parts in isolation and thus to overlook their relational and dialogical character. In both instances Goethe is addressing the disparity between the knowing subject's *inclinations*, on the one hand, and the *phenomenon* that the subject is attempting to grasp, on the other. Moreover, in both instances, he regards this disparity as methodological *and* epistemological. Thus although in the latter part of "The Experiment as Mediator," Goethe focuses on scientific procedures and biases, the insight with which he commences the essay remains relevant, namely that the natural *dispositions* of cognition are problematic.

This highlights an important difference between Goethe and Kant. For Goethe, the disparity is not—as it is for Kant—between our cognitive *ability* (the structure of cognition which we cannot change) and reality, but rather between our *dispositions* or *procedures* and reality. The implication is that we *can* and indeed *should* transform these procedures to better capture the phenomena before us.

In "The Experiment as Mediator," Goethe offers some insights into how the experiment (and possibly also the essay) can play the role of mediating element and thereby overcome this disparity. As he sees it, one must undertake as many experiments as possible, in order to discern the phenomenon in as many variations, relations, and contexts as possible. The goal, however, is not to rest content with this manifoldness, but to arrive at a "whole." This whole is identified with a "higher sort" of empirical evidence in contrast to the evidence achieved through only one or a couple of experiments (FA 25, 34).

Now given that the whole is not the result of any one experiment, but of all the experiments together, simply taking note of the results of these experiments is not enough. In addition, we must find a way to connect the experiments and their results. We must develop a narrative—to invoke the other meaning of *Versuch*—through which we can discern how the experiments are related to one another, how the one illuminates, builds on, or challenges the other. Or, as Goethe had done with the leaves of the date palm, we must place the results of the different experiments side by side, and thereby grasp how they are related, how they are manifestations of the "one phenomenon."

This requires reflection and imagination. For what we need to do is move from regarding the various parts (the various results of the experiment) in isolation to regarding them as expressions of one phenomenon. We cannot do this by simply dwelling on the individual parts (results). Yet this is precisely what our "natural disposition" moves us to do. We must, therefore, consciously seek to overcome our inclination—and find a way by which to "see" the various parts (results of experiments) in relation to one another. We must, in other words, develop a hermeneutic approach to understanding the meaning and significance of experimental results.

Though the essay is suggesting what Goethe will later describe as intuitive judgment or knowledge with the mind's eye, at this stage he does not offer much guidance in terms of what this form of knowledge involves or requires. However, he does offer a clue in his (uncharacteristically) positive assessment of the mathematical procedure:

> From the mathematician we must learn the meticulous care required to connect things in unbroken succession, or rather, to derive things step by step. Even where we do not venture to apply mathematics we must always work as though we had to satisfy the strictness of geometricians. (FA 25, 34)[28]

The natural researcher must seek to imitate the meticulousness of the mathematician, who does not miss a step in developing the sequence of a proof. The narrative that the natural research must develop, in other words, must not overlook one transition, relation, or point of connection.

Of course, there are significant differences between the object of mathematics and that of the empirical sciences. The object of mathematics is entirely intellectual—it is not given to the senses but must be constructed by the mind. By contrast, the object of empirical science must be given to the senses. Furthermore, in mathematics the formula is (usually) given and the aim is to construct *out of* the formula. In the empirical sciences, by contrast, the goal is to *discover* the formula (the archetypal phenomenon) through following the sequences.[29]

These differences imply that the two sciences cannot proceed in an entirely identical manner and point to a number of difficulties in the empirical sciences that are not encountered in mathematics. Above all, the fact that what is given to the senses is in space and time means that objects are apprehended as spatial and temporal—one object or part appears (to us) *after* (in both the spatial and temporal senses) another object or part. This sequential apprehension of objects, however, conflicts with our scientific and cognitive aims, where the goal is to grasp the totality of the phenomenon, and not simply regard its parts in sequence. Or, as Goethe puts it in "Doubt and Resignation," there is a fundamental conflict between our "experience" of an object and our "idea" of it, one that has to do with our spatiotemporal mode of apprehension. He writes:

> This difficulty of uniting idea and experience presents obstacles in all scientific research: the idea is independent of space and time, while scientific research is bound by space and time. In the idea, simultaneous elements are closely bound up with sequential ones, but in experience they are always separated; we are seemingly plunged into madness by a natural process which must be conceived of in idea as both simultaneous and sequential. The understanding [*Verstand*] cannot think of something as united when the senses present it as separate, and thus the conflict between what is grasped as experience and what is formed as idea [*zwischen Aufgefaßtem und Ideiertem*] remains forever unresolved. (FA 24, 450)

In this passage Goethe sheds new light on the challenges facing the student of nature. Through our senses objects appear purely sequentially; in the idea, however, the various parts are both sequentially and nonsequentially related. As we have seen in the preceding chapter, "idea" does not refer to a Kantian (regulative) idea, and is not simply the outcome of reason's interests. Rather, the idea (as *Typus* or *Urbild*) has an ontological significance, even if it does not refer to any physical object. We will return to this. For now, it is important to emphasize that Goethe is pointing to the dissonance between experience and idea that prevents us from properly grasping the phenomenon and must therefore be overcome.

But how is this overcoming to proceed and what does it involve? One answer would be: the idea should conform to experience. This answer can be described as loosely empiricist. Here the claim is that all our ideas come from experience, such that whatever ideas we construct, they should mirror the structure of the sensibly given. Thus, if nature appears to us sequentially, the *idea* of nature cannot contradict that. Our idea of nature, in other words, must be that nature is sequential. On this view, no conflict would arise between experience and idea. By contrast, a Kantian interpretation would argue that because experience gives us objects in a sequential manner, we do not have cognitive access to anything that is nonsequential, i.e., ideas. Ideas therefore cannot play a determining role in our experience or cognition.

For Goethe both responses are problematic. The empiricist response is problematic because it fails to distinguish between what is given to us in experience and reality. Simply because we apprehend in a certain way does not mean that our apprehension conforms to reality. The Kantian response is problematic not because it naively fails to distinguish between apprehension and reality, but because it fails to account for the fact that although we apprehend sequentially, we somehow *recognize* nonsequential relations in nature, e.g., in organized beings. In other words, although our apprehension is sequential, we have some way by which to access the nonsequential structure of living beings—an access which Kant leaves largely implicit.[30]

Despite the differences between the empiricist and Kantian responses, they are united in one respect: neither sees it as relevant that living beings *do not* emerge purely sequentially or that the *relations* between the parts (of living beings and of nature as a whole) are not solely sequential. Thus, by regarding the parts merely sequentially, both fail to offer an adequate account of the relations within and among living beings, i.e., an account of *how* their parts are in dialogue with one another, and how these relations are not purely sequential. For this reason, Goethe could not agree with either.

Accordingly, we must find a way to grasp *both* sequential and nonsequential development and relations, to see how the parts emerge "one after the other" and "one from the other" *and* how they do not simply emerge in this way, i.e., how their developmental relations are nonlinear. In other words, we must find a way by which to grasp sequential and nonsequential relations *together*, as aspects of one process. Only then can we see how the parts that are yet to come (e.g., fruit) are anticipated by the parts presently before us (e.g., the flower) and are thus "part of" the sequential development, even if their influence does not follow the linear sequence.[31] Only then can we properly grasp the plant as a developmental process, rather than as a static substance, composed of purely externally related units.

In light of this, we must pose the question again: how can we overcome the disparity between experience and idea? If the empiricist and Kantian solutions do not resolve the difficulty, then we must find another way. This way cannot, however, take us in the opposite direction, where experience is discounted entirely in favor of the idea—a direction which we might call the idealist or rationalist solution. For Goethe's goal was to find a way to bring experience and idea together—without reducing the one to the other. Thus the question is: how can we wed experience and idea such that the two inform and complement one another?

In "Doubt and Resignation" Goethe does not offer a straightforward answer. In fact, the essay could be read as an extremely pessimistic take on what can be achieved in knowledge. Not only is this negative attitude evident in the essay's title, but also in Goethe's cited statement, which seems to resign the knower to a state of madness and irresolution.

One reason for Goethe's despairing remarks might have to do with the fact that the sequential structure of *The Metamorphosis of Plants* cannot—on its own—capture the way in which sequential and nonsequential development occur simultaneously. The text *aims* to demonstrate this by, for instance, pointing to the similarities between the different stages of plant development (e.g., the aggregating leaves of the cotyledon and the calyx) and highlighting the way in which one part can be seen in and through another part (e.g., how the stamen resembles a contracted petal). However, as an essay that proceeds step by step, following each part of the plant as it emerges, *The Metamorphosis of Plants* cannot *embody* or *perform* before the reader the nonlinear character of plant development. Only the reader can enact this process through the "eye of the mind."

Goethe concludes "Doubt and Resignation" by, as he puts it, turning "to the sphere of poetry."[32] While from a philosophical perspective, this turn might appear as a refusal to deal with the problem, in light of the difficulty that Goethe outlines and the solution he attempted in *The Metamorphosis of Plants*, it makes perfect sense, and can be regarded as exemplary in addressing the problem.

4.7. The Poetic Metamorphosis of the Plant

"Doubt and Resignation" ends with a specific poem, one that Goethe had begun to compose in the early 1770s, but which first appears (with significant revisions) in this essay, and then again under the title "Antepirrhema," in his collection *God and World* [*Gott und Welt*]:[33]

> So schauet mit bescheidnem Blick
> Der ewigen Weberin Meisterstück,
> Wie ein Tritt tausend Fäden regt,
> Die Schifflein hinüber herüber schießen,
> Die Fäden sich begegnend fließen,
> Ein Schlag tausend Verbindungen schlägt. (MA 12, 100)[34]

Already in the first line of the poem, Goethe thematizes seeing. The focus is on the "Blick," the "gaze" (or eye), of the observer. Furthermore, and also in the first line, there is an implicit imperative concerning seeing. The observer looks with "unassuming gaze," which can also be translated as "modest" or "humble gaze." The implication is that only such a gaze is able to grasp the complex and multiple connections in nature, to recognize the way in which each thread in nature is interwoven with countless others.

This dual character of the poem—as both a description of nature and a reflection on the activity of observing nature—is at the heart of other poems that Goethe publishes in *On Morphology*. "Epirrhema," which appeared in the second issue of the first volume with no title,[35] begins with an imperative regarding observation: "Müsset im Naturbetrachten / Immer eins wie alles achten [In observing nature, / one must pay attention to one and all]" (MA 12, 92). The observer *must* observe the one and all. Or, as the poem at the end of the "Zwischenrede" puts it, "Willst Du ins Unendliche schreiten, Geh im Endlichen nach allen Seiten [If you want to stride into the infinite, then follow the finite in all directions]" (MA 12, 93).

By homing in on the active character of seeing, Goethe is drawing attention to the fact that if the observer simply proceeds according to the "natural" or "usual" way of observing, her observations will be far from adequate. Accordingly, Goethe's opening lines place a demand on the observer, first by making her conscious of the extent to which observation is active (as opposed to passive), and second by speaking in terms of an imperative that seeks to accord with nature, with the "one and all" or the "thousand strands." The observer thus becomes aware of her responsibility to grasp the successive and simultaneous character of natural development—a responsibility that emerges from the demands that nature places upon the knowing subject.

Importantly, these statements are parts of poems, and poems generally place greater interpretive demands on the reader than other forms of writing. Poetry engages with language in a far more creative way than the usual scientific essay, and makes use of bolder and more complex metaphors. The reader must attend to the poem, its nuances, the connections it is drawing, the relations between sound, meter, rhythm, and meaning, in a way that she does not need to when reading an essay. The poetic form thus makes the reader more aware of her responsibility as a reader—and thereby draws greater attention to her active participation in the process of knowing.

The poem's form is, of course, sequential. But it is not only sequential. For although it proceeds sequentially, its various elements relate to one another in a nonsequential manner. The sound, rhythm, line, meter, and meaning work together to illuminate one another, such that the different elements of the poem act as clues to one another. They must be read and understood in their various and multiple relations. In this way, the poem is like the living organism, whose various parts are fundamentally interlinked and can only exist with and through one another.[36] Or, as Goethe puts it in "Epirrhema," nothing living is only one; it is always many: "Immer ist's ein Vieles." Similarly, no line of a poem is singular in meaning, nor are its relations linear. Rather, the line's meanings are manifold, and its relations multidirectional. Furthermore, the art of reading a poem involves being able to behold all the different relations and implications *together*, i.e., to behold the sequential movement of the poem *and* the nonsequential elements and relations, so that each of the lines illuminates all the others and also expresses the whole within itself: in the same way that each of the parts of the plant illuminates the others, and is also an expression (a modification) of the one organ.

While the essay on the metamorphosis of plants certainly *sought* to achieve this, the poem's form *consciously* or *explicitly* demands it—such that the reader is *expected* to perform the imaginative seeing of the simultaneous and sequential at once. Only in this way can the reader grasp the poem.

The poem that most vividly articulates these points might be none other than Goethe's 1798 "The Metamorphosis of Plants [*Die Metamorphose der once*, by beholding their transforming shapes in one gaze, Goethe was able to see how all the parts were members of one transforming form (the date leaf tree), of one "uninterrupted activity." And in so doing, he arrived at the archetypal phenomenon.

What this shows is that the archetypal phenomenon is *achieved* through the work of the knower: through her ability to see and discern unity in the multiplicity. Accordingly, the archetypal phenomenon does not exist *prior* to this work—whether in the physical entity (e.g., as the fundamental animal form) or in a supersensible realm (a Platonic heaven). Rather, it *emerges* through the activity of knowing. More specifically, it emerges through *collaboration* between knower and known—between Goethe and the date palm tree.

To explicate what I mean, it is helpful to draw on a very concrete and well-known example from the Preface to the *Theory of Colors*. Goethe writes,

> all of our attempts to describe a person's character are in vain, but when we draw together his actions, his deeds, then an image of his character will emerge. (FA 23/1, 12)

Goethe's point here is that if we want to know a person's character, we must begin by observing her actions, behaviors, and gestures. Anything else would be useless, because anything else would give us an empty universal—a description that can be said of hundreds, if not thousands, of people. Saying, for instance, that she is gregarious, or awkward, or astute, does not convey her character to us. By contrast, describing her acts, behaviors, and gestures in different circumstances—how she carries herself, how she sits, responds to a question, etc.—vividly conveys her character, portraying a concrete, living person. By ordering and reordering these descriptions, we begin to discern her character *in and through* them. We begin to "see" her with our mind's eye.

Now although these descriptions are particular, they are not *accidental*. That is to say, the particular descriptions capture and convey something *essential* about this person. There is, thus, no conflict between the particular and the essential. Rather, it is in the particular that the essential emerges.

Furthermore, these descriptions offer an image, which is to say, an idea of her character, that we must conjure for ourselves—visualize as one uninterrupted activity. This idea is, importantly, also real. For the idea brings together the many descriptions that capture something fundamental about the person. Accordingly, the outcome of the descriptions is an *ideal reality*. It is ideal insofar as it involves "drawing together" the various particulars—the particulars that are not accidental—and understanding them in relation to one another. As such, it requires the active participation of the knower. In turn, this idea is real insofar as it discerns and captures what is essential *about* the phenomenon. It is an ideal that captures the real, or, put differently, the archetypal phenomenon is the result of the coming together of the ideal and real—the knower and the known.

When speaking of the archetypal plant, Goethe explains that it is an image not seen with his physical eyes, but through his "organ of visualization [*Sehorgan*]," and has its "roots in many years of contemplation of the metamorphosis of plants" (MA 12, 353–54).[19] This means that the *Urphänomen* does not refer to any "object out there," i.e., a physical entity that is separate from my organs of visualization.[20] It also means that the *Urphänomen* is not a general concept that simply aims to subsume the particular. Or, to put it in different terms: the *Urphänomen* does not simply exist in nature, but it is also not merely the achievement of the knower alone. Rather, the *Urphänomen* is the achievement of the knower *in collaboration with nature*. Or, as Frederick Amrine puts it, "As the Urphänomen is not an abstract terminus (in either sense of the word) but a pure activity, it can be accessed and realized only through practice."[21]

To think of the *Urphänomen* as a collaboration *between* the knower and the known sheds important light on its epistemological and ontological status.[22] For collaboration implies that the *Urphänomen* is the outcome of an ongoing effort between two collaborators—the knower and the known—and is thus realized only through this effort. Accordingly, it has a distinctive ontological and epistemological status. Ontologically, it does not exist in any physical object, but also it does not exist in a purely ideal world. Furthermore, insofar as it does not simply "exist" or "subsist," but emerges through a collaborative effort, it is best construed as an ongoing activity, which requires a genuine coming together of the two parties.

Epistemologically, as the outcome of a collaboration between the ideal (mind of the knower) and the real (the phenomenon), the *Urphänomen* is both real and ideal *at once*. This makes sense in light of the example from the *Theory of Colors*. For while it is our responsibility to draw together the various actions, behaviors, and gestures of a person, and visualize this person before our mind's eye, the character that emerges through this work *should* say something essential *about* the person. It is not, in other words, an arbitrary or accidental characterization.

This is, in fact, how Schiller came to understand the *Urphänomen* and how he explicated it in his January 1798 letter to Goethe. In contrast to his critical remarks from 1794, Schiller writes to Goethe in 1798 that his (Goethe's) method is alone capable of "fully preserving the rights of the object," to which he adds that the pure phenomenon is "one with the objective laws of nature" (MA 8/1, 499).

There is no doubt that by that point, Schiller had come a long way from the skeptical stance he had originally adopted toward Goethe's notion of the *Urpflanze*. There is no doubt that Goethe too had come a long way. Not only does Goethe distinguish two forms of seeing, but he also makes his methodology far more explicit, with the intention of demonstrating to his reader how one ought to proceed in the search for the *Urphänomen*. However, despite his increasing familiarity with philosophy and philosophical vocabulary, Goethe does not make a point of situating his method in relation to (and in contrast with) other philosophical schools or traditions. Such a contextualization might, nonetheless, serve both Goethe's purpose and ours. For the method of rational empiricism clearly bears connections to rationalism and empiricism. In departing from them, however, his method charts a new path. To explicate this path, Schiller—in his letter to Goethe—takes the time to provide this philosophical-historical context. And because this context might help us to better understand Goethe's place in the history of philosophy, it is worthwhile to turn, even if only briefly, to Schiller's letter.

5.3. Schiller on the *Urphänomen* and Rational Empiricism

The letter begins with Schiller suggesting to Goethe that the best way by which to understand the distinction between the three kinds of phenomena—the empirical, the scientific, and the pure—is by considering them in light of the table of categories, i.e., in light of the kinds of judgments that the various phenomena allow us to make.[23] This means considering each of the phenomena according to the categories of quantity, quality, relation, and modality (i.e., the division of judgment that goes back to Aristotle, and forms the basis for Kant's table of judgments).

The empirical phenomenon is the focus of empiricism (which Schiller appears to identify with a vaguely Lockean account of empiricism), and concerns that which is immediately seen or sensed, what is here and now. In terms of quantity, the empirical phenomenon can only yield *singular* (rather than universal) judgments (*this* table here is green; *this* man is tall). And, in terms of quality, it can only assert the existence of things (x *is* y) rather than negate them (x is *not* y), oppose them to other things (x is *non*-y), or compare them with other things (x is *like* y). When it comes to relation, common empiricism runs the risk of confusing what is accidental for what is essential (e.g., all swans that I've seen are white, therefore all swans are white) but does not actually commit the error, because it remains on the level of "*this* swan is white"—it never moves to the universal judgment "all swans are white." Finally, in terms of modality, the empirical phenomenon is only about what is actual (what is in front of me now), and thus cannot think in terms of the possible (what may be the case) or the necessary (what must be the case). There are significant limitations to common empiricism. However, it does have one important virtue. Because it remains bound to the phenomenon in its most immediate form, it does not ascend to the level of general judgment—to making claims beyond the singular. For there lies the source of error, which emerges when we move to the scientific phenomenon, i.e., rationalism.

Rationalism is the source of error, because it is less focused on what is before the knower, and more concerned with the laws of thought—with what we can *think* rather than *perceive*. Thought and perception are, Schiller emphasizes, not the same, and the problem emerges when we mistake thought for reality (MA 8/1, 497).

But rationalism has numerous advantages. For one, it yields plurality rather than simple singularity (*many* men are tall). However, Schiller warns, it should resist going further, to totality (*all* men are tall), which would clearly result in error. In turn, rationalism allows for negation. Nonetheless, Schiller adds, it should be wary of isolating and separating those things which are, in nature, fundamentally connected. In terms of relation, rationalism aims to regard all things in causal terms, but Schiller once again warns that rationalism should be careful not to overdetermine everything in causal terms, as that would yield a purely linear picture of natural relations: nature as an endless chain of causes and effects. Finally, rationalism abandons the actual (which is far too contingent for its purposes) but is unable to arrive at the necessary (because it can only consider plurality, rather than totality). This means that it is only concerned with the possible—i.e., the realm of logical possibility (MA 8/1, 497–98).

In contrast to both the empirical and the scientific phenomenon, the pure phenomenon, Schiller writes, is "one with the objective laws of nature." With the pure phenomenon emerges rational empiricism, the approach that Schiller ascribes to Goethe, and which involves conjoining empiricism and rationalism. Only such an approach, Schiller argues, can grasp the objective laws of nature because it remains with what is given (via empiricism) but, through the capacities of reason, is able to note differences, draw comparisons, and arrive at what is essential. Or, as quoted above, "it preserves fully the rights of the object " (MA 8/1, 499). How, according to Schiller, does it do this?

First, rational empiricism moves beyond both singularity and plurality, to unity, because it is concerned with what is essential and constant in the various manifestations before us. As Schiller explains, it aims to discern the unity *in* the multiplicity. In turn, rational empiricism is not concerned with mere affirmation (x is y) or mere negation (x is not y) but limitation, which involves seeing how things are both like and unlike other things, drawing connections rather than simply affirming or negating. When it comes to relation, rational empiricism pays attention to both the causal nexus of objects—determining their causal relations to other objects—*and* to their independence, i.e., to the fact that they are *not merely* effects or causes, but *also* integral wholes, which are themselves *loci* of causal relations (e.g., an animal body is seen as an integral whole, rather than a mere outcome of various external causes). As such, Schiller explains, rational empiricism does not simply regard nature as an endless chain of cause and effect, but also discerns nature's "breadth," the diversity and uniqueness of individual beings. It sees objects *for themselves*—and not merely as points in a chain. Finally, precisely because rational empiricism is concerned with what is essential, it arrives at necessity, at what *must be* rather than what is here and now—which can be accidental—or what may be—which is speculative.

Schiller contends that Goethe's method is capable of preserving the rights of the object because it discerns the essential *in* the empirical phenomena. Accordingly, the necessary here is not the *logically* necessary (i.e., necessity achieved through logical derivation and which has nothing to do with the empirically real). Rather, the necessary is found in the real. It is for this reason that rational empiricism is a form of empiricism. But unlike common empiricism, it does not remain with the singular, but arrives at the essential, i.e., the fundamental character of its object. This makes it rational. What Schiller has come to understand, then, is that the *Urphänomen* is indeed an idea, but it is an objective or real idea: it delivers essential insight into the phenomenon. It is, to put it simply, *ideal* and also essentially *real*.

5.4. Goethe's Environmental Ethics and the Source of Responsibility

While Schiller's explication helpfully contextualizes Goethe's method and his notion of the *Urphänomen* in relation to other philosophical schools and traditions, Goethe's methodology is—I believe—not only historically significant and unique, but also relevant today. Indeed, to recall the opening remarks of this chapter and to echo Eckart Förster's closing statement in his book, Goethe's approach has the potential to offer important insights and responses to contemporary questions and concerns. Although I think that Goethe's methodology can fruitfully address a number of contemporary discourses—including biology's attempt to conceptualize the relationship between organism and environment, which will be discussed in Chapter 6— I will here focus on the environmental discourse.[24]

As we saw in Chapter 3, in his 1795 essay on comparative anatomy and osteology Goethe offers important reflections on his methodology. Specifically, he claims that he arrived at the notion of an "animal type (*Typus*)" by reaching a higher standpoint. Looking back at this moment, Goethe notes that it was precisely through this higher standpoint that he also began to think about ethical matters. "Bit by bit," he writes, "I elevated my standpoint in order to draw judgments on scientific and ethical actions" (MA 12, 181).

Interestingly—and as we shall elaborate in the chapters to come—Goethe wrote this essay on the bidding of the two Humboldt brothers, Alexander and Wilhelm. Whether Goethe's ethical interests were inspired by the Humboldt brothers, or vice versa, it is impossible to know. However, one thing is certain: for both Goethe and Alexander von Humboldt, ethical considerations cannot be divorced from epistemological or ontological questions. This view is founded on their understanding of knowledge: knowledge involves and draws on the individual scientist's capacities and judgments—and her willingness to transform these capacities in light of the task at hand.

From a contemporary perspective, Goethe's emphasis on the individual scientist and his view that aesthetic education plays a crucial role in the transformation of the scientist seems to be, at best, quaint, and, at worst, problematic. After all, the goal of science—we have come to believe—is to arrive at objective knowledge, i.e., knowledge that is not only entirely separable from the subject of knowledge and the circumstances of this subject, but also from the specific circumstances of the object (i.e., what Herder describes as its "world"). Goethe, by contrast, emphasizes both: the knower plays an essential role in the formation of knowledge, and the object of knowledge (the phenomenon) should always be grasped in relation to its context rather than beyond it.

There is, nonetheless, reason to believe that Goethe's form of science, his emphasis on the individual scientist and on aesthetics, has a role to play in the world today. This is not only because scientists themselves are reaching out to the arts,[25] or because we live in a postpositivist age.[26] Although both of these are significant, I believe that Goethe's approach to nature is relevant because it offers a new way by which to establish environmental ethics.

Traditionally, environmental ethics has proceeded on the assumption that we can only be held responsible toward a nonhuman being (e.g., a horse, a river, a tree) only once we have established its moral worth. Accordingly, discussions of responsibility are dependent on the (prior) justification of a being's moral status, such that it is *only once* it has been granted moral status, that we become morally responsibility toward it.[27] Thus within environmental ethics, a crucial question has been: how do we determine this moral status? On what grounds can we designate nature or particular natural beings as morally relevant? Is it because they have value for us (e.g., economic or ecological value)? Is it because they are ends in themselves (i.e., possess value irrespective of our needs and interests)? Or is it because they experience pain and pleasure, have interests and goals, to which we must pay heed?

Despite their differences, these approaches share two crucial features. The first is that they seek to *extend* human values (e.g., "rights") to the more-than-human world. Accordingly, the ideals and norms which they apply to the more-than-human world have their source in human concepts, ideals, and norms. The assumption is that these concepts, ideals, and norms are adequate for understanding and taking account of the more-than-human world. This assumption is, however, not self-evident and thus requires justification.[28]

The second problem concerns the fact that any attempt to "represent" or "speak on behalf of" the natural world—whether in an ethical context or in a court of law—assumes that what is represented (a horse, a tree, a river) cannot speak on its own behalf, that it is "deaf," "mute," or "vegetable."[29] This, however, robs the natural world of the ability to speak or represent itself, and, as Eva Giraud notes, can lead to "forms of political ventriloquism that reinscribe inequalities rather than overturning them."[30] Goethe's ethics avoids both of these pitfalls, while also generating crucial insights into the meaning and sources of ethical responsibility.

As suggested in the preceding chapter, in the opening lines of *On Morphology* Goethe furnishes his methodological manifesto—an outline of the crucial elements in his approach to nature. According to Goethe, knowledge depends on the active participation of both subject *and* object; it requires an infinite education on the part of the knowing subject; and this education involves the transformation of sensibility and judgment and the emergence of new cognitive capacities.

While the claim that knowledge involves both subject *and* object does not sound new or radical, there is, in fact, something fundamentally radical about it. For Goethe is not simply claiming that the subject requires the object in order to know it, or that knowledge ought to be "objective," i.e., *about* the object. His claim, rather, is that the subject *and* the object are *collaborators* in the ongoing (indeed infinite) process of knowledge. Accordingly, the "object," or better, the phenomenon, is an active participant in the process of knowing. It places demands on the knower, and it is in light of these demands that the knower recognizes that she is ill-equipped and must educate herself, develop new capacities. The knower, in turn, is also active, insofar as she must engage with the object of knowledge and transform herself—in accordance with the object's demands—in order to achieve knowledge. After all, while the phenomenon challenges the knower—revealing to her how she is not prepared to grasp the phenomenon properly—*how* the phenomenon will ultimately appear depends on the tools and capacities that the knower possesses.

Returning to Kant momentarily, we can say that for Kant, the knower does not have a proper grasp of organization in nature to begin with. Rather, she assumes that all beings can be understood according to the laws of mechanism and efficient causality. However, in her encounter with "certain entities" she finds that the tools that she is employing are inadequate—the bird's structure, for instance, remains unintelligible, despite her best efforts. She is being challenged by the phenomenon. The question is: can she rise to meet the challenge? Can she develop "new forms of grasping and responding" that *can* make the phenomenon intelligible?

These questions, and Goethe's account of knowledge as collaboration, imply, first, that neither subject nor object is more significant in the process of knowledge. In fact, the usual roles are reversed: it is not the knower who places demands on the object, but the object that places demands on the subject.[31] They also imply that the object does not disappear from the process of knowledge: the phenomenon is not replaced by an abstract law, a category, or a figure in a statistical table. Rather, the phenomenon—as collaborator—remains. In fact, it is the task of the knower to make sure the phenomenon does not disappear and to maintain an ongoing relationship with it—to allow the phenomenon to continually challenge the knower. Thus, one can begin by stating that Goethe's science is, first and foremost, a science of encounter, where the fundamental goal is to remain with and be challenged by the phenomenon that is encountered.

This emphasis on encounter—on attending to the phenomenon—is evident in Goethe's understanding of the experiment and his critique of the idea (developed by Newton) of the "crucial experiment."[32] The view that knowledge can be achieved through a crucial experiment encourages the swift move away from phenomenon—what the experiment is investigating—to the construction of a system or a law that is supposed to explain this phenomenon. Thus, instead of remaining with the phenomenon, the notion of a crucial experiment takes us away from it—from its many and manifold manifestations—to the abstract concept, category, or law arrived at through this one experiment.

In "The Experiment as Mediator," Goethe argues that science should not rely on one crucial experiment. Rather, he contends that science is the outcome of many experiments, which build upon, deepen, and illuminate one another. This delivers a distinctive picture of science. For it implies that the goal is to bring together (narrate, present) the results of the various experiments and see them in relation to one another. Science is a "beholding" of experimental findings, and through this beholding we arrive at what Goethe describes as a "higher sort" of empiricism, i.e., the *Urphänomen* (FA 25, 34).

This means that for Goethe science is not predictive, nor does it aim to arrive at a set of true (but abstract) propositions about a reality outside of us. Rather, science is an active contemplation, which consists in the scientist bringing together various results, *seeing* them in relation to one another, and *discerning* the essential in them individually and in their unity. Above all, science consists in paying heed to, indeed "saving," the phenomena.

This is why Goethe, in the *Theory of Colors*, likens science to art. For, he writes, "we must conceive of science as an art if we are to expect any kind of holistic results [*wenn wir von ihr irgend eine Art von Ganzheit erwarten*]"

(FA 23/1, 605). Both involve beholding or seeing. Both seek to discern the essential in the particular. And both emphasize the need to remain with the phenomenon.

In a time of general alienation of nature, where our experiences of the more-than-human world are increasingly mediated, and our very concept of nature leads us to unconsciously assume that nature is something "out there," outside the walls of "culture," the emphasis on encountering and remaining with the phenomena poses an important challenge and corrective. Indeed, this is how Goethe understood his work in relation to Newton's—as a challenge and a corrective.[33] The crucial problem with Newton, as Goethe saw it, was methodological: Newton and his school took us away from the phenomenon and replaced it with an abstraction (whether a mathematical formulation or a hypothesis).[34] The goal of science should, however, be the opposite: to dwell with the phenomenon, to *discern* lawfulness *in the phenomenon* itself.

While a number of environmental thinkers have noted the problems with abstraction—especially in relation to the concept of nature—and the way it can obstruct ethical and political action, few have offered positive alternatives.[35] Goethe's methodology does precisely that. In the place of an abstract concept of nature from which we are alienated, Goethe offers us "nature" as a concrete and experienced reality, a reality composed of dynamic beings that address us and place demands on us. What Goethe's methodology thus furnishes is a way by which to *return to the concrete*, to engage with the world around us in a meaningful and ethical way.

But where exactly does the ethical significance of knowledge emerge? To answer this question, we must consider Goethe's understanding of knowledge as collaboration more carefully. If knowledge involves not only the knower, but also the known, it follows that the activity of knowledge is a relationship between the two. This relation is a *collaboration* insofar as the known is not a passive entity, but is actively involved, and plays a role in determining the framework of the relationship—for instance, by requiring the knower to transform herself. If the knower does not abide by this framework (if she refuses to acknowledge the demands placed upon her), then the goal of this relation (knowledge) cannot be fully or properly realized.

Underpinning this conceptualization of the knowledge relation is the idea that the knower implicitly agrees to the framework of the relationship. In entering the relationship, the knower puts herself in a position of obligation. She is bound to the framework of the knowledge relation, its parameters and expectations, and this means that she ought to fulfill the demands placed upon her. Thus, once she becomes aware of these demands, she has a choice to make: she can fulfill them or ignore them. She can transform herself and her capacities, or she can remain unchanged. She can choose to know well or to know badly.

The question thus is: to whom does she bear the responsibility of knowing well? If, in other words, she chooses to know badly—she chooses not to transform her cognitive capacities—then to whom is she responsible? Is it only to herself, insofar as she sets a task for herself and in failing to achieve it, she fails herself? Or is it also a responsibility that she bears to her community, insofar as her bad knowledge is likely to influence their knowledge as well—potentially leading them in false directions? Both are clearly the case. In knowing badly, the knower is not only failing herself (failing to meet her own presumed goal); she is also failing the community, in which she makes a claim to knowledge. For as soon as she presents herself as a knower to others, she implicitly takes on the responsibility to know well. She is, in a sense, asking her community to entrust her with the task of knowledge. By choosing not to transform, by choosing not to know well, she is failing in her responsibility to her community and undermining the community's trust in her. Without trust, the relationship cannot continue. In turn, if her community is a community of knowers (e.g., a scientific community), she is also undermining the community, which can only exist on the basis of trust.

Already we can sense that the responsibility to know well cannot be simply an epistemological responsibility. For as soon as knowing involves others, virtues such as honesty and truthfulness can no longer be purely epistemic virtues, but become social and ethical ones: they are necessary to uphold and maintain communities. By choosing to know badly, the knower can damage a relationship and a community, and the consequences of this damage include undercutting the community or individual members within it (e.g., those who particularly trusted her, or who based their own work on hers).

While Goethe was certainly interested in the sociology and history of science, and the role of the individual scientist in the development of science,[36] these considerations do not capture the full extent of responsibility that his statement implies or its significance for environmental ethics. For what we have thus far outlined is an account of ethical responsibility that does not consider the most crucial element in the production of (natural-scientific) knowledge—the main collaborator in this relationship—the known phenomenon, the natural world. My claim is that Goethe's statement puts the knower in a position of ethical responsibility not only to other knowers, but also to the phenomena that are to be known: the oak tree, the river, the horse. How can this be the case?

This conceptual possibility arises once we conceive of the phenomenon as a collaborator. For in that case, we begin to think of the phenomenon as actively involved in determining the framework and expectations of the relationship. Accordingly, in entering the relation of knowledge, the knower is implicitly agreeing to abide by the demands and expectations of the phenomenon. In other words, the knower puts herself in a position of obligation *toward the phenomenon*—her collaborator. If she does not follow the demands of her collaborator, she is not upholding her part of the deal. If she knows badly, in other words, she is acting unfaithfully toward her fellow collaborator. This undermines the relationship of knowledge into which they have both entered. It can also lead to false or incomplete understanding, which can have devastating consequences for the collaborator.

These consequences, in turn, can be morally relevant. After all, *how* we know determines how the object *appears*, and how it *appears* determines how we *treat* it. Consider, for instance, a bird, which—depending on our cognitive tools, skills, and habits—can appear either as a machine or as a sentient being. If, to recall Kant, we invoke purely mechanical principles, then it will appear to us to be a machine. Thus, despite clear indications from the bird that our tools are inadequate—that the framework we are using is not making it any more intelligible—we ignore these indications and proceed with what we already have. By contrast, if we follow the bird's indications—allow it to show us that our tools and habits are inapt, allow it to place demands on us to invoke different principles, develop new capacities (e.g., intuitive understanding)—then we might begin to see it differently: as a self-organizing being, with itself (its life) as its own end. Thus, with our different tools and new capacities, the bird no longer appears to have an end outside itself but is its own end. It is, furthermore, striving to realize this end. Accordingly, it has interests and purposes. In contrast to a machine, which does not have itself as its end, which does not strive toward self-preservation, a being that strives may be worthy of our moral consideration. If we had continued to use our old tools, the moral status and significance of the bird would not have emerged as a topic. This makes evident that moral consideration cannot be divorced from our cognitive tools, skills, and habits, i.e., from knowing well and knowing badly.

This, however, is not the full extent of Goethe's statement, nor does it uncover his statement's its most radical aspect. For underpinning the above reflections is the assumption that a being becomes morally relevant once we have determined its ontological status, i.e., whether it strives or has goals, whether it suffers and is sentient, or whether it has certain capabilities.[37] On this view, it is only *after* we have determined the moral status of the bird (e.g., *it is morally relevant, because it is sentient and suffers*), that we hold ourselves responsible to it. Goethe's claim, however, is that there is a more fundamental (ethical) question that needs to be raised—a question that specifically concerns the act of knowledge itself and *its* ethical status. In other words, the primary question is not whether non-human beings possess certain (human) qualities or capacities, which might lead us to grant them moral status. Rather, the primary question is whether *we*, as knowers, bear responsibility to the world we wish to know.

Accordingly, the foundation of environmental ethics—from a Goethean perspective—is not in principles derived from human ethical norms, and (sometimes problematically) applied onto the more-than-human world, but in epistemological and ontological questions, and in *their* ethical status. What is being interrogated is not whether any particular being is worthy of moral consideration (because it is, in some way, *like* us). Rather, what is being interrogated is whether *our* (epistemological) comportment toward this being is *moral*, i.e., whether we are upholding our part of the collaboration. The justification for this view is Goethe's understanding of the enterprise of knowledge—as situated, dialogical, and responsive—and of what it entails for the knower—education, transformation. Thus, Goethe's nascent environmental ethics emerges out of an *ecological conception* of knowing and being.

This demands a shift in our understanding of the relationship between knowledge and ethics. Rather than first seeking to establish the moral status of a being in order to justify responsibility toward it, Goethe begins with responsibility (the responsibility of the knower), and on that basis grants moral status. Precisely because the activity of knowledge is a collaboration, the phenomenon (the known) places a demand on the knower, and the knower is responsible to meet this demand. In other words, the knower bears responsibility to whatever she seeks to know such that *all known beings are morally relevant*.[38] This is because the relationship of knowledge is based on trust, and the implicit agreement to comply with the demands placed on the knower in this relationship.

This allows us to address the matter of representation more directly. Precisely because the known is a collaborator, who is actively engaged in framing the relationship of knowledge and determining its principles and expectations, the known cannot be regarded as mute. This implies that upon entering this relationship, the knower is under the obligation to *listen* to the known. In other words, precisely because the knower is guided by the known, and indeed transformed by this encounter, the knower does not aim" to speak on behalf of" the known. In fact, the goal of this collaboration is not a re-presentation of the known, but its self-presentation, achieved through the mediation of the knower. The knower aims to allow the phenomenon to come to presentation *in and through* her "natugemäße Darstellung" of the phenomenon. Put differently, the knower aims to present the phenomenon *through* the *Urphänomen*, which is nothing other than the outcome of a successful collaboration between knower and known.

By conceiving of knowledge in this way, Goethe demonstrates that the activity of knowing cannot be carried out in the abstract "amoral" sphere. As such, he extends the insights of feminist philosophers of science, but from a different angle.[39] For the claim is not simply that knowledge always takes place in a particular context, and is therefore never only for the sake of knowledge. The claim is, additionally, that knowledge must (also) be *for the sake of the known*.

The ethical significance of Goethe's methodology is thus to be found in the ways in which he develops the notion of responsibility. In the first instance, responsibility is understood not only as a moral ideal that concerns actions and behaviors, but also as an epistemic virtue—i.e., the responsibility to know well. This means that we cannot treat epistemic, ontological, and ethical questions in separation from one another, or regard our knowledge activity as occurring in an amoral context. Knowledge is always *for* an end, and, as Goethe suggests, it must always be *for the known*. This leads to the second way in which he develops the notion of responsibility. For responsibility, on Goethe's account, is not only directed toward beings that are "like us," and which are regarded as "moral subjects" or subjects worthy of moral consideration. Rather, responsibility is shown to be an *emergent property* that belongs to relations: it emerges in and through the relations we have with our collaborators. Accordingly, responsibility is toward our collaborators, whomever they may be.

Once we begin to think of knowledge as collaboration, and to recognize nature as collaborator, we open up a new path for environmental ethics. Environmental ethics no longer needs to be about adjudicating moral status to the more-than-human world. Rather, it can now focus on our responsibilities to our fellow collaborators. In turn, given that the activity of life itself is an ongoing collaboration with other beings, it follows that responsibility pervades living activity more generally. We are, in a sense, always entering relations of responsibility toward the more-than-human world. Accordingly, the genuine ethical question does not aim to determine *whether* we are responsible, but rather *how to respond* to this responsibility. That is, the goal of environmental ethics should be to understand *how best to respond* to the demands placed upon us by our collaborators. Transforming our cognitive habits and developing our perception and understanding are, certainly, the first, and perhaps most important, step in this response.

While Goethe did not possess the words "ecology" and "environment," his understanding of the relationship of knowledge signals the emergence of what we today would call an "ecological" or "environmental consciousness." By placing the natural world, the phenomena, at the center of his thinking and demanding that the knower pay head to phenomena, Goethe furnished crucial insights into how to understand the human-nature relationship and human responsibility toward the more-than-human world. Though many of Goethe's contemporaries were not always interested in these questions, one of them took notice: Alexander von Humboldt.

6
Organism and Environment
The Aesthetic Foundations of Humboldt's Ecological Insight

Often described as the "father of environmentalism" and the founder of modern ecology, Alexander von Humboldt is perhaps the first European thinker to develop a comprehensive, empirically grounded vision of nature as a dynamic, organized, and developing unity.[1] Although it was Ernst Haeckel who coined the term "ecology [*Oecologie*]" some seven years after Humboldt's death (in his 1866 *General Morphology* [*Generelle Morphologie*]), it was Humboldt's way of thinking and his understanding of the natural world that made Haeckel's coinage of the term possible. In fact, Haeckel seems to have had Humboldt in mind when he wrote that "by ecology, we understand the whole science of the relationships between organisms and their surrounding external world, which we could count as their 'conditions of existence' in a wider sense."[2] Thus, while Haeckel gave us the term *ecology*, it was Humboldt who elaborated the idea of nature as a dynamic "household (oikos)" in which living beings mutually influence and support one another.[3] As Humboldt put it in one of the first statements of his five-volume *Kosmos* (*Cosmos*) (1845–56): "nature is, for thinking observation [*denkende Betrachtung*], unity in multiplicity, the connection of the many in form [*Form*] and mixture, of natural objects and natural forces, as one living whole [*als ein lebendiges Ganzes*]" (*Kosmos* 1, 10).[4]

But it was well before the publication of *Kosmos* that Humboldt began to conceive of nature as a living unity, composed of mutually influencing and supporting members. His first concrete ecological observations go back to his time in South America. In March 1800, Humboldt and his scientific companion, Aimé Bonpland (1773–1858), arrived in Lake Valencia, or Lake Tacarigua, in present-day Venezuela. In contrast to their expectations, they encountered a region suffering from drought. Through conversations with Indigenous locals, Creole farmers, and his own investigations, Humboldt came to a surprising conclusion: the felling of trees, and the replacement of forests by farms, had fundamentally transformed the climate and the soil. What was once a verdant area, with regular rain, had become a desert.[5] This is how he puts it:

> When forests are destroyed . . . as they are everywhere in America by the European colonists, the springs . . . dry up, or become less abundant. The beds of the rivers, remaining dry during a part of the year, become torrents whenever heavy rain falls on the heights. With the disappearance of sward and moss from the sides of the mountains, the waters falling in rain are no longer impeded in their course: and, during heavy showers, instead of slowly augmenting the level of the rivers by progressive filtrations, they furrow the sides of the hills, bear down the loosened soil, and form those sudden inundations that devastate the country. And so it results that the destruction of the forests, the want of permanent springs, and the existence of torrents are three phenomena closely connected to one another. (PNW 4, 143–44; translation altered)

In this statement, which had a profound impact on environmental policy across the world—from the United States to India—Humboldt points to two crucial, but hardly recognized, facts: the influence of trees (forests) on the environment and the influence of human beings on the environment.[6] While Humboldt's predecessors (including Buffon, Kant, Herder, and Goethe) had recognized that living beings are affected by their environments, they had not considered how living beings themselves affect their environments: that is, how living beings, including humans, fundamentally transform the climate, soil, plants, and animals of a region.

Accordingly, and along lines broached by Herder in his articulation of the notion of an animal's "world," Humboldt came to realize that the relationship between a living being and its context (organism and environment) is not unilateral but bilateral. This means, Humboldt emphasized, not only that living beings are inextricably linked to their contexts (as a bee is to the beehive) but also that the context is the *outcome* of the activity of living beings. The climate of Lake Valencia cannot exist without the trees—and vice versa: the trees cannot exist without this climate. The implication is that what we call the "environment" is not a static backdrop that preexists living beings, but a dynamic relationship *between* living beings and their surroundings over long periods of time.

Humboldt's insight was radical for his time.[7] What is surprising is that his insight remains radical today. Although it might appear to us as entirely straightforward, we continue to find it difficult to conceptualize the dynamic relationship between living beings and their environments. As biologist Sonia Sultan puts it in her 2015 book, *Organism and Environment*, while "conceptualizing the relationship between organisms and their environments is pivotal for both ecological and evolutionary investigations," it remains the case that "[i]n both disciplines, this relationship is generally seen as an interaction between separate entities, in the sense that an individual whose traits are *internally* (i.e., genetically) determined confronts an *externally* defined and measurable environment."[8]

In other words, some two hundred years after Humboldt, we remain bound to a notion of the "environment" that fails to take account of his ecological insight. For what he saw is that the "environment" is not an unchanging stage for animal (and plant) activity, but an ongoing dynamic collaboration between living beings and their surroundings. This means that the two—organism and environment—are absolutely interdependent. The one cannot exist without the other: the climate and soil of Lake Valencia cannot exist without the trees—and vice versa: the trees cannot exist without regular rain and nutrient-rich soil. To conceive of them as *originally* separate entities that *then* somehow come together is to misunderstand them and their relation.

The question then is: How did Humboldt come to see organisms and their environments as a dynamic collaboration? How did he come to recognize that a particular environment does not preexist its inhabitants, and that the inhabitants do not preexist the environment? What were Humboldt's methods and tools, and what concepts, frameworks, and approaches did he develop in order to discern and communicate the dynamic relation between living beings and their surroundings? Finally, what are the implications of Humboldt's ecological insight: for our understanding of the world, and for our understanding of ourselves in the world?

These are the questions we will consider over the next two chapters, beginning with an investigation of Humboldt's methodology. As I will argue, Humboldt's approach to the study of nature is fundamentally aesthetic, in both senses of the term. On the one hand, it is based on the view that perception and sensibility more generally are crucial for grasping the natural world. Like Goethe, Humboldt aims to remain with the phenomena. Accordingly, he distinguishes his approach from what he calls the "rational science of nature," which seeks to derive or construct nature from abstract rational principles. In contrast, Humboldt contends, knowledge of nature must always remain tethered to what is seen and felt, i.e., to the phenomenon and to lived experience.

On the other hand, Humboldt's methodology is aesthetic in that it emphasizes impressions and feelings and is modeled on an artistic view of nature. Specifically, Humboldt draws on the ways in which certain artistic media (in particular landscape painting and literature) are able to capture a natural environment in "one glance" or "at once"—and thereby present to the viewer (or reader) the ongoing, manifold, and multidirectional relations that make up an environment. Importantly, the arts present these relations concretely—in their very form. Precisely because the aesthetic integrity of a work of art is not merely abstract and formal, works of art are able to convey, in their very form, the integrity of the environment that is depicted. For this reason, Humboldt argues, the scientist must learn from the artist *how* to look at nature.

Humboldt's aesthetic approach to nature might make some readers uneasy. By using various artistic media to orient the scientist, Humboldt appears to be challenging some of the most basic modern scientific principles and ideals. After all, landscape painting is situated: what is depicted depends on where the painter happens to be and when. Further, much of what is conveyed in a landscape painting is difficult to pin down and articulate in objective terms. The *feeling* of a place, its character, involves the viewer as much as it involves the view. What is captured in the painting appears to lie somewhere between objectivity and subjectivity. For it refers to *both* the particular place that is depicted *and* the impressions and feelings that this place evokes—impressions and feelings that are *of* this place, that reveal something *about this place*, but which nonetheless belong to a human subject.

As I will argue in this chapter, however, it was precisely this aesthetic approach that enabled Humboldt to come to his ecological insight. In other words, my claim is that there is a crucial and largely understudied *aesthetic element* at the very heart of ecology. And, as I will argue in the next chapter, this aesthetic element must be resuscitated in our present time of ecological crisis.

6.1. Thinking Observation: Goethe and the Origins of Humboldt's Methodology

In the Introduction to *Kosmos*, Humboldt distinguishes his approach from both rationalism and empiricism. He writes: the "physical description of nature . . . makes no claims to be a rational science of nature [*rationale*

Wissenschaft der Natur]" because "it is a thinking observation of the appearances given empirically as the whole of nature [*es ist die denkende Betrachtung der durch Empirie gegebenen Erscheinungen, als eines Naturganzen*]." Accordingly, Humboldt continues, while a rational science of nature aims to arrive at "a general description of nature," which is the result of "derivation from a few, rational principles [*Ableitung aus wenigen, von der Vernunft gegebenen Grundprinzipien*]," his approach rests on the "level of the empirical [*Stufe der Empirie*]" (*Kosmos* 1, 22). This, however, is not to identify his methodology with empiricism, or what he calls "raw and incomplete empiricism" (*Kosmos* 1, 13). Rather, Humboldt's approach involves "a thinking treatment [*denkende Behandlung*] . . . a meaningful ordering [*sinnvolle Anordnung*] of the appearances of nature . . . [that is] deeply penetrated with the belief in an ancient internal necessity [*eine alte innere Notwendigkeit*]" (*Kosmos* 1, 22).

Humboldt's methodology bears clear affinity to the approach that Schiller dubbed "rational empiricism." E. C. Otté, one of Humboldt's English translators, may have picked up on this, as she uses precisely this phrase to render Humboldt to an Anglophone audience (CE 1, 49).[9] In turn, the notion of "thinking observation" clearly resonates with Goethe's statement that thinking must become more perceptual and perception more thought-like.[10] Humboldt is not shy about acknowledging Goethe's influence, especially on his methodology.[11] As he puts it in a letter to Caroline von Wolzogen from May 14, 1806:

> From the forests of the Amazon to the tops of the high Andes, I saw how, from pole to pole, all things are as if ensouled by a breath, how only one life pours out into rocks, stones, animals and in the swelling breasts of humans. Everywhere I was aware of the extent to which my connections to Jena had affected me, how I had been raised through Goethe's views of nature [*Naturansichten*], how I had been granted new organs [*mit neuen Organen ausgerüstet*]![12]

Goethe's "views of nature" (a phrase that Humboldt will use as the title of his first book of essays) seem to have provided Humboldt with a new perspective on nature. Specifically, through encounters with Goethe, Humboldt claims, he developed "new organs" of perception.

Humboldt first met Goethe in March 1794, while visiting his brother Wilhelm in Jena. Immediately the two found much to discuss and like about one another, and in December of that year, when Humboldt was in Jena again, Goethe spent three days with the two brothers. It is very likely that during this visit, Goethe discussed his work on the animal type, leading Wilhelm and Alexander to urge Goethe to put down his ideas in writing. For just a month later, in January 1795, Wilhelm sends a letter to Goethe containing an "osteological schema" of a peacock.[13] As Wilhelm explains, this schema was inspired by their conversations. To this he adds: "I have not yet done anything about the description of the goat, because I regard it as necessary for me [first] to become familiar with the essay you left behind and with your spirit of investigation" (LA 2/9A, 442).

Goethe himself records this moment in *On Morphology* as follows:

And so I spent my time, until 1795 when the Humboldt brothers, who have been illuminating dialogue partners throughout my life, were in Jena for a while. In this context, the mouth could not withhold that which fills the heart, and I took the opportunity to present my type often and intrusively, before they impatiently demanded that I should write down these thoughts. (MA 12, 181)

As noted, in 1795 Goethe was working on his essay on comparative anatomy and osteology, in which he explicates and justifies his understanding of the animal type (*Typus*). We can now add that the essay appears to have been written on the bidding of the Humboldt brothers. And, as we have also seen, it was at this same time that Goethe began to think about the ethical implications and obligations of scientific knowledge (MA 12, 181).[14] Whether Goethe reached this view on his own, or through conversation with the Humboldt brothers, it is impossible to know. What is worth noting, however, is the parallel between Humboldt's and Goethe's thinking on these topics. Like Goethe, Humboldt drew on the idea of form; and also like Goethe, he came to the conclusion that the separation of ethical and scientific questions was impossible and its presumption dangerous.

Humboldt returned to Jena at the end of March 1795, remaining there until May 2. This longer stay gave him and Goethe the opportunity to meet regularly and undertake experiments. They spent whole days together, days which provided Goethe with much-needed companionship. Their most important exchange—for Humboldt at least—happened two years later in 1797. This was also to be their last encounter before Humboldt's journey to South America two years later.[15]

Over several months—from March to May—Humboldt shuttled back and forth between Jena and Weimar, often spending several days in Weimar, where he undertook experiments on galvanism and muscle irritability.[16] On the basis of these experiments, Humboldt went on to compose what has been described as his "major work" in morphology.[17]

In this work, titled *Versuche über die gereizte Muskel- und Nervenfaser* [*Essays on the Irritability of Muscle and Nerve Fibers*] (1797–98), Humboldt invokes the notion of an animal "type" and explains the relations between animals in terms that recall Goethe's approach in his search for the intermaxillary bone in the human being. As Goethe had recognized, the bone is present more or less explicitly in different animals, depending on their overall structure. Or, in Humboldt's words, "what is often only alluded to in one animal, becomes fully explicit in another."[18] Accordingly, to discern the bone in the human being, it was necessary to consider the structure of the human body as a whole. For, as Goethe had argued in his 1795 essay on comparative anatomy and osteology, by positing an ideal "anatomical type," we are able to discern how the various empirical animals relate to one another.[19]

It is this attempt to grasp the relations between the different parts in light of an ideal type that Humboldt found so important and impressive, concluding in his 1797–98 essay that "this as yet under-developed field of zoonomy can be happy about the rich inheritance which Mr. Goethe will offer it, once he finally decides to make public his careful anatomical studies of skeletal formations [*Knochenbildungen*], and his account of general metamorphosis in the animal kingdom."[20] Humboldt's estimation of the significance of Goethe's notion of type or form did not change over the years, and in some ways became even more explicit.[21] As he puts it in the Introduction to *Kosmos*, Goethe's greatest contribution to science amounts to the "solution" he offered to the "problem of metamorphosis." This solution, Humboldt writes, is nothing other than the notion of "an ideal form that corresponds to certain fundamental types [*auf gewisse Grundtypen entspricht*]" (*Kosmos* 1, 22).

Let us consider this point carefully. When Humboldt figuratively raises his cup to toast Goethe's "solution" to the "problem of metamorphosis," locating this solution in the notion of an "ideal form," he situates the problem within a larger historical and scientific context. As Humboldt explains in the remarks preceding his mention of Goethe, the problem of metamorphosis has to do with the dual difficulties of the proliferation of organic forms (the infinite diversity of nature—as Kant had put it) and the relation between the currently existing organic forms and those long extinct. The two difficulties, which were intensified through European exploration and recent geological discoveries, amount to the problem of unity and multiplicity, or better, the problem of discerning unity, relation, connection in an ever-changing, dynamic nature. It is, in other words, the very same problem that Buffon, Kant, Herder, and Goethe had articulated and sought to resolve.

Following his affirmation of Goethe's "solution" to the "problem" of metamorphosis, Humboldt quotes the landscape painter and physician Carl Gustav Carus (1789–1869). Carus, who had invoked the Greek conception of *physis*, describes it as "the eternally growing, eternally in the process of forming and unfolding [*das ewig Wachsende, ewig im Bilden und Entfalten Begriffene*]" (*Kosmos* 1, 18). According to this definition, nature (*physis*) is eternally growing, and doing so *in form* (*Bild*). Thus, despite the multiplicity and ever-transforming character of living beings, despite the changes that have happened over millennia, we can see that there are connections, continuities, and relations. And these connections are to be discerned through *forms*. It is, in other words, *in and through* form that we begin to discern unity across geographic and historical distances.

Goethe's notion of form, as Humboldt emphasizes, is "an ideal"—it does not physically present itself to the sensible eyes but must be imagined through the mind's eye. In turn, if Goethe's notion of form provides the "solution" to the problem of unity and diversity, it follows that the work of seeing unity, connection, and relation among living forms of vastly different regions and across historical epochs requires more than simple observation: it also requires imagination, and—as Humboldt will argue—the tools of landscape painting.

Humboldt's interpretation of form seems to accord with our presentation of Goethe in the preceding chapters. But it also reveals the significance of form for Humboldt's own project. Or, as Humboldt puts it in *Ideen zu einer Geographie der Pflanzen* [*Ideas for a Geography of Plants*] (1807), the goal of the geography of plants is to discern nature's "fundamental forms [*Urformen*]" (DA 1, 53; EGP 67; translation altered). This might be surprising. After all, studies of form focus on individual organisms, while an ecological account of nature aims to highlight relations between organisms and between organisms and their context (environment). The implication is that an ecological perspective is not interested in form. In fact, it is precisely on account of its disinterest in form that it becomes ecological, i.e., focused on relations.

This, in fact, is one way of interpreting the crucial difference between Goethe and Humboldt. While Goethe is interested in the structure and character of individual beings, the argument goes, Humboldt focuses on their relations in the wider world.[22] And it is precisely in moving beyond individual forms that Humboldt makes his most important contribution. In other words, it is in departing from Goethe's focus on individual beings and their forms that Humboldt establishes ecology.

There is some truth to this interpretation. Goethe was perhaps less interested than Humboldt in landscapes and relationships between living beings and their surroundings. But he was not entirely uninterested. After all, it is precisely the relationship between plants and their context that led Goethe to think about plant form during his Italian journey, and he continued to investigate questions concerning this relationship well after his return from Italy. In the 1795 essay "Preparations for a Physiology of Plants [*Vorarbeiten zu einer Physiologie der Pflanzen*]," Goethe contends that there are two factors that any student of nature must take into account: first, the internal structure or form of the living being, and second, its relation to its external environment (LA 1/10, 135). Thus, while it is true that Goethe focused on this relationship to a lesser degree than Humboldt, he had recognized its significance and—as we shall shortly see in more detail—sought to theorize it.

But the more important point that challenges this understanding of the difference between Goethe and Humboldt has to do with Humboldt specifically. By regarding Humboldt's most significant move beyond Goethe as consisting in his emphasis on environmental conditions, this interpretation lends itself to overlooking the genuinely radical nature of Humboldt's ecological insight. After all, the idea that living beings must be grasped within their contexts was a basic premise of research well before Humboldt, in both Europe (as evident in Buffon's and Herder's works) and South America.[23] Although Humboldt went beyond Herder and Buffon in crucial ways— for instance, through precise empirical observations and measurements, through gaining access to flora and fauna that they could not have imagined—this is not the extent of his contribution. Rather, what distinguishes Humboldt from these thinkers was his understanding of the relationship between a living being and its environment as *reciprocal*. It is not only that living beings are shaped by their environments; it is also the case that they actively shape their environments. Importantly, Humboldt came to this insight through the notion of form.

If we go back to the first statement quoted above from *Kosmos*, Humboldt's claim is that thinking observation regards nature as "unity in multiplicity," to which he then adds, "the connection of *form* and mixture." In other words, the new organs of perception, which are connected to seeing forms in nature, are *also* the means by which to arrive at an ecological understanding of the world, of seeing "unity in multiplicity." This was already suggested in Humboldt's letter to Wolzogen, where he maintains that the new organs of perception enabled him to see nature as imbued with "one breath." Humboldt makes the point more explicit in *Kosmos*, where he writes that it is through the "discovery of new means of sensible perception, indeed of new organs [*neuer Organe*]," that "knowledge of nature as a whole [*Erkenntnis eines Naturganzen*]" is possible (*Kosmos* 2, 241). The new organs of perception, then, grant insights into nature as a dynamic and interrelated unity *of forms*.

How are we to understand this? How, in other words, are we to understand Humboldt's ecological insight *in connection to* his emphasis on form? To answer this question, we have to take a few steps back: first to Kant, and then to Goethe. For it is in their conceptualization of the relationship between form and context, between the internal structure of the organism and its external world, that we find the challenges that come with attempting to grasp this relationship, and the potential solutions to these challenges.

6.2. External Teleology: Kant's Either/Or

As discussed in Chapter 1, Kant consider the question of the relationship between living beings and their contexts in Section 63 of the *Critique of the Power of Judgment*. This relationship, Kant contends, is a form of external purposiveness, which contrasts to the internal purposiveness that he regards as unique to organized beings. In contrast to internal purposiveness, external purposiveness aims to understand ("explain") the living being through something external to itself. There are two kinds of external purposiveness—two ways of explaining the organism through something outside itself. The first, which interests us here, concerns the relationship between organisms and their environment.[24] There are two ways to understand this relationship: either the organism is understood as determined by some other organism in its environment or it is understood as determined by its environment more generally. The claim is that the organism is what it is *because of* these external factors.

Now this *because of* can be understood in terms of services (e.g., the flower is what it is *because of* the services it renders to bees) or in terms of the laws governing its environment (e.g., a flower is what it is *because of* the laws of motion in space). In either case, the claim is that a living being is what it is *because of* a relationship with something outside itself. This relationship is entirely mechanical (i.e., in terms of both function and the relations among the various constitutive parts) if there is no intention involved. Insofar as we cannot ascribe an intention to nature, it follows that it is mechanical (and thus explicable through the laws of motion and efficient causality). This means that explaining organized beings through this relationship amounts to explaining them through mechanical principles. However, if, as Kant contends, organized beings are not mechanically explicable, then they cannot be externally purposive, i.e., explicable through their environments. Rather, as "cause and effect of themselves," and "self-organizing," they are *internally* purposive.

Kant's claim, then, is that internal purposiveness and external purposiveness are mutually exclusive: *either* living beings are self-causing (organized), *or* they are caused by something outside of themselves (the environment or interaction with other beings). The disjunctive in Kant's argument has to do with the meaning of internal purposiveness, which implies, first, that organisms are not mechanically explicable, and second, that they are not passive, but actively self-organizing. Environmental external purposiveness, however, implies both: mechanical explicability *and* passivity.

For this reason, Kant suggests that if we are to make sense of the organism-environment relation, i.e., of the fact that organisms are not isolated beings, but *active* members *of* their environments, then we must think of the environment—i.e., of nature as a whole—differently: not as an amalgamation of mechanical relations and forces, but as an organized unity. He writes, "this concept [of self-organization] necessarily leads to the idea of the whole of nature as a system in accordance with the rule of ends, to which idea all of the mechanism of nature in accordance with principles of reason must now be subordinated" (AA 5, 379).

As we have seen, however, Kant was ultimately ambiguous as to the status of organization in nature. The question of whether organized beings *are* reducible to mechanical forces remains unanswered. If they are reducible, then there would be no need to develop a conception of nature as organized—and external purposiveness would suffice to explain their structure and function. If they are not reducible—if they are internally purposive—then such a need would emerge. Kant gestures in both directions, thereby failing to take a clear stance on this crucial point in the Antinomy of Teleological Judgment. Nonetheless, from the preceding we can conclude that for Kant the most relevant point is this: *if* we are to conceive of organisms as self-organizing, then they cannot exist in a nonorganized context. Accordingly, the only way by which to conceive of organisms *in* nature is to conceive of nature as an organized whole. However, what this organized whole *looks like*, *how* organisms interact with one another and within it, and *what kinds* of relationships they develop with and through their environments are questions that Kant does not address. This is not surprising, and not only because the statement is based on a conditional, but also because for Kant nature as organized is an idea of reason. As such, it is not something that can be seen, described, or investigated. Or, as he puts it, "nature as a whole is not given [*gegeben*] as organized" (AA 5, 398).[25]

Thus although Kant offers important insights into the problems that emerge when we begin to conceive of living beings in their environments, he does not provide any clear solutions to these problems. In turn, while many of Kant's contemporaries—as well as Kant himself in his work on physical geography—were offering detailed accounts of living beings in their contexts, none considered the difficulty in the terms Kant articulated in the third *Critique*. For the problem, as Kant saw it, ultimately has to do with whether living beings are conceived as active or passive, as self-organizing or as externally organized. Despite its significance, this question did not emerge as a concern for the majority of thinkers writing on natural history and physical geography, who were more interested in describing living beings in relation to one another and to their contexts than they were with addressing difficult conceptual questions. Goethe and Humboldt were important exceptions.

6.3. Conditions Rather Than Causes: Goethe's Critique of External Teleology

Goethe felt a strong connection to the *Critique of the Power of Judgment*, in large part because it treated nature and art in the same work, regarding them as connected through the faculty of reflecting judgment.[26] This was not, however, the only reason. In addition, Goethe regarded Kant's critique of external teleology as profoundly important. As he explains in "Influence of the New Philosophy," "The antipathy I felt toward ultimate causes [*Endursachen*] was now put in order and justified. I could make a clear distinction between purpose [*Zweck*] and effect [*Wirkung*], and I saw why our human understanding so often confuses the two" (MA 12, 96).[27]

Though Kant had not used the terms that Goethe invokes here, the distinction between purpose and effect roughly maps onto Kant's distinction between external and internal purposiveness. While "purpose" implies an externally determined cause, "effect" speaks of the *acts* of living beings—their effects in the world—and thus alludes to what Kant calls self-organization. Nonetheless, it is interesting that Goethe does not use Kant's terminology. In fact, Goethe rarely uses the words "self-organizing" or "internal purposiveness," preferring instead to use the terms "organisms," "living beings," "*Bildungen*," and above all, "metamorphosis." This preference goes hand in hand with Goethe's approach to the matter of external teleology.

In the 1795 essay on comparative anatomy and osteology, Goethe challenges (external) teleological conceptions of the organism's relation to its environment. To do so, he distinguishes two statements that describe an organism's relation to its environment. In the first statement, we are told that "the fish is for the water [*der Fisch ist für das Wasser*]." This claim, Goethe contends, implies external teleology because the fish is designated as being *for* the water. Thus, the fish exists *for* an end, the water, and insofar as the water is outside of the fish, the end is external. The implication is that the fish *is what it is because* of the (influence of) the water. Its *form* is reduced to its *context*, such that the fish (the form) is taken to be *explicable* through the water (the context). This roughly maps onto the conception of external teleology discussed above and articulated in Section 63 of the third *Critique*.

Following this brief explication, Goethe offers another statement which describes the fish's relation to the water in a different way. He writes, "the fish is in the water and there through the water [*der Fisch ist in dem Wasser und durch das Wasser da*]." This statement, Goethe maintains,

> expresses far more clearly what the first statement leaves hidden in the dark, namely: the existence of a being that we call fish is only possible under the condition of its element that we call water, not only in order to be in it, but also to become in it [*drückt viel deutlicher aus, was in dem erstern nur dunkel verborgen liegt, nämlich die Existenz eines Geschöpfes das wir Fisch nennen, sei nur unter der Bedingung eines Elements das wir Wasser nennen, möglich, nicht allein um darin zu sein, sondern auch um darin zu werden*]. (FA 24, 212)

In the first statement, water is regarded as the external *cause* of the fish. In the second, water is its *condition*. The difference might not seem significant, because we often think of condition *as* cause, or vice versa. In Goethe's time, for instance, various external conditions (above all climate) were regarded as *causes* of different skin colors. As "causes," these climatic conditions are used to *explain* differences. Goethe's point is that we must not confuse condition and cause—a point that is closely linked to his methodology and his critique of a certain form of "explanation," which does not explain but rather explains *away*.

If we return to the first statement, it seems to imply that water, as a cause of the fish, *explains* the fish. This means that the fish's form, growth and development, behavior and activity, are *explicable* through the water. As we have seen, for Goethe, such an "explanation" is no explanation at all. This is because it requires us to "look behind" the phenomenon in order to "explain" it. By explaining the fish through something outside of it, we are no longer investigating the fish (the phenomenon), analyzing its distinctive structure and exploring its relation to its context. Rather, we are turning away from the phenomenon to its explanandum—the water.

The primary problem with external teleology, then, is that it claims to offer an explanation when in fact it does no such thing. By moving away from the phenomenon to something outside or behind it, this form of explanation fails to offer substantial insights into the phenomenon. For this reason, Goethe emphasizes that in morphology "we do not look for causes, but rather the conditions under which the phenomenon appears [*wird nicht nach Ursachen gefragt, sondern nach Bedingungen, unter welchen die Phänomene erscheinen*]" (FA 25, 126).

What then is the difference between cause and condition? And how does investigating conditions, as opposed to causes, allow us to remain with the phenomenon? Let us briefly go back to Goethe's remarks in Italy. A plant's form—its structure—differs depending on its location. Plants of the same species (not to mention leaves on the same plant) look significantly different depending on whether they are growing at the top of the mountain or at its bottom. The geographic location is the condition, the element, in which a plant grows. Accordingly, a plant's form is deeply connected to its condition. The same, Goethe maintains, holds for fish in relation to water. Water is the condition, the element, in which fish live. Without water, fish would be something very different. Their structure—and their parts, the gills, eyes, scales, etc.—would not be what they are outside the water. Accordingly, the way the fish appears (its form) is fundamentally connected to its element, the water.

When we investigate plants and fish in this way, we are not moving beyond the phenomena. Rather, what we are doing is seeing the phenomenon (the form of the plant, the form of the fish) *in* its context, and on that basis recognizing a *relation* between the phenomenon and its context. This contrasts with the view that the water is the *cause* of the fish, which leads us to look "behind" the phenomenon, behind the fish or the plant, to the water or the mountain, in order to "explain" it.

Furthermore, by focusing on the condition of the phenomenon and seeing the phenomenon *in* its condition, Goethe's methodology allows us to see how the condition is not something *outside* the phenomenon, but is internal to it—literally inscribed on its very form. A tree's structure, growth and development are inextricably linked to its context—such that the way it *looks* (its branches, trunk, crown) is crucially dependent on *where* it is. When densely planted, for instance, trees grow long straight trunks and small canopies, but when planted in a grass field, they grow shorter stems and broad crowns.

While a cause is understood as something external to the fish or the plant, such that studying it leads the observer to look beyond the phenomenon, a condition is both external and internal. The plant's form is fundamentally in-formed by its altitude, soil, climate, water, and so on. The same holds for the fish. Its form is in-formed by its condition. By thinking in terms of conditions, we begin to recognize that both plant and fish *express* their context in their very form.[28]

The aim of morphology is to capture precisely this expressiveness of living beings. As Goethe explains, "morphology rests on the conviction that everything that exists must express and indicate itself [*sich anzeigen und deuten muss*]" (LA 1/10, 128). The emphasis on visibility and expressiveness recalls Goethe's terms in "Influence of the New Philosophy," and illuminates why Goethe chose these terms rather than Kant's. As he put it in that essay, the difference is between *purpose* and *effect*. Kant's terms were, by contrast, external purposiveness and internal purposiveness. *Effect* refers to something that can be seen, while *internal* purposiveness refers to something hidden—*internal*—and thus places much less emphasis on expression and visibility. Furthermore, the term *purpose*—whether external or internal—continues to imply an invisible *cause* (an end) that is taken to provide an *explanation* of the form. Goethe's goal was to eliminate all such hidden or occult "causes"—which purport to offer explanations—and instead focus on the phenomenon that appears before us.[29]

By highlighting and explaining the difference between cause and condition, Goethe was able to do precisely that. This distinction also allowed him to take account of the ongoing reciprocal determination that occurs between living being (form) and its condition (context)—*without* reducing the one to the other, i.e., without seeing the living being as "caused" by its context. As Goethe puts it in the passage cited above, water is not an element in which the fish *is* but in which it *becomes*. The fish, in other words, transforms *in* the water (though not *because* of it). The emphasis on *becoming* is important. For it implies that the fish is not a passive being that is simply *caused* by its external element. Rather, as *becoming* the fish is regarded as part of an ongoing relationship *with* the water. For to *become*, the fish must be capable of *responding* to the water in an integrated and unified way. This means that the fish *as a whole organism* is responding to the water.[30] In other words, *all of its parts* are working together, as if in dialogue with one another, in their response. This means, however, that the parts are *parts of* an integrated unity, parts *of* a whole. Only as such can they respond in an integrated and coherent way. Only as such can the fish be understood as an *active* agent in dialogue with its context. By contrast, if the fish were the "outcome" of preexisting parts, which randomly come together and whose relations are solely determined by the external laws of motion, then the fish could not *respond* to its context in a coherent and integrated way. Only *one* of its parts would (randomly) change, and that change would be entirely passive—the outcome of external shaping forces. By contrast, Goethe contends, the fish is actively engaged with its context—and this can be seen in the fact that *all of its parts* reflect the context, and appear to be working together in this response.

By drawing the distinction between cause and condition, and seeing the fish in its condition, Goethe offers a way by which to understand the fish as an integrated unity (a whole) that is also in its context. This significantly alleviates Kant's worries. Kant, however, did not make this distinction. While he acknowledged the need to situate organized beings *within* nature, his insistence that organized nature is an *idea* that cannot be studied or described implies the impossibility of investigating the organism in its context, i.e., of *seeing* it in its context and *seeing* its context within it. In turn, despite acknowledging the need to conceive organized beings within nature—as members of a larger context—Kant's hard-and-fast distinction between organization and nonorganization leads in the opposite direction. For the implication is that organized beings cannot be significantly related to their nonorganized

192   ROMANTIC EMPIRICISM

contexts, which in turn means that organized beings are somehow isolated, apart from the world. This isolation is suggested by Kant's terminology. "Cause and effect of itself" and "*self*-organizing" both denote an inwardness, a turn away from the world that nourishes and maintains the organized being.[31] While Kant's worries about the organism-environment relationship are significant, his solution—or lack thereof—has undesirable implications. By conceiving of the organism as turned inward and failing to develop an account of living beings *in* their environments, Kant inadvertently furnishes a picture of organisms that makes little sense—and which both Goethe and Humboldt reject.[32]

6.4. The *Urformen* of Plants: Capturing the Trees *and* the Forest

In January 1806, Humboldt delivered his first lecture after returning from South America at the Prussian Academy of the Sciences in Berlin. The lecture, which was published in Humboldt's "favorite work," *Ansichten der Natur* [*Views of Nature*] (1808; 1826; 1849), provides insights into Humboldt's methodology and the knowledge he gained during his travels.[33] Titled "Ideen zu einer Physiognomik der Gewächse [Ideas for a Physiognomy of Plants]," the lecture introduces Humboldt's audience to a new way of looking at the natural world: a way that he calls "physiognomy."

Just as we discern a person's character through her gestures, body language, and expressions, so the physiognomist of nature—the new scientist that Humboldt wants to establish—discerns the character of a landscape through the expressions and gestures of plant and animal life. Accordingly, the physiognomist of *plants* is interested in what Humboldt calls the *form* of the plant—those aspects of a plant that make the greatest impression on the viewer: whether it attains to great heights like palms or twists and turns like lianas, whether its leaves are broad like those of the banana tree or narrow like conifer needles. But this is not all. In addition, Humboldt contends that it is through the physiognomy of plants that we can go on to develop a physiognomy of *nature*—that is, an understanding of the contexts, regions, or environments in which the plants grow.

What exactly does Humboldt mean by plant form? And how are we supposed to discern this form? In turn, how is the "science of plant forms" that Humboldt aims to develop different from botany? And how does studying the form of plants lead to the study of the "environment" in which the plants grow?

Humboldt gives a first response to these questions in an early passage in "Ideen zu einer Physiognomik der Gewächse"—a passage that is as complex as it is insightful. He writes,

> whoever is able to grasp [*umfassen*] nature with *one* look [*mit* einem *Blick*] and knows to abstract localized phenomena will see how, with the increase in invigorating heat from the poles to the equator, there is also a gradual increase in organic power and abundance of life. But with this increase, certain beautiful aspects are reserved to each different section of the earth: to the tropics, the diversity and immensity of plant forms; to the north the aspect of meadows and the periodic reawakening of nature upon the first breaths of the spring airs. Besides its particular advantages, each zone has its own character [*Charakter*]. The old and profound power of organization [*die urtiefe Kraft der Organisation*], despite a certain liberty in the abnormal development of specific cases, binds all animal and vegetable life forms to firm, perpetually returning types [*alle tierische und vegetabilische Gestaltungen an feste, ewig wiederkehrende Typen*]. In the same way that one discerns a certain physiognomy in individual organic beings, just as descriptive botany and zoology, in the strict sense of the word, are the analysis of animal and plant forms, so too there is a *physiognomy of nature that applies, without exception, to each aspect of the earth*. (DA 5, 181; VN 160; final emphasis added)

We are told, first, that the "physiognomy of plants" aims to grasp nature with "one look." Reiterating the aim articulated by Buffon, Herder, and Goethe, Humboldt emphasizes vision and the ability to see the many *in* one, or *at once*. This seeing with "one look" is not a compilation of random facts. Rather, the goal is to discern the "character" of a geographic region or zone. This means seeing how the various parts of a region (the various plants) work *together* and *together* make up the region. Accordingly, the goal is to discern continuity and relationality within and across regions, despite "a certain liberty" within nature. In other words, the goal is not simply to observe and collect data, but to grasp how the various parts influence and transform one another, and how *together* they contribute to an integrated and dynamic unity. Seeing, then, is not simply seeing, or—to speak with Goethe—there is a difference between "seeing and seeing." The seeing that Humboldt is invoking here recalls the "thinking seeing [*denkende Betrachtung*]" that he describes in the Introduction to *Kosmos*: a seeing that—through the activity of thinking—detects similarities and differences, draws judgments, and thereby recognizes how the various parts address, respond to, anticipate, or reiterate one another.

Now, to grasp continuity and relationality within a geographic region—and thereby arrive at the "character" of a region—involves, as Humboldt puts it, discerning the "perpetually returning types" of animals and plants. The notion of perpetually returning types echoes Herder's attempt to discern the *Hauptform* in its infinite reiterations. The science that Humboldt aims to develop is a science of appearances and, more specifically, of *reappearing forms*. By studying these reappearing forms, Humboldt claims, we will also be able to study a region or a landscape. In other words, to grasp the distinctive character of a natural environment, it is necessary to discern the forms that emerge within it and understand their relations to one another and to their context.

From this we can surmise the following: Humboldt's idea of plant geography involves discerning the appearance of certain *Urformen* across regions. Once we have determined which basic forms reappear across the earth, and in which relations and contexts, we can move to consider whether there is a relationship between *form* and *context*, i.e., whether certain plant forms grow next to certain other plant forms; which climate, altitude, latitude, and what kind of soil lend themselves to which forms; and, whether certain forms reappear across vastly different geographic contexts, and under which conditions. By posing and responding to these questions, we begin to develop a picture of the relationship between forms and their contexts, and are thereby able to distinguish contexts not only in terms of climate or soil, but also on the basis of the plants (and animals) that inhabit them. These insights will, eventually, lead us to pose the more complex—and crucial—question: how does a particular context exert influence on a particular form, and vice versa, how does a particular form exert influence on its context?

To respond to these questions, we must consider Humboldt's notion of form and its relation to the physiognomy of nature more carefully. As noted above, physiognomy involves discerning character through gesture, body language, and expression. Thus, physiognomy implies visibility and expressiveness. This means that the aims of the physiognomist of nature are to focus on what is most expressive, most striking, what has the greatest "mass

[*Masse*]"—and to locate *therein* the character of the region. As Humboldt puts it,

> physiognomy bases its division, its choice of its types, upon everything that has mass: upon the stem, the branches and appendicular organs (leaf form, leaf position, leaf size, composition and the luster of the parenchyma), that is, upon the now so suitably named "vegetation organs," the organs upon which the preservation (nourishment, development) of the individual depends. (DA 5, 295; VN 239)

This emphasis on immensity, on what is most visible and striking, strongly contrasts with the interests of the botanist, who generally focuses on small, almost hidden parts of the plant—the sexual organs or, at times, the fruit. Thus, while the botanist homes in on what is not impressive, it is precisely "impression" that guides the work of the physiognomist.

This gives us a first insight into what form and physiognomy imply. But it also leaves us with questions. After all, the methodology of the physiognomy of plants is working with the assumption that the external characteristics of a plant, its overall structure and gesture, say something *about* the plant (and also about its context)—an assumption that clearly echoes Goethe's methodology and its concern with what "expresses and indicates itself." How does Humboldt justify this assumption?

As the subtitle of *Kosmos* indicates, Humboldt's goal is to offer a "physical description of the world [*physische Weltbeschreibung*]." A physical *description*, Humboldt emphasizes, differs from a *history*, in that its concern is not with determining the "obscure beginnings of a history of organisms [*den dunkeln Anfängen einer Geschichte der Organismen*]" (*Kosmos* 1, 178–79).[34] Rather a physical description aims to remain with what is visible, expressive, and not move to explain the phenomenon through something invisible, or offer a historical-diachronic account of its origins. Accordingly, Humboldt's choice of words in speaking about his methodology is worth noting. Distinguishing his methodology from "abstraction [*Abstraction*]," he writes that the goal of physical geography is to "depict [*schildern*]" and "observe [*betrachten*]" (*Kosmos* 1, 27–28).

For Humboldt this means focusing on form. Thus, rather than replacing phenomena with something other than themselves (whether a conjectured history, or an external cause), we observe forms and their relations and discern fundamental laws therein. In other words, through forms we arrive at the most important insights *without* losing sight of the visible phenomenon: insights into both the relations between forms (i.e., between living beings) and between forms and their habitats (between living beings and their environments).

But how exactly is the new scientist supposed to discern forms *and* gain insight into the distinctive character of the landscape *through* these forms? Specifically, how is this new scientist to grasp the relationship between a living being and its environment *without* reducing the one to the other (Kant's worry) or regarding them as originally separate entities that come together only after they have independently developed (Sultan's worry)? In other words, how can the physiognomist see the two as members of an ongoing dynamic collaboration—where the one cannot exist without the other?

Humboldt's answer to these methodological questions is art, and more specifically, landscape painting. He contends that the distinctive approach to the natural world cultivated by landscape painting is one that the physiognomist of nature must also seek to cultivate. Why?

For one, the landscape painter is interested in the overall impression that a landscape makes on the viewer. This means that she is interested in the most expressive aspects of a landscape, which give the landscape its unique character. Furthermore, and in contrast to a botanist, who aims to categorize, distinguish, and separate plants, the landscape painter, Humboldt remarks, "binds them" together. Thus, even when the landscape painter portrays different species of plants—for instance palm and fern—she portrays them in their relation to one another, as members of the same context. In turn, when presenting plants of the same genus, or plants that strikingly resemble one another, the painter does not offer outlines of separate trees, but allows them, as Humboldt puts it, to "run one into the other," and thereby portrays them as *members of a forest* (DA 5, 184; VN 162).

To give his audience a concrete sense of what he means, Humboldt considers the diverging ways that a painter and a botanist treat leafy hardwoods. While the botanist distinguishes different hardwoods (oak, beech, walnut), the landscape painter allows them "to run one into the other." This is because the painter is interested in the overall impression that hardwoods make on the viewer—an impression that has to do with their distinctive form *and* with the way in which this form is *informed* by their context. By homing in on form and seeing form in its larger context, then, the landscape painter reveals something that would otherwise be missed: form is inextricably linked to context. *How* a plant *appears*—the size of its leaves and trunk, the shape of its crown, its growth pattern—has to do with *where* it appears, and vice versa—*how* a context *appears* (the kind of impression it makes on us) has to do with the plants that inhabit it.

In this way, a landscape painter captures trees *in* the forest, and captures the forest *through* the trees. This means, however, that she is working with a crucial premise concerning the relationship between trees and forests. For to capture the trees in the forest and the forest through the trees implies that the trees *express* their forest environment, and the forest environment is an *expression* of its trees. In other words, by working with forms, expressions, and gestures, and discerning relations *through* these forms—by showing how the trees are informed by the forest and vice versa—the landscape painter reveals the significance of form and visibility. As such, landscape painting offers a kind of demonstration of Humboldt's assumption concerning expressiveness: we should take expression seriously precisely because the *form* of the tree tells us something not only about the individual tree, but also about its context. But this is not all that landscape painting offers. By presenting trees and forest as interdependent realities—as members of an ongoing collaboration, in which the one can only emerge with and through the other—the landscape painter showcases and highlights the relationship, which is so difficult for us to conceptualize. It is precisely this ability to see and depict the one in and through the other, and to grasp them in one glance, that the new scientist, Humboldt contends, must develop and emulate.

6.5. Plant Forms and Contexts

In the lecture he gave at the Prussian Academy of Sciences, the essay based on the lecture, as well as the essay, *Ideen zu einer Geographie der Pflanzen* (1807) [*Géographie des Plantes* (1805)], Humboldt enumerates different plant forms and considers them in relation to their contexts.[35] These forms are based on "impressions," i.e., the gesture of a plant, and its most striking external characteristics. Accordingly, they do not generally align with taxonomic categories. In turn, following the example of landscape painting, Humboldt's contention is that plant forms will not only teach us about the distinct plants, but also about the landscape in which they grow.

In the essay on plant physiognomy, Humboldt enumerates sixteen plant forms. In the French edition of *Ideen zu einer Geographie der Pflanzen*, i.e.,

Géographie des Plantes, he distinguishes fifteen forms, while in the German edition, he offers seventeen forms.[36] Humboldt is clear that his list is incomplete given that new plants will be discovered and perhaps also new forms. Furthermore, he emphasizes that the forms he distinguishes are based on *his* knowledge—whether gained through personal experience or through reading others' descriptions. This means that there is always the possibility of adding more forms.

When he distinguishes a form, Humboldt describes both its individual characteristics—detailing, for instance, the shape of its leaves, its usual size (height and width), its overall gesture—and its growth patterns—where and when it grows, under which conditions, next to which other plants, and so on. His aims are, he explains, "to dare to come to a recognition of the laws that determine the physiognomy of nature, the scenic vegetational character of the entire surface of the earth, and the vital impression evoked by the aggregation of contrasting forms in various zones of latitude and elevation" (DA 5, 295; VN 239). While the latter two goals might seem to be nonscientific—concerned with understanding the "scenic character" of the earth and the "vital impression" that emerges through careful observation—Humboldt insists that all three go together, such that the first (most scientific sounding) of the goals is only achievable through the latter two.

To understand how these three goals go together, and how studying sixteen or seventeen plant forms will enrich our understanding of nature, it is necessary to consider in some detail a few of the plant forms that Humboldt distinguishes. This will allow us, on the one hand, to gain a concrete sense of how his notion of form differs from taxonomic categorization and, on the other, to understand the connection between the physiognomy of *plants* and the physiognomy of *nature*. In other words, it will allow us to grasp how discerning the "character" of individual plants makes it possible for us to develop a "total impression" of the landscape and thereby discern its character. This, ultimately, will lead us to the "laws" of nature that Humboldt wants to distill.

I will focus on three forms: the conifer (*Nadelholz*), the tall grasses (*Grasform*), and the myrtle (*Myrten-Gewächse*).[37] These three forms are of particular interest because they do not coincide (whether explicitly or implicitly) with any taxonomic categories. Furthermore, in his consideration of the three forms, Humboldt describes both the form itself and its relation to its larger context. Significantly, each of the three forms appears to embody (and thus demonstrate) a different relationship to its context: while one form only appears in a particular context, another appears across vastly different regions. Accordingly, in considering these three forms, we are able to assess Humboldt's goal of trying to understand a region through its plant forms.

The conifer form, which Humboldt identifies with trees bearing needle-shaped leaves (*Nadelholz*), is perhaps the most well-known of the plant forms that Humboldt discusses, at least in the Northern Hemisphere.[38] Pines only appear in the Northern Hemisphere, although other conifers are found in the Southern Hemisphere, and Humboldt notes that they grow in the high mountains of Peru and Mexico. Conifers have, as Humboldt puts it, a "singular appearance." This has to do with their unusual heights (think of the California redwoods), the width of their girth, and "the almost umbrellalike spread of the horizontal or uplifted branches" (DA 5, 273; VN 224). But it also has to do with their needle-like leaves, which Humboldt describes as expressions of the "greatest contraction [*größte Zusammenziehung*]" (DA 5, 276; VN 226). Furthermore, Humboldt notes that conifers are "social plants [*gesellige Pflanzen*]"—a category he develops—insofar as they always grow together. There are whole forests composed of only one or two conifer species (pine forests, for instance), in contrast to the highly heterogeneous rain forests of South America.

In Mexico and Peru, conifers can only be found in the highest (and coolest) regions. This corresponds to conifer growth in Europe, whether on the Pyrenees, the Alps, or in Lapland, which suggests a relationship between conifers and altitude, and allows Humboldt to take "a broad view" of the plant form—a view from which he is able to consider the relationship between conifer and elevation (DA 5, 265; VN 219).

First, he considers the relationship between conifers and the snow line. While in the Pyrenees and Alps, conifers are the trees that reach the highest point before the snow line, in Lapland the birch (a hardwood) reaches further up. Thus as we climb the mountain, we encounter conifers, and then birches. However, upon descending the mountain, we note uniformity in growth. For what *comes after* conifers as we go down is *always* the same. In the Swiss and Italian Alps, and in the Pyrenees, Humboldt notes, conifers are followed by "alpine roses and *Rhododendra*" (DA 5, 266; VN 291).[39] In Lapland, the same pattern is found, but with a different species of rhododendrons. The same, strikingly, applies in Mexico and Peru. In these regions too, we find that blossoming shrubs begin to appear immediately after conifers as we descend the mountains. In this instance, however, the blossoming shrubs do not belong to the genus Rhododendra or even the family Ericeae, but to an entirely different taxonomic family.[40] Humboldt writes:

> Should we wish to pursue this last zone of vegetation before the line of perpetual snow all the way to the tropics, by our own observations we would name in the Mexican tropics, *Cnicus nivalis* and *chelone gentianoides*; in the cold mountainous regions of New Granada, the woolly *Espeletia grandiflora, E. corymbosa*, and *E. argentea*; in the Andes of Quito, *Culcitium rufescens, C. ledifolium*, and *C. nivale*—yellow-blossomed Compositae, which here take the place of the somewhat more northerly hairy-leaved shrubs of New Granada that are so physiognomically similar to them, the *Espeletia*. (DA 5, 266; VN 219)

Cnicus nivalis and *Espletia grandiflora*, which grow in Mexico and Peru, belong to the Daisy family, while the flowers in the north largely belong to the Ericeae family. Nonetheless, they bear clear physiognomic resemblance to one another. They are all shrubs with blossoms. Furthermore, they all make for a striking contrast with the blossomless conifers that come before them. Thus, Humboldt concludes, "Such replacement and repetition of similar, almost identical forms in regions separated by oceans or broad expanses of land is a wondrous law of nature. It holds sway even over the most peculiar types of flora" (DA 5, 266; VN 219). By focusing on form, rather than taxonomic categories, Humboldt recognizes a pattern across the various regions: in Mexico and Peru, just as in the Swiss and Italian Alps, the Pyrenees and Lapland, conifers are followed by bushy shrubs with striking blossoms.

This should give us some pause. For not only do we find plants of different species and families bearing strong physiognomic resemblance to one another. We also find that these physiognomic resemblances have some relation to *where* the plants grow (i.e., on a mountain, at a certain altitude) and *next to whom*. Conifers on mountains are followed by *the same form*: that of bushy shrubs with striking blossoms. What Humboldt is pointing to is a *physiognomic pattern* that reveals relationships *between* different plants and *between* plants and their regions. By focusing on form, Humboldt discerns a "reiteration" of forms and relations across regions. The daisies in the Southern Hemisphere *replace* and *repeat* the rhododendrons in the Northern Hemisphere.

A similar insight, Humboldt writes, can be gained if we consider the form of the long grasses, where the same form—though not the same species—reappears in different regions. While the Bambusa (bamboo) is "completely absent from the New Continent," the Guadua—an extremely strong grass that can become very tall like the Bambusa—is "exclusively indigenous to it" (DA 5, 281–82; VN 230). Tall grasses of different species, which strikingly resemble one another, appear in distant regions of the world under similar climatic conditions. As in the case of the conifers in relation to the shrubs, so here we find a *repetition and replacement of form*. Tall grasses appear in the tropics and in Asia, and their appearance is connected to a number of geographic factors, including soil, climate, humidity, latitude, and altitude.

The same is the case if we consider the myrtle form, which Humboldt does not identify with either the taxonomic family Myrtaceae or the genus Myrtus, but with those plants that exhibit "a delicate form with stiff, gleaming, densely packed, mostly nonserrated, small, and foraminous leaves" (DA 5, 288; VN 235).[41] By disentangling the myrtle form from a taxonomic category, Humboldt finds myrtles in different regions across the earth. Myrtle plants, he writes,

> give a distinct character to three regions of the earth's surface: southern Europe, especially the islands (limestone cliffs and trachyte rocks) that rise up from the basin of the Mediterranean; the continent of Australia, adorned with Eucalyptus, Metrosideros, and Leptospermum; and a section of land that lies between the lines of the tropics, which is partly low and flat, and partly elevated nine to ten thousand feet above sea level—the high comb of the Andes in South America. (DA 5, 288; VN 235)

The European myrtle plant and the Australian species are part of the same taxonomic family, Myrtaceae. However, the plants found near Quito in Ecuador, the third of the regions Humboldt lists, do not belong to the family Myrtaceae, but are "of myrtlelike appearance" (DA 5, 289; VN 235). These plants, Humboldt writes, are "physiognomically so reminiscent of the myrtle form" that they must be regarded as members of it.

As in the previous two cases, Humboldt is pointing to physiognomic similarities that are independent of taxonomic categories. By focusing on form, we are surprised to find variations of the same forms repeated across vastly distant regions. While numerous species and families are indigenous to only one part of the world, forms *are not* indigenous, but are found in many different parts of the world. One can thus draw the conclusion that there are certain fundamental forms (*Urformen*), which, as Humboldt puts it, "morphologically replace one another in the different parts of the world" (DA 5, 281; VN 230).

What does this tell us? What do we learn by focusing on plant forms in relation to their region and geographical distributions? What, in other words, is the significance of the "wondrous law of nature," of the fact that certain forms reappear across distant zones, at times in different contexts?[42]

When considering the conifer form, a certain pattern becomes apparent, which we would have otherwise missed. If we did not think in terms of forms, but rather in terms of species or genus, we would not have noticed that blossoming shrubs on mountains always come after conifers. Accordingly, by focusing on form, we begin to see that *certain forms* occupy *certain regions* in *certain ways*. This allows us to discern a relationship between form and context. We see that the form conifer and the form blossoming shrub often appear together, and they appear in cool, mountainous regions.

By contrast, if we look at the myrtle form, it appears as if there is no connection between form and context. In this case we find the same form appearing in very different contexts: in almost impenetrable forests (Australian eucalyptus forests) and in sparser regions near the water (Southern Europe). This seems to suggest that form is *independent* of context. Indeed, some of Humboldt's statements might be read to imply precisely that.

Speaking of the willow form, for instance, Humboldt writes that "among willows of the most contrasting climates, the similarity of the foliage, the branching, and the whole physiognomic formation is exceedingly great, perhaps greater even than that of the conifers" (DA 5, 287; VN 234). Furthermore, Humboldt insists that while we can explain the increase or decrease in *populations* through environmental factors, we cannot explain *form* through environmental factors. This is how he puts it:

> The composition of the soil and the conditions of temperature and humidity, upon all of which the nourishment of plants depends, certainly promote the thriving and increase in the number of individuals that make up a species; the tremendous height, however, to which the trunks of only a few ascend while in the midst of many closely related species of the same genus is not determined by soil and climate, but rather, in the plant and animal kingdoms, by a *specific organization, by innate natural qualities* [*spezifische Organisation, durch innere Naturanlagen bedingt*]. (DA 5, 273; VN 224; emphasis added)

In other words, while geographic and climatic conditions play a role in determining whether a population thrives, they do not "explain" the specific organization or innate natural qualities of living beings. While we can draw on these conditions to explain why there are so many conifers in a particular region and so few in another, we cannot draw on them to "explain" the distinctive form of the conifer.

Immediately after this passage, Humboldt offers an example to illuminate what he means by "specific organization" and "innate natural qualities." He distinguishes two very short trees: a two-inch willow that has been "stunted by cold or the mountain altitude," and a small phanerogam, native to the southern tropics, which "reaches a height of barely three French lines [i.e., a quarter of an inch]." The two trees are very short, but their shortness is accounted for differently. The two-inch willow is not short *by its specific organization*. Rather, its shortness is clearly due to geographic and climatic influences. The phanerogam's height, by contrast, has to do with its specific organization.

It is striking that Humboldt turns to the willow to make this point—i.e., the form which he also describes as the "most persistent." The willow's growth is significantly stunted by certain climatic influences, and it does not achieve its usual heights. Even the most persistent form is affected by its geographic and climatic conditions. And so the implication is that form—as persistent as it might be—is *also* sensitive and plastic, growing in dialogue with its context.

What exactly is the nature of this dialogue? If we observe the two-inch willow, we see that every one of its parts is affected by its conditions: not only its branches and leaves, but also its trunk and roots are extremely small. This shows that its parts are not acting separately, but in unison. Thus, although the roots are not as affected by the strong winds and high altitude as the other parts of the tree, they do not grow large, but achieve a size that is commensurate with the rest of the plant. Accordingly, the willow's parts respond to their context *together*. In other words, they act as parts *of* a whole, which emerge and grow in dialogue with one another. This reveals—along the lines articulated by Goethe in his explication of the fish in water—that it is the willow *as a whole* that responds to its environment. Otherwise, the various parts would not act in unison, and the roots would grow in ways that do not cohere with the branches and leaves, for instance. But that is not how the willow develops. For this reason, *each* of the willow's parts is an expression of both the willow form *and* the willow's context. *Each* of the parts tells the story of the willow as it responds to its context.

This gives us a better understanding of Humboldt's conception of form. For form does not imply an isolated being that is morphologically distinguished from its environment. Rather, form points to *both* the distinctive internal organization of a living being *and* the ways in which this internal organization responds to its environment. In the case of the two-inch willow, we see in the willow itself—inscribed in its very structure—not only the distinctive willow shape, but also the environment in which the willow has developed.

That form is an expression of both a living being and its context is also evident in leafy hardwoods—to return to the example Humboldt invokes when speaking of the landscape painter. Consider the oak. A solitary oak growing on a hill looks decisively different from an oak growing in a forest. The crown of a solitary oak spreads out in all directions, eventually achieving a dome shape. By contrast, the forest oak develops a small crown, and its growth is patterned on the growth of the other trees in the forest. An oak in a hardwood forest is an expression not only of the individual tree or the species oak, but also of the forest itself. The forest is not "outside" the individual oak tree, but literally inscribed in it its very form—in the same way that the mountain and the wind are inscribed on the two-inch willow. Ultimately, then, form tells us the story of the plant *and* its world.

This has significant implications for understanding the relationship between living beings and their environment. For one, it reveals that the relation between them is not and indeed cannot be an either-or relation, as Kant had put it in his critique of external teleology. For Kant, the problem was ultimately logical or definitional: the definition of an organized being as "cause and effect of itself," as self-causing, excludes the possibility of external conditions being causes of the organism. From this perspective, only the disjunctive either-or is coherent. *Either* organisms are self-organizing, *or* they are caused by something external to themselves. Kant realized that this either-or was untenable: clearly organisms are *both* self-organizing *and* influenced by their environment. However, he found no way by which to accommodate these apparently conflicting claims.

Humboldt's focus on forms offers a way out of Kant's dilemma. On the one hand, it allows us to see how forms *reappear* across the earth. This shows that forms persist. The implication is that they are not mere outcomes of their surroundings, but, as Humboldt puts it, possess "specific organization" and "innate natural qualities." On the other hand, the reappearance of forms across the earth happens *differently*. Either the form is affected by its context (e.g., the two-inch willow or the oak) or it appears in relation to other forms and in specific geographic locations (e.g., the conifer and shrub). Living beings, in other words, are sensitive to their surroundings—they are changed by climate, soil, altitude, geography, and human activity—even if they are not reducible to their surroundings.

In contrast to Kant, Humboldt does not offer an argument, but a perspective—mirroring the perspective of the landscape painter—from which we are able to see that living beings express *both* themselves *and* the world in which they live. By taking up this perspective, we do not commit the two usual mistakes: of either regarding the living being in opposition to its context (as an autonomous, enclosed entity, or as somehow existing before its context) or seeing it as a mere outcome of its context. Rather, the focus on form allows us to see living beings *in relation* to their context. Thus, in the place of the logical disjunctive, *either-or*, this perspective offers a *both-and*: living beings are *both* self-organizing *and* formed by their context.

Through the both-and perspective, logical oppositions are reconciled. The idea of a self-organizing being or a persisting form no longer appears to contradict the notion of a living being that responds to and modifies in relation to its context. Rather, from this perspective, the two are shown to *go hand in hand*. And they go hand in hand both epistemologically (i.e., for us knowers) and ontologically (for the forms). Epistemologically, we cannot separate the two because it is only by recognizing the persistence of form that we are able to discern how forms adapt or modify in varying contexts. To return to the willow, we (as knowers) are able to discern climatic influence *only because* we know the form (i.e., the willow form). If we were not familiar with the willow form, we would not be able to discern the influence of the environment on this particular willow—and would erroneously assume that the willow is by its "specific organization" and "innate natural qualities" short.

Ontologically, the persistence of form is precisely what *enables* the form's plasticity, i.e., its ability to respond to and modify in relation to its context. For it is only if the form is persistent—if the living being is a unity composed of integrated parts—that it can *respond* to its context. As we have seen, it is the two-inch willow *as a whole* that responds to its context. Not just one of its parts, but all of its parts, express both the willow and the willow's context.

By turning our attention to form, we begin to recognize something that we would otherwise miss: living beings are neither passive in relation to their environments—the mere outcome of their environments—nor self-enclosed entities that are separate from their environments. Rather, they are *both* possessive of innate qualities *and* sensitive to their contexts. By taking up the *both-and* perspective that the notion of form affords us, by beholding the two *at once*, we begin to see that it is *precisely because* living beings are integrated unities that they can *also* respond to their environments. In other words, through this double focus we are able to overcome the conceptual problem that Kant had elaborated—a problem that may perhaps be impossible to overcome if we remain on the level of definition or argument. In the place of conceptual distinctions, Humboldt offers a perspective, a point of view, from which living beings are revealed as *transforming forms,* as *both* self-organizing *and* open, integrated *and* porous. Or, as Humboldt puts it, "In all living organisms... are paired the fixed and the fluid" (DA 5, 116; VN 107).

6.6. The Physiognomy of Plants: The Physiognomy of Nature

Thus far we have considered how focusing on forms allows us to understand living beings in relation to their surroundings. This is not, however, the extent of Humboldt's goal. In addition, he contends that the focus on form allows us to grasp the "physiognomy of nature." Accordingly, the question is: why do we need *form* to understand not only living beings but also their world?

As noted earlier, Humboldt writes that the goal of the physiognomy of plants is to "dare to come to a recognition of the laws that determine the physiognomy of nature in general," which involves taking in "the scenic vegetation character of the entire surface of the earth, and the vital impression evoked by the aggregation of contrasting forms in various zones of latitude and elevation" (DA 5, 294; VN 239). The aim, in other words, is not to rest contented with the sixteen or seventeen plant forms that he outlines, but to discern *through* these forms and their relations the scenic character of "the entire surface of the earth." Accordingly, the goal is to see the different forms together, and more specifically to see how *together* they make up a landscape or region. In taking up this perspective, we arrive at the physiognomy of *nature*.

As noted earlier, the physiognomy of nature concerns the most expressive elements of a particular landscape—mass, height, gesture, and so on. An "Italian landscape" looks decisively different from a "tropical landscape," and the physiognomist of nature homes in on those features that most clearly embody and express the different landscapes. The underlying assumption is that the expressive elements of a landscape—the size and shape of its trees, for instance—tells us something *about* the landscape. In other words, the assumption is that the impression that plants *together* make tells us something about the *context* in which they grow. On what grounds is this assumption justified?

The answer to this question is connected to Humboldt's general interest in and emphasis on plants, and his claim that the physiognomy of *plants* will naturally lead to the physiognomy of *nature*. Accordingly, a first answer to this question involves exploring the distinctive character of plants—and how they differ from animals.

Perhaps the most obvious difference involves place and movement. Although as seeds, plants can travel vast distances, once in the soil, they are largely sessile.[43] Recalling Herder's elucidation of the different ways that living beings inhabit their worlds, Humboldt writes in *Kosmos* that once plants "have taken root, they become dependent on the soil and on the strata of air surrounding them. Animals, on the contrary, can at pleasure migrate from the equator toward the poles" (*Kosmos* 1, 183). Although not all animals can easily migrate—and many can only travel short distances in their brief lifetimes—it is certainly the case that animals are not rooted in a particular location in the way that plants are. This (greater) independence from any one location is evident in the fact that animals maintain a metabolic system that is (largely) detached from their surroundings. While this is most clear in warm-blooded animals, even cold-blooded animals, Humboldt contends, exert some control over their body temperature—through movement. By going into the sun, they are able to regulate their body temperatures. In this way, animals express a form of self-sovereignty and self-regulation that plants do not.

In contrast to animals, Humboldt elaborates, plants "live primarily in and through their outer surface," i.e., through leaves and stomata. In other words, plants' most important organs—their vital organs—are not hidden or invisible but turned outward, facing their environment. This morphological fact reveals plants' distinctive dependence "upon their surrounding medium" (DA 5, 246; VN 206). In fact, the deep connection between plants and their contexts makes it extremely difficult to draw a hard-and-fast distinction between the individual plant and its environment.[44] And it is also the reason why plants are not only expressions of their species, but also of their specific contexts—the two-inch willow does not only tell us the story of the willow, but also the story of its environment (and environmental change). This context is in turn not expressed in only one of its parts (e.g., its crown or roots), but in *every part*: the roots of the plant as well as its crown and branches manifest its context.

While animals also express their contexts, they do so with far less specificity and less visibility. For instance, a fish's form clearly expresses its element, the water. But it does not express the *specific* body of water that it inhabits. This makes sense in light of animals' migratory nature. Furthermore, although specific parts of animals (such as bones and tooth enamel) tell us something about their history, they do not tell the story of a *specific* context (region, environment), but relate the *individual* animal's story, i.e., its overall health, its nutrition, its stress levels, and so on.[45] These parts are, also, far less visible than the outwardly turned parts of the plants, and thus do not make a strong impression on the viewer. In the plant, *every part* is an expression of the plant's history *and* specific context. From roots to branches, to rings, foliage, and canopy, the plant *as a whole* expresses the *particular place* it inhabits.

Plants are, however, not only receptive in relation to their surroundings; they are also active within it. The *kind* of forest that we encounter—whether it is cool and humid, or temperate and dry, whether its soil is nutrient rich or poor, how much carbon it stores, and how much rain it receives—depends on the plants that make it up. The forest environment, in other words, is largely realized in and maintained through the activities of its trees. Of course, animals also shape their environments (e.g., beavers building dams). However, they do not do this to the same extent or degree as plants. A region *is* what it is (cool and humid, for instance) because of the kinds of plants within it (bearing large leaves which provide shading and evaporation, for example). Or, alternately, a region changes because of the disappearance of plants. As Humboldt notes, "if a region has lost all of its plants, if the sand is shifting and lacks all sources of water, then the hot, vertically rising air hinders the precipitation in clouds, and millennia must pass before organic life presses into the interior of the waste from its green shores" (DA 5, 181; VN 159). Similarly, plants are not only influenced by the quality of the soil, but also influence the soil: either by transforming it in ways that prohibit other plants to grow or by making it fertile, thereby paving the way for future plants. Heaths, for instance, make the soil sterile, and for this reason, Humboldt notes, "have dominated these regions completely" (DA 1, 51; EGP 66). By contrast, cryptogams in the Northern Hemisphere and mosses and lichens in the tropics "prepare the soil for the growth of grasses and herbs," thereby playing a determining role in the region's future (DA 5, 104; VN 99).

What does this deep connection between plants and their contexts tell us? First, it confirms Goethe's distinction between condition and cause. To speak of environments as somehow "causing" plants is a mistake, because it implies that environments precede the plants that make them up. The truth, however, is the opposite: what we mean by "environment" is inextricably tied to the living beings, and in particular the plants, that make it up. Accordingly, an environment is *not* independent of its vegetation. It is not a stable backdrop for animal and plant activity. Nor is vegetation (and animal life) independent of the environment. Thus, with Goethe, we can say that plants and their contexts are reciprocally conditioning, or that each is a condition in and through which the other flourishes—or not. Perhaps we can say that living beings and their environments are *collaborators*, insofar as the one can only be what it is through the other. Neither causes nor precedes the other; rather, each is influenced by and influences the other, and the two can only exist *together*. This was the ecological insight at the heart of Humboldt's investigations at Lake Valencia. Without the trees, the climate and soil fundamentally transformed.

This also tells us why the study of plant *forms* is integral to—and a necessary first step toward—the study of nature more generally, i.e., the physiognomy of nature. For one, plants have a deep connection to their context, which involves both dependence on and sensitivity toward context *and* the ability to bring about major transformations in that context. Furthermore, this deep connection is expressed in the structure of the plant. This has to do, first, with plant morphology—plants are turned outward and their vital organs are visible—and second, with the fact that plant forms shift in relation to their context (i.e., plants of the same species look decisively different at the top of the mountain than they do at its bottom). All of this means that there is nothing strange or arbitrary about studying plant forms in order to study regions. It makes perfect sense, insofar as the form of the plant is *informed* by where the plant grows, and, vice versa, the form of the region is *informed* by the kinds of plants that inhabit it. The physiognomy of plants directly leads to the physiognomy of nature. The form of the one is inextricably linked to the form of the other. By studying form, then, we achieve a higher perspective—a perspective from which we can see how the living being is an expression of its context, and how the context is an expression of its living beings.

6.7. Humboldt's Ecological Insight

Humboldt's emphasis on plants was, in many ways, novel. For although many thinkers before him had examined the relationship between animals and climate or soil—Buffon, Herder, Kant, and Eberhard Zimmermann (1743–1815)—few had focused on the relationship between plants and geography.[46] In turn, while European and Creole botanists such as Carl Ludwig Willdenow (1765–1812) and Francisco José Caldas (1768–1816) emphasized context, they did not see the relationship between plants and their environments as reciprocal.[47] This insight, however, is precisely what Humboldt sought to articulate.

By coupling Herder's and Goethe's notion of form with the perspective of landscape painting, Humboldt developed what we might describe as an "expanded conception of form," that is, an understanding of form as an expression of the manifold and multidirectional relations between a living being and its context. Specifically, through the double focus that the expanded notion of form enables, Humboldt overcame the difficulties that our usual cognitive procedures encounter—of seeing objects as originally separate, and regarding their relations in terms of external causality, i.e., in linear or one-sided terms. By focusing on form, Humboldt was able to see plants as both active and passive in their contexts, see how they are both creators and receivers—and in this way challenge reductive accounts of living beings *and* static conceptions of their relations. Thus, by working with the idea of form, which at first appears to stand in opposition to a modern ecological interest, Humboldt was able to better grasp the distinctive relationship that plants have to their context, and thereby provided crucial clues for understanding the relationship between living beings and environments more generally.

In important ways, Humboldt brought Goethe's distinction between cause and condition to further realization. Living beings are not caused by their environments. Rather, their environments are the conditions in which they develop. To this Humboldt added: living beings are *also* the conditions in which environments develop. There is no relation of external causality here, i.e., between two originally separate entities. Rather, what he discerned is a productive relating over time that resembles the causal nexus that Kant had reserved for organized beings.

What Humboldt saw, then, and what he tells the reader in *Kosmos*, is that integrated unities are not only to be found in living beings, but also in the relations between living beings and nonliving beings, in the relations between trees, water, soil, altitude, latitude, human activity, and so on. To understand life, Humboldt concluded, it is not adequate to conceive of life as something separate, inwardly turned, and independent from what is not-life. Rather, to understand life requires recognizing that life and not-life engage in ongoing, lifelike processes or relations which we call nature. This was, and remains, Humboldt's most important ecological insight.

7
Embodied Cognition
Humboldt and the Art of Science

In August 1794, five years before sailing to South America, Humboldt drew up a list of the scientific tasks that he wished to accomplish. The list was part of a letter to Schiller, whom Humboldt had met two years earlier, in July 1792. Schiller invited Humboldt to contribute to his journal, *Die Horen*, and Humboldt's letter was, in part, a response to this invitation. Though *Die Horen* was publishing works by other young authors—including women, such as Caroline von Wolzogen, Sophie Mereau, and Amalie von Imhoff—Humboldt was the only scientist to have ever been invited to contribute. He jumped at the opportunity, and the letter—as well as the long list—evidence his enthusiasm.

It is perhaps surprising that Humboldt's scientific goals were articulated in a letter to Schiller, a poet and philosopher who had distinguished himself from Goethe on the grounds that while Goethe defended the rights of nature, he (Schiller) defended the rights of freedom. Even more surprising is the manner in which Humboldt addresses Schiller, and the way in which he enlists Schiller to his projects. Following a quotation from Pliny's *Natural History*, Humboldt turns to Schiller, as if to an intimate friend, and writes: "You sense with me that there is something higher to look for, and to find" (JB 346).[1] This desire to form a connection with Schiller is made even more evident in the following sentence, where Humboldt places Schiller in the same camp as Aristotle and Pliny, who stand in contrast to the "contemporary archivers of nature." Humboldt writes: "Aristotle and Pliny who had connected human aesthetic sense and education with the description of nature [*Naturbeschreibung*], certainly had a more expansive perspective than our contemporary archivers of nature [*Registratoren der natur*]." In other words, Humboldt—and Schiller—are to be aligned with the expansive science developed by Aristotle and Pliny: a science that couples "aesthetic sense and education" with "the description of nature." The "contemporary archivers of nature" lack this aesthetic sense and education, and thus fail to develop a capacious science.

In the lines that follow, Humboldt offers a sense of this science:

> The general harmony in form, the problem of whether there is an original plant form [*ursprüngliche Pflanzenform*] which manifests itself in a thousand gradations; the distribution of these forms across the earth; the different impressions of happiness and melancholy that plants inspire in the sensitive person; the contrast between the dead, unmoving rock-masses, between the apparently inorganic tree trunks and living plants, which gently cover corpses with mitigating flesh; the history and geography of plants, or the historical presentation of the general distribution of herbs on the earth, an unstudied part of general world history; exploration of the oldest plants in their tombs (fossils, stone coal, turf, etc.); the gradual hospitability of the earth; the immigration and succession [*Züge*] of social and isolated plants; maps about which plants followed which peoples; a general history of agriculture; comparison of cultivated plants with pets, the origin of both; extinction; which plants hold more firmly, and which more loosely, to the law of similar form; the wilding of cultivated plants . . . [the clearing up of] general confusions in the geography of plants through colonization. These appear to me to be the objects that are worthy of further thought and which have hardly been considered. (JB 346–47)

At first sight, it is not only the length of Humboldt's list that is striking, but also the apparent disparity between the different tasks he enumerates. How, one might wonder, are "the impressions of happiness and melancholy" in any way connected to the "immigration and succession of social and isolated plants," and why are "apparently inorganic tree trunks" related to the history of human immigration and the geography of plants? The list, in other words, seems just that: a list of unrelated tasks that Humboldt wishes to pursue. However, Humboldt's opening lines suggest that these tasks are not at all disparate. They are deeply connected—and it is in discerning their connection that science becomes capacious.

The claim, then, is that Aristotle and Pliny achieved this capacious form of science by joining "aesthetic sense and education with the description of nature." Through this joining, they were able to consider a multitude of natural phenomena, find harmony among them, discern their many forms and relations (including their relations to the human mind), discover connections between feeling and knowing, and trace the ways in which human history has affected natural history, and vice versa. Why does Humboldt enlist Schiller to his project of developing a capacious science—and how does this relate to Humboldt's sense for the need to find "something higher," which they apparently share?

Clearly, Humboldt is presenting his own program, which he goes on to carry out over the next decades, beginning with his travels in South America. Furthermore, Humboldt is expressing his intuition that art and artistic tools are necessary for the realization of this program. But this is not all. By addressing Schiller as a comrade of sorts, Humboldt is suggesting that Schiller has some understanding of this capacious science and has perhaps even contributed to it. As Humboldt puts it, Schiller *senses* with him that there is something higher to look for, and to find. Schiller, it appears, may know what Humboldt is looking for—and may have already indicated *how* to find it.

In 1794, Schiller was working on the *Letters on the Aesthetic Education of Humanity* [*Über die ästhetische Erziehung des Menschen in einer Reihe von Briefen*] (1794–95). In these letters, he argues that aesthetic experience and education are uniquely able to overcome the conflict between the intellectual and sensuous sides of human nature—or, as he calls them, the "form drive [*Formtrieb*]" and the "sense drive [*Sachtrieb*]" (NA 20, 344). In enabling us to overcome this conflict, Schiller contends, aesthetic experience and education have a singular moral significance. This is because so long as we do not overcome the conflict between our opposing drives, we are unfree. One part of our selves remains subordinated to another part. Either our sensuous side compels our intellectual side, as is the case when we are driven to act in hedonistic ways, or our intellectual side compels our sensuous side, as when we coerce ourselves to follow the moral law. In both cases, there is an internal conflict, which keeps us from acting out of our *whole* selves. This means that our actions are not founded on harmony and unity within ourselves. Yet, Schiller contends, this unity is the ground of moral freedom (NA 20, 373). Unless we can act out of our *whole* selves, we are not free—but remain constrained (by one or the other of the two drives)—and it is only by overcoming this inner conflict that we are in a position to achieve moral freedom: to act *as whole human beings*.

What makes art so significant in this regard has to do with the fact that it is both sensuous and meaningful: a sensuous appearance that has assumed a meaningful form. As such, it engages both our sensible and our rational sides, and does so in a harmonious way. In a work of art, the sensuous appearance does not stand in opposition to the meaningful form, and vice versa. Rather, the two work together. For this reason, a work of art differs from both merely agreeable works and merely intellectual ones. While a merely agreeable work only moves our senses, a merely intellectual one only moves our intellect. Both, then, fail to harmonize the sensuous and the intellectual. A work of art does this because it is able to engage our intellectual and sensuous sides in a way that allows them to work together, rather than stand in conflict with one another. And through this experience, we overcome the conflict within ourselves and achieve a higher standpoint (NA 20, 360). Schiller's claim, then, is that aesthetic experience has the potential to lead to a higher synthesis within the human being, and artworks are an expression (a "symbol") of this higher synthesis that we, as individuals, should strive to achieve (NA 20, 353).

As we have seen, Humboldt was interested in the arts, and in their potential to transform scientific inquiry. Landscape painting provides the student of nature with crucial insights into *how* to look at nature and *what* to look for. However, Humboldt's interest in the arts—and in aesthetic experience more generally—extends beyond landscape painting and its significance for science. His own writings were, in a significant sense, works of art.

In the Preface to *Ansichten der Natur*—whose title intimates vision and the visual arts—Humboldt explains that his essays seek to offer an "aesthetic treatment of great scenes of nature." To describe the essays, he coins the term *Naturgemälde*, which literally means nature paintings, and alludes to portraiture in the visual arts.[2] The essays certainly possess a painterly quality, in that they furnish a view or a portrait of a particular aspect of nature, and thereby mirror the aims of landscape painting. Just as a painting depicts a specific landscape—a mountain or a valley, a desert or an ocean—so also the essays consider a particular kind of geographic region or zone: steppes and deserts, waterfalls and rivers, volcanoes, jungles, and so on.

However, in addition to being aesthetic works that aim to heighten the reader's sense of a place through vivid depictions, the essays are, Humboldt emphasizes, works of science. In the Preface to the second and third editions, he writes of the "dual direction" of the book, noting that the essays seek to join a "literary with a purely scientific goal." Accordingly, each essay has *both* aesthetic and scientific ends. Or, as he puts it, he wishes "to occupy the imagination and at the same time, through the increase of knowledge, to enrich life with ideas" (DA 5, xi; VN 27). This is because Humboldt's aim is to offer a "living depiction [*lebendige Schilderung*]" of nature—not a dead one (DA 5, 142; VN 159; see also *Kosmos* 1, 55). His goal, in other words, is to depict nature as dynamic and developing, as an expressive reality of which we are part, and to which we belong—not as a static, mute, and indifferent object.

Humboldt dedicates *Ansichten der Natur* to "embattled minds." By following him "into the thickets of the forest, into the immeasurable steppes, and out upon the spine of the Andes range," Humboldt writes, these embattled minds will arrive at a higher standpoint. Though this higher standpoint is not explicitly identified with a moral standpoint, Humboldt's concluding remarks point in that direction. The Preface to the first edition ends with a passage from Schiller's 1803 play, *The Bride from Messina* [*Die Braut von Messina*], which begins with the line "In the mountains is freedom" (DA 5, x; VN 26). The implication is that the aesthetic experience of nature carries moral significance—or, more specifically, that through an aesthetic experience of nature we are able to arrive at a higher standpoint ("the mountain"), in which conflicts are reconciled, and new light is shed not only on nature, but also on our relation to nature, and our moral lives. Embattled minds, in other words, might find solace and moral hope, even freedom, in the experience of nature.

From this we can conclude that, for Humboldt, the aesthetic experience of nature plays a crucial role in the realization of both *scientific* and *moral* ends. In turn, by aesthetic experience, Humboldt means the direct experience of being in nature as well as the indirect experience of nature through works of art. In fact, Humboldt maintains that his own writings strive to provide a substitute for the direct experience of nature—and they do this *precisely because* they are also works of art (DA 1, 66; EGP 75).

Immediately several questions arise. Why does Humboldt regard aesthetic experience—whether immediate or mediated—as crucial for both science and morals? And how does he justify this view? In turn, what exactly does Humboldt mean by aesthetic experience? Finally, and perhaps most crucially, how do his essays seek to realize his many goals? How, in other words, do Humboldt's *Naturgemälde* aim to offer a "living depiction" of nature, which both expands our understanding of the natural world *and* stimulates moral reflection?

These questions will be the focus of this chapter and answering them will (in part) involve an examination of how Humboldt took up and expanded Schiller's insights concerning aesthetic experience and its significance. While Humboldt does not follow Schiller's conceptualization of aesthetic experience and its significance to the letter, he does so in spirit. In his writings, Humboldt describes the landscapes that he experienced with a vivid concreteness that aims to imaginatively place the reader on the foot of the granite mountain that separates the lush valleys of Caracas and the arid steppes, in the narrow and crowded canoe that flowed down the Orinoco for weeks on end, in the jungle at midnight, where, suddenly, hundreds of animals begin to shriek and cry, and in the contrasting stillness of the midday silence. His aim is to capture the full experience of *being there*, of smelling, hearing, touching, and seeing the landscape. In other words, his aim is to develop an *embodied* aesthetics, one which speaks to the *whole individual*—the individual not merely as a sensuous or as an intellectual being, but as *both*.

Humboldt's interest in developing an embodied aesthetics that addresses the whole individual is based on his view that genuine knowledge of nature is not purely intellectual, but also aesthetic and thus embodied. In other words, knowledge involves the senses, feeling, and imagination, and cannot be divorced from lived experience. As I will argue in the following, it is precisely in his conceptualization *and* realization of this insight that Humboldt remains relevant for contemporary environmental concerns.

7.1. "Truth to Nature": Humboldt's Understanding of Truth in Art

Humboldt is hardly known as a philosopher or historian of art and aesthetics. Yet, the second volume of *Kosmos* offers a lengthy exploration of the relationship between the history of art and the history of science. As Humboldt explains in volume 3 of *Kosmos*, while the first volume examines "the pure objectiveness of external phenomena," in the second, his aim is to consider nature "as the reflection of the image impressed by the senses upon the inner man, that is, upon his ideas and feelings" (*Kosmos* 3, 386). The goal, in other words, is to see nature *through* human ideas and feelings *about* nature, which are most clearly and eloquently expressed in art.

This makes the second volume a bit of an outlier in the five-volume set. Why, many have wondered, has Humboldt suddenly turned away from a direct exploration of nature to an examination of art and art's relation to knowledge? Some have gone so far as to state, in the words of Michael Dettelbach, that this part of Humboldt's *Kosmos* is the "least durable."[3] After all, Humboldt's concerns are with the study of nature, and so it is not at all clear how the study of the history of art, and artistic depictions of nature, can contribute to his project. This confusion makes sense in light of the fact that traditionally studies in the history of science have largely ignored the history of the arts (and vice versa).

However, more recent work in the history of science has come to share Humboldt's view that the history of science must be understood in relation to the history of the humanities—and that anything else would be deeply anachronistic.[4] Like Humboldt, these scholars have pointed to the ways in which artistic methods, skills, and devices directly contributed to the investigation of nature. Still, despite clear affinities with Humboldt's approach, this more recent work is limited in its scope, and its thesis is not as radical as Humboldt's. For Humboldt's claim is not only that the tools developed by artists played an important role in the development of science, but also that the feelings and impressions that artworks convey and inspire are critical for understanding nature. In this way, Humboldt challenges the premise—articulated by both Edmund Burke and Kant—that pleasure in nature and intellectual interest in nature occupy two different (and unrelated) spheres in the human mind (*Kosmos* 2, 189).[5]

Humboldt begins volume 2 by drawing on Schiller's distinction between "naive" and "sentimental" poetry, as articulated in his 1795-96 work *On Naive and Sentimental Poetry [Über naive und sentimentalische Dichtung]*. According to Schiller, naive poetry offers direct descriptions of its object, and expresses a sense of unfreedom (on the part of the subject) in relation to the object (NA 20, 435). By contrast, sentimental poetry is attuned to the subjective experience of the object (that comes with a sense of a separation between subject and object) and is thus far more self-aware and reflective (NA 20, 441). The two artistic dispositions thus manifest a different relationship between the human being (the subject) and the natural world (the object), and, when regarded historically, reveal shifts in our relationship to nature and our sense of our self in nature. Historically, Schiller associates naive poetry with ancient Greek poetry, and sentimental poetry with modern European poetry.

While Humboldt agrees with Schiller's historicization of art, he is aware of its limits. For it only holds for European art, and thus says nothing about the human relation to the natural world outside of Europe.[6] Examining poetry from the Hindu Vedas, for instance, Humboldt remarks on their vastly different interest in nature, which contrasts not only to Greek and Roman poetry, but also to Hebrew poetry. While the Greeks expressed little—if any—interest in direct depictions of the natural world, Humboldt notes that in the Vedas, the "main subject . . . is the veneration and praise of nature" (*Kosmos* 2, 206; CE 2, 50). Accordingly, a more sensitive approach to the history of art would not be only historical but also comparative.

In light of this, Humboldt goes on to distinguish crucial moments in the history of art and situates them in their larger historic and geographic context. In so doing, he connects transformations in artistic depictions of nature to transformations in our knowledge about nature. Speaking of the emergence of landscape painting in the seventeenth century, for instance, he writes, "as the riches of nature became more known and more carefully observed, the feeling of art was likewise able to extend itself over a greater diversity of objects, while at the same time, the means of technical representation had simultaneously been brought to a higher degree of perfection" (*Kosmos* 2, 228). In this way, Humboldt traces the emergence of landscape painting in relation to increased understanding of the natural world, which was achieved through travel and exploration, and the development of new instruments and tools for measurement and observation.

But Humboldt's interest in art is not purely historical. He is also interested in analyzing the artistic medium, and in understanding how certain artworks can offer a "living depiction" of the natural world. In this instance, Humboldt's concern is less about noting differences between historical epochs and cultures, and more about discerning similarities—across epochs and cultures. For what Humboldt recognizes is that, despite historical and geographic distances, certain works of art achieve "truth to nature [*Naturwahrheit*]."[7]

Humboldt introduces the idea of "truth to nature" in his examination of the Vedic poem "The Messenger of Clouds [*Megaduta*]." Composed by the fourth-century Sanskrit poet Kalidasa, the poem, Humboldt writes, "describes with admirable truth to nature [*Naturwahrheit*] the joy which, after long drought, the first appearance of a rising cloud is hailed as the harbinger of the approaching season of rain" (*Kosmos* 2, 207). This brief description might give us some pause. What is described as "truth to nature" is not only a portrait of a natural event but also of the "joy [*Freude*]" associated with it. To this Humboldt adds a reference to the Sanskrit scholar Theodor Goldstücker. According to Goldstücker, the poem depicts "the influence of external nature on human feelings" (*Kosmos* 2, 209). And, Goldstücker elaborates,

"In his longing for his beloved, from whom he is separated, [the narrator] entreats a passing cloud to convey to her tidings of his sorrows and describes to the cloud the path which it must pursue, depicting the landscape as it would be reflected in his deeply excited mind [*tief aufgeregten Gemüthe*]" (*Kosmos* 2, 209). Clearly, whatever Humboldt means by "truth to nature," it is not an "objective" truth, in which human feeling and experience are taken out of the picture.

Not all writing, Humboldt emphasizes, achieves "truth to nature." He criticizes Buffon's works, for instance, on account of their "style and rhetorical pomp." Buffon's overly stylized prose inspires a feeling of the "sublime" in the reader—a feeling, Humboldt argues, that has less to do with what is being presented, and more to do with Buffon's style. Accordingly, Buffon's writings do not present a "visible picture of the actual life of nature [*anschauliche Schilderung des wirklichen Naturlebens*]," nor do they "convey to the senses the echo, as it were, of reality" (*Kosmos* 2, 220).

By contrast, Humboldt continues, the works of Rousseau, Bernardin de St. Pierre, and Chateaubriand express a "depth of feeling" through "individualizing true depictions [*individualisirend wahr*]" (*Kosmos* 2, 220). What distinguishes Buffon from these authors is not a sterile objectivity, on the one hand, and an overly sentimental depiction, on the other. All of them express and inspire feeling. What distinguishes them is the richness of their descriptions and the relationship between these descriptions and the feelings they inspire. Buffon's works inspire a feeling of sublimity. This feeling, however, has nothing to do with the phenomena depicted. In the works of these authors, the feelings depicted are inspired by the landscape and thus speak *of* and *about* the landscape.

Humboldt describes St. Pierre's 1788 novel *Paul et Virginie* as possessing "inimitable truth [*unnachahmlicher Wahrheit*]" (*Kosmos* 2, 221). This is because it captures the character of the tropics in such a way that the reader is able to experience *what it is like* to be in the region. The work brings the landscape to life by allowing the reader to hear "the rustling of the air amid the crowded bamboos," and to see "the waving of the leafy crown of the slender palms." Drawing on his own experience of reading the work, Humboldt remarks how "often . . . in the calm brilliancy of a southern sky, or when, in the rainy season, the thunder re-echoed, and the lightning gleamed through the forests that skirt the shores of the Orinoco, we [i.e., Humboldt and Bonpland] felt ourselves penetrated by the marvelous truth with which tropical nature is described, with all its peculiarity of character, in this little work" (*Kosmos* 2, 221). During his travels, Humboldt realized the truth of the novel's depictions: the extent to which they conveyed the experience of *what it is like* to be in tropics.

In his discussion of Portuguese poetry, Humboldt similarly notes how concrete description and feeling intersect and deepen one another. Referring to the sixteenth-century epic poem *The Lusiad*, he speaks of "the individual truth to nature, which emerges from one's own perception [*jene individuelle Naturwahrheit, die aus eigner Anschauung entspringt*]," adding that

> in the descriptive portions of the work, the enthusiasm of the poet, the ornaments of diction, and the sweet tones of melancholy never impede the accurate representation of physical phenomena, but rather, as is always the case where art draws from a pure source, heighten the animated impression of the greatness and truth of the pictures of nature [*wie dies immer der Fall ist, wenn die Kunst aus ungetrübter Quelle schöpft, den belebenden Eindruck der Größe und Wahrheit der Naturbilder erhöht*]. (*Kosmos* 2, 216–17)

As in the other works, so also here we find a consonance between careful description of the landscape and the feelings inspired by the landscape. Insofar as the feelings conveyed emerge in the encounter with the landscape, they speak *of* the landscape. As such, they are neither subjective and interior feelings (having only to do with the specific individual experiencing them) nor arbitrary (random associations, for instance). Rather, they reveal something about the landscape. To this we can also add that these feelings, as Humboldt puts it, *heighten* one's experience of the landscape. Precisely because they are *of* the landscape, the feelings draw the observer's attention toward the landscape, leading her to become more interested in it.

But as feelings, they also belong to a human subject. What Humboldt means by truth to nature, then, occupies a space between inner and outer, subjective and objective. Or, to borrow from Gernot Böhme, works that achieve truth to nature depict experiences that are "quasi-objective."[8] And this, for Humboldt, is their greatest strength.

Literature, Humboldt suggests, is the medium that most readily lends itself to capturing and conveying this form of human participation in nature— this human expressiveness of the natural world. This suggestion is made throughout the second volume of *Kosmos*, where Humboldt offers detailed considerations of literary works, but hardly discusses landscape painting or visual art more generally. The few pages he dedicates to landscape painting are surprisingly scant. At first, one might assume that this brevity has to do with the fact that landscape painting is a modern art form and has therefore supplied fewer examples than literature. However, Humboldt also claims that "landscape poetry," as he calls it, is a "modern genre." This does not stop him from considering it at length or going back to retrieve such poetry in fourth-century India or sixteenth-century Portugal—a move that conflicts with his claim that it is a modern genre. Furthermore, while Humboldt offers some insights into what constitutes a successful landscape painting, he is equivocal with regard to the success of actual landscape artists and paintings.

Another surprise has to do with the fact that in volume 2 of *Kosmos* Humboldt does not mention the work of the German painter Johann Moritz Rugendas. Rugendas was deeply influenced by Humboldt, whom he met in Paris in 1825. In 1830, Rugendas traveled to Mexico with Humboldt's assistance.[9] This was followed by trips to Chile and Argentina. By being in the actual landscape, Rugendas was able to do what earlier European landscape painters had not done: see the landscape for himself. Furthermore, Rugendas's work was precise, based on careful measurement, and proportionate, taking account of the distance between the phenomena he depicted.[10] Many of his paintings were sold to the Berlin Museum in 1843 and were on display throughout the decade. Yet, although volume 2 of *Kosmos* was published in 1847, it does not include a discussion of Rugendas's works. Humboldt does mention Rugendas, but in volume 5, where he focuses on scientific (rather than artistic) representation of nature. Pointing to Rugendas's painting *Landscape around the Colima Volcano near Tonila* [*Landschaft um den Vulkan Colima bei Tonila*] (1830), Humboldt writes, "in the true and exceedingly artistic views of the volcano of Colima, drawn by Moritz Rugendas and preserved in the Berlin Museum, we distinguish two adjacent mountains,—the true volcano, which constantly emits smoke, and is covered with but little snow, and the more elevated Nevada, which rises far into the region of perpetual snow" (CE 5, 280). The brevity of these remarks and the fact that they appear in volume 5 do not suggest that Humboldt was unimpressed by Rugendas, but that in volume 2, he was interested in works that are not only precise and rigorous, but that also enable a lived experience of nature.

By focusing on literature in the second volume of *Kosmos*, then, Humboldt appears to be suggesting that literature has been more successful at achieving this goal. After all, literature lends itself more easily to conveying the feelings and moods of the narrator, and to conveying transformations—in the landscape (e.g., seasonal changes) and also in the narrator's feelings and impressions in relation to the landscape. Furthermore, on account of its generality, the linguistic medium can point to connections (e.g., between landscapes), draw comparisons, and arrive at wide-ranging and far-reaching conclusions with greater facility than the visual arts. These might be the reasons why Humboldt's historical account is more focused on literature, and why Humboldt chose to compose essays. For, it may be the case that the literary medium is more amenable to realizing Humboldt's aim "to occupy the imagination and at the same time, through the increase of knowledge, to enrich life with ideas" (DA 5, xi; VN 27).

To get a fuller sense of Humboldt's reasoning, and his own artistic choices, it is important to understand the larger context to which he contributed—and the ongoing debate concerning the differences between paining and poetry.

7.2. Poetry versus Painting: Lessing, Schiller, and Humboldt

In his 1766 *Laocoon: or on the Limits of Painting and Poetry* [*Laokoon: oder über die Grenzen der Mahlerey und Poesie*], Gotthold Ephraim Lessing (1729–1781) launched an attack on what he regarded as a problematic confusion of artistic genres. His critique was leveled against the notion that poetry and painting are alike—an idea that goes back to Horatio's "*ut pictura poesis* [as is painting, so is poetry]."[11] Lessing's aim was to distinguish the two art forms, establish what "rightly" belongs to one and what does not, and thereby draw a clear distinction between the subject matter and the capacities of painting and poetry.

Lessing begins the essay by remarking that "the first who compared painting with poetry was a man of fine feeling," but not a critic or a philosopher.[12] This is because painting and poetry have different capacities. As a pictorial art, painting is spatial. It is therefore most capable of depicting what appears in space, what is visible, i.e., corporeal reality. Poetry, by contrast, is not spatial, and is thus less suited to representing objects in space. Its procedure, moreover, is temporal, because it depends on the succession of words, lines, and sounds. Accordingly, Lessing concludes, poetry's primary concern is (or should be) what is nonspatial and invisible.

This is not to deny that language can describe bodies. It can. However, Lessing adds, "I deny that this power exists in language as the instrument

[*Mittel*] of poetry."[13] In other words, poetry's distinctive capacity is not capturing what is visible and embodied. And this has to do with the fact that "the coexistence of the body comes into collision with the sequence of the words."[14] Precisely because poetry proceeds successively, its form is less apt at depicting a scene or a corporeal whole at once or "in one glance." Thus, Lessing concludes, "To try to present a complete picture to the reader by enumerating in succession several parts or things which in nature the eye necessarily takes in at a glance, is an encroachment of the poet on the domain of the painter."[15]

Ultimately, Lessing's point is that poetry (and language more generally) should be responsible for representing what takes place in time (e.g., action), while painting (and sculpture) should be responsible for representing what appears in space (e.g., bodies).

To some extent, Humboldt agrees with Lessing. His interest in landscape painting, and his view that landscape painting offers important tools for observing a region and discerning the relations between its living beings, suggest that landscape painting has a unique capacity to portray in "one glance" or "at once" something that other artistic media, in particular literature, cannot do. However, Humboldt was not entirely convinced by Lessing's distinction. For one, in his exposition of the two art forms in *Kosmos*, Humboldt assesses them according to the same criterion. The implication is that when it comes to the presentation of nature, painting and poetry should strive to achieve the same goal: truth to nature. While the two media have different tools (color, shape, perspective, brushstrokes versus words, metaphor, sound, line, and rhythm), their aim is to convey a natural phenomenon through a seamless joining of concrete detail and quasi-objective impressions and feelings. Furthermore, Humboldt's coining of the term *Naturgemälde* to describe his literary productions suggests that he saw in literary works the capacity to paint or portray nature. As indicated, Humboldt's essays seek to emulate landscape painting in their focus on one aspect of nature—one geographic region or zone. In turn, in his historical account of literary depictions of nature, Humboldt contends that literature *has* offered vivid, contemplative, and arresting portrayals of corporeal nature, which are in important respects superior to the achievements of landscape painting.

There was, however, yet another flaw with Lessing's conceptualization of the two art forms. By drawing a hard-and-fast distinction between painting, as the representative of the corporeal, and poetry, as the representative of the temporal, Lessing made it impossible to capture what is *both* corporeal *and* temporal. In other words, Lessing made it impossible to represent the *living body*, or what Schiller described in the *Aesthetic Letters* as "living form [*lebende Gestalt*]" (NA 20, 355).[16] The question then is: which artistic medium is most capable of depicting forms that *transform* in time and place?

As we saw in the preceding chapters, Goethe sought to capture the transforming forms of plants through language: whether in the essay on the metamorphosis of plants, with its distinctive temporal structure, or the elegy "The Metamorphosis of Plants," which uses sound, rhythm, line, and meaning to capture the transforming plant form and the transformative experience of the student of nature. In working with poetry Goethe took advantage of the medium's temporal structure. The sequential character of the poem reflects the sequential development of a plant. At the same time, Goethe sought to make up for poetry's deficiency—i.e., the fact that it cannot present the whole plant "at once"—by placing a demand on the reader to *imagine* the interconnected character of the plant in her mind's eye.

Humboldt, as we have seen, was less interested in depicting the development of a single plant, and more interested in capturing the relations between plants and between plants and their region. Accordingly, whatever art form he is to use, it must be able to present this larger relational context, to convey transforming forms *in place*. Furthermore, given that Goethe did not *present* the relations between the plant's parts but *pointed to* them, placing upon the reader the responsibility to visualize them for herself, the question for Humboldt is: can literature, as a medium, also *point to* the relations *between living beings*, and *between living beings and their surroundings*? And what kind of responsibility does that place upon the reader?

In addition to working on the *Aesthetic Letters* in 1794, Schiller composed a review of the poetic writings of Friedrich von Matthisson (1761–1831). Many of Matthison's poems were of natural scenery or landscape, and so Schiller took the opportunity to consider the aporia of writing nature poetry, in light of Lessing's distinction. "The poet," Schiller writes, "finds himself in a certain disadvantageous situation in comparison to the painter." This is because, he continues, "a large part of the effect [of nature] rests on the simultaneous impression of the whole, which he, however, can only bring together *successively* in the imagination of the reader." In other words, a crucial aspect of our experience of nature revolves around our being able to see it "in one glance," grasping the whole *at once*. Poetry's successive character limits its ability to do this, and places upon the reader the responsibility to imagine it. This, however, also reveals poetry's distinctive advantage. For,

Schiller elaborates, "the concern of the poet is not to represent to us what is, but rather what *happens* [*geschieht*]." Accordingly, if the poet "understands his advantage, then he will limit himself to those objects, which are capable of a *genetic* presentation" (NA 22, 274).

This means, Schiller continues, that while a natural landscape is "a whole given at once in appearances [*ein auf einmal gegebenes Ganze von Erscheinungen*]" and is thus most suited to the medium of painting, poetry has the advantage of being able to portray the *change* that a landscape undergoes. For, Schiller notes, the natural landscape "is also a successively given whole, because it is in continuous change, and is thus suitable to the poet" (NA 22, 274). The poet's object, Schiller concludes, "is the *moving* rather than the still nature" (NA 22, 275).

Schiller agrees with Lessing that the two art forms have different capacities. This does not mean, however, that poetry ought not to present corporeal reality. Nor does it mean that poetry cannot be painterly, or seek to approximate, in its own way, the imagistic character of painting. Rather, Schiller grants to poetry a significant role in the presentation of nature: poetry's temporal character means that it can capture change and transformation, and thus depict a dynamic or living nature, rather than a static or dead one.

Schiller goes even further in the *Aesthetic Letters*, where he contends that the various art forms must seek to overcome their inherent limitations and approximate one another. As he puts it, "This, precisely, is the mark of the perfect style in each and every art: that it is able to remove the specific limitations of the art in question without thereby destroying its specific qualities." The plastic arts, he continues, "must become music and move us by the immediacy of their sensuous presence. Poetry, when most fully developed, must grip us as powerfully as music does, but at the same time, like the plastic arts, surround us with serene clarity" (NA 20, 380–81). In the hands of a master, every art form should be able to achieve *more* than what Lessing had accorded to it. And it can do this by approximating other art forms: poetry should strive to become more *painterly*, and painting should strive to become more *musical*.[17]

A few years later, in 1799, Humboldt's brother, Wilhelm, takes up the question of poetry versus painting in his review of Goethe's play, *Hermann and Dorothea* [*Hermann und Dorothea*] (1797). In agreement with Schiller, Wilhelm von Humboldt writes that "movement is distinctive to poetry."[18] For this reason, he continues, poetry's "images are not mere groupings, in which one form hangs onto another; [rather] they also approximate perfectly structured chains, in which movement emerges out of movement, figure emerges out of figure [*sie gleichen auch vollkommen gegliederten Ketten, in welchen Bewegung aus Bewegung, Figur aus Figur entspringt*]."[19]

According to Wilhelm von Humboldt, it is the task of the artist to "bring human beings into the closest and most manifold connection with nature." To achieve this, it is not enough simply to present the natural world, but also to present it in a way that allows the reader or viewer to enter into a relation with nature. This means that the artist must, at one moment, convey the sensible objects, and in the next moment, turn to the "inner mood [*innere Stimmung*]." Or in Schiller's articulation, the artist must join landscape painting's ability to portray with music's ability to emotively engage. Thus, Humboldt continues, by proceeding "simultaneously imagistically and with attunement [*zugleich bildend und stimmend*]," the artist is able to "present the object and prepare the subject, to enter into relation [with the object]."[20] By working with both the imagistic character of landscape painting and the emotive character of music, the artist produces a work that enables the reader to enter into relation with nature.

However, Humboldt adds, the widespread view of poetry is that it is largely emotive, connected to feeling and mood. For this reason, poets have shown little interest in concrete descriptions of nature, focusing instead on expressing feeling. But Humboldt asks rhetorically, "How much more would it be, if we could add careful observation [to poetry]!"[21] In other words, how much more would poetry be able to achieve if, in addition to suggestively evoking a mood, it were able to portray and present the world?

Alexander von Humboldt was familiar with Schiller's writings on the topic and with his brother's essay and quotes from both in *Kosmos*. Furthermore, in his essays he attempts to achieve the two goals that his brother sets forth for poetry: presenting the phenomenon and articulating a distinctive feeling or mood in relation to it. However, perhaps even more influential on Humboldt's thinking than either Schiller's or his brother's theoretical writings was a poem in which Schiller sought to realize these goals, his 1795 "Elegy [*Elegie*]," which he renamed "The Walk [*Der Spaziergang*]" in 1800.[22] Turning to this poem, and comparing it to Humboldt's essays, will allow us to better appreciate what Humboldt took from Schiller and how he went beyond him.

7.3. Embodied Landscapes: Schiller's "Walk" and Humboldt's *Views*

In Schiller's poem, the narrator is a wanderer, and as he walks through a landscape, he describes what he sees and the feelings that these various views inspire in him. He often stops to reflect on the changing scenery, from the idyllic pastoral scenes of country life to the colorful and bustling city. Walking, as the revised title indicates, is a central feature of the poem, and the narrator's bodily movement punctuates and animates the poem's structure. As he moves, the narrator registers his moods and feelings, and the impact that the landscape has on them. His movement, in turn, is captured within the landscape, and as a response to it. By describing movement and change—in the landscape, in the narrator, and in the narrator's feelings toward the landscape—the poem conveys precisely what a landscape painting cannot: transformation.

The reader is invited to imaginatively follow in the narrator's footsteps: as he smells, feels, touches, and observes various natural events and objects—the sun's rays on his face, the wind waving through the grass, the night closing in around him—the reader imaginatively smells, feels, touches, and observes. Furthermore, as the narrator makes his way from the country to the town—at one time he is walking, at another looking up at the sky, at yet another bending down to the grass—the reader is invited to imaginatively do the same.

Embedded within these descriptions of sensation and corporeal movement are descriptions of the feelings and reflections that the landscape inspires. For instance, as the narrator walks past thick forests, he observes which paths he can and cannot take, suggesting his sense of potential danger. But the feelings that he shares are not only related to his own sense; they also convey the moods that particular places express. Villages are "cheerful [*muntre Dörfer*]," while the sound of wind through branches is "jovial [*fröhlich*]."[23] These moods, in turn, offer pedestals for reflection. Thus as the narrator takes in the varying landscapes, he considers the different ways in which human beings inhabit and relate to the natural world: those who live outside the city, we are told, are "fortunate [*glücklich*]" because they are "Not yet to freedom awakened [*Noch nicht zur Freiheit erwachet*]." This is because, to recall Schiller's distinction between naive and sentimental poetry, they have not yet experienced alienation from the natural world.

As the wanderer approaches the city ("From the craggyest core to'ring the *city* does rise [*Aus dem felsigten Kern hebt sich die thürmende Stadt*]") he observes how the surrounding wall creates significant distance between human culture and nature, thereby transforming the human experience of both. Schiller writes: "To the wild outside are the woodland fawns now ejected [*In die Wildniß hinaus sind des Waldes Faunen verstoßen*]." And to this he adds: "Man is brought closer to mankind. Around him everything narrows, / In him the world now awakes [*Näher gerückt ist der Mensch an den Menschen. Enger wird um ihn, / Reger erwacht, es . . . sich in ihm die Welt*]." Our experience of ourselves and of other humans shifts within the city walls.

While many of the depictions of life in the city are filled with joy ("So there the markets are swarming, alive with joyful existence [*da wimmeln die Märkte, der Krahn von fröhlichem Leben*]"), the narrator's reflections lead him to the French Revolution and the Reign of Terror—thoughts that are prompted by the reality of city life. For, Schiller notes, it is within the closed walls of the city, where human beings are at such close proximity to one another, and where exchange between them is so frequent, that the desire for freedom emerges. "Freedom, reason cries out, freedom the savage's passions, / Out from Nature august, strive forth in greed to be free [*Freiheit ruft die Vernunft, Freiheit die wilde Begierde, / Von der heil'gen Natur ringen sie lüstern sich los*]." Within the city walls, however, no clear resolution to these cries appears to be possible. In the last lines of the poem, Schiller turns not to the city and its busy streets, but to nature, which alone offers hope in the midst of suffering. "Ever the self-same [*Immer dieselbe*]," nature's lawfulness contrasts with the chaos of human civilization. In nature's "ever repeating form [*ewig wiederholte Gestalt*]," the narrator appears to find some consolation and meaning. For, despite differences among us, we share the same blue sky and green earth. Or, as Schiller puts it, "Homer's fair sun, also is shining on us [*Und die Sonne Homers, siehe! sie lächelt auch uns*]."

What Schiller attempts to portray in this poem is a changing world that is experienced by a changing narrator. The changes that are observed in the natural world align with—and are reflected in—changes in the narrator's feelings and moods. There is, in other words, a consonance between what is "out there" and what is "in here." Thus the natural landscape is not experienced as an indifferent object, but as something that is seen, felt, and enjoyed by a particular individual. (Nature only becomes something "out there" once we enter the walled city.) In fact, nature is often the source of the feelings, observations, and reflections, and it is the reader's privilege to see, hear, feel, and think with the narrator-wanderer. Crucially, the poem offers portraits of various landscapes, in the way that landscape painting does. However, while painting would have to stretch itself in order to portray the smells and sounds of a place, and may not be able to describe humidity, or the cool breeze of the ocean, the poem can easily do these things. Similarly, while painting may be able to capture night and day (for instance, by depicting night on one panel and day on another), it cannot easily capture the transformation as it occurs, or the changes in the shapes of animals, plants, and humans over a day or a year. Poetry can do all of that—and more.

By invoking a narratorial I, and by noting a parallel between the subject's feelings, thoughts, movements, and the landscape and its movements, the poem alludes to what Humboldt calls the "mysterious interworking" between the human mind and the natural world (DA 5, 183; VN 161). In other words, poetry can depict and attend not only to what can be seen, but also to what cannot be seen: to what is felt and understood, and to the way in which feelings and thoughts can be expressive of the world in which they emerge.

That Humboldt appropriated some insights from this poem is highly likely. In his own depictions of nature, Humboldt invokes a narratorial I, a wanderer, who follows in Humboldt's footsteps. This narrative voice is often walking, climbing, listening, or smelling. Movement, and bodily movement in particular, structures and animates Humboldt's essays. Moods, feelings, observations, and thoughts emerge in relation to these movements. In his various accounts, Humboldt is not only interested in depicting the corporeality of the natural world, but also human corporeality, and the ways in which the body is a participant in this larger corporeal reality. In so doing, he focuses on those aspects of our experience of nature that are more difficult to depict visually: the relations between bodies (including the human body) as they move alongside or with other bodies, their transformations over time, and their (sensual and intellectual) effects on the wanderer.

But Humboldt also differs from Schiller in important ways. Although Schiller's depictions might refer to a particular region—perhaps Jena, perhaps Stuttgart—Humboldt's are clearly connected to specific landscapes. His aim is to reveal to his readers what certain regions in the world look, smell, and feel like. This allows him to provide vivid and rich details, in ways that Schiller's elusive references do not. Furthermore, Humboldt is interested in both the specificity of the landscapes and their commonality: the repetition of certain forms across regions, the ways in which certain landscapes, despite their differences, evoke similar feelings in the observer. In turn, on the basis of these "quasi-objective feelings," Humboldt draws connections between landscapes—connections that, on the surface at least, are not self-evident. Thus, feelings and impressions make way for discerning similarities and differences between landscapes, and drawing conclusions on the basis of these reflections. These modes of reflection are not present in Schiller's poem, largely because Schiller does not have the scientific interest that Humboldt does.

Furthermore, while Schiller moves from nature to city, and forms his moral and political outlook in his reflections on city life, Humboldt does not focus on the cities he visited, such as Havana or Cumana. Rather, the landscapes that interest him the most are inhabited (or were once inhabited) by Indigenous Americans. Thus, when he discusses culture, Humboldt's focus is on the Indigenous cultures that lived with, rather than beyond, the natural world.[24] Finally, while Schiller, in his turn to nature, emphasizes the "selfsameness" of the natural world—the blue of the sky and the green of the earth—Humboldt is attuned to change in nature, brought about by plants, animals, and also humans.

It is also important to note that the two use different media. Schiller's work is a poem, while Humboldt's works are essays. Although his essays are imagistic, they do not have the formal character of a poem. This does not mean, however, that they lack form altogether. They have form, but their form does not clearly align with any traditional forms or genres, and significantly departs from travel narratives despite superficial resemblance to this genre. While travel narratives proceed chronologically and follow the footsteps of their author, Humboldt's essays do not. Rather, and as Ottmar Ette has noted, they look both forward (anticipating what is to come) and backward (reflecting on what has occurred), developing a nonlinear structure that allows for comparisons across vast geographic and temporal distances. Furthermore, and again in contrast to travel narratives, Humboldt's persona—Humboldt the traveler—is not clearly present. While the essays appear to follow in his footsteps, he is rarely named, and in his place emerges a neutral "wanderer."[25]

Humboldt explicitly distinguishes his writings from travel narratives, noting in the 1852 Introduction to *Personal Narrative* that his works seek to achieve a "unity of composition," something that the majority of travel narratives, in their linear descriptions, fail to achieve (PNR, xix). Unity of composition, Humboldt explains, requires bringing together, in an uninterrupted way, two crucial elements: the experience of being in nature and the insights that emerge from this experience. It requires, in other words, finding a way by which to convey the feelings, sensations, and moods associated with a particular place, alongside an understanding of this place. These two components must, furthermore, be conveyed in a manner that captures the reader's attention and inspires scientific and moral interest. Success depends on the integration of these elements in a seamless manner.

In "Das nächtliche Tierleben im Urwald [The Nocturnal Wildlife of the Primeval Forest]," included in the second edition of *Ansichten der Natur*, Humboldt describes the harmonious coalescing of these elements as "truth to nature." Thus in addition to what we have surmised regarding truth to nature above, we can now say that truth to nature also involves determining what is essential for expressing nature by way of narrative, and ordering those essential aspects in the right way: in a way that allows descriptions to deepen and enliven feelings and reflections, and vice versa. Or, as Humboldt puts it in *Kosmos*, the author must order the ample material she has collected according to a "leading idea [*leitende Idee*]" (*Kosmos* 1, 12). The essay's structure, the details that are conveyed, the insights that are gained, are determined by this leading idea— by the picture that the author wishes to present. This picture becomes "living," however, only if it "excites the mind." Accordingly, the leading idea must be made concrete through vivid detail—detail that is founded in observation, and that draws on the feelings that observation inspires. Or, as Humboldt puts it in his assessment of *Paul et Virginie*, the work's power lies in its ability to grasp "individualities, without destroying the general impression of the whole, and without depriving the subject of a free inner animation of poetical imagination" (*Kosmos* 2, 221). The question then is: does Humboldt himself successfully achieve "truth to nature" in his writings?

7.4. Steppes, Deserts, Jungles, and Waterfalls: Humboldt's Embodied Aesthetics

Humboldt opens *Ansichten der Natur* with the essay that he later described as his most "daring" (DA 5, 128; VN 117). Titled "Über die Steppen und Wüsten [Concerning the Steppes and Deserts]," the essay begins by situating the reader, imaginatively placing her in a particular spot: the foot of a high granite mountain—or as Humboldt describes it, a granite spine. Immediately, the reader is invited not only to *picture* the mountain, but also to *stand* at its foot.

From there her gaze turns southward, and rests on "a broad, immeasurable plain," the steppes or Llanos. What the reader sees is not a God's-eye view of the landscape, but the steppes as they appear from a particular angle. This angle colors her impression. The steppes *seem* to "climb and dwindle into the horizon." Having walked to the steppes from the lush valleys of Caracas, the reader is also struck by the sudden change in landscape from the "luxuriant fullness of organic life" to "the barren edge of a sparse and treeless desert" and feels astonished (DA 5, 3; VN 29).

In this opening paragraph, Humboldt makes no mention of himself. The reader presumes, however, that what is being described is the path that Humboldt had trodden, and the view he had seen. However, by the end of the paragraph, any evidence of Humboldt, the explorer, disappears and in his place stands the "astonished wanderer." That Humboldt invokes the astonished wanderer—rather than himself—allows the reader to take on the perspective of the wanderer, to imaginatively *become* the wanderer. In turn, by appealing to all of the reader's senses, her feelings and imagination, as well as her body, the essay—from this first paragraph to its final descriptions—invites the reader to see, smell, touch, and listen to what the wanderer sees, smells, touches, and hears. With the wanderer, the reader imaginatively walks from the verdant valleys to the starkly barren steppes and feels astonished; watches the clouds thickening overhead, portending months of rain, and senses the constriction in the atmosphere; smells the oncoming deluge, and observes with wonder the changed behavior of the animals. In reading these descriptions, the reader does not only *think* about the particular aspect of nature, nor does she simply *see* it from a specific standpoint. She also imagines herself *in* the landscape, experiencing it in an embodied and emotive way.

Throughout the reader is not an outside observer, but an embodied wanderer, fully involved in the landscape as she walks, climbs, or rides through it. At one time, she imagines herself traveling in east Asia, in "low-slung Tartar carriages over the trackless parts of these herb-covered steppes." To take a look at the ground beneath her feet, she has to *stand upright* in the carriage, because it is the only way that one can "orient oneself and thus see the densely packed forest of plants that bow before the wheels" (DA 5, 5; VN 31). At another time, she is walking through the South American steppes, and senses a change in the light and air and notes the sudden formation of clouds.

Interwoven with these vivid descriptions of embodied experience are careful observations and detailed measurements of various natural phenomena, as well as comparative, historical, and geographical analyses. The technical details and scientific explanations are not separated, however, from the embodied experiences, but emerge from them.

This is particularly clear in Humboldt's description of the sudden shift in atmosphere preceding an electric storm. This passage is, in fact, referred to in *Kosmos* immediately after Humboldt describes "The Messenger of Clouds" as an expression of truth to nature. As in "The Messenger of Clouds," so here what is being observed is the formation of clouds and the coming of rain. The accuracy of Humboldt's description, and its epistemic value, are indicated in the fact that he included it in other works, and contemporary authors referenced it when discussing the phenomenon of electrical storms.[26]

Furthermore, and just as in "The Messenger of Clouds," so also here the description is imbued by the feelings of the observer. While in "The Messenger of Clouds," the landscape is depicted through a "deeply excited mind [*aufgeregten Gemüth*]" (*Kosmos* 2, 209), in "Über die Steppen und Wüsten" the experience is colored by a sense of "constriction." This is how Humboldt puts it in the essay:

> When the charred grass falls to dust under the vertical rays of the sun, the hardened earth gapes open as if shaken by powerful tremors. Should it then be touched by opposing currents whose conflict equalizes in circular motion, the plain takes on a curious appearance. In the form of funnel clouds with their tips gliding across the earth, the sand rises like steam through the airless, electrically charged center of the vortex, like the hissing waterspouts feared by experienced boatmen. A hazy, almost straw-colored half-light is thrown by the seemingly low-hanging heavens on the desolate plain. The horizon suddenly draws nearer. It *constricts the steppe and the mood of the wanderer* as well. The smothering heat of the air is increased by the hot, dusty earth floating in the atmosphere, which is veiled as if by fog. Instead of cooling, the east wind brings only more warmth as it blows across the long-heated ground. (DA 5, 14; VN 37; emphasis added)

As the narrator watches the clouds thicken over the steppes, he feels constricted. This feeling, while belonging to the narrator, also belongs to or speaks of the natural processes occurring around him. This is because the feeling emerges in the encounter with the natural phenomenon. The formation of low-hanging clouds, the narrowing of the horizon, the thickness of the air, the smothering heat and dust, are the sources of the sense of constriction, which, while felt internally, also reflects the surrounding events.

By following these descriptions, the reader observes the phenomenon and also imaginatively senses the internal constriction that the narrator feels. By taking note of the change in the light and the formation of the clouds, of the different air currents coming through, and the smothering heat and dust, the reader imaginatively senses a tightening of chest and breathing difficulties. Thus, by the time the reader is *told* about the feeling of constriction, she is already aware of this feeling. In this way, the reader recognizes that there is nothing random about the feeling: it is *inspired by* the natural process and thus reveals—via the medium of feeling—something about it.

But more is at work in this passage. For the feeling of a constricted atmosphere motivates careful observations of cloud formation before an electric storm, which Humboldt includes in his accounts of the process of cloud formation in relation to electricity.[27] The feeling, in other words, makes way for, indeed incites, careful scientific observation. In this passage, then, Humboldt manages to convey aesthetic feeling *and* enrich our understanding of a natural phenomenon—seamlessly moving from feeling to understanding. Thus one can say that this passage embodies the "dual direction" that Humboldt's essays aim to achieve.

This dual direction is not, however, unique to this passage but permeates the essay as a whole. For instance, the feeling of shock at the sudden deluge leads to insights about animal adaptation, how the cows and horses that had for months survived in arid conditions had suddenly become amphibian-like, struggling with new predators, in a new habitat. Or, as Humboldt puts it, the sight of horses and cattle fighting crocodiles in their new watery home "irresistibly reminds the observer of the flexibility with which all-providing Nature has endowed certain animals and plants" (DA 5, 16; VN 39). In their ability to adapt to a vastly changed environment, the animals that live in the steppes reveal an astounding ability to change their behaviors, habits, their very ways of life for a part of the year.

In turn, when the wanderer journeys from South America to Africa, she is surprised by the vastly different impressions that their respective landscapes inspire. This leads her to reflect on their deep histories and geographies and to offer reasons for why the African desert, the Sahara, is so arid in comparison to the South American one.

These feelings are not mere stimulants, which are put aside once scientific explanation begins. They remain and serve to anchor scientific insights in the reality of lived experience. As responses to the world, openings onto phenomena, the feelings and impressions reveal something about the phenomena. The astonishment that we feel in suddenly gazing on the vast, barren steppes has to do with their stark difference in character from the lush valleys, while the sense of constriction before an electric storm reflects the heaviness of the air, the sudden closeness of the horizon, and the intensifying clouds. In and through these feelings, the landscape expresses itself to the attentive wanderer, and thereby ceases to be a mute, indifferent object.

But just as feeling anchors scientific insight, so insight informs and shifts feeling. In witnessessing the adaptability of animals in the flooded steppes, for instance, surprise and wonder make way for considered reflection. Throughout, feeling and reflection enable, expand, and transform one another.

This is perhaps most vivid in Humboldt's description of the practice of so-called horse-fishing, where wild horses are corralled into a pond filled with electric eels. The idea is that in electrocuting the large animals, the eels will exhaust themselves, and can then be easily caught. In the instance Humboldt describes, horse-fishing was undertaken on his bidding, as he was fascinated by the phenomenon of animal electricity.

To begin with, we sense a certain excitement and curiosity in connection with the strangeness of the phenomenon of electric fish. However, as we observe the horses' repeated attempts to flee the scene, witness their strained bodies, and the panic in their eyes, excitement wanes, and in its place emerge shock and concern. What we feel disrupts the narrative, and as we read the essay's final paragraphs, the panic in the horses' eyes, and the feeling it evokes, haunt our reflections. In this instance, feeling challenges thinking, calling upon us to reflect on the implications of our actions, and their worth.

What we find in Humboldt's essays, then, are *scientific works of art*—however contradictory this term might at first appear—works in which feeling and thinking are in the service of one another, where each is willing to be challenged, expanded, and transformed by the other. Feeling is not a mere means by which to communicate the data that Humboldt collected. Rather, it inspires, shapes, and transforms intellectual and moral consideration—as it is also shaped and transformed by them.

7.5. The Ecological Significance of Embodied Aesthetics

From this, we can conclude that Humboldt did achieve "truth to nature." Still, one might wonder *why* Humboldt sets this goal for himself in the first place. Why, in other words, does he regard it as important and relevant to portray nature in a "living" way? Why not simply write a scientific paper? Some might worry that by associating knowledge with feelings and impressions, Humboldt undermines the knowledge that he is seeking to impart. After all, it was during Humboldt's lifetime that the standard of objectivity in science became normative, such that knowledge came to be understood as separate from emotion and independent of personal experience.[28] Humboldt explicitly resists this move. And so the question is: why does Humboldt insist, contra many of his contemporaries, that moods, feelings, and impressions are integral to our understanding of nature, and our understanding of ourselves in nature?

A first answer to this question leads us back to Schiller, and in particular to Schiller's argument in the *Aesthetic Letters*. According to Schiller, and as briefly discussed above, aesthetic experience uniquely allows us to overcome the conflict between our intellectual and sensual sides. As a sensuous appearance in meaningful form, the work of art engages our two sides at once, and does so in a way that allows them to work together. The sensuous character of art is not disconnected from its intellectual character, but is crucial to it, and vice versa: the intellectual character of art deepens and expands its sensuous side. Accordingly, in contemplating works of art, the two aspects of ourselves are no longer in conflict with one another, and we achieve a state of equilibrium. We are not consumed by either our intellectual or our sensuous side—we are neither abstracted from life, nor controlled by sensuous desires. Precisely because the intellectual does not *force* itself upon the sensuous, or vice versa, we are in a situation in which duty (intellectual side) and desire (sensuous side) work together. This makes way for ethical life. Aesthetic experience thus contributes to the formation of individuals who do not experience a conflict between duty and inclination.[29] We act in the world not as divided individuals (where duty must subjugate desire, for instance), but as *whole* individuals. And this is the beginning of moral freedom.

While Schiller's account emphasizes the moral and political significance of aesthetic experience, it does not enter into a discussion of the ways in which aesthetic experience can deepen and transform knowledge. A Kantian, Schiller remained wedded to the view that aesthetic experience is noncognitive.[30] Humboldt, by contrast, regarded aesthetic experience as essential for *understanding* nature—and thus extended Schiller's articulation of its significance while also drawing on his exposition of its value.

In the essays collected in *Ansichten der Natur*, Humboldt appeals to both our sensuous and our intellectual sides, seeks to engage body and mind in an integrated way, with the goal of achieving—as he puts it in the letter to Schiller—"something higher." This something higher recalls what Schiller (and Otté's Humboldt) describes as "rational empiricism," that is, the synthesis of what is given to the senses and what is discerned through the understanding. By conveying an embodied experience that seamlessly takes the reader to moments of scientific explanation and insight, which are concretized and thus deepened by embodied experience, Humboldt's essays realize this (aesthetic) ideal. They engage our rational and sensuous sides harmoniously, allowing them to extend and enhance one another. Accordingly, the significance of Humboldt's essays does not simply lie in their ability to convey aesthetic feeling *and* to impart scientific knowledge, as if the two enterprises were separate. Rather, their significance lies in their ability to *join* aesthetics and science in such a way that they are both transformed, so that they become "something higher."[31] This "something higher" is a new *kind* of knowledge: an *embodied* knowledge that appeals to our *whole* selves.

In this way, Humboldt's essays reveal a different way of being in and understanding the world, a way that is not neutral and detached, but passionately involved in and affected by a dynamic world. And they do this not purely theoretically. By addressing the reader as a sensing, feeling, and thinking being—as a *whole* self—the essays *generate and enact* this richer way of being in and knowing the world. By reading the essays, we begin to experience thinking and feeling in a new way—not as conflicting aspects of ourselves, calling us in opposite directions, but as interdependent, mutually supportive elements. We begin to see how an impression is deepened and confirmed through understanding, and how understanding is enlivened through the impression; to sense how feeling can stimulate thinking, and how thinking can remain anchored in feeling.

While the essays communicate information—where certain flora grow and in relation to which factors; what the causes of the animals' midnight cries might be; or how, when the steppes are suddenly flooded during the rainy season, the animals quickly adapt to their changed home—this information is not preseted as a list of facts. Rather, it is presented as part of a larger experience. The observer of this information, in turn, is not a netural observer, but an immersed participant who is *affected* by what he witnesses. In other words, "information" is not presented in a distant and objectifying way, but as emerging from and relevant to lived experience.

This gives the reader a distinctive form of access to knowledge, allowing her to realize that, like the narrator, she is not indifferent to what she sees, hears, and touches. In other words, she realizes that she is—in a significant sense—*moved* by the natural world. By following in the narrator's footsteps, the reader begins to experience herself not as an outsider contemplating a distant and neutral object, but as a *passionate participant* in a world that speaks to her. She becomes aware of the ways in which she is affected and changed by the world just as the horses and cows are affected and transformed by the sudden downpour on the steppes. She realizes that *who* she is inextricably connected to the world in which she lives.

By allowing us to experience nature and ourselves in nature in this way—by addressing us as whole individuals—Humboldt's essays lead us to deeper insights about ourselves and our relation to the world. They reveal something that the mere communication of information cannot: we are not outside nature, but inside it as much as it is inside us. They thus demonstrate, in a visceral and embodied way, that the destruction of nature necessarily results in the destruction of culture.[32] As beings who are deeply affected by nature, we cannot presume anything else.

Throughout his work, Humboldt draws attention to this fact, but it is in his political writings that he homes in on the mismanagement of the natural world by colonial administrators in South America, and demonstrates its devastating effects not only on nature, but also on culture. Though he notes that these effects are most acutely felt by Indigenous Americans, he is clear that it is human culture at large that will suffer from the destruction of nature. Whether it is the mass deforestation that seems to be connected to the Spanish desire to transform the South American landscape to resemble "in every way the soil of Castile, arid and devoid of vegetation," or the thoughtless construction of new cities, dams, and underground tunnels, the destruction of nature has been catastrophic for all cultures (KNS 1, 328). Or, as he puts it in *Personal Narrative*,

> The changes which the destruction of forests, the clearing of plants and the cultivation of indigo have produced within half a century—in the quantity of water flowing in, on the one hand, and on the other, the evaporation of the soil and the dryness of the atmosphere—present causes sufficiently

powerful to explain the successive diminution of the lake of Valencia. I am not of the opinion of M. Depons (who was in these countries after I was there) "that to set the mind at rest, and for the honour of science," a subterranean issue must be admitted. By felling the trees which cover the tops and the sides of mountains, men in every climate prepare at once two calamities for future generations: want of fuel and scarcity of water. (PNR 2, 9; translation altered)

In contrast to Depons, a scientific traveler who claims that significant changes to the natural landscape should be accepted for the "honour of science," Humboldt points to something that is more important than this "honour"—the calamities that scientific goals can result in. Thus, and in agreement with Goethe, Humboldt is claiming that we must hold the scientific enterprise to account. In turn, the calamities to which he points are just two among the many of which we are keenly aware today. Yet, despite our knowledge of them, we have taken little action. Why is this the case?

This is perhaps *the* question of our era, and everything from human psychology to short-term economic thinking have been offered as responses. While these various explanations illuminate aspects of our contemporary situation, they do not get to the crux of the question, which concerns the relationship between knowledge and action. We *know*. However, *despite* our knowledge, we *do* very little.

This implies a rift between what we *know* and what we *do*. Or better, it is as if we know but don't *really* know. There is, in other words, a chasm *within us*, within our knowledge. The fact that we "know" but also don't *really* know suggests that we know *in a limited way*—a way that does not seem to affect our actions or motivate us. We know intellectually, through data, graphs, and numbers. But we don't know in an embodied and visceral way. We don't know as *whole human beings*.

Perhaps Humboldt had a premonition of this when he chose to engage his readers' whole selves, and thereby show them the extent to which they are part of nature—and that the destruction of nature is also, and inextricably, the destruction of culture. His goal was not simply to communicate information, but to convey and impart a different *kind of knowledge*—a knowledge that is not purely intellectual, but also sensual and embodied. And this knowledge, which addresses our whole selves, has the potential to reach us in ways that graphs, numbers, and theses cannot—and thereby bring about a shift in our sense of ourselves and our relation to the natural world.

Humboldt's writings and the *kind of knowledge* they seek to embody and realize suggest a different approach to the environmental crisis. For what is at stake is the *way we know*—our practices of knowing. The claim is that these practices are themselves part of the problem. So long as we continue to know in an abstracted and distanced way, we will continue to imagine ourselves as *outside* nature, as beings who are not fundamentally affected by what happens "out there." Humboldt's form of knowledge, which speaks to our whole selves, has the potential to move and motivate us, because it reveals—in a visceral and embodied way—that nature's fate is *also* our fate.

7.6. The Moral Significance of Embodied Aesthetics

In the concluding remarks of "Über die Steppen und Wüsten," Humboldt contrasts animal to human struggles, writing that "though tiger and crocodile battle horses and cattle in the steppe, we see on its forested bank, in the wilderness of Guyana, man forever armed against man." The human being, even in "the vainglory of his elevated civilization," can only "make for himself a wearisome life" (DA 5, 19; VN 41). Over and over again, and across the globe, Humboldt remarks, the wanderer will witness the same scene of eternal struggle—one that will sap any hope for the future of humanity. For this reason, Humboldt continues,

> He who seeks spiritual peace amidst the unresolved strife between peoples therefore gladly lowers his gaze to the quiet life of plants and into the inner workings of the sacred force of nature, or, surrendering to the instinctive drive that has glowed for millennia in the breast of humanity, he looks upward with awe to the high celestial bodies, which, in undisturbed harmony, complete their ancient, eternal course. (DA 5, 19; VN 41–42)

The study of nature, then, offers a way beyond the sorry reality of humanity, beyond ceaseless human conflicts.

Reminiscent of the closing lines of Schiller's poem, these statements might suggest a form of quietism and complacency—by turning to nature, to its "eternal laws," we can escape the tumult of politics. But Humboldt's intention appears to be the very opposite. As stated in the Preface to the first edition of *Ansichten der Natur*, the contemplation of nature can, and should, lead us to a higher (moral) perspective. "In the mountains is freedom!" he writes, quoting Schiller (DA 5, x; VN 26). The implication is that by reading the essays—by following Humboldt "into the thickets of the forest, into the immeasurable steppes, and out upon the spine of the Andes range"—we arrive at a standpoint from which we can better grasp, and realize, our moral vocation (DA 5, x; VN 25). How might this be the case? And how might these moral concerns reflect back on Humboldt's portrayal of the disquieting struggle between horses and eels?

In the concluding remarks of "Das nächtliche Tierleben im Urwald," Humboldt describes the human being as the one who can listen to nature's many voices, tune in to both the cries of animals at night, and the midday silence. For even in this silence, Humboldt writes, "everything announces a world of active, organic powers. In every shrub, in the cracked bark of the trees, in the loose earth where live the hymenoptera, life audibly stirs." And, he adds, these silent expressions are "one of the many voices of nature, discernible to the solemn, receptive mind of humanity" (DA 5, 165; VN 147; translation altered). Echoing Herder's notion of *Besonnenheit* and his view that the human being inhabits an expressive and meaningful world, Humboldt describes the human being as the listener, observer, and describer of nature, whose vocation is to reflect nature.

But reflection—like much of human activity—is a double-edged sword, as evident in the meanings of the term. For to reflect means, in the first instance, to shed light on. The human being reflects nature through observation and descriptions, through feelings, ideas, and images. In this mode, the human being is giving expression to nature in and through the human form—in the feelings that emerge through an encounter with a natural event, or in the ideas that illuminate the event. But to reflect also means to turn back, to turn inward. Whether it is our feelings or images, our ideas or observations, our reflections on nature also belong to us, and reveal something about ourselves: that we are feeling and thinking beings. Accordingly, in turning to reflect on nature, we also turn to reflect on ourselves, and on our relationship to nature.

This reveals that the human relation to nature is dual. We are, on the one hand, of and in nature. In this mode, our feelings and ideas *speak of* and *participate in* the natural world. On the other hand, we can turn away from nature, toward ourselves. In this mode, we can become divorced from the reality around us. Our ideas and feelings can become untethered from our observations. We forget that we are participants in nature and take ourselves to be abstract knowers, somehow positioned outside the reality that touches and transforms us. It is in light of this dual posture that, I believe, Humboldt's own position must be understood.

In his description of the "wondrous struggle of horses and fish," Humboldt places himself outside of the struggle, and observes it with enthusiastic wonder. As an observer who is not implicated, he fails to consider the way in which his interests affect those of horses and eels. This contrasts with the overarching perspective that he develops, in which all beings are understood as interrelated and mutually supportive, such that the destruction of one will affect all the others. In this instance, however, Humboldt loses his grounding, and becomes an abstracted knower, almost unwilling to tune into the relations that he has elsewhere remarkably demonstrated.

Yet, Humboldt was not entirely abstracted. For as he describes the struggle, he pauses to take note of the panic in the horses' eyes. And it is this description—and this momentary pause—that remains with the reader, even as the narrative moves on. Accordingly, in witnessing the struggle, the reader/knower not only attends to the wondrous law of nature which the struggle appears to confirm (i.e., electricity), but also to the panic in the horses' eyes, the exhausted eels, and the two drowned horses.[33] In this momentary observation, the reader is brought back to the world of which she is part and called upon to examine her involvement and complicity in the violence before her.

Humboldt suggests in the closing lines of "Über die Steppen und Wüsten" that the awareness of human strife gives no solace. This might have to do with the fact that human beings repeatedly make Humboldt's mistake. We can get lost in purely intellectual pursuits, which dislodge us from the reality of which we are a part, allow us to forget that, as listeners, we must repeatedly and with care attune ourselves, our capacities, to listening: to the animals at night, and at midday, but also to the cries of the horses and the panic in their eyes.

The moral significance of embodied aesthetics, then, is that it retethers us to the natural world, reminds us that our feelings and thoughts should not become abstract, but remain close to the world, and be moved and challenged by the embodied experiences that inspired them.[34] For Humboldt, as for Goethe, knowledge is a moral act, because *how* well we know affects *what* we know. If our knowing is abstracted, then we will not concern ourselves with the suffering of the horses. If it is embodied, then we will concern ourselves, and this concern will challenge us to think carefully about human actions and their value, animal suffering and its need.

What Humboldt's writing and his aesthetics reveal, then, is that different forms of knowledge have significantly different results, which deeply affect our way of being in the world. With Goethe we can say that there is a difference between "seeing and seeing," or between "knowing and knowing." Knowing *well* is *embodied knowledge*: knowledge that addresses our *whole* selves—our sensibility, imagination, and understanding. It is a knowing that anchors us in the world, reminding us that it is not only our fate, but also the fate of many others, that depends on how well we listen.

Conclusion

The Relevance of Romantic Empiricism

The goal of this book is in part revisionary. By shedding light on an understudied philosophical tradition, and demonstrating a methodological continuity between four key thinkers, I have sought to offer a new history of German philosophy, one in which empiricism (albeit a distinctive form of empiricism) plays a far more significant role than otherwise recognized, and in which thinkers often relegated to the sidelines of the history of German philosophy (with the exception of Kant) are shown to have made crucial contributions to that history. Furthermore, by homing in on their methodologies, and showing how these methodologies sought to overcome fundamental philosophical difficulties, my aim is to open up a new way of reading the work of these four thinkers and assessing its significance.

My goals, however, are not purely historical, as the romantic empiricist approach remains relevant on a number of counts. First, romantic empiricism offer us insights into how we might be able to overcome fundamental oppositions—between diversity and unity, fixity and flux, sensibility and understanding, contingency and necessity. Second, it allows us to move beyond the one-sidedness of reductive empiricism, on the one hand, and abstract rationalism, on the other. Third, and perhaps most importantly, the romantic empiricist approach challenges us to think differently about the practices and ideals of knowledge, and about the relationship between epistemology, ontology, aesthetics, and ethics.

It is in relation to this last point that this book aims to contribute to environmental thought and action widely construed. After all, and as Val Plumwood put it, the environmental crisis is not only a biophysical crisis, but also, and more significantly, a crisis of reason: a crisis that is inextricably connected to the concepts and frameworks we use in order to understand the natural world and our place within it.[1] Accordingly, to address the environmental crisis, we must critically examine the concepts and frameworks that have led to our current situation.

The fields of environmental philosophy and environmental ethics emerged in light of this view, and have been built around the goal of, on the one hand, challenging certain concepts and frameworks, and, on the other, offering alternatives to them. Thus, concepts such as mechanism, or frameworks such as anthropocentrism, are replaced with, for instance, organicism and eco- or biocentrism, respectively. The conviction is that these concepts and frameworks are the source of our problematic behaviors toward the more-than-human world, such that their replacement with better concepts should have transformative effects on our behaviors.

Some practitioners in these fields have agonized over their lack of success.[2] What is striking is that in reflecting on their apparent failures, few have considered the possibility that the ecological crisis has less to do with any *one* concept or ideal, and more to do with the *way in which we know*, with our very practices of knowing.

Recent environmental thinkers have begun to address this point. This is particularly evident in critiques of the concept of nature, which, in the words of Timothy Morton, is a "transcendental idea in a material mask."[3] In other words, the problem has to do with the way in which we take abstract concepts to refer to real objects—an argument that recalls Herder's critique of hypostatization. Thus *nature* appears to refer to a concrete reality, when in fact it is an abstraction. And, the argument goes, it is precisely because *nature* is not a concrete reality that affects us, and that we can defend, that it has been a source of ethical and political inaction.

While this analysis is illuminating, it too stops short. For these critiques do not consider the possibility that nature is not the only problematic concept, and that the problem lies in the *ways* in which we know—in our tendency to abstract, to distance ourselves from the phenomena. Instead, they simply furnish another, equally abstract concept in the place of nature (e.g., ecology).

However, and as Danielle Celermajer has recently argued in relation to the catastrophic 2019–20 Australian bushfire season, it is only if our knowing ceases to be the abstracted transmission of information, that we will properly grasp the existential reality that is global climate change.[4] This means, to return to Plumwood's statement, that the environmental crisis is not only a crisis of reason, but also of sensibility and imagination, or more accurately, of the separation of knowing from sense, feeling, imagination, and action. What is needed, then, is a new approach to knowledge—a new practice of knowing.

The romantic empiricists offer a new approach to knowledge. They do not furnish a better concept or framework, but a new way of knowing and being in the world—a way that remains anchored in the phenomena and in lived experience.

By seeking to join what is given to the senses with what is known through the understanding, the romantic empiricists articulate and instantiate a different picture of what knowledge is, and what it involves. Knowledge is a practice, and as such, requires constant attention as well as formation or education. Specifically, it requires the education of our cognitive capacities. This education must be aesthetic, because it is only through aesthetic experience and insight that we can overcome our natural tendency to separate what is connected, and to regard dynamic and ongoing processes and relations as fixed and completed objects. Furthermore, by engaging our sensibility and understanding at once, aesthetic education anchors reflection in lived experience. This means that aesthetic education is necessary if we want to overcome the problems of abstraction and their consequences—everything from genuine misunderstanding to ethical and political inaction. In other words, aesthetic education is necessary if we are serious about addressing the crisis of sensibility, imagination, and understanding that lies at the heart of the environmental crisis.

In turn, by distinguishing between knowing well and knowing badly, the romantic empiricists reveal—in a new and exemplary way—how we, as knowers, are implicated in the act of knowing. In so doing, they demonstrate the extent to which our ideals and practices of knowing impact us and the world that we wish to know. After all, depending on *how* we know the phenomenon—the lens through which we regard it—the phenomenon will appear differently. And the manner in which it appears will impact our moral considerations. The romantic empiricists thus shed important light on how our moral responsibility extends to our cognitive practices—and how we, as knowers, are responsible to know *well*.

While much has changed since the time of Herder, Goethe, and Humboldt, their approach to nature and knowledge can inspire us to develop new ideals and practices of knowledge—and in this way help us to address the crises in which we find ourselves entangled today.

Notes

Introduction

1. Sankar Muthu, *Enlightenment against Empire*, 1.
2. See Dalia Nassar, "Pure versus Empirical Forms of Thought."
3. Kant and Herder are most often associated with the late Enlightenment, with Herder usually identified as a "critic" of the Enlightenment. Goethe is a key figure in Weimar classicism, while Humboldt is associated with both Enlightenment and romanticism. On this last point, see Michael Dettelbach, "Alexander von Humboldt between Enlightenment and Romanticism."
4. See Marion Heinz, "Philosophie. Einleitung." In the last few years, three major monographs on Herder were published in English alone: Kristin Gjesdal, *Herder's Hermeneutics*; Michael Forster, *Herder's Philosophy*; and Rachel Zuckert, *Herder's Naturalist Aesthetics*. In addition, Anik Waldow and Nigel DeSouza coedited the anthology *Herder: Philosophy and Anthropology*.
5. Eckart Förster, *The Twenty-Five Years of Philosophy*. I have also drawn it out in a number of works; see esp. *The Romantic Absolute*.
6. Andrea Wulf, *The Invention of Nature*. See also Laura Dassow Walls, *The Passage to Cosmos*, Joan Steigerwald, "The Cultural Enframing of Nature," and Elizabeth Millán, "Saving Nature from Vicious Empiricism."
7. Two important exceptions to this trend are Peter Hanns Reill's *Vitalizing Nature in the Enlightenment* and Michael Bies, *Im Grunde ein Bild*. Reill's study, which considers Kant, Herder, Goethe, and Humboldt, among many others, provides an important historical context for their work. However, in its historical focus, it does not provide systematic interpretations of their methodologies or of the (ethical and epistemological) implications of these methodologies. Furthermore, Reill's claim that these thinkers are part of a larger "Enlightenment" tradition, while interesting insofar as it extends the Enlightenment all the way to 1850, unwittingly repeats the problematic distinction between Enlightenment and romanticism that it attempts to challenge and does not pay adequate attention to the distinctively *new* elements that Kant, Herder, Goethe, and Humboldt introduce—elements that distinguish them from the French Enlightenment. Finally, by bringing these thinkers under the umbrella of "vitalism," Reill's study does not adequately acknowledge important differences *between* the four thinkers, such that what we have on his account are *echoes* rather than individual writers and scientists who were collaborating with and challenging one another in important and interesting ways. Bies's study does not consider Herder, focusing instead on Kant, Goethe, and Humboldt. Furthermore, Bies does not make the claim that these thinkers are part of a distinctive tradition, nor does he draw out the

various (epistemological, ethical) implications of their approach. Nonetheless, I am sympathetic to Bies's careful and illuminating analyses.

8. This is an interpretation that goes all the way back to Kant's critical reviews of Herder's *Ideas for a Philosophy of History of Humanity* [*Ideen zur Philosophie der Geschichte der Menschheit*] (1784–1791). It has been challenged by John Zammito, who has shown that—despite their strong rivalry—Kant and Herder *also* learned from one another. See Zammito, *The Genesis of Kant's "Critique of Judgment"* and *Kant, Herder and the Birth of Anthropology*.

9. An excellent example of this interpretation is Robert Richards, *The Romantic Conception of Life*.

10. Hans-Dietrich Irmscher's influential studies of Herder and Goethe do not consider these points. See Irmscher, "Goethe und Herder" and "Goethe und Herder im Wechselspiel von Attraktion und Repulsion."

11. This is the case in the two recent monographs on Humboldt: Walls, *The Passage to Cosmos* and Wulf, *The Invention of Nature*. Millán's article on Goethe and Humboldt is an exception. See Millán, "The Quest for the Seeds of Eternal Growth."

12. Scholars have shed important light on the ways in which the Jena romantics challenged the methodology of transcendental idealism, by showing how Friedrich Schlegel and Novalis, for example, criticized idealist system-building and a priori principles. This is an important step in the effort to discern differences in methodologies among philosophers of this period. See esp. Manfred Frank, "*Unendliche Annäherung*" and Frederick Beiser, *German Idealism*.

13. On Herder's influence on the romantics, see Michael Forster, *German Philosophy of Language*, Part 1. On Goethe's influence, see my *The Romantic Absolute*.

14. Germaine de Staël's work *De l'allemagne* (1810) played a crucial role in cementing the distinction between classicism and romanticism—a distinction that has since become commonly accepted. Staël, *De l'allemagne*, 144–45. Contrary to Staël, I agree with studies which have shown that when it comes to understanding nature, there is more commonality between the "classical" and the "romantic" than might otherwise be the case. See esp. Richards, *The Romantic Conception of Life* and Zammito, *The Gestation of German Biology*.

15. By contrast, in studies of British poetic romanticism, the distinction between romanticism and empiricism has not been as strong. See Gavin Budge, *Romantic Empiricism*. See also comparative studies of British and German romanticism, such as Kate Rigby, *Topographies of the Sacred*.

16. For an explication of Schlegel's "romantic empiricism," see my "Friedrich Schlegel, 1770–1829." However, in Schlegel's case, the focus is on the study of literature (and its history), the study of philosophy (and its history), and the study of languages, as opposed to nature and natural history. Accordingly, he does not develop a philosophy of nature in the same way that Kant, Herder, Goethe, and Humboldt do.

17. Buffon, *Histoire naturelle, generale et particulière*, vol. 14, 22–23.

18. I am drawing on the title of Rachel Zuckert's book, the only one in English that considers both parts of the third *Critique*. See Zuckert, *Kant on Beauty and Biology*.

19. And, as Zammito has shown, under pressure from Herder. See Zammito, *The Genesis of Kant's "Critique of Judgment,"* 10.
20. It is worth mentioning that the term "scientist" did not exist in English until 1834—i.e., two years after Goethe's death. It was coined by William Whewell, historian and philosopher of science, and headmaster at Trinity College, Cambridge, on analogy with the term "artist."
21. See Lorraine Daston and Glenn W. Most, "History of Science and History of Philologies."

Chapter 1

1. The phrase "human art [*menschliche Kunst*]" suggests that Kant does not intend the fine arts in this context, but the arts more generally, including crafts. Accordingly, it is likely the case that here the analogy to nature is to end-oriented practical activity (to making in general), rather than to the fine arts specifically. See also AA 5, 193.
2. As John Zammito has noted, the First (unpublished) Introduction was composed in May 1789, while the published Introduction was written in the last phase of composition, in 1790. Zammito, *The Genesis of Kant's "Critique of Judgment"*, 7–8.
3. The emphasis on "certain things [*gewisse Dinge*]" comes a few pages later, where Kant writes: "No one has doubted . . . the fundamental principle that certain things in nature (organized beings) and their possibility must be judged in accordance with the concept of final causes" (AA 5, 389).
4. Eric Watkins contends that in Section 71, Kant's justifies mechanism by appealing to the sensible world, because mechanism is "firmly rooted in the sensible world, which must form the basis for any 'interconnected experiential cognition.'" See Watkins, "The Antinomy of Teleological Judgment," 207.
5. See Angela Breitenbach, "Mechanical Explanation of Nature and Its Limits in Kant's *Critique of Judgment*," esp. 708–9. Breitenbach's contention is that all empirical laws of nature are left underdetermined by the transcendental structure of experience. This means that the a priori laws of the understanding cannot be identified with what Kant calls mechanism in the third *Critique*.
6. As Kant puts it, symbolic presentation "proceeds in a way merely analogous to that which it observes in schematization, i.e., it is merely the rule of this procedure, not of the intuition itself, and thus merely the form of the reflection, not the content, which corresponds to this concept" (AA 5, 351). See also Henry E. Allison, *Kant's Theory of Taste*, 264.
7. Kant, *Logik-Vorlesung*, 110. See Samantha Matherne, "Kant on Cognition by Analogy."
8. The brevity of my construction of this argument has to do with the fact that my goal here is not to analyze Kant's understanding of beauty as a symbol of morality, or to investigate the fact that there is an analogy in our manner of reflection on the two, but rather to explicate how analogy as symbolic presentation plays a role in expanding

our understanding of nature. For a more detailed account of the symbolic relation between beauty and morality, see Allison, *Kant's Theory of Taste*, 255–56.
9. Andrew Chignell similarly notes the significance of the object in Kant's account of analogy and symbol in Section 59. Chignell, however, does not emphasize the structural point. See Chignell, "Beauty as Symbol of Natural Systematicity."
10. Matherne introduces this distinction in her account of Kant's understanding of analogy. See Matherne, "Kant on Cognition by Analogy."
11. The exact sense in which we can "experience" organisms *before* we invoke symbolic presentation—i.e., analogical reflection—is unclear and contested in the scholarship. On the one hand, we need to have some intimation of them as having a specific structure in order to claim that they are inexplicable according to mechanical principles *and* to go on and invoke teleological judgment. On the other hand, as Kant claims here, "even the thought of them" is impossible for us without the idea of intention (AA 5, 398), such that prior to invoking the symbol of a purpose, organized beings in nature might appear to us as merely contingent. Accordingly, we can only say that they are *inexplicable* according to mechanical laws, but not add the further claim that this inexplicability *demands* the use of teleological judgment. After all, chemical phenomena are also inexplicable according to mechanical laws, but this does not demand the use of teleology. This difficulty comes down to the fact that Kant's argument is disjunctive and based on a hidden major premise: *either* mechanism *or* teleology. However, it is not clear that this is justified—there is no reason to assume that because certain beings are inexplicable from mechanical principles, only teleological ones will do.
12. On Herder's student years and his relationship to Kant in Königsberg, see Zammito, *Kant, Herder, and the Birth of Anthropology*, esp. chapter 4.
13. See Reill, *Vitalizing Nature in the Enlightenment*.
14. Buffon, *Histoire naturelle*, vol. 1, 50–51. On Buffon's influence on both French and German philosophies of nature, see Zammito, *The Gestation of German Biology*, chapters 3 and 6.
15. Linnaeus dropped the category "quadruped" in 1758, and in its place introduced "mammalia."
16. Buffon, *Histoire naturelle*, vol. 1, 20.
17. Buffon, *Histoire naturelle*, vol. 1, 16.
18. For an account of Buffon's distinction between "real" and "abstract" truths, see Philip Sloan, "Buffon, German Biology, and the Historical Interpretation of Biological Species."
19. According to Hans-Dietrich Irmscher, Wolff's use of *Witz* is connected to the notion of knowledge as creative, or as Wolff puts it, *Witz* is the "art of invention [*Kunst der Erfindung*]." Hans-Dietrich Irmscher, "Beobachtungen zur Funktion der Analogie im Denken Herders," 89–90.
20. Christian Wolff, *Vernünftige Gedanken von Gott, der Welt und der Seele des Menschen, auch allen Dingen überhaupt*, §363.
21. It is worthwhile to note that this need not be considered a case of analogy, but rather of simple application, i.e., the counting of money is the *application* of mathematics.

22. Johann August Eberhard, *Von dem Begriffe der Philosophie und ihren Theilen. Ein Versuch*, 22.
23. Buffon, *Les Époques de la nature*, vol. 1, 1. Quoted in Jacques Roger, *Buffon: A Life in Natural History*, 402. As Roger notes, Buffon's *Époques* was presented before the Academy of Sciences, Arts and Belles-Lettres of Dijon in 1773.
24. Buffon, *Histoire naturelle*, vol. 1, 30.
25. Philip Sloan, "The Buffon-Linnaeus Controversy," 370.
26. An earlier version of *Thoughts on the Interpretation of Nature* was published in late 1753 under the title *De l'Interprétation de la Nature*; however, the book as it is known today was published in early 1754 under the new title.
27. Denis Diderot, *Pensées sur l'Interprétation de la Nature*, 6, paragraph II; *Thoughts on the Interpretation of Nature*, 35.
28. Diderot, *Pensées*, 24, paragraph VII; *Thoughts*, 39.
29. Diderot, *Pensées*, 18–19, paragraph VI; *Thoughts*, 37–38.
30. Buffon, *Histoire naturelle*, vol. 14, 22–23.
31. Diderot and Buffon also emphasized the role of the imagination in grasping whole objects. See Jessica Riskin, *Science in the Age of Sensibility*, 98, 210–11. On the importance and widespread use of analogy in eighteenth-century life science, see Reill, *Vitalizing Nature in the Enlightenment*.
32. Buffon, *Histoire naturelle*, vol. 1, 50–51.
33. Buffon, *Histoire naturelle*, vol. 7, 22.
34. Kant, *Logik-Vorlesung*, 477–78.
35. Thus Herder's view that human history must be regarded as part of natural history is—for Kant—the outcome of an unjustified analogy. As Herder unequivocally puts it in the *Ideas*: "the entirety of human history is a pure natural history of human powers, activities, and drives according to place and time" (FHA 6, 568).
36. Kant's conception of construction in the *Metaphysical Foundations* is a topic of debate, and I will not enter into the debate here. In *Kant's Construction of Nature*, Michael Friedman challenges the view that by construction Kant means (only) mathematical construction. Friedman acknowledges that given Kant's statements in the Preface—where he identifies rational construction with mathematics— it is "natural" to assume that Kant's conception of construction is mathematical. But, Friedman argues, in the Dynamics section Kant is constructing matter nonmathematically; thus, construction is not bound to mathematics. This implies that Kant gives up on necessity, which is the defining feature of what he calls "proper science [*eigentliche Wissenschaft*]" (AA 4, 468). Indeed, Friedman claims that for Kant the dynamic character of matter is "contingent." He writes, "Kant explicitly recognizes, in particular, that this [dynamic] analysis is, in an important sense, contingent, insofar as there is an alternative mechanical concept in accordance with the system of absolute (as opposed to relative) impenetrability. And his choice of this preferred (dynamical) concept over the alternative (mechanical) concept rests, in the end, on nothing more nor less than the empirical success of Newton's theory in comparison with the opposing mechanical philosophy." *Kant's Construction of Nature*, 569.

37. As Rachel Zuckert explains, "on the physical-mechanical view . . . matter is understood as thoroughly homogeneous, as composed of homogeneous parts (i.e., space-filling parts) related to one another in virtue of the same forces that render them material." *Kant on Beauty and Biology*, 109.
38. Breitenbach, "Mechanical Explanation of Nature," 701.
39. See for instance, Henry Allison, "Kant's Antinomy of Teleological Judgment," and more recently, Breitenbach, "Mechanical Explanations of Nature."
40. Kant uses the expression "physical-mechanical" in a number of contexts in order to distinguish between physical-mechanical laws and those laws that "produce an organic body" (AA 2, 436). See also AA 8, 179. See Zuckert's account of Kant's understanding of the term, and of the important connections between the third *Critique* and the *Metaphysical Foundations*. *Kant on Beauty and Biology*, chapter 3.
41. For Aristotle, all four causes are inherently connected; for our purposes, however, the most important point concerns the relationship between structure (form) and purpose, which are brought together in Kant's conceptualization of internal purposiveness.
42. Peter McLaughlin has also pointed to the fact that what Kant at times means by final cause appears to be much closer to formal cause. However, in contrast to McLaughlin, I think internal purposiveness is not separate from formal causality. McLaughlin, *Kant's Critique of Teleology*, 153–154.
43. This is a point that Hannah Ginsborg emphasizes in her argument that there are two kinds of mechanical inexplicability, one of which concerns purposive machines. See Ginsborg, "Two Kinds of Mechanical Inexplicability in Kant and Aristotle."
44. Zuckert has also emphasized that what makes organized beings mechanically inexplicable is not only the specific part-whole structure that they exhibit, but also their distinctive temporal character. *Kant on Beauty and Biology*, 137–44.
45. In a letter to Christian Garve from 1798, Kant asserts that it was his discovery of the antinomy of pure reason that resulted in his awakening from his dogmatic slumbers (AA 12, 257–58). I thank Simon Kiorgaard for pointing this out to me.
46. Eric Watkins has argued that despite all the efforts to deliver a resolution to the antinomy of teleological judgment, the "challenge is still outstanding." Watkins, "The Antinomy of Teleological Judgment," 220.
47. Watkins provides an analysis of the most convincing attempts up to the publication of his article (2009). Watkins, "The Antinomy of Teleological Judgment." More recent efforts include Angela Breitenbach, "Two Views on Nature: A Solution to Kant's Antinomy of Teleological Judgment," which contends that mechanical judgment and teleological judgment offer "two perspectives" on nature—a scientific perspective (that of mechanical judgment) and one that conforms to our everyday experience (teleological judgment). The problem with this solution is that both forms of reflective judgments are regarded as directives for *scientific* (rather than purely everyday) practice. Breitenbach says as much when she notes that the antinomy presents "a conflict between the principles telling us how to go about in our search for knowledge of the natural laws" (355). In addition, Eckart Förster has offered a more comprehensive

attempt at a solution in *The Twenty-Five Years of Philosophy*, which I will discuss below (an earlier one is analyzed by Watkins).
48. See McLaughlin, *Kant's Critique of Teleological Biology* and Breitenbach, "Two Views on Nature."
49. This is close to the view espoused by McLaughlin, who argues that the resolution to the antinomy is based on the fact that the thesis concerns phenomena which discursive human understanding *can* explain, while the antithesis speaks of phenomena that we cannot explain. Thus the thesis is not so much prioritized, as *recognized*, for its explanatory (discursive) powers. *Kant's Critique of Teleology*, 162. This is, however, by no means the consensus account of Kant's resolution. Again, see Watkins, "Kant's Antinomy of Teleological Judgment."
50. One can add that it is also imperative to uphold the a priori construction of nature achieved in the *Metaphysical Foundations*, given that it is what Kant designates as "proper science." On that account, it is clear that mechanical explanations must be prioritized, insofar as they belong to proper science.
51. Förster, *The Twenty-Five Years of Philosophy*, chapter 6.

Chapter 2

1. Diderot, *Pensées*, 18–19, paragraph IV; *Thoughts*, 37–38.
2. That reflective judgment is itself inherently hermeneutical brings Kant even closer to Diderot. See Rudolf A. Makreel, *Imagination and Interpretation in Kant*. Makreel's analysis does not go into teleological judgment, however.
3. For this reason, I disagree with interpretations (such as Reill's) that place Kant and Buffon in the same camp. While Buffon clearly influenced Kant, Kant's ultimate ambivalence toward analogy and reflecting judgment in the study of nature strongly distinguishes him from Buffon. See Reill, *Vitalizing Nature in the Enlightenment*.
4. As Zammito has put it, in the eighteenth century the natural scientist became more than an *observateur* of nature; she became an *interprète* of nature. Zammito, *Kant, Herder and the Birth of Anthropology*, 229.
5. Herder's hermeneutic approach to nature can also be connected to an older (theological) tradition which regards nature as a book to be read, i.e., the Book of Nature. There are, however, crucial differences between this tradition and Herder's hermeneutical approach, and for this reason the two should be distinguished. First, Herder's approach is founded on his hermeneutical methodology, which he developed in response to the challenges of interpretation. Accordingly, it is not simply an adoption or adaption of an earlier conception of nature as "readable," and expressive of the voice of God. Rather, it is a creative appropriation of hermeneutics for the study of nature. Second, the trope of the Book of Nature implies that God *wrote* nature, and thus assumes that nature is something *created* and *finished*. For Herder, by contrast, nature is not a finished product. Thus, if we are to use the trope of writing, we are better off speaking of nature as "self-scripted." See Kate Rigby, "Earth's Poesy: Romantic

Poetics, Natural Philosophy, and Biosemiotics," 55. Finally, in the eighteenth century, the trope of the Book of Nature was invoked—as Axel Goodbody has argued—to distinguish scientific research from poetic writing. Goodbody, *Natursprache,* 29–30. For Herder, however, this distinction makes no sense. The poetic was necessary for scientific investigation. For all these reasons, it is imperative to recognize the difference and the *newness* of Herder's interpretive approach to nature.

6. Johann Gottfried Herder, *Herders Briefe,* 179–80. Quoted in Michael Forster, *After Herder,* 66. Translation modified.

7. Following Spinoza's distinction in the *Ethics* Herder argues in his 1787 *God: Some Conversations* [*Gott. Einige Gespräche*], through the voice of one of the interlocutors, that Spinoza's God or Nature (*Deus sive Natura*) is not an "abstract, lifeless deduction from the world," but the dynamic "cause of all being" (FHA 4, 726).

8. As we have seen, Kant's reviews criticize Herder's emphasis on the similarity between the human and the animal form, and in this respect positions Herder as a "naturalist." Furthermore, Herder appears to align himself with naturalist accounts of the origin of language, although, as we will see, with significant qualification. It is important to emphasize, however, that Herder's naturalism is not reductive. Kant, in his reviews, argues that Herder is reductive insofar as he seeks to "derive" human reason from the upright posture. As Kant sees it, Herder's account of the human being in nature implies that the human being "obtained reason through the erect posture, as the natural effect of the very same arrangement which was needed merely for letting him walk upright" (AA 8, 48). This reductive form of naturalism is, as I will argue, far from Herder's form of naturalism—and Kant's interpretation is misguided. It is for this reason also important to distinguish Herder's naturalism from twentieth-century forms of naturalism (indeed, the very term "naturalism" is a twentieth-century term), in that these more recent naturalisms (such as Quine's) are reductive. As I will show, Herder's relevance lies less in any alignment with recent naturalist views and more in the fact that he is critical of the abstract concept of nature and offers an important alternative to it. On the effort to align Herder with Quine, see Rachel Zuckert, "Herder and Philosophical Naturalism." Zuckert's more recent book on the topic argues that Herder's naturalism is nonreductive (might best be described as "emergentist") and is more closely connected to "normative naturalism." See Rachel Zuckert, *Herder's Naturalist Aesthetics.*

9. Buffon, *Histoire naturelle,* vol. 14, 22–23.

10. Buffon, *Histoire naturelle,* vol. 1, 4.

11. On Herder and Hamann's connection to Buffon, see Eugen Sauter, *Herder und Buffon,* 6–11. It is important to note that Sauter's account is missing Herder's first reference to Buffon, made in his 1768 essay on Thomas Abbt (Sauter claims, by contrast, that the first mention is from the 1769 *Journal of my Travels* [*Journal meiner Reise*]). Furthermore, though Hamann may certainly have mentioned Buffon to Herder, given the popularity of the *Histoire naturelle,* Herder may have come to Buffon through other sources. On Herder in Paris, see Zammito, *The Gestation of German Biology,* 180.

12. On Buffon's account of the influence of food and climate on the "degeneration" of species, see Philip Sloan, "The Idea of Racial Degeneracy in Buffon's *Histoire naturelle*." Thanks to Jennifer Mensch for directing me to this article.
13. According to Jacques Roger, Buffon's notion of "climate" changed over the years, such that by 1775, it denoted temperature alone. Roger, *Buffon*, 415.
14. Buffon, *Histoire naturelle*, vol. 4, 215. Buffon provides an account of the influence of climate on every species he examines.
15. Roger, *Buffon*, 178; Sloan, "The Idea of Racial Degeneracy," 307–9.
16. See for instance Chenxi Tang, *The Geographic Imagination of Modernity*. Tang argues that Herder's view of nature as "a dynamic system of forces" strongly contrasts with "a static surface lending itself to schematic description in the manner of Bergman, Buffon, and other descriptive geographers" (108).
17. As Kristin Gjesdal puts it, "genius, for Herder, is not understood as an ability to produce original works of art without reference to existing culture, but as an ability to rework, from within a culture, the available resources of tradition in an individualized and novel way, thus expanding the horizon of symbolic expressions and models of understanding." Gjesdal, *Herder's Hermeneutics*, 135.
18. For a more comprehensive account of the main differences between ancient Greek and Shakespearean tragedy according to Herder, see Michael Forster, *After Herder*, 172. See also Herder's critique of Winckelmann's assessment of ancient Egyptian and ancient Greek sculpture. Herder argues that Winckelmann's account does not adequately consider the culture in which the respective sculptures emerged, and thus does not recognize that there is a fundamental difference in the goals of Greek and Egyptian sculpture. As Forster notes, according to Herder, Winckelmann fails not only in his interpretation of these works, but also in his valuation of them. *After Herder*, 173–75.
19. See also Gjesdal, *Herder's Hermeneutics*, 135–37.
20. When writers realized that meaning need not be sequentially ordered, but is in a significant sense also nonsequential, they began to compose nonsequential works, which "begin" at the "end," i.e., the end of the story, and proceed "backward" to its "beginning."
21. The question posed by the Academy is as follows: "En supposant les hommes abandonnés à leurs facultés naturelles, sont-ils en état d'inventer le langage? Et par quels moyens parviendront-ils d'eux-mêmes à cette invention? [Abandoned to their natural capacities, would human beings be in a condition to invent language? And by what means could they achieve this invention on their own?]"
22. This view is denoted as Epicurean because of Epicurus's argument, in the *Letter to Herodotus*, that language originated in animal-like expressions of emotion, and was followed by a process through which different entities became distinct and this eventually led to the ability to denote abstract entities.
23. The primary aim of Rousseau's *Discourse* was not to consider the question of the origin of language, but the question of inequality and whether it is authorized by natural law.
24. Here I am following Avi Lifschitz's account of Rousseau's challenges to naturalistic views of language. See Lifschitz, *Language and Enlightenment*, esp. 78–80.

258   NOTES

25. Lifschitz, *Language and Enlightenment*, 79.
26. Jean-Jacques Rousseau, *Oeuvres complètes*, vol. 3, 149.
27. As Lifschitz recounts, "Rousseau's exasperation at the difficulties posed by the human invention of language became a focal point for conservative authors, from Beauzée to de Maistre," and ultimately led to Süßmilch's argument for the divine origin of human language. Lifschitz, *Language and Enlightenment*, 79; see also 83–87.
28. As Herder puts it, on account of Rousseau's and Condillac's failures, he will "need to begin from rather far back [*muß also etwas weit ausholen*]" (FHA 1, 711; HPW 77).
29. See also Lifschitz, *Language and Enlightenment*, 183–86.
30. Herder's discussion of the animal's "circle [*Kreis*]" or "world [*Welt*]" comes very close to later (twentieth-century) discussions of the notion of an animal environment or *Umwelt*, a term coined by Jakob von Uexküll to describe the intimate connection between the animal's capacities and its habitat. See, for instance, Uexküll's account of the tick, in which—along the same lines as the ones Herder offers here—he describes the intimate connection between the tick's perceptual capacities and its world. Jakob von Uexküll, *A Foray into the World of Animals and Humans*.
31. This insight is further elaborated by Humboldt in his account of the relationship between a living being and its context. See chapter 6. Herder's perspective on the bee-beehive relation corresponds to the view that the beehive (or ant colony) should be regarded as a "superorganism," and the bee as an essential member of this larger context. The claim is that the bee is irreducibly part of the beehive, and the beehive is irreducibly dependent on the bee. It is a relation of absolute reciprocity such that it is impossible to separate the two, and regard the one as the antecedent (i.e., efficient) cause of the other. See, for instance, William Morton Wheeler, "The Ant Colony as Organism," and T. D. Seeley, "The Honey-Bee Colony as a Superorganism."
32. See FHA 4, 661. Herder's goal, as I will explicate below as well as in chapter 3, is to discern lawfulness in nature through careful observation, description, and analogical reflection. The law, in other words, is to be found immanently in the phenomena, rather than beyond them, whether the beyond signifies an efficient cause that stands outside of the phenomena or a *causa occulta*, which must be posited but can never be known.
33. As recent work in theoretical biology has argued, it is the animal as a *whole* that must be accounted for if we are to understand it as a being that is transformed by its world, but that also *actively* transforms its world. See, for instance, Patrick Bateson, "The Return of the Whole Organism," and, more recently, Daniel J. Nicholson, "The Return of the Organism as a Fundamental Explanatory Concept in Biology."
34. "Taking awareness" is the translation offered by Michael Forster in HPW.
35. On Herder's interest in contemporary physiology, see Stefanie Buchenau, "Herder: Physiology and Philosophical Anthropology." On his emphasis on the "figuration" of sensation, prior to conceptualization, and the significance of analogy in this regard, see Amanda Jo Goldstein, "Irritable Figures: Herder's Poetic Empiricism," 284–85.
36. Thus he writes: "One will never get to the bottom of these forces if one merely treats them superficially as ideas that dwell in the soul, or worse still, separates them from

one another as walled up compartments and considers them individually in independence" (FHA 4, 356; HPW 210).
37. On this point, see also Anik Waldow's analysis in *Experience Embodied*, esp. chapter 5.2.
38. The German *alläosieren* has also been translated as *alloisizing*. See Goldstein, "Irritable Figures," 286. My preference for translating it with *allocating* has to do with the fact that *alläosieren* is usually translated as such, and also that *allocating* makes more evident the connection between *alläosieren* and *translation*, which, as Goldstein also notes, are used synonymously by Herder.
39. It is interesting that Kant at no point directly criticizes this claim. While in the first review, which was published in March 1785 and considers the first volume of the *Ideas*, Kant cites this passage without a critical discussion, in the second review, published in November of that year, and focusing on the second volume of the *Ideas*, Kant notes that Herder locates the origins of reason in human culture. This means, Kant continues, that Herder does not find reason in "the human species' own faculty, but rather entirely outside it, in a teaching and instruction by other natures" (AA 8, 63). It is very likely that Kant's reworking of the first *Critique* in 1787 (i.e., the B edition of the first *Critique*) and in particular his writing of the B Deduction—in which he speaks of the "epigenesis of pure reason" (B167)—was an attempt to challenge precisely this view. See Daniela Helbig and Dalia Nassar, "The Metaphor of Epigenesis: Kant, Blumenbach and Herder." On Kant's conceptualization of reason as "self-born [*Selbstgebärung*]" (A765/B793) and its significance for the B Deduction, see Jennifer Mensch, *Kant's Organicism*.
40. As Marion Heinz points out, Herder disagrees with Locke's empiricism, on the one hand, and Leibniz's rationalism, on the other. Heinz, *Sensualistischer Idealismus*, 109–17. Nonetheless, Heinz contends that Herder's position is quite close to Leibniz's view regarding the original unity of sensation and cognition, but that he departs from Leibniz in one important respect: in the way he justifies his position. Leibniz relies on the doctrine of pre-established harmony. In contrast, Heinz argues, Herder aims to *show* that there is an original unity between mind and body which in turn implies a unity between sensation and cognition. In other words, Herder must somehow explain how sensations *become* ideas. Herder's answer, I believe, rests on his view that cognition is essentially analogical, i.e., it translates sensations into ideas. On Heinz's account of Herder's relation to and departure from Leibniz, see *Sensualistischer Idealismus*, 121–22.
41. The dualist position was espoused by Johann Georg Sulzer (1720–1779), who won the Berlin Academy's 1778 prize, for which Herder had composed "On Cognition and Sensation." See Heinz, *Sensualistischer Idealismus*, 109–17, 133–35.
42. As Herder puts it, "the invention of language is . . . as natural for him as is his being a human being!" (FHA 1, 722; HPW 87).
43. As he puts it in the *Ideas*, an animal's capacities are "in harmony with its entire way of life [*seiner ganzen Lebensweise harmonisch*]" (FHA 6, 127).
44. On the emergence of "dynamic" natural history and its influence on modern geography, see Tang, *The Geographic Imagination of Modernity*, chapter 1. Tang maintains

that Herder was the first to contribute to the dynamicization of natural history (108). Eugen Sauter similarly maintains that Herder played an important role in the emergence of modern geography, above all through influencing the geographer Carl Ritter. Sauter, *Herder und Buffon*, 88.
45. The most famous example here is Aldo Leopold, whose notion of "land" emphasizes this inherent relation between a place and its inhabitants.

Chapter 3

1. Newton, *Philosophical Writings*, 115–16.
2. Blumenbach, *Über den Bildungstrieb*, 25–26.
3. For a comprehensive account of Herder's various conceptions of force and his uses of force, see Robert J. Clark Jr., "Herder's Conception of 'Kraft.'"
4. In other words, Blumenbach was not the only eighteenth-century thinker to make use of Newton's *hypotheses non fingo*. On the widespread use of Newtonian analogies, see Charles T. Wolfe, "On the Role of Newtonian Analogies in Eighteenth-Century Life Science."
5. On the significance of the notion of force (and the various forces that were posited in the late eighteenth century to account for living beings) for the development of biology, see Zammito, *The Gestation of German Biology*. While Zammito is right to emphasize that force was a significant factor in the emergence of biology as a distinct discipline, my point is that Herder and Goethe had good reason to emphasize form. Furthermore, I do not think it is entirely accurate to claim that force was the most significance concept for the emergence of biology. As Hans Driesch put it in his 1907 Gifford Lectures: "it is *form* particularly which can be said to occupy the very centre of biological interest; at least it furnishes the foundation of all biology." Hans Driesch, *Science and Philosophy of the Organism*, 17.
6. This was of course the context in which Kant was writing and which ultimately resulted in his ambivalent conclusions regarding the status of both teleological judgment and organization in nature. For an account of the "problem" of animal generation in the early modern period, see Justin Smith, *The Problem of Animal Generation*.
7. See Stephen Gaukroger, *The Collapse of Mechanism and the Rise of Sensibility*, 357ff.
8. Albrecht von Haller, "Reflections on the Theory of Generation of Mr. Buffon," 320. For a detailed account of the debate between the two most well-known proponents of preformation (Haller) and epigenesis (C. F. Wolff) on the question of animal generation, see Shirley Roe, *Matter, Life, and Generation*.
9. On the differences between Kant and Blumenbach on this issue, see Robert Richards, "Kant and Blumenbach: A Historical Misunderstanding."
10. Importantly, Herder distinguishes his metaphysics from his methodology, because, as H. B. Nisbet explains, for Herder "scientific investigation can take place only 'von außen,'" such that "Herder's conception of 'Kraft' . . . has no scientific status whatsoever." Nisbet, *Herder and Scientific Thought*, 9. As I have indicated above, Herder

is clear about the fact that we cannot investigate forces, and repeatedly emphasizes that scientific research must be concerned with what appears. Thus while it is fair to claim that Herder had a metaphysics of forces, it is not fair to claim that this metaphysics was at the heart of his *approach* to nature or to argue that his dynamic conception of nature is based on his metaphysics. Rather, as I have shown in the preceding chapter, Herder arrived at his dynamic conception of nature through the notion of world, which he developed in his work in hermeneutics. Nigel DeSouza has a slightly different, even if ultimately concurring, interpretation. He argues that for Herder "human language . . . can only depict how things appear, i.e., 'according to their form,'" and only a divine perspective can grasp "how things 'were formed,'" i.e., how the forces brought them about. Nigel DeSouza, "Herder's Theory of Organic Forces and Its Kantian Origins," 122.

11. Goethe offers critical remarks on both Caspar Wolff's notion of *Lebenskraft* and Blumenbach's notion of *Bildungstrieb* in an essay he published in On Morphology titled "*Bildungstrieb*." Similarly, Humboldt, who originally regarded the notion of a life force as essential for explicating the difference between life and nonlife—as evident in his early essay "Die Lebenskraft oder der Rhodische Genius. Eine Erzählung [The Life Force or the Rhodian Genius: a Tale]," published in Schiller's *Die Horen* in 1795—retracts this view. Both argue that the notion of a life force or drive fails to explain what it purports to explain, i.e., "life." For an analysis of their critiques, see Dalia Nassar, "The Challenge of Plants: Goethe, Humboldt and the Question of 'Life.'"
12. Herder to Hamann, in *Herders Briefe*, 231; quoted in Richards, *The Romantic Conception of Life*, 369.
13. Nicholas Boyle, *Goethe: The Poet and the Age*, vol. 1, 97.
14. For an account of the differences in the methods and assumptions of Goethe, Camper, and Blumenbach on this point, see Ryan Feigenbaum, "Toward a Nonanthropocentric Vision of Nature." Feigenbaum, however, contests Goethe's interpretation of the history of science, arguing that for Camper and Blumenbach the intermaxillary bone did not serve as the distinguishing feature of the human. Rather, it was the upright posture or gait. On Goethe's interpretation of this moment in the history of science, see above.
15. Goethe composed a brief treatise on his discovery in 1786 which he sent to the most important anatomists of the time—Camper, Blumenbach, and Sömmering—all of whom altered their view of the bone in the coming years. For an account of Goethe's influence on comparative osteology, see Richards, *The Romantic Conception of Life*, 372–75.
16. Goethe to Knebel (November 1784) in *Briefwechsel zwischen Goethe und Knebel*, 55.
17. As Craig Holdrege puts it, "In his studies of living nature Goethe considered how every part of a larger whole is truly a member of that whole and expressive of it. All the bones in the human frame are related to our upright posture. It's not a particular bone that makes us human but how the individual bones are configured within the context of the whole organism." Holdrege, "Goethe and the Evolution of Science," 12.
18. Richards, *The Romantic Conception of Life*, 374.

262   NOTES

19. As we will see in the chapters to follow, Goethe's conceptualization of *Typus* is not of a static structure. Rather, and as Goethe emphasizes when he distinguishes *Gestalt* from *Bildung*, the idea of the archetype points to a living, dynamic reality that is in dialogue with its context. See esp. chapter 5, section 5.2.

Chapter 4

1. *On Morphology* [*Zur Morphologie*], also known as the "Morphologische Hefte," was published in two volumes (with each volume having two issues). Volume 1 appeared between 1817 and 1822 and volume 2 appeared between 1823 and 1824.
2. Although the English term "scientist" did not exist in Goethe's time, I am using it, for the sake of brevity, to describe the student of nature, a category that closely corresponds to the idea of the natural scientist.
3. The most influential interpretation is perhaps Eckart Förster's. See *The Twenty-Five Years of Philosophy*, chapters 11 and 12. While Förster offers crucial insights with regard to both Goethe's place in the history of German idealism and his methodology, he does not consider the significance of education in Goethe's epistemology—and thus also overlooks the ways in which it distinguishes him from his idealist contemporaries. See also Gunnar Hindrichs, "Goethe's Notion of an Intuitive Judgment," and Brady Bowman, "Goethean Morphology, Hegelian Science: Affinities and Transformations." Important exceptions to this trend among philosophical interpretations are Jost Schieren, *Anschauende Urteilskraft* and Frederick Amrine, "The Metamorphosis of the Scientist," both of whom emphasize the role of education in Goethe's epistemology and methodology. Schieren argues that Goethe's notion of intuitive judgment is not something that we are born with or even truly achieve, but must constantly strive toward realizing. See Schieren, *Anschauende Urteilskraft*, 230.
4. As Baumgarten puts it in his *Philosophical Letters*, aesthetics does not only concern the arts, but also "the weapons of the senses or those instruments through which we are enabled to receive a clear perception when the perception would have otherwise remained dim for us." Alexander Baumgarten, "Philosophischer Briefe zweites Schreiben," 2.
5. As Gabriel Tropp has noted, there are at least four ways in which the morphological poems relate to Goethe's science: (1) mimetic in content: they offer summaries of Goethe's scientific findings; (2) mimetic in form: they equate the form of poetry with the forms (and transformations) of nature; (3) productive or generative: they offer a means for "cognitive training"; (4) metaphilosophical: they illustrate the principles, trajectories, histories, and effects of morphological observation on the scientist. Tropp, "Poetry and Morphology," 398–99. My considerations in the following will focus on number 2 and number 3, which I regard as deeply related. For it is precisely through their form that poetic works contribute to "cognitive training," i.e., the education of the senses and judgment. A similar take on the importance of poetic form, and in particular Goethe's poem "Metamorphosis of Plants [*Metamorphose der*

Pflanzen]," for cognitive education can be found in Gernot Böhme, "Die Einheit von Kunst und Wissenschaft im Zeitalter der Romantik." The final section of this chapter offers a discussion of this poem.

6. Goethe returned to Weimar in 1788 and at that point turned to reading the *Critique of Pure Reason*. As the publisher of the widely read *Teutscher Merkur*, Christoph Martin Wieland, writes to his son-in-law, the Kantian Karl Leonard Reinhold, in February 1789: "Goethe has been studying Kant's *Critique* for some time with great application, and he has resolved to have a conference with you about it in Jena." Quoted in Wolf, *Streitbare Ästhetik*, 417.

7. Goethe published a shorter version of the essay in the first volume of *On Morphology* (1817) and a longer version in 1831. In both, he remarks on the significance of his time in Italy for the development of his botanical research. In the longer essay, however, he offers more detail, and for this reason, I will reference the longer (1831) version, which bears the title "The author relates the history of his botanical studies [*Der Verfasser teilt die Geschichte seiner botanischen Studien mit*]," and can be found in LA 1/10, 319–38.

8. This passage appears in a number of Goethe's writings, including the *Italian Journey*, "History of My Botanical Studies," and in a letter to Knebel. Within the *Italian Journey*, it is part of a 1787 report titled "Disruptive Observations of Nature [*Störende Naturbetrachtungen*]," which immediately follows Goethe's introduction of the idea of an *Urpflanze* and his description of it as a "proteus." In this context, he makes no mention of Kauffmann. However, in "History of My Botanical Studies," Goethe situates his encounter with the proliferous carnation in Kauffmann's garden. See FA 24, 750–51 and LA 1/10, 336.

9. Johann Heinrich Tischbein, with whom Goethe shared an apartment, introduced Goethe to a number of German artists living in Rome, including Kauffmann, Friedrich Bury, Johann Georg Schütz, Johann Heinrich Lisp, the sculptor Alexander Trippel, and the artist and teacher Heinrich Meyers. For the full list, see HA 14, 419. Goethe moved into Tischbein's apartment on October 30, 1786.

10. Although Goethe had attempted drawing before going to Rome, while in Rome he dedicated himself in a more concerted way to drawing, painting, and sketching, and sought out a tutor. In a letter to Duke Carl August (March 17, 1788) Goethe relates that he has discovered himself anew as an artist—and specifically as a visual artist (FA 30, 394–95).

11. Goethe writes that "I count the day I entered Rome as my second natal day, a true rebirth" (FA 15/1, 158).

12. As noted in the preceding chapter, Goethe develops the notion of *Typus* in that essay as a way for dealing with the impossible task of accounting for every species and seeking to find continuity among them. As he puts it, "Hence, an anatomical archetype [*anatomischen Typus*] will be suggested here, a general picture containing the forms of all animals as potential, one which will guide us to an orderly description of nature" (MA 12, 122). See chapter 3, section 3.4.

13. A helpful account of *Steigerung* can be found in Astrida Orle Tantillo, *The Will to Create: Goethe's Philosophy of Nature*, chapter 2.

14. Date palms do not have branches, such that the resemblance of the mature leaves' form to the form of branches might suggest not only an approximation to the form, but even a kind of replacement of it.
15. The most important exception is Alexander von Humboldt, whom we will discuss in chapters 6 and 7. There were other important exceptions, however, including botanists with whom Goethe worked closely, such as A. J. G. K. Batsch, who founded a botanical garden and a natural history society in Jena, and F. J. Schelver, a former student of Schelling's who succeeded Batsch as director of the botanical garden in 1803. On Goethe's friendship and work with both, see Nicholas Boyle, *Goethe: The Poet and the Age*, vol. 2, 206 and 783; on Goethe's relation to Schelver, see Förster, *The Twenty-Five Years of Philosophy*, 288–91.
16. For such a reading, see, for example, Boyle, *Goethe: The Poet and the Age*, vol. 2, 82.
17. Another famous instance of this interpretation is found in Schiller's distinction between "naive" and "sentimental" poets. While Goethe is cast as upholding the naive tradition of poetry, Schiller is, by contrast, regarded as the herald of the modern, or sentimental poetry, i.e., poetry that emphasizes a disconnection between self and nature, a turn to subjectivity, even as it also strives for unity. Goethe seems to agree with this description, writing in "Influence of the New Philosophy," while Schiller "preached the gospel of freedom, I wanted to preserve the rights of nature" (MA 12, 97). However, in both this statement and in the claim that he possesses no "organ for philosophy," there is no indication that Goethe did not grasp fundamental epistemological and methodological difficulties facing the study of nature. Rather, both statements refer to Goethe's lack of a certain philosophical attitude—which one might describe as an abstract way of approaching the world—and a philosophical vocabulary. While Goethe certainly did not possess the former, it was not for naive but rather for studied reasons; the latter, as I will argue below, became an important tool for Goethe in his later writings. For a similarly non-naive interpretation of Goethe's development, see Frederick Amrine, "Goethean Intuitions."
18. On this point, see esp. Luke Fischer, "Goethe contra Hegel: The Question of the 'End of Art.'"
19. When Goethe republished the essay in *On Morphology*, he placed it alongside a number of methodological essays, as well as poems, many of which highlight the role of the knower in the act of knowing, and investigate the historical, cultural, and sociological context in which knowledge is produced. For this reason, Goethe has been referred to as the first sociologist of science. See Fink, *Goethe's History of Science* and Dorothea von Mücke, "Goethe's Metamorphosis." Although Goethe does not make any changes to the content or structure of the original essay, he does add introductory and concluding remarks (sometimes in the form of short essays) that might help prepare the reader to engage with the work—including the remarks quoted at the beginning of this chapter.
20. In his ruminations on the "fate" of the text, Goethe notes that *The Metamorphosis of Plants* did not fare well in part because of his renown as a poet. While I do not wish to contest this explanation altogether, I want to add that a year earlier, in 1789, Erasmus Darwin delivered his scientific research and investigations in verse form,

titled "The Botanic Garden." This work was well-received. Though there are significant differences between Goethe's and Darwin's works, there is reason to believe that the lack of enthusiasm for *The Metamorphosis of Plants* did not *only* have to do with the fact that Goethe was a poet, but also, as I argue above, with the *kind of* work it is and the *expectations* it places on its reader. On Erasmus Darwin's "The Botanic Garden," see Amanda Jo Goldstein, *Sweet Science*, chapter 1.

21. As Ronald Brady notes, the meaning of the "symbolic plant" in this essay is not at all clear. Brady, "The Causal Dimension of Goethe's Morphology," 334. Put in the context of Goethe's epistemological writings, however, it gains some clarity—as will be elaborated in chapter 5.

22. Goethe's comparative work in 1784 focused on mammals, and the intermaxillary bone is a mammalian bone.

23. As Goethe recounts in the Preface to the 1817 edition of *The Metamorphosis of Plants*, his critical attitude toward preformationist theories of generation may have been another reason for the unpopularity of the text. However, it is important to note that Goethe's views on this question may be easily missed, given that *The Metamorphosis of Plants* does not explicitly engage with the debate.

24. For a lengthier account of the debate see chapter 3, section 3.1. See also Shirley Roe, *Matter, Life, and Generation*.

25. Quoted in Wolf, *Streitbare Ästhetik*, 417.

26. While the title of the essay suggests Kant's influence on Goethe, it is important to note, first, that Goethe's understanding of the difference between subject and object does not map onto Kant's—as we will see in what follows—and second, that Goethe had already thematized the separation of subject and object well before his acquaintance with the first *Critique*. As Fink notes, the problem of the subject-object separation was one which Goethe had thematized in some of his earliest poetry. However, it was not until 1792/1793 that Goethe explicitly took it up and attempted to articulate it theoretically. Fink, *Goethe's History of Science*, 6.

27. Förster, *The Twenty-Five Years of Philosophy*, 254–65. Goethe's interest in Spinoza, which may have been sparked by Herder, goes back to the mid-1780s. See Förster, "Goethe's Spinozism," 86.

28. This positive assessment of the mathematical procedure is another indication of the influence of Spinoza on this essay. See Förster, "Goethe's Spinozism," 92–93.

29. There is, of course, the other possibility in mathematics as well: we do not begin with the formula, but rather must discover it by following the arithmetical sequence. This would be more aligned with the procedure of the empirical sciences.

30. See chapter 1, especially the discussion of the Antinomy of Teleological Judgment. See also Dalia Nassar, "Sensibility and Organic Unity: Kant, Goethe, and the Plasticity of Cognition."

31. As Förster puts it, "Goethe is convinced that what makes a plant a plant is the ideal whole that determines the parts and their succession and is simultaneously at work through that succession, so that *the earlier states are just as determined by the later ones as the later ones are determined by the earlier ones*: Not only does the formation of the petals, for example, presuppose the formation of the stem and the leaves; the

possibility of the later formation of the fruit is already formatively at work in the development of the pistils and stamens in the blossom" (*The Twenty-Five Years*, 275 n. 17; emphasis added). In other words, what the usual procedure of experience misses is the fact that all the parts are informed by one another, such that none can be understood outside of their mutually formative relationships within the whole.

32. A turn that is echoed in the essay titled "Problems [*Probleme*]" (1823), where Goethe writes, "There may be no escape from this difficulty without recourse once more to artifice [*künstliches Verfahren*]" (MA 12, 295).

33. On the history and publication of this poem, see Regina Sachers, *Goethe's Poetry and Philosophy of Nature*, chapter 4.

34. A translation of this poem: "Thus view with unassuming gaze / The Weaver Woman's masterpiece: / One pedal shifts a thousand strands, / The shuttles back and forward flying. / Each fluent strand with each complying, / One stroke a thousand links commands."

35. As with "Antepirrhema," so "Epirrhema" is the title which Goethe gives the poem in *God and World*.

36. On the ways in which poetry (in general) mirrors the form of living beings, see Günther Müller, "Morphologische Poetik."

37. An English translation of the poem (by Frederick Turner and Zsuzsanna Ozsvàth) is provided below. This translation can be found at https://poems.com/poem/the-metamorphosis-of-the-plants/

I will not use this translation in my interpretation of the poem above, but provide my own (less eloquent, but more straightforward) translations.

> You are perplexed, my love, by this thousandfold mixed profusion,
>   Flowering tumultuously everywhere over the garden grounds;
> So many names you are hearing, but one suppresses another,
>   Echoing barbarously the sound makes in the ear.
> Each of their shapes is alike, yet none resembles the other,
>   Thus the whole of the choir points to a secret law,
> Points to a holy puzzle. I wish, lovely friend, that I were able to
>   Happily hand you at once the disentangling word!—
> Watch now and be transformed, how bit by bit the plant-form,
>   Guided stepwise, builds to emerge in blossom and fruit!
> Out of the germ it unfolds, the moment the still and fertile
>   Lap of the earth has lovingly let it go out into life,
> There where the charm of light, the holy eternal mover
>   Now ushers in the most delicate structures of burgeoning leaves.
> This was a power that simply slept in the seed; a prototype
>   Lay there closed and curled up in itself inside the husk,
> Leaf and taproot and seed, as yet half-formed and colorless;
>   Thus the dry kernel holds and protects the dormant life,
> Then it gushes, heaving up, trusting to milder moistures,
>   Lifts itself all at once out of the enveloping night.
> Still, though, it simply retains the form of its first appearance,
>   Thus the infant reveals and betrays itself under the new plant.
> Soon after that, a following impulse, renewing, throws upward

Knot upon towering knot, in still the original shape.
Never the same, though; for always its self-generation is manifold,
    Always the following leaf, you see there, is fully informed:
Notched, expanded, and split into apex and branched divisions,
    That which in embryo rested curled up in the organ below.
Now it achieves for the first time its highly-determined completion,
    Which in some species can leave you astonished and awed.
Fretted and tuned all over its mastlike and bristling surface,
    Now in full force appears the drive to be endlessly free.
Here, though, Nature with mighty hand halts the upbuilding,
    Leading it gently on until its full form is complete.
So with more measure it guides the sap and tightens the vessels,
    Suddenly blazoning out the pattern's more dainty effects.
Silently now the drive ebbs from the leading edges,
    Letting the vein of the stem build itself fully out.
Leafless and swiftly, though, rises the stalk in its greater elegance,
    Where the observer is drawn to a yet more miraculous form:
Ringed in a circle, each petal, in number defined or left open,
    Sets itself, smaller at first, by its twin that emerged before.
Crowding around the axle, the mounting cup comes to decision,
    Which, in its highest form, releases its colorbright crown.
Nature thus boasts now a nobler and fuller manifestation,
    Stepwise arraying organ on organ in ordered display.
Always you're freshly amazed when the flower on its stem, now open,
    Sways there above the slender scaffold of altering leaves.
Now, though, this splendor becomes a new shaping's annunciation,
    Yes, the bright-tinted petal feels the hand of God;
Swiftly it draws itself in, and then the tenderest of structures
    Bifold strive to emerge, determined to make themselves one.
Intimate now they stand, the lovely couples together,
    Round the sacred altar in order arranging themselves.
Hymen floats nearby, and heavenly fragrances violently
    Pour their sweet and quickening odors all through the air.
Germ cells at once swell up now, each an individual,
    Lovingly wrapped in the waxing fruits of the mothering womb.
Here, then, Nature closes the ring of eternal forces;
    Still, a new one promptly fastens itself to the old,
So that the chain might extend itself onward all through the ages,
    And that the whole be revitalized, as is the single one.
Turn now, beloved, your eyes to these blooming and colorful multitudes,
    See how, perplexing no longer, they stir there in view of your soul!
Every plant announces, to you now, the laws eternal,
    Every flower louder and louder is speaking with you.
You but decipher here the holy glyphs of the Goddess,
    Everywhere, though, you see her—in even their changing itself.
Slow crawls the caterpillar, in haste the butterfly flutters,

>   Man the adaptable changes himself the foreordained form.
>   Think then also, my love, how from the germ of acquaintance
>   Little by little in us a familiar dearness springs up,
>   Friendship unveils itself in power from our inner concealment,
>   Till like Eros at last it procreates flower and fruit!
>   Think how soon these forms and those, in their manifold course of emerging,
>   Gently have lent to our feelings the presence of Nature herself!
>   So then, rejoice—and rejoice for today! Love in its holiness
>   Strives to the highest fruit of the same movement of thought,
>   Same outlook on things, in harmonic contemplation,
>   Thus the pair make their bond, and find out a loftier world.

38. As Goethe puts it in *On Morphology*: "every living thing is not an individual, rather a plurality [*kein Einzelnes, sondern eine Mehrheit*]; even if as it appears to us as an individual, it remains an assembly of living, independent beings [*Versammlung von lebendigen selbständigen Wesen*], which—according to the idea, the predisposition—are the same, but in the appearance can be either the same or like one another, or different and unlike one another. Some of these beings are already bound together from the start, some find and conjoin one another. They divide, seek each other again, and in this way effect an endless production in every way and in every direction" (MA 12, 14).

39. Goethe writes in a letter to Knebel that the poem is "an attempt [*Versuch*] at representing the experience [*Anschauen*] of nature, if not poetically then at least rhythmically." Goethe to Knebel (June 29, 1798) in *Briefwechsel zwischen Goethe und Knebel. 1774–1832*. Part 1, 1774–1806, 178.

40. I thank Luke Fischer for his help with the formal qualities of the poem. See also Bernhard Kuhn, *Autobiography and Natural Science in the Age of Romanticism: Rousseau, Goethe, Thoreau*, 78 and Müller, "Goethes Elegie die 'Metamorphose der Pflanzen.'"

41. Müller, for instance, notes that the three parts of the poem indicate a "spiralling tendency" such that in each phase of development we witness a reiteration that is also an intensification. See Müller, "Goethes Elegie" 369.

42. As Müller puts it, "These observations and considerations should show that the plant elegy . . . [is] a pure poetry, which is clearly organized through words and sentences, but which cannot be grasped through the summation of isolated sentences. Rather, [it is grasped] through the sensibly apprehended organic unity of form, through the distinctive relation between the parts and through the unity of the movement, which proceeds from beginning to end." "Goethes Elegie," 372.

Chapter 5

1. As Goldstein points out, Goethe was keen to make sure that the emphasis was not placed solely on the "objective" but also on the active *coming together* of thinking and perceiving (or, in Goldstein's translation, "intuiting"). Goldstein, *Sweet Science*, 130.

2. Förster, *The Twenty-Five Years of Philosophy*, 377.

3. Förster writes: "what is being elaborated here is the project of a Spinozist *scientia intuitiva* on the basis of Kant's characterization of the intuitive understanding." *The Twenty-Five Years of Philosophy*, 254.
4. This is how Förster puts it: "the methodological peculiarities" of intuitive understanding are "(a) that the object's properties can be derived from its essence (Spinoza); (b) that the whole makes the parts possible and conditions them (Kant); and (c) that the methodological path lies in the observation of transitions (Goethe)." *The Twenty-Five Years of Philosophy*, 265.
5. On Goethe's reading of Jacobi's 1785 *On Spinoza's Doctrine* [*Über die Lehre des Spinoza*], see Förster, "Goethe's Spinozism."
6. That the majority of philosophical interpretations focus on Kant and the Kantian context is not surprising, given that most philosophers are familiar with Kant. Even Förster, who pays attention to Spinoza's influence, redescribes Goethe's intuitive judgment as "intuitive understanding"—to align it with the term that Kant introduces in Section 77 of the third *Critique*. Other relevant philosophical interpretations of intuitive judgment include Schieren, *Anschauende Urteilskraft*; Amrine, "Goethean Intuitions"; Bowman, "Goethean Morphology, Hegelian Science"; Iris Hennigfeld, "Goethe's Phenomenological Way of Thinking and the Urphänomen"; and Gunnar Hindrichs, "Goethe's Notion of an Intuitive Judgment." These more recent interpretations contrast with earlier studies, such as Nisbet's, which situates Goethe in the context of Neoplatonism, and early modern rationalism and empiricism. H. B. Nisbet, *Goethe and the Scientific Tradition*.
7. See also Schieren, *Anschauende Urteilskraft* and Amrine "The Metamorphosis of the Scientist." Amrine, though, does not discuss the essay on intuitive judgment in this context. Furthermore, neither considers the role of aesthetic education in the development of intuitive judgment.
8. Hindrichs, "Goethe's Notion of an Intuitive Power of Judgment," esp. 57–58.
9. Goethe uses the term *belauschen*, or "eavesdropping," in *The Metamorphosis of Plants*, where he speaks of petals, writing that "their fine organization, their colors, their fragrance, would make their origin impossible for us to recognize, if we were not able to eavesdrop on nature in several extraordinary cases" (MA 12, 41, no. 41). He also describes the work of the artist as involving "eavesdropping" on nature, writing in an introductory essay on the sculptor Philip Hackert (1737–1807) (with whom he became acquainted in Rome): "It is a requirement that the artist not only choose his perspective so that the objects stand together in a good connection, and make a pleasant grouping in the details. Rather, [the artist] must also eavesdrop on nature, to determine which light results in the best effect, whether it is early in the morning or later in the evening at sunset ... [The artist] can also come back on another day at the same time, in order to eavesdrop on the effect yet again, until he has come so far, that he believes he has achieved the completed image in accordance with his imagination" (FA 19, 585).
10. For Kant education plays no role in the development of our cognitive capacities. In the first *Critique* he describes the power of judgment as a form of "mother-wit," which "cannot be made good by any school" (A133/B172). In *Anthropology from a*

Pragmatic Point of View, he identifies "wit" as the ability "to note the identity of a manifold that is different in part" (AA 7, 201), the capacity to "draw comparisons" (AA 7, 220), emphasizing that wit is a "natural predisposition [*natürliche Anlage*]" or "gift of nature [*Naturgabe*]," which cannot be taught or learned (AA 7, 220).

11. For this reason, I do not fully agree with Daston and Galison's placement of Goethe under the same rubric as Linnaeus, which they call "truth to nature." While both Goethe and Linnaeus sought to achieve true insight into the natural world through an experience-based approach that aims to arrive at a fundamental ideal reality, Linnaeus—as Daston and Galison put it—"aggressively" focused on the regular, excluding all irregularities. Goethe, by contrast, was also interested in irregularities (he was, for instance, interested in the proliferous rose and carnation, and the atypical tulip), in difference, and in the clues that irregularities and differences give us about form and formation. By focusing on difference and seeing similarity in and through difference, Goethe was able to arrive at the concept of metamorphosis, and, as I will argue in what follows, develop a distinctive notion of the *Urphänomen*. Daston and Galison, *Objectivity*, esp. 55–62.

12. As Brady notes, for Goethe intuitive judgment is not only the capacity to detect but also to generate insight. Brady, "Goethe's Causal Morphology," 339.

13. The essay's title in the WA and the LA editions is "Erfahrung und Wissenschaft [Experience and Science]," while in the FA it is titled "Physik Überhaupt [Physics in General]." I have followed the WA and LA title. The essay appears with an additional title "Das reine Phänomen [The Pure Phenomenon]" in the LA. The essay can be found in LA 1/11, 39–40 and FA 25, 125–27.

14. This is how the notion of archetype was historically received, and how historians of science have often interpreted Goethe's contribution to biology and morphology. Thus Richard Owen's notion of "type," which attempts to reduce difference in order to arrive at "a fundamental or general type," is often regarded as continuous with Goethe's notion of archetype. Robert Richards, for instance, writes that "Richard Owen . . . followed the German lead in constructing his own quite celebrated theory of the archetype," and goes on to note that Owen invoked the "Platonic Idea" to establish his theory. *The Romantic Conception of Life*, 528–29. However, as I will argue, there is a crucial difference between Owen's static conception of, for instance, a "typical vertebra," where obvious differences between vertebral structures are dismissed, and Goethe's understanding of the archetypal phenomenon, which seeks to hold on to and capture these differences. See also Brady, "Goethe's Causal Morphology," esp. 329.

15. In addition, it is important to note that the general concept achieved through induction does not achieve necessity, insofar as it is always possible to falsify it through an empirical counterexample. The classic case is, of course, the statement that "all swans are white." Schiller draws attention to this in his explication of Goethe's rational empiricism, as we will see below.

16. In contrast to Kant and Blumenbach, who drew a hard-and-fast distinction between organic and anorganic, Goethe sees in the anorganic world a dynamism and even a drive to transformation that mirrors the formative drive that Blumenbach regards

as the distinguishing feature of living beings. Thus, Goethe writes in *Maxims and Reflections* [*Maximen und Reflexionen*] (1833), "The most beautiful metamorphosis in the anorganic realm occurs when the amorphous assumes a structure as it comes into being. Every material [*Masse*] has the right and drive [*Trieb*] to do so" (FA 13, 72). In the poem "Dauer im Wechsel (Permanence in Change)," which appeared in *God and World*, Goethe invokes the Heraclitean idea that you can never step in the same river twice to make this point (FA 2, 493). See also Goethe's statement in his writings on geology, "All matter appears to us formless, if we are not attentive. However, it has an irresistible tendency toward self-formation [*eine unwiderstehliche Neigung, sich zu gestalten*]" (LA 1/2, 111).

17. These two different conceptions of morphology are reiterated some one hundred years later by Hans Driesch in his lectures on the history of vitalism. Driesch bases his distinctions on two different ways of conceiving the whole: a static whole, in contrast to one that is inherently transforming. For Driesch, only the latter can properly capture living beings, because the former regards the living form as a product based on a blueprint—i.e., as a structure produced in accordance with an idea that is external to it. This means that the whole is not itself productive or capable of internal transformation. Such a conception fails to capture the character of living beings, which are not finished products, but producers, shifting and transforming over time and in relation to place. Driesch, *Geschichte des Vitalismus*, 5–6. Goethe would argue that nonliving beings also exhibit such shape-shifting characteristics, even if to a lesser extent. See note 16 above.

18. Jakob Ziguras has offered one of the most comprehensive arguments against identifying intuitive judgment with inductive reasoning. See Ziguras, "Archē as Urphänomen: A Goethean Interpretation of Aristotle's Theory of Scientific Knowledge," and "Aristotle's Rational Empiricism," esp. 23–24.

19. See also Ziguras, "Aristotle's Rational Empiricism," 72.

20. As we have seen in chapter 3, Goethe emphasizes in his essay on osteology that the archetype cannot be identified with any particular animal, because "the particular can never serve as a measure for the whole" (MA 12, 122).

21. Amrine, "The Metamorphosis of the Scientist," 198.

22. As Ina Goy points out, several interpretations of Goethe's notion of the *Urpflanze* come to the conclusion that it is a kind of force or a cause, albeit a formal one. While this is in some sense right, it is also wrong, in that it overlooks the active participation of the knower. Furthermore, it overlooks Goethe's explicit statements that morphology is not a science concerned with "causes" but only with "conditions" (LA 1/11, 40). In turn, although Goy agrees with this interpretation, she points to a crucial difficulty which it faces: how to integrate the *Urpflanze* as a formal principle with the material reality of the plant. In other words, the notion of a (formal) cause or force ends up creating a dualism between form and matter, which seems to go against Goethe's fundamental intentions. Ina Goy, "'All Is Leaf': Goethe's Plant Philosophy and Poetry," 165–66.

23. This section is an expansion of a previously published essay. See Dalia Nassar, "Rational Empiricism?"

24. Goethe has received a fair bit of attention from an environmental perspective in recent years. Works include the special section of volume 22 of the *Goethe Yearbook* edited by Luke Fischer and Dalia Nassar, and the coauthored introduction to the section, which investigates a number of ways in which Goethe's approach to the natural world can be brought to bear on environmental questions and concerns. See Fischer and Nassar, "Goethe and Environmentalism." See also the essays published in the section, such as Kate Rigby's "Art, Nature, and the Poesy of Plants in the *Goethezeit*," and Ryan Feigenbaum's "Toward a Nonanthropocentric Vision of Nature." In German, Gernot Böhme has been an important voice in bringing Goethe's ideas into dialogue with environmental thought. Böhme's angle is particularly relevant for our purposes, given his focus on aesthetics (broadly speaking) and its role in transforming our ways of thinking and behaving. See Böhme, *Atmosphäre: Essays zur neuen Ästhetik*.
25. As, for instance, reported in a recent article in *Nature*: https://www.nature.com/articles/d41586-021-00469-2.
26. See John Zammito, *A Nice Derangement of Epistemes*.
27. As Richard Routley argued, the only way by which to found an "environmental ethic" is by regarding the environment itself as a moral object. Accordingly, the question which environmental ethicists have been attempting to answer since the publication of Routley's article in 1973 has been: on what basis do we *grant* moral status to nature (or particular objects in nature)? The answers have been many, but in the early debates they revolved around two options: inherent value (e.g., Tom Regan) and instrumental value (e.g., John Passmore). Goethe offers an entirely different approach to environmental ethics which, as I will argue, has the potential to steer environmental ethics in new, more productive directions. Routley, "Is There a Need for a New, an Environmental, Ethic?"
28. As Danielle Celermajer et al. have recently argued, what is urgently needed is not an extension of human ideals and norms to the more-than-human, but their genuine *transformation*. Danielle Celermajer et al., "Justice through a Multispecies Lens."
29. As Christopher D. Stone puts it in his influential (but problematic) 1972 paper, "One ought, I think, to handle the legal problems of natural objects as one does the problems of legal *incompetents*—human beings who have become *vegetable*. If a human being shows signs of becoming senile . . . those concerned with his well-being make such a showing to the court, and someone is designated by the court with the authority to manage the incompetent's affairs." Stone, "Should Trees Have Legal Standing," 464; emphasis added.
30. Eva Giraud, *What Comes after Entanglement?*, 26.
31. In this regard, one can think of Francis Bacon's statement in the *Great Instauration* (1620) that his goal is not to regard nature "free and at large" but rather "under constraint and vexed; that is to say, when by art and the hand of man she [nature] is forced out of her natural state, and squeezed and molded." Francis Bacon, *Selected Philosophical Works*, 82. While Bacon was himself critical of Aristotle for forcing nature into abstract categories and schemas, Goethe is critical of both the abstractions that one witnesses in scientific systematization (Linnaeus is a clear example here, but also Newton—as we will briefly note below) and the desire to dominate nature evident

in statements like Bacon's. Goethe, however, was not entirely negative about Bacon; he notes that Bacon heralded a new (anti-Newtonian) phase in science, which was, nonetheless, often broken and made impossible through theoretical tendencies (FA 13, 243). In contrast to the approach that seeks to manipulate and dominate nature, Goethe writes in *Maxims and Reflections*, "Nature will reveal nothing under torture; its frank answer to an honest question is "Yes! Yes! No! No! Anything more is evil" (FA 13, 14). This goes hand in hand with Goethe's "gentle empiricism [*zarte Empirie*]" that aims to make the knower "identical" with the known (FA 13, 149).

32. For a discussion of Goethe's critique of Newton's crucial experiment, see Dennis L. Sepper, *Goethe contra Newton*, esp. chapter 4.

33. Sepper puts Goethe's polemics with Newton in the following way: "Goethe was chiefly interested in exploring precisely those properties and relationships of color that escape the rather elementary mathematics of the Newtonian theory," adding that in the essay "The Experiment as Mediator," Goethe is primarily concerned with "the question of how one keeps one's *experience* of phenomena and experiments separate from what one *thinks* and *hypothesizes* about them." Dennis L. Sepper, "Goethe against Newton: Towards Saving the Phenomena," 181–82.

34. Thus Goethe writes: "Newton and his school believe they see with their own eyes what they have theorized into the phenomenon, that is precisely what one is complaining about" (FA 23/1, 386; paragraph 217). For a discussion of Goethe's critique of abstraction, see also Roger Stephenson, *Goethe's Conception of Knowledge and Science*, chapter 2.

35. See, for instance, Kate Rigby, "Writing after Nature"; Kate Soper, *What Is Nature?*; Raymond Williams, "Ideas of Nature"; and Val Plumwood, "Toward a Progressive Naturalism." Timothy Morton goes further, arguing that the idea of nature is nothing but a "transcendental term in a material mask," and for this reason the concept must be eliminated from environmental thought. Morton, *Ecology after Nature*, 14.

36. For Goethe, a crucial aspect of being a scientist involved understanding one's prejudices. Accordingly, he saw it as necessary that scientists study the history of science, in order to familiarize themselves with the implicit premises with which they are working and thereby become aware of their unconscious biases. As he famously puts it in the Preface to the *Theory of Colors*, "the history of science is itself science" (FA 23/1, 16). Some scholars have developed Goethe's "ethics" of science, i.e., his ideal vision of how scientists should proceed in relation to one another and their community. See, for instance, Sepper, *Goethe contra Newton*, 189–95. As Sepper notes, and as I will note below, Goethe's normative vision is based on his view that the scientist is ultimately in the service of the phenomena.

37. The majority of animal ethics has been founded on this approach, i.e., of determining how animals are "like us" and, on the basis of likeness, granting moral status. Earlier influential theories include Tom Regan's argument for animal rights on the basis of the intrinsic value of animal lives, and Peter Singer's (contrasting) focus on suffering and "sentience." See Regan, *The Case for Animal Rights*, and Singer, *Animal Liberation*. More recent work, while in some ways more sophisticated, remains tethered to this approach. Martha Nussbaum, for instance, extends her capabilities approach

to include animals who are capable of having a social life and experiencing joy and sorrow, while Christine Korsgaard argues that we have duties to animals on account of their ability to have a "point of view" and "evaluate" their world (as more or less good for them). Both rely on the human form (and the human relation to the world) in order to determine what makes a life worth living and thus morally relevant. See Nussbaum, *Frontiers of Justice*, and Korsgaard, *Fellow Creatures*.

38. In this way, Goethe's view is much closer to Indigenous and feminist approaches to environmental ethics, which emphasize the notions of stewardship and relationality. Stewardship "refers to acknowledgement of one's place in a web of interdependent relationships that create moral responsibility, and ... recognizes that there are methods and forms of expertise involved in carrying out such responsibilities." Kyle Powys Whyte and Chris J. Cuomo, "Ethics of Caring in Environmental Ethics: Indigenous and Feminist Philosophies," 238.

39. See, for instance, Kristen Intemann, "25 Years of Feminist Empiricism and Standpoint Theory."

Chapter 6

1. Several studies in English have attributed to Humboldt the status of the founder of both environmentalism and ecology. See, for instance, Aaron Sachs, *The Humboldt Current*, which offers a nuanced account of Humboldt's influence on key figures in the American environmental movement; Andrea Wulf, *The Invention of Nature*, which traces Humboldt's influence on lesser known, but equally significant figures in the environmental movement; and Laura Dassow Walls, *The Passage to Cosmos*, which investigates Humboldt's impact on American writers, especially Henry David Thoreau.

2. Ernst Haeckel, *Generelle Morphologie der Organismen*, vol. 2, 286. As ecologists, Juli Pausas and William Bond put it, "Ernst Haeckel was thinking of Humboldt's work when he coined the term 'ecology.'" Pausas and Bond, "Humboldt and the Reinvention of Nature," 1031.

3. In a footnote in which he elaborates on the title of *Kosmos*, Humboldt directly connects it to the Greek οἰκονομία, citing the work of the historian of ancient Greece August Böckh. Humboldt writes that two inscriptions in ancient Greece identify *Kosmos* with οἰκονομία (*Kosmos* 1, 33 n. 27). References to *Kosmos* will include the volume number, although the edition I am citing includes all five volumes in one book.

4. Or as he puts it some pages later in the Introduction, "nature is not a dead aggregate," and goes on to quote Schelling's statement that nature is "to the enthusiastic researcher ... the holy, eternally creative power [*Urkraft*] of the world, which brings forth all things from itself" (*Kosmos* 1, 25; see also *Kosmos* 1, 38).

5. Humboldt's claim has been recently reconfirmed by research in the southern Amazon, which demonstrated the influence of trees on the wet season. Transpiration during the late dry season brings the dry-to-wet transition forward by two to three

months, such that the loss of trees does not only mean drought, as Humboldt had realized, but may also trigger a collapse in the rainforest and the development of savannah. Without trees, the wet season would start when the Atlantic intertropical convergence zone arrives during its annual southward migration. Fu et al. "Increased Dry-Season Length over Amazonia."

6. The national parks' movement in the United States and Britain was strongly supported by Humboldt's explication of the relationship between trees and rain. In an 1847 speech to the US Congress, the congressman George Perkins Marsh—an avid reader of Humboldt's works—described the negative impact of human activity on the environment, focusing on deforestation, and three years later, in 1850, the US commissioner of patents, Thomas Ewbank, cited Humboldt's observations at Lake Valencia in support of the campaign for national parks. Yellowstone National Park was established in 1872—the first in the world—though the campaign for designating it a national park had begun in the 1860s. See Matthew Lindstrom, *Encyclopedia of the U.S. Government and the Environment*, 836. In 1890 Yosemite became a national park through the work of John Muir, who was also deeply influenced by Humboldt—however, as Aaron Sachs notes, by the later stage of his life, Muir had moved away from his Humbolditan origins, in that he came to prioritize nature over the human cultures that inhabited it. See Sachs, *The Humboldt Current*, 28. See also Wulf, *The Invention of Nature*. For Humboldt's influence on India, see Richard Grove, "Colonial Conservation, Ecological Hegemony and Popular Resistance," 22.

7. There has been a debate concerning the "originality" of Humboldt's thought, focusing on the extent to which Humboldt learned from scientists he met in South America, in particular, the Colombian Francisco José de Caldas (1768–1816). Caldas met Humboldt in 1801 and joined Humboldt's party for several weeks. A self-taught naturalist and astronomer, Caldas had developed a novel way by which to measure air pressure in relation to elevation. He was deeply familiar with South American vegetation and studied it in relation to climate and altitude. There is no doubt that Humboldt learned from Caldas—and vice versa. For instance, Caldas learned the formal elements of botany from Humboldt and Bonpland. On this reciprocal influence, see John Wilton Appel, *Francisco José de Caldas*. Some scholars have argued that Humboldt's biogeographical maps, which order living beings in accordance with elevation, were stolen from similar work that Caldas was undertaking (and which he eventually published). See for instance, Margarita Serje, "The National Imagination in New Granada." As Jorge Cañizares-Esguerra has shown, however, in late eighteenth-century South America, the Andes were regarded as a "microcosm" of the universe, and the assumption was that studying their vegetation in relation to altitude would yield knowledge about other similar environments. Thus a more accurate picture would be that Humboldt learned not specifically from Caldas, but from the wider South American intellectual tradition. See Jorge Cañizares-Esguerra, "How Derivative Was Humboldt?" While these are crucial points and should be part of any discussion of Humboldt's maps, including his famous depiction of Chimborazo, it is worthwhile to note that Humboldt's basic goal of developing a geography of plants had been outlined before he set foot in South America, and was partly inspired by his journey along the

Rhine with Georg Forster (in 1790) and his reading of Friedrich Willdenow's 1787 study of Berlin flora. This is evident not only in the kinds of instruments that he took with him to South America (which measure elevation and air pressure), but also in his various descriptions of his goals. In a letter to the Spanish king from March 11, 1799, for instance, Humboldt writes that his reasons for seeking permission to travel to South America have to do with his interest in "analyzing the atmosphere," and "recognizing the general relationships that bind organized beings." This reiterates statements made in Humboldt's August 1794 letter to Schiller, in which he relates that his goal is to discern historical and geographic connections between plants, animals, and people—through, among other things, the use of maps. For Humboldt's exchange with the Spanish king, see Miguel Ángel Puig-Samper, "Humboldt, un Prusiano en la Corte del Rey Carlos IV," 337. For the letter to Schiller, see JB 346–47. Furthermore, the specific insight that I am exploring here, and which I have called Humboldt's "ecological insight," does not simply involve ordering plants and animals in accordance with altitude (or other ecological factors). Rather, it involves regarding living beings and their environments as members of an ongoing relationship. In other words, the crucial insight rests on the fact that neither living beings nor environments are static; that environments are as much an outcome of the activity of living beings, as living beings are of their environments.

8. Sultan, *Organism and Environment*, 31.
9. Hanno Beck also describes Humboldt's methodology as a "rational empiricism." Beck, *Alexander von Humboldt*, vol. 1, 105. The passage from Otté's translation of *Kosmos* reads as follows: "Devoid of the profoundness of a purely speculative philosophy, my essay on the *Cosmos* treats of the contemplation of the universe, and is based upon a rational empiricism, that is to say, upon the results of the facts registered by science, and tested by the operations of the intellect." As Alison Martin notes, Otté was both a more present and more creative translator than Edward and Elizabeth Sabine, who had done an earlier translation, on Humboldt's bidding. See Martin, *Nature Translated*, chapter 6. For this reason, some of Otté's translations do not clearly map onto the original German. This is one such case. My guess is that the translated passage refers to the following: "Was ich physische Weltbeschreibung nenne . . . macht daher keine Ansprüche auf den Rang einer *rationellen Wissenschaft der Natur*; es ist die denkende Betrachtung der durch Empirie gegebenen Erscheinungen, als eines Naturganzen" (*Kosmos* 1, 22).
10. Hartmut Böhme similarly draws a connection between Humboldt's "denkende Betrachtung" and Goethe's intuitive judgment. See Hartmut Böhme, "Alexander von Humboldts Entwurf einer neuen Wissenschaft," 506.
11. Though I discuss Goethe's connection to (and influence on) Humboldt, there is no doubt that Herder also played a significant role in the development of Humboldt's thought. My focus on Goethe, however, has to do, first, with the fact that—as demonstrated in the preceding chapters—Goethe himself was collaborating with, and influenced by, Herder, such that tracing Goethe's influence on Humboldt implies Herder's influence, and second, that Humboldt is more forthcoming when it comes to acknowledging Goethe's significance. By contrast, his references to Herder are

sparse, and largely indirect. And when they are made, they are later omitted. For instance, in the 1806 lecture on the physiognomy of plants, as well as in the first and second editions of *Ansichten der Natur* [*Views of Nature*] (1808, 1826), Humboldt cites Herder as one of his foremost influences (along with Buffon, Bernardin de St. Pierre, and Chateaubriand). Humboldt, *Ansichten der Natur mit wissenschaftlichen Erläuterungen*, 1, 176. Surprisingly, however, Herder's name is taken out of the third edition (1849). For this reason, as one scholar puts it, Herder is often "the unnamed" influence on Humboldt's thinking. See Eberhard Knobloch, "Naturgenuss und Weltgemälde." As I have intimated, Herder's notion of a "world" is a clear forerunner of Humboldt's dynamic conceptualization of the natural world, and his idea of a *Kosmos*. On the reasons why Herder's name was omitted, see Bernhard Hunger, "Alexander von Humboldt und Johann Gottfried Herder." On Herder's influence on Humboldt, see Hanno Beck, "Kommentar," in Alexander von Humboldt, *Studienausgabe in sieben Bänden*, 287–328, and Annette Graczyk, *Das literarische Tableau*, esp. 290–91. Accordingly, in my analysis, I do not wish to underestimate Herder's influence. Rather, I see it as actualized in Goethe's influence on Humboldt.

12. Alexander von Humboldt, *Aus meinem Leben*, 180.
13. As the editors of the LA note, "after he [Goethe] lectured to the Humboldt brothers from his sketches and—as Wilhelm relates (in a letter from the end of January 1795)—gave them the manuscript to transcribe, they bade him to write about *the matter of type* in a longer text" (LA 2/9A, 593).
14. See chapter 5, section 5.4.
15. After his return from the Americas, Humboldt visited Jena/Weimar three times: December 1826, January 1831 (the last time he saw Goethe), and finally, shortly after Goethe's death in 1832. See Ottmar Ette, *Humboldt-Handbuch*, 224.
16. As recorded in Goethe's TAG, they met on the following dates: March 1, 3, 4–6, 8, 11, 16, 19, 27 in Jena; April 19–21 and 23–25 in Weimar; and May 23, 26, 29 in Jena.
17. Adolf Meyer-Abich, *Die Vollendung der Morphologie*, 121.
18. Alexander von Humboldt, *Versuche über die gereizte Muskel- und Nervenfaser*, vol. 2, 285.
19. On Goethe's use and justification of "type" in this essay, see chapter 3.
20. Humboldt, *Versuche über die gereizte Muskel- und Nervenfaser*, vol. 2, 285.
21. There are numerous studies of Humboldt's relationship to Goethe, the majority of which emphasize Goethe's influence on Humboldt. Fewer studies consider Humboldt's influence on Goethe. My approach to the matter of influence is less concerned with locating the source of ideas, and more focused on discerning a continuity, a shared way of thinking and approach to the natural world. Thus, the crucial point is to see how Goethe and Humboldt collaborated with one another to arrive at complementary insights and methodologies. Scholarship on their relationship includes Ilse Jahn and Andreas Kleinert, *Das Allgemeine und das Einzelne*; Bies, *Im Grunde ein Bild*; Elizabeth Millán, "The Quest for the Seeds of Eternal Growth"; and Meyer-Abich, *Die Vollendung der Morphologie*.
22. The majority of interpretations of Goethe and Humboldt see Humboldt's originality in precisely this interest in relations beyond the individual organism. See for instance,

Michael Bies who writes that while Humboldt aims to achieve "a description of the whole tropical nature," Goethe, "in his writings on metamorphosis looks only at the individual plant." *Im Grunde ein Bild*, 251. Anne Buttimer similarly argues that Humboldt went beyond Goethe in his greater sensitivity toward "scale, spatial distribution . . . temporality, rhythmicity . . . [and] social worlds" and "succinct graphic expressions of landscapes and lifeways." Anne Buttimer, "Beyond Humboldtian Science and Goethe's Way of Science," 114. In turn, while Joan Steigerwald recognizes the importance of form for Humboldt, she does not regard it as a defining feature of his approach. She writes, "But Humboldt's was a singular vision, which, unlike Goethe's, focused upon vegetation in relation to the environment and how the physiognomy of plants was modified by the particular conditions of a particular region." Steigerwald, "The Cultural Enframing of Nature," 473.

23. See note 7 above.

24. The second, which was discussed in chapter 1, invokes the artifact model to explain living beings (i.e., living beings are made according to an idea or a blueprint which originates in the mind of the maker). For a more detailed consideration of Kant's conception of external purposiveness, see chapter 1, section 1.4.

25. See also Angela Breitenbach, *Die Analogie von Vernunft*, 137–40, and Naomi Fisher, "Organisms and the Form of Freedom in Kant's Third *Critique*."

26. As Géza von Molnár's publication of Goethe's copy of the third *Critique* shows, Goethe read the third *Critique* very carefully and was particularly struck by Kant's understanding of the artist (genius), his account of symbol, his conceptualization of the organized being, and his notion of intuitive understanding. See Géza von Molnár, "Goethes Studium der *Kritik der Urteilskraft*."

27. In his autobiographical text, *Campaign in France* [*Kampagne in Frankreich*] (1792), Goethe puts the matter in the following way: "When in his *Critique of the Power of Judgment* Kant places aesthetic judgment alongside teleological judgment, it is clear that he wishes to allude to the following: a work of art should be treated as a work of nature and a work of nature should be treated [*behandelt*] as a work of art, and the worth of each should be developed out of itself and considered in itself" (FA 16, 491).

28. Or, as biologist J. S. Haldane put it in his 1917 book, "In a living organism, the past lives on in the present" such that "it is literally true of life, and no mere metaphor, that . . . each moment of the past [is] in each moment of the present." Haldane, *Organism and Environment*, 98. Every living being can thus be said to "carry" its context within itself, in its very form.

29. See chapter 3, note 11.

30. On the importance of the *organism as a whole* in understanding the organism-environment relationship, see chapter 2, note 34. As Nicholson explains, the "return of the organism" in biology requires fundamental shifts in the way that biology is done—above all, a shift in our understanding of the relation between part and whole. The whole, in other words, must be taken *as a whole*, and not as simply "caused" by its various parts. He writes, "Understanding the whole requires studying the whole. It means recognizing that by virtue of the organization of the whole, the parts interact nonlinearly causing qualitatively new properties to emerge that are not possessed by

the parts, neither when considered individually nor when assembled in other combinations." This is precisely what the romantic empiricists sought to realize, and why Goethe drew the distinction between cause and condition. For by understanding the organism in its condition, he allows for "studying the whole," and this means studying the organism as a whole (an agent) participating in a reciprocally determining relation with its context. See Nicholson, "The Return of the Organism," 352.

31. Or as Foucault puts it in his description of the emergence of biology as a distinct discipline: an organized being "wraps itself in its own existence." Michel Foucault, *The Order of Things*, 299. Although Foucault does not speak of Kant here, Amanda Jo Goldstein has made the connection, noting the significant difference between Kant and Goethe on this count. Goethe, in contrast to Kant, emphasizes the visible and expressive, while Kant's terminology and his lack of a conception of the organism "in the world" took him in the opposite direction. See Goldstein, *Sweet Science*, 48–49 and 79.

32. While Kant provides an account of organized beings *in* their contexts in his noncritical writings, in particular his lectures on physical geography and his essays on race, these works do not address his worries about environmental reductionism, such that it is not clear how the pictures of living beings in their environments articulated in the noncritical works relate to Kant's (justified) concern, as outlined in the third *Critique*. Goethe's distinction between cause and condition and Humboldt's emphasis on form address precisely this concern, and thereby provide a way beyond the dilemma Kant articulates.

33. See Humboldt's letter to Varnhagen von Ense (October 15, 1849). *Briefe von Alexander von Humboldt an Varnhagen von Ense*, 244.

34. Humboldt's desire to emphatically distinguish "history" and "description" is also evident in the chagrin he expressed toward the first English translation of *Kosmos*, done by Augustin Prichard and published by Baillière. Prichard translates *Beschreibung* in the subtitle of *Kosmos* as "history." Humboldt practically begs Edward and Elizabeth Sabine to undertake a second translation, writing to Edward that "I have striven to demonstrate that *Weltbeschreibung* is not *Weltgeschichte*, that the history of the revolutions which our planet has undergone, as exemplified by the Milky Way, should not be confused with the description of the earth and of the celestial spaces, which does not hinder Mr. Baillière from adulterating them, even right down to the title of my book: instead of physical description of the universe he has made of it a physical history. I hardly dare complain about what will surely humiliate me before an English public." Quoted in Martin, *Nature Translated*, 203.

In *Kosmos* he explicates the distinction as follows: "A physical description remains tied clearly [*nüchtern*] to reality, not from modesty, but according to the nature of its content and its limits, and it is alien to the obscure beginnings of a history of organisms [*den dunkeln Anfängen einer Geschichte der Organismen fremd*], if the word 'history' is accepted here in its most useful sense. But world description may thereby remind us that in the inorganic layer of the earth [*Erdrinde*] are encountered the same basic elements [*Grundstoffe*] which form the framework of animal and plant organs. It teaches us that in these, as in those, the same forces [*Kräfte*] govern, which combine and separate matter, and shape and liquify it in organic tissues. . . . The nature-contemplating tendency of our minds is thus a necessity, which is to be followed from the physical appearances of the earth to its highest summit, to the development [*Erzeugung*] of the forms of plants, and from its self-determined motions into animals. In this way the geography of organic life (the geography of plants and animals) is connected to the description [*Schilderung*] of inorganic natural appearances" (*Kosmos* 1, 178–79).

35. The *Ideen* was originally composed and published in French in 1805 with the title *Géographie des Plantes*. The essay appeared in a multivolume work titled *Voyage de Humboldt und Bonpland*. Humboldt himself translated it into German over a few months in 1805, though it was published in German two years later. The German version was published as a self-standing essay, and was not part of a larger work. In an important sense, Humboldt did not simply *translate* the French into German, but *wrote* the German edition anew. There are significant differences between the two editions, including the fact that in the German edition Humboldt describes seventeen fundamental forms of plants, while in the French he speaks only of fifteen.

36. In the German edition, Humboldt adds the aloe, the lily, and the fungus forms, and takes out the orchid form (See DA 1, 62–64; EGP 73–74). In the essay on plant physiognomy (delivered 1806), he brings back orchids, adds willow, myrtle, and laurel, but takes out mosses, lichens, and fungus. See also note 35.

37. I will follow the names and spellings that Humboldt uses, rather than adjust them to contemporary taxonomic spellings. This is because the names that he uses are not always clearly connected to contemporary nomenclature, and even in instances where there is a connection, there are ambiguities (e.g., it is not always clear whether Humboldt is referring to the species or the family).

38. In German, *Konifere* and *Nadelbaum* are both used to refer to the English *conifer*. Humboldt's choice to use the term *Nadelholz* goes hand in hand with his focus on form. He only discusses trees that bear needle-like leaves, and does not consider shrubs that are taxonomically classified as conifers, but that do not have a clear resemblance to these other conifers. Furthermore, Humboldt closely connects conifers to other trees bearing needle-like leaves, including the Australian casuarina (commonly known as the Australian pine), which taxonomically belongs to an entirely different clade, given that the casuarina—unlike conifers—flowers (is an angiosperm). See, for instance, his statement that the leaves and branches of both trees (the conifer and the casuarina) express the "greatest contraction" (DA 5, 188; VN 165–66). Accordingly, although the term "conifer" might suggest that Humboldt is describing the taxonomic category, *Coniferae*, he is, in fact, not doing this.

39. These species all belong to the Ericeae family, which is taxonomically classified as a member of the heaths. Humboldt, however, resists this identification, instead identifying the *form* of the heath with "the very consistent and characteristic form of the Erica species, including Calluna" (DA 5, 259; VN 214). He places the rhododendrons and other plants from the Ericeae family under the *myrtle* form. This has significant consequences, as we will consider below.

40. Ericeae, like Rhododendra, are categories that are no longer used, but were used by Humboldt, and are used in the most recent English translation (see VN 219). Ericeae refers to the Ericaceae family, which is commonly known as the heath family, while Rhododendra refers to the genus rhododendrons. The translators of EGP provide a list of synonyms for Humboldt's terms in contemporary taxonomy. See EGP 198-220. However, as the translator notes, the list is not exhaustive and includes names and spellings different from the ones Humboldt uses in *Ansichten der Natur*.

41. See also Humboldt's discussion of the aloe form, which includes species from a variety of families (Liliaceae, Asphodeleae, Pandaneae, Amaryllideae, and Euphorbiaceae), but all of which are characterized by "the candelabra form of the aloe plants" (DA 5, 279-80, VN 228-29).

42. As Hanno Beck notes, in pointing to this "wondrous law of nature," in which the same forms (but not the same taxonomic categories) repeat or reiterate themselves, Humboldt paved the way for what the influential twentieth-century geographer Carl Troll (1899-1975) came to describe as "convergent life forms." Troll was deeply influenced by Humboldt, and it was in the Andes that he developed his notion of convergent life forms. See Hanno Beck, *Ansichten der Natur*, 266-67. For Troll, see "Die tropischen Gebirge." Before Troll coined the phrase, the Swiss botanist Augustin de Candolle (1778-1841)—who was also very interested in Humboldt's idea of reiterating plant forms—articulated the view that species with no evident common evolutionary ancestor strongly resemble one another. On Condolle's interest in Humboldt, see Anne Marie Clara Godlewska, "From Enlightenment Vision to Modern Science?"

43. I want to emphasize that plants are largely but not exclusively sessile, because they do move—in relation to the sun or in relation to other plants. However, as Humboldt notes, their movement is invisible to us. This is because the pace of their movement is extremely slow—in contrast to that of animals—and so we fail to see it. Thus he writes in *Kosmos*: "if nature had endowed us with microscopic powers of vision, and the integuments of plants had been rendered perfectly transparent to our eyes, the vegetable kingdom would present a very different picture from the apparent immobility and repose in which it appears to our senses. The interior portion of the cellular structure of their organs is incessantly animated by the most varied currents, either rotating, ascending and descending, ramifying, and ever changing their direction, as manifested in the motion of the granular mucus of marine plants . . . and in the hairs of phanerogamic land plants" (*Kosmos* 1, 179).

44. Plant biological individuality has long been a significant challenge for botanists. As Alexander Braun (1805-1877) put it, "individuality in plants is as obscure and ambiguous as in animals it appears clear and simple." Alexander Braun, "The Vegetable Individual in Its relation to Species," 300. A striking example comes from Tasmania: a particular strand of Huon Pine on Tasmania's Mt. Read has been reproducing vegetatively for over 10,000 years. Branches that touch the ground form roots and are eventually detached from the original stem, making it difficult to determine whether they are individual trees. Similar questions come upon when considering a forest of aspens, which appears on the surface to be composed of individual aspen trees. However, the trees are not at all separated from one another, but are connected underground by

282 NOTES

multicellular runners. Through these runners, the "individual" trees share nutrients and other resources with one another, making what appears to be a superorganism. See Ellen Clarke, "The Problem of Biological Individuality."
45. Through analysis of human teeth, for instance, researchers have been able to trace the Irish potato famine. See Beaumont and Montgomery, "The Great Irish Famine."
46. Humboldt sought to emulate Zimmermann's work on animal (bio)geography but for plants. As Humboldt puts it, "Zimmermann's classic work presents animals according to the differences in their geographic location on the earth," adding that his own goal is to do the same in relation to plants (DA 1, 149; EGP 132). The classic work to which Humboldt refers is *Geographische Geschichte des Menschen, und der allgemein verbreiteten vierfüßigen Thiere* (1780). In addition to Zimmermann, Treviranus is regarded as a founder of the field of biogeography. See Zammito, *Gestation of Biology*, 243–44.
47. Willdenow's 1787 study of Berlin flora (*Flora Berloinensis*) introduced Humboldt to botany and inspired him to focus on plants, while his 1792 *Grundriss der Kräuterkunde* included a significant account of plant geography. See Frank N. Egerton, *Roots of Ecology*, 121. On Caldas, see note 7.

Chapter 7

1. The passage that Humboldt quotes comes from the Preface of Pliny's *Natural History*. In Humboldt's quotation, it is significantly abbreviated and comes from Herder's translation of Pliny, which appears as the epigraph of the third volume of Herder's *Ideas* (1787): "*Res ardua vetustis novitatem dare, omnibus naturam et naturae suae omnia* [It is clearly a difficult undertaking to make old matters new ... and in one word, to reduce all to their own nature]." Buffon had quoted the same passage in *Histoire naturelle* (vol. 1, 3). Humboldt returns to Pliny throughout *Kosmos*, and indeed the epigraph of the work comes from Pliny: "*Naturae vero rerum vis atque majestas in omnibus momentis fide caret, si quis modo partes ejus ac non totam complectatur animo* [in fact the power and greatness of nature lack credibility if only parts of it, and not the whole, are observed by the mind]" (*Kosmos* 1, title page).
2. *Gemälde*, which comes from the verb *malen*, to paint, generally denotes a painting. Humboldt also uses the term *Naturgemälde* to describe his visual depictions of landscapes, including his famous portrait of Chimborazo. In the French edition of EGP, Humboldt uses the term *tableau physique*, again suggesting the painterly and artistic quality of his compositions. For an account of the significance of the notion of *tableau* for these visual depictions, see Sylvie Romanowski, "Humboldt's Pictorial Science." I will not consider the *tableau physique*, as my focus here is on Humboldt's literary productions and their aesthetic significance.
3. Michael Dettelbach writes in his 1997 Introduction to volume 2 of *Cosmos*, "The first section of volume 2, 'The Incitements to the Study of Nature,' seems perhaps the most puzzling and least durable part of *Cosmos*, fitting uncomfortably between the portrait

of nature and the historical development of that portrait." Dettelbach, "Introduction to the 1997 Edition," xxvi–xxvii.
4. See Daston and Most, "History of Science and History of Philologies."
5. Humboldt specifically criticizes Burke's view that the pleasure taken in nature is distinct from (and indeed opposed to) research into nature—an objection he could have made against Kant as well: "I cannot agree with Burke when he says 'it is our ignorance of natural things that causes all our admiration, and chiefly excites our passions'" (*Kosmos* 1, 18). This coincides with Kant's distinction between "free" and "dependent" beauty, and his claim that a botanist cannot enjoy an experience of "free beauty" when considering a flower, because she encounters the flower intellectually. See Section 16 of the *Critique of the Power of Judgment*.
6. Following a long quotation from *Naive and Sentimental Poetry*, Humboldt writes: "However much truth and excellence there may be in these remarks, they must not be extended to the whole of antiquity; and I moreover consider that we take a very limited view of antiquity, when, in contradistinction to the present time, we restrict the term exclusively to the Greeks and Romans" (*Kosmos* 2, 191). As he goes on to explain, while Schiller was right in his assessment of the Greeks ("the description of nature in its manifold richness of form, as a distinct branch of poetic literature, was wholly unknown to the Greeks"), he was mistaken in assuming that all ancient cultures mirrored Greek culture (*Kosmos* 2, 191).
7. *Naturwahrheit* can also be translated as "true to nature." The category comes from the visual arts, and was particularly important in Renaissance art, though it was likely inspired by Greek and Roman art and philosophy. See Walter Paatz, *The Arts of the Italian Renaissance*, 13. It is also one of the categories that Daston and Galison use to describe science before objectivity and which they identify with Goethe's approach. Daston and Galison, *Objectivity*, chapter 2.
8. Gernot Böhme's notion of "quasi-objective" atmospheres refers both to the mood of a particular place (e.g., a forest, a museum, or a party) and to the way in which the individual takes up and reflects this mood (e.g., upon arriving at a lively party, a person's mood suddenly shifts and becomes the mood of the party). As Böhme puts it, atmospheres are "neither subject nor object—yet not nothing." Böhme, *Atmosphäre*, 66.
9. Humboldt influenced a number of landscape painters in the nineteenth century, many of whom he did not meet or support in the immediate way that he did Rugendas. These include the American Frederic Edwin Church, who also traveled to South America. See Edmunds V. Bunkse, "Humboldt and an Aesthetic Tradition in Geography."
10. Interestingly, in his own pictorial depictions, Humboldt chose not to be realistic, or draw to scale. In his Chimborazo drawing, he depicts two volcanoes: Chimborazo and, behind it, Cotopaxi. However, as Humboldt writes, "In reality, Cotopaxi is not as close to Chimborazo as it seems in my picture," noting that if he had sought to "preserve the true horizontal distances . . . and . . . represent the irregularity of the ground in a given region," he would have instead depicted the Carihuairazo volcano. Importantly, Humboldt adds, "I had a very powerful reason for preferring Cotopaxi.

I heard the underground groans of this volcano when I was in the port of Guayaquil undertaking the first sketch of this tableau" (DA 1, 78; EGP 84). In other words, his pictorial depiction is imbued by his own lived experience.
11. On the history and changing meaning of the phrase, see Henryk Markiewicz and Uliana Gabara, "Ut Pictura Poesis . . . a History of the Topos and the Problem."
12. Gotthold Ephraim Lessing, *Laokoon: oder über die Grenzen der Mahlerey und Poesie*, vol. 1, 2.
13. Lessing, *Laokoon*, vol. 1, 171.
14. Lessing, *Laokoon*, vol. 1, 172.
15. Lessing, *Laokoon*, vol. 1, 177. Interestingly, this point was made well before Lessing, by Leonardo da Vinci, who wrote: "Using language to reproduce the described object, can easily divide it into parts, but putting them together is exceedingly difficult, if not impossible." Quoted in Markiewicz and Gabara, "Ut Pictura Poesis," 540.
16. Living form, according to Schiller, is the object of the play drive (*Spieltrieb*), which unites the object of the sense drive—life—with the object of the form drive—form. Accordingly, living form is the beautiful itself.
17. In the twentieth century, Paul Klee expanded this view in relation to painting. In a famous diary entry, Klee speaks of improvising freely on his color keyboard (*Farbklavier*) and describes his work as "polyphonic painting." In lectures he argues that there are important analogies between the two art forms, including the way in which a line in a painting eventually becomes part of a figure, just as a musical motif becomes a theme. See Paul Klee, *The Dairies of Paul Klee*, 244, no. 873; 374, no. 1081.
18. Wilhelm von Humboldt, *Ästhetische Versuche. Erster Theil. Über Göthe's "Herrmann und Dorothea,"* 60.
19. Wilhelm von Humboldt, *Ästhetische Versuche. Erster Theil. Über Göthe's "Herrmann und Dorothea,"* 58.
20. Wilhelm von Humboldt, *Ästhetische Versuche. Erster Theil. Über Göthe's "Herrmann und Dorothea,"* 44.
21. Wilhelm von Humboldt, *Ästhetische Versuche. Erster Theil. Über Göthe's "Herrmann und Dorothea,"* 45.
22. Humboldt also quotes from this poem in *Kosmos*. See *Kosmos* 1, 16. See also Bettina Hey'l, *Das Ganze der Natur und die Differenzierung des Wissens*, 156–58 and Graczyk, *Das literarische Tableau*, 272.
23. The poem appears in NA 1, 260–66 under the title "Elegie." The translation I quote from is by Marianna Wertz and can be founded in the Archive of the Schiller Institute: https://archive.schillerinstitute.com/fid_97-01/973_schiller_walk.html. Accessed November 16, 2020.
24. It is important to emphasize that here I am speaking of Humboldt's text, *Ansichten der Natur*, and not his other writings, which do include detailed descriptions of city life and the lives of European colonists. See for instance his *Essay on the Kingdom of New Spain*.
25. Ottmar Ette has argued that in the same way that there is a distinctive form of science that Humboldt carried out—i.e., "Humboldtian science" as named by the historian of science Susan Faye Cannon—so there is also a distinctive form of writing, which Ette

has called "Humboldtian writing." According to Ette, Humboldtian writing involves the experiences of an impersonal self (not Humboldt in particular, but a narratorial I), movement, comparison, and temporal flexibility. While I agree with Ette's analysis, and will similarly draw out these important points, in what follows I will argue that what Humboldt's writing style enables is an *embodied* experience of the natural world, which addresses the *whole* self. This has not been widely recognized. See Ottmar Ette, "Eine 'Gemütsverfassung moralische Unruhe'—Humboldtian Writing." See also Vera M. Kutzinski and Ottmar Ette, "Inventories and Inventions: Alexander von Humboldt's Cuban Landscapes," xvii–xix.

26. Humboldt included it in volume 1 of *Kosmos* and in his 1827 essay on geographical differences in climate, *Über die Haupt-Ursachen der Temperatur-Verschiedenheit auf dem Erdkörper*. See *Kosmos* 1, 176. The 1832 edition of the *Edinburgh Encyclopedia* references Humboldt's description of cloud formation and electrical storms in its section on Physical Geography. David Brewster, *The Edinburgh Encyclopedia of Philosophy*, vol. 15, 589.

27. In *Über die Haupt-Ursachen* (see note 26), in which Humboldt includes this description, he remarks that the beginning of the rainy season in the equatorial regions, which is determined by the changing direction of the sun and the modification of air currents, also influences the "electric explosions" that occur in the air. The regularity of these events, and their connection to cloud formation, Humboldt adds, provides the traveler with the same exactness of orientation as a compass. Humboldt, *Über die Haupt-Ursachen*, 309.

28. See Daston and Galison, *Objectivity*, 212.

29. In *On Grace and Dignity [Über Anmut und Würde]* (1793), Schiller describes this state of acting out of our whole selves as the "beautiful soul" (NA 20, 287).

30. As Frederick Beiser notes, "Like Kant, Schiller distinguishes aesthetic judgment from *all* forms of cognition, from *all* judgments of theoretical reason." Beiser, *Schiller as Philosopher*, 63.

31. For this reason, I disagree with Hartmut Böhme's claim that Humboldt's essays, in particular "Über die Steppen und Wüsten," fail to achieve the goal of uniting aesthetics and science, insofar as most of the science is placed in the "Annotations" after the essays. Hartmut Böhme, "Ästhetische Wissenschaft: Aporien der Forschung im Werk Alexander von Humboldts," 17. Although Böhme is right to highlight these annotations, I do not see them as undermining the unity of the essays, insofar as (1) the annotations need not be read as parts of the essays, and (2) they are not the sole source of science in the essays. As we have seen, the "science" is strewn throughout Humboldt's writings in a way that challenges a strong distinction between science and art. Furthermore, many of the annotations are written with the same kind of care that we find in the essays. They are not only imparting scientific information, but often invoke Humboldt's and Bonpland's lived experience, and thus, in both form and content, are continuous with the essays. The examples of such annotations are many and include the following passage from "Ideen zu einer Physiognomik der Gewächse": "The luminosity of the ocean counts as one of those gorgeous occurrences in nature that give rise to wonderment, even when one has watched it return nightly for months.

In all climates the sea phosphoresces, but who has not observed the phenomenon in the tropical latitudes (especially in the Pacific) has only an incomplete notion of the majesty of this grand spectacle" (DA 5, 205; VN 177). My claim, then, is that what Humboldt does in the essays is not so much join disparate disciplines but *transform* them—and this is the essence of the *embodied cognition* that he aims to impart.

32. As Richard Grove remarks in his article on the rise of environmentalism in the West, while French thinkers—from Rousseau to Bernardin St. Pierre—had drawn connections between human activity (especially colonial activity on the island of Mauritius) and the destruction of nature, it was Humboldt who first drew the connection between the destruction of nature and the destruction of human culture. Richard Grove, "Origins of Western Environmentalism."

33. Humboldt's account of this episode in *Personal Narrative* goes beyond his description in the essay. In the longer work, he describes not only the panic in the horses eyes and their repeated attempts to escape, but also their "panting," and their "haggard eyes," their expressions of "anguish," and their "stumbling" as they seek to flee, and, finally, their exhaustion. Within five minutes, he notes, two horses were drowned. PNW 1, 349.

34. On the importance of this retethering experience for moral and environmental action, see Eduardo Kohn, *How Forests Think*, Introduction.

Conclusion

1. See Val Plumwood, *Environmental Culture*.
2. See, for instance, Eugene Hargrove, "After Twenty Years," 340.
3. Timothy Morton, *Ecology without Nature*, 14.
4. See Danielle Celermajer, *Summertime*.

Works Cited

Allison, Henry E. "Kant's Antinomy of Teleological Judgment." *Southern Journal of Philosophy* 30 (1991): 25–42.
Allison, Henry E. *Kant's Theory of Taste: A Reading of the Critique of Aesthetic Judgment.* Cambridge: Cambridge University Press, 2001.
Amrine, Frederick. "Goethean Intuitions." *Goethe Yearbook* 18 (2011): 35–50.
Amrine, Frederick. "The Metamorphosis of the Scientist." *Goethe Yearbook* 5 (1990): 187–212.
Appel, John Wilton. *Francisco José de Caldas: A Scientist at Work in Nueva Granada.* Philadelphia: American Philosophical Society, 1994.
Bacon, Francis. *Selected Philosophical Works.* Edited by Rose-Mary Sargent. Indianapolis: Hackett, 1999.
Bateson, Patrick. "The Return of the Whole Organism." *Journal of Bioscience* 30.1 (2005): 31–39.
Baumgarten, Alexander. "Philosophischer Briefe zweites Schreiben." In *Texte zur Grundlegung der Ästhetik*, edited and translated by Hans R. Schweizer. Hamburg: Meiner, 1983.
Beck, Hanno. *Alexander von Humboldt.* Volume 1, *Von der Bildungsreise zur Forschungsreise, 1769–1804.* Wiesbaden: Franz Steiner, 1959.
Beck, Hanno. "Kommentar." In Alexander von Humboldt, *Studienausgabe in sieben Bänden.* Edited with a commentary by Hanno Beck, 287–328. Darmstadt: Wissenschaftliche Buchgesellschaft, 1989.
Beaumont, Julia, and Janet Montgomery. "The Great Irish Famine: Identifying Starvation in the Tissues of Victims Using Stable Isotope Analysis of Bone and Incremental Dentine Collagen." *PLOS ONE* 11.8 (2016).
Beiser, Frederick. *German Idealism: The Struggle against Subjectivism.* Cambridge, MA: Harvard University Press, 2002.
Beiser, Frederick. *Schiller as Philosopher.* Oxford: Oxford University Press, 2005.
Bies, Michael. *Im Grunde ein Bild: Die Darstellung der Forschung bei Kant, Goethe und Alexander von Humboldt.* Göttingen: Wallstein, 2012.
Blumenbach, Johann Friedrich. *Über den Bildungstrieb.* 2nd ed. Göttingen: Johann Christian Dieterich, 1789.
Böhme, Gernot. *Atmosphäre. Essays zur neuen Ästhetik.* Frankfurt am Main: Suhrkamp, 2013.
Böhme, Gernot. "Die Einheit von Kunst und Wissenschaft im Zeitalter der Romantik." In *Für eine ökologische Naturästhetik*, 96–120. Frankfurt am Main: Suhrkamp, 1989.
Böhme, Hartmut. "Alexander von Humboldts Entwurf einer neuen Wissenschaft." In *Natur und Figur*, 495–512. Munich: Fink, 2016.
Böhme, Hartmut. "Ästhetische Wissenschaft: Aporien der Forschung im Werk Alexander von Humboldts." In *Alexander von Humboldt—Aufbruch in die Moderne*, edited by Ottmar Ette, Ute Hermanns, Bernd M. Scherer, and Christian Suckow, 17–32. Berlin: Akademie Verlag, 2001.

Bowman, Brady. "Goethean Morphology, Hegelian Science: Affinities and Transformations." *Goethe Yearbook* 18 (2011): 159–81.
Boyle, Nicholas. *Goethe: The Poet and the Age*. Volume 1, *The Poetry of Desire (1749–1790)*. Oxford: Oxford University Press, 1997.
Boyle, Nicholas. *Goethe: The Poet and the Age*. Volume 2, *Revolution and Renunciation (1790–1803)*. Oxford: Oxford University Press, 2000.
Brady, Ronald. "The Causal Dimension of Goethe's Morphology." *Journal of Social Biological Structure* 7 (1984): 325–44.
Braun, Alexander. "The Vegetable Individual in Its relation to Species," *American Journal of Science and Arts* 19 (1855): 297–318.
Breitenbach, Angela. *Die Analogie von Vernunft und Natur*. Berlin: de Gruyter, 2009.
Breitenbach, Angela. "Mechanical Explanation of Nature and Its Limits in Kant's *Critique of Judgment*." *Studies in History and Philosophy of Biological and Biomedical Sciences* 37 (2006): 694–711.
Breitenbach, Angela. "Two Views on Nature: A Solution to Kant's Antinomy of Teleological Judgment." *British Journal for the History of Philosophy* 16 (2008): 351–69.
Brewster, David, ed. *The Edinburgh Encyclopedia of Philosophy*. Volume 15. Philadelphia: Joseph and Edward Parker, 1832.
Buchenau, Stefanie. "Herder: Physiology and Philosophical Anthropology." In *Herder: Philosophy and Anthropology*, edited by Anik Waldow and Nigel DeSouza, 72–93. New York: Oxford University Press, 2017.
Budge, Gavin, ed. *Romantic Empiricism: Poetics and the Philosophy of Common Sense, 1780–1830*. Lewisburg, VA: Bucknell University Press, 2007.
Bunkse, Edmunds V. "Humboldt and an Aesthetic Tradition in Geography." *Geographical Review* 71.2 (1981): 127–46.
Buffon, Georges-Louis Leclerc, Comte de. *Les Époques de la nature*. Paris: L'Imprimerie Royale, 1780; original 1778.
Buffon, Georges-Louis Leclerc, Comte de. *Histoire naturelle, generale et particulière*. 36 volumes. Paris: L'Imprimerie Royale, 1749–78.
Buttimer, Anne. "Beyond Humboldtian Science and Goethe's Way of Science: Challenges of Alexander von Humboldt's Geography." *Erdkunde* 55.2 (2001): 105–20.
Cañizares-Esguerra, Jorge. "How Derivative Was Humboldt?" In *Nature, Empire, and Nation: Explorations of the History of Science in the Iberian World*, 96–111. Stanford, CA: Stanford University Press, 2006.
Celermajer, Danielle. *Summertime: Reflections on a Vanishing Future*. Sydney: Penguin, 2021.
Celermajer, Danielle, et al. "Justice through a Multispecies Lens." *Contemporary Political Theory* 19 (2020): 475–512.
Chignell, Andrew. "Beauty as Symbol of Natural Systematicity." *British Journal of Aesthetics* 46.4 (2006): 406–15.
Clark, Robert J., Jr. "Herder's Conception of 'Kraft.'" *PMLA* 57.3 (1942): 737–52.
Clarke, Ellen. "The Problem of Biological Individuality." *Biological Theory* 5.4 (2010): 312–25.
Daston, Lorraine, and Peter Galison. *Objectivity*. Boston: Zone Books, 2007.
Daston, Lorraine, and Glenn W. Most. "History of Science and History of Philologies." *Isis* 106 (2015): 381–82.

DeSouza, Nigel. "Herder's Theory of Organic Forces and Its Kantian Origins." In *Kant and His German Contemporaries*, volume 2, *Aesthetics, History, Politics, and Religion*, edited by Daniel O. Dahlstrom, 108–27. Cambridge: Cambridge University Press, 2018.
Dettelbach, Michael. "Alexander von Humboldt between Enlightenment and Romanticism." *Northeastern Naturalist* 8 (2001): 9–20.
Dettelbach, Michael. "Introduction to the 1997 Edition." In Alexander von Humboldt, *Cosmos: A Sketch of a Physical Description of the Universe*, volume 2, edited and translated by E. C. Otté, with an Introduction by Michael Dettelbach, xxvi–xxvii. Baltimore: Johns Hopkins University Press, 1997.
Diderot, Denis. *Pensées sur l'Interprétation de la Nature*. Paris: n.p., 1754.
Diderot, Denis. *Thoughts on the Interpretation of Nature and Other Philosophical Works*. Translated by Lorna Sandler. Manchester: Clinamen Press, 1999.
Driesch, Hans. *Geschichte des Vitalismus*. Leipzig: J. A. Barth, 1922.
Driesch, Hans. *Science and Philosophy of the Organism*. London: Adam and Charles Black, 1908.
Eberhard, Johann August. *Von dem Begriffe der Philosophie und ihren Theilen. Ein Versuch*. Berlin: Christian Friedrich Doß, 1778.
Egerton, Frank N. *Roots of Ecology: Antiquity to Haeckel*. Berkeley: University of California Press, 2012.
Ette, Ottmar. "Eine 'Gemütsverfassung moralische Unruhe'—Humboldtian Writing: Alexander von Humboldt und das Schreiben in der Moderne." In *Alexander von Humboldt—Aufbruch in die Moderne*, edited by Ottmar Ette, Ute Hermanns, Bernd M. Scherer, Christian Suckow, 33–42. Berlin: Akademie Verlag, 2001.
Ette, Ottmar, ed. *Alexander von Humboldt-Handbuch: Leben-Werk-Wirkung*. Stuttgart: Metzler, 2018.
Feigenbaum, Ryan. "Toward a Nonanthropocentric Vision of Nature: Goethe's Discovery of the Intermaxillary Bone." *Goethe Yearbook* 22 (2015): 73–93.
Fink, Karl J. *Goethe's History of Science*. Cambridge: Cambridge University Press, 1992.
Fischer, Luke. "Goethe contra Hegel: The Question of the 'End of Art.'" *Goethe Yearbook* 18 (2011): 127–57.
Fischer, Luke, and Dalia Nassar. "Goethe and Environmentalism." *Goethe Yearbook* 22 (2015): 3–22.
Fisher, Naomi. "Organisms and the Form of Freedom in Kant's Third *Critique*." *European Journal of Philosophy* 27 (2019): 55–74.
Förster, Eckart. "Goethe's Spinozism." In *Spinoza and German Idealism*, edited by Eckart Förster and Yitzhak Melamed, 85–99. Cambridge: Cambridge University Press, 2012.
Förster, Eckart. *The Twenty-Five Years of Philosophy: A Systematic Reconstruction*. Translated by Brady Bowman. Cambridge, MA: Harvard University Press, 2012.
Forster, Michael. *After Herder: Philosophy of Language in the German Tradition*. Oxford: Oxford University Press, 2010.
Forster, Michael. *Herder's Philosophy*. Oxford: Oxford University Press, 2018.
Foucault, Michel. *The Order of Things: An Archaeology of the Human Sciences*. New York: Routledge, 1989.
Frank, Manfred. *"Unendliche Annäherung". Die Anfänge der philosophischen Frühromantik*. Frankfurt am Main: Suhrkamp, 1997.
Friedman, Michael. *Kant's Construction of Nature: A Reading of the Metaphysical Foundations of Natural Science*. Cambridge: Cambridge University Press, 2013.

Fu, Rong, et al. "Increased Dry-Season Length over Southern Amazonia in Recent Decades and Its Implication for Future Climate Projection." *Proceedings of the National Academy of Sciences* 110.45 (2013): 18110–15.
Gaukroger, Stephen. *The Collapse of Mechanism and the Rise of Sensibility: Science and the Shaping of Modernity, 1680–1760.* Oxford: Oxford University Press, 2010.
Ginsborg, Hannah. "Two Kinds of Mechanical Inexplicability in Kant and Aristotle." *Journal of the History of Philosophy* 42 (2004): 33–65.
Giraud, Eva. *What Comes after Entanglement? Activism, Anthropocentrism, and an Ethics of Exclusion.* Durham, NC: Duke University Press, 2019.
Gjesdal, Kristin. *Herder's Hermeneutics: History, Poetry, Enlightenment.* Cambridge: Cambridge University Press, 2017.
Godlewska, Anne Marie Claire. "From Enlightenment Vision to Modern Science? Humboldt's Visual Thinking." In *Geography and Enlightenment*, edited by David N. Livingstone and Charles W. J. Withers, 236–75. Chicago: University of Chicago Press, 1999.
Goethe, Johann Wolfgang von. *Begegnungen und Gespräche.* Volume 5, *1800–1805.* Edited by Ernst Grumach and Renata Grumach. Berlin: de Gruyter, 1985.
Goethe, Johann Wolfgang von. *Briefe Goethe's und der bedeutendsten Dichter seiner Zeit an Herder.* Edited by Heinrich Dünzer and F. G. von Herder. Frankfurt am Main: Meidinger Sohn, 1858.
Goethe, Johann Wolfgang von. *Briefwechsel zwischen Goethe und Knebel, 1774–1832.* Part 1, 1774–1806. Edited by G. E. Gurhauer. Leipzig: Brockhaus, 1851.
Goethe, Johann Wolfgang von. *Goethes Werke* (Weimarer Ausgabe). Edited by P. Raabe et al. Weimar: Hermann Böhlau, 1887–1919.
Goethe, Johann Wolfgang von. *Sämtliche Werke: Briefe, Tagebücher und Gespräche* (Frankfurter Ausgabe). Edited by H. Birus et al. Frankfurt am Main: Deutscher Klassiker Verlag, 1985–2003.
Goethe, Johann Wolfgang von. *Sämtliche Werke nach Epochen seines Schaffens* (Münchner Ausgabe). Edited by K. Richter et al. Munich: Carl Hanser, 1985–98.
Goethe, Johann Wolfgang von. *Die Schriften zur Naturwissenschaft* (Leopoldina Ausgabe). Edited by D. Kuhn et al. Weimar: Hermann Böhlaus Nachfolger, 1947–.
Goethe, Johann Wolfgang von. *Tagebücher.* Edited by W. Albrecht and E. Zehm. Stuttgart: Metzler, 2000.
Goethe, Johann Wolfgang von. *Werke* (Hamburger Ausgabe). Edited by E. Trunz et al. Hamburg: Christian Wegner Verlag, 1949–71.
Goldstein, Amanda Jo. "Irritable Figures: Herder's Poetic Empiricism." In *The Relevance of Romanticism: Essays on German Romantic Philosophy*, edited by Dalia Nassar, 273–292. New York: Oxford University Press, 2014.
Goldstein, Amanda Jo. *Sweet Science: Romantic Materialism and the New Logics of Life.* Chicago: University of Chicago Press, 2017.
Goodbody, Axel. *Natursprache. Ein dichtungstheoretisches Konzept der Romantik und seine Wiederaufnahme in der modernen Naturlyrik (Novalis—Eichendorff—Lehmann—Eich).* Neumünster: Karl Wachholtz, 1984.
Goy, Ina. "'All Is Leaf': Goethe's Plant Philosophy and Poetry." In *Philosophy of Biology Before Biology*, edited by C. Bognon-Küss and C. T. Wolfe, 146–69. London: Routledge, 2019.
Graczyk, Annette. *Das literarische Tableau zwischen Kunst und Wissenschaft.* Munich: Wilhelm Fink, 2004.

Grove, Richard. "Colonial Conservation, Ecological Hegemony and Popular Resistance: Towards a Global Synthesis." In *Imperialism and the Natural Word*, edited by John MacKenzie, 15–50. Manchester: Manchester University Press, 1990.

Grove, Richard. "Origins of Western Environmentalism." *Scientific American*, July 1992: 42–47.

Haeckel, Ernst. *Generelle Morphologie der Organismen*. Volume 2. Berlin: Georg Reimer, 1866.

Haldane, J. S. *Organism and Environment as Illustrated by the Physiology of Breathing*. New Haven: Yale University Press, 1917.

Haller, Albrecht von. "Reflections on the Theory of Generation of Mr. Buffon." In *From Natural History to the History of Nature: Readings from Buffon to His Critics*, edited and translated by J. Lyon and P. R. Sloan, 214–327. Notre Dame, IN: University of Notre Dame Press, 1981.

Hargrove, Eugene C. "After Twenty Years." *Environmental Ethics* 20 (1998): 339–40.

Heinz, Marion. "Philosophie. Einleitung." In *Herder Handbuch*, edited by Stefan Greif, Marion Heinz, and Heinrich Clairmont, 41–47. Paderborn: Fink, 2016.

Heinz, Marion. *Sensualistischer Idealismus. Untersuchungen zur Erkenntnistheorie des jungen Herder (1763–1778)*. Hamburg: F. Meiner, 1994.

Helbig, Daniela, and Dalia Nassar. "The Metaphor of Epigenesis: Kant, Blumenbach and Herder." *Studies in History and Philosophy of Science* Part A 58 (2016): 98–107.

Hennigfeld, Iris. "Goethe's Phenomenological Way of Thinking and the Urphänomen." *Goethe Yearbook* 22 (2015): 143–67.

Herder, Johann Gottfried. *Herders Briefe*. Edited by Wilhelm Dobbek. Weimar: Volksverlag, 1959.

Herder, Johann Gottfried. *Philosophical Writings*. Edited and translated by Michael Forster. Cambridge: Cambridge University Press, 2002.

Herder, Johann Gottfried. *Sämtliche Werke*. Edited by Bernard Suphan. Berlin: Weidmann, 1877–1913.

Herder, Johann Gottfried. *Selected Writings on Aesthetics*. Edited and translated by Gregory Moore. Princeton, NJ: Princeton University Press, 2006.

Herder, Johann Gottfried. *Werke in zehn Bänden*. Edited by Jürgen Brummack and Martin Bollacher. Frankfurt am Main: Deutscher Klassiker Verlag, 1985–2000.

Hey'l, Bettina. *Das Ganze der Natur und die Differenzierung des Wissens: Alexander von Humboldt als Schriftsteller*. Berlin: de Gruyter, 2007.

Hindrichs, Gunnar. "Goethe's Notion of an Intuitive Judgment." *Goethe Yearbook* 18 (2011): 51–65.

Holdrege, Craig. "Goethe and the Evolution of Science." *In Context* 31 (2014): 10–23.

Humboldt, Alexander von. *Ansichten der Natur mit wissenschaftlichen Erläuterungen*. Tübingen: Cotta, 1808.

Humboldt, Alexander von. *Aus meinem Leben*. Edited by Kurt-R. Biermann. Leipzig: Urania Verlag, 1987.

Humboldt, Alexander von. *Briefe von Alexander von Humboldt an Varnhagen von Ense*. Edited by Ludmilla Assing. Leipzig: Brockhaus, 1870.

Humboldt, Alexander von. *Cosmos*. Volume 1. Edited and translated by E. C. Otté. Reprint: Baltimore: Johns Hopkins University Press, 1997. Original: London: Bohn, 1849.

Humboldt, Alexander von. *Cosmos*. Volume 2. Edited and translated by E. C. Otté. Reprint: Baltimore: Johns Hopkins University Press, 1997. Original: London: Bohn, 1850.

Humboldt, Alexander von. *Cosmos.* Volume 3. Edited and translated by E. C. Otté. London: Bohn, 1851.
Humboldt, Alexander von. *Cosmos.* Volume 5. Edited and translated by E. C. Otté and W. S. Dallas. London: Bohn, 1858.
Humboldt, Alexander von. *Darmstädter Ausgabe.* Edited with commentary by Hanno Beck. 7 volumes. Darmstadt: Wissenschaftliche Buchgesellschaft, 2018.
Humboldt, Alexander von. *Essay on the Kingdom of New Spain.* Volume 1, *A Critical Edition.* Edited with an Introduction by Vera M. Kutzinski and Ottmar Ette. Chicago: University of Chicago Press, 2019.
Humboldt, Alexander von. *Die Jugendbriefe Alexander von Humboldts 1787–1799.* Edited by Ilse Jahn and Fritz Lange. Berlin: Akademie Verlag, 1973.
Humboldt, Alexander von. *Political Essay on the Island of Cuba: A Critical Edition.* Edited by Vera M. Kutzinski and Ottmar Ette. Translated by J. Bradford Anderson, Vera M. Kutzinski, and Anja Becker. Chicago: University of Chicago Press, 2011.
Humboldt, Alexander von. *Versuche über die gereizte Muskel- und Nervenfaser nebst Vermuthungen über den chemischen Process des Lebens in der Thier- und Pflanzenwelt.* 2 volumes. Posen: Decker und Compagnie/Berlin: Heinrich August Rottman, 1797–1798.
Humboldt, Alexander von. *Über die Haupt-Ursachen der Temperatur-Verschiedenheit auf dem Erdkörper.* Berlin: Preussische Akademie der Wissenschaften, 1830.
Humboldt, Alexander von. *Views of Nature.* Edited by Stephen T. Jackson and Laura Dassow Walls. Translated by Mark W. Person. Chicago: University of Chicago Press, 2014.
Humboldt, Alexander von, and Aimé Bonpland. *Essay on the Geography of Plants.* Edited with an introduction by Stephen T. Jackson. Translated (from French) by Sylvie Romanowski. Chicago: University of Chicago Press, 2009.
Humboldt, Alexander von, and Aimé Bonpland. *Personal Narrative of Travels to the Equinoctial Regions of America, during the Years 1799–1804.* Edited and translated by Helen Maria Williams. 7 volumes. London: Longman, Hurst, Rees, Orme, and Brown, 1814–29.
Humboldt, Alexander von, and Aimé Bonpland. *Personal Narrative of Travels to the Equinoctial Regions of America, during the Years 1799–1804.* Edited and translated by Thomasina Ross. 3 volumes. London: Bohm, 1852–53.
Humboldt, Wilhelm von. *Ästhetische Versuche. Erster Teil. Über Göthes "Herrmann und Dorothea."* Braunschweig: Vieweg, 1799.
Intemann, Kristen. "25 Years of Feminist Empiricism and Standpoint Theory." *Hypatia* 25 (2010): 778–96.
Irmscher, Hans-Dietrich. "Beobachtungen zur Funktion der Analogie im Denken Herders." *Deutsche Vierteljahrsschrift für Literaturwissenschaft und Geistesgeschichte* 55 (1981): 64–97.
Irmscher, Hans-Dietrich. "Goethe und Herder." In *Johann Gottfried Herder. Aspekte seines Lebenswerkes*, edited by M. Keßler and V. Leppin, 232–269. Berlin: de Gruyter, 2005.
Irmscher, Hans-Dietrich. "Goethe und Herder im Wechselspiel von Attraktion und Repulsion." In *"Weitstrahlsinniges" Denken. Studien zu Johann Gottfried Herder*, edited by M. Heinz and V. Stolz, 335–368. Würzburg: Königshausen und Neumann, 2009.
Jahn, Ilse, and Andreas Kleinert, eds. *Das Allgemeine und das Einzelne—Johann Wolfgang von Goethe und Alexander von Humboldt im Gespräch.* Halle: Leopoldina, 2003.
Kant, Immanuel. *Critique of Pure Reason.* Edited and translated by Paul Guyer and Allen Wood. Cambridge: Cambridge University Press, 1998.

Kant, Immanuel. *Critique of the Power of Judgment*. Edited by Paul Guyer. Translated by Paul Guyer and Eric Matthews. Cambridge: Cambridge University Press, 2000.

Kant, Immanuel. *Gesammelte Schriften*. Edited by Preußische Akademie der Wissenschaft. Berlin: de Gruyter, 1900–.

Kant, Immanuel. *Logik-Vorlesung, Unveröffentlichte Nachschriften II. Logik Hechsel, Warschauer Logik*. Edited by Tillmann Pinder. Hamburg: Felix Meiner Verlag, 1998.

Klee, Paul. *The Dairies of Paul Klee, 1898–1918*. Edited with an Introduction by Felix Klee. Berkeley: University of California Press, 1964.

Knobloch, Eberhard. "Naturgenuss und Weltgemälde: Gedanken zu Humboldts *Kosmos*." *Humboldt im Netz* 5.9 (2004): 33–47.

Kohn, Eduardo. *How Forests Think: Toward an Anthropology beyond the Human*. New York: Columbia University Press, 2013.

Korsgaard, Christine M. *Fellow Creatures: Our Obligations to Other Animals*. Oxford: Oxford University Press, 2018.

Kuhn, Bernhard. *Autobiography and Natural Science in the Age of Romanticism: Rousseau, Goethe, Thoreau*. London: Routledge, 2016.

Kutzinski, Vera M., and Ottmar Ette. "Inventories and Inventions: Alexander von Humboldt's Cuban Landscapes." In Alexander von Humboldt, *Political Essay on the Island of Cuba: A Critical Edition*, edited by Vera M. Kutzinski and Ottmar Ette, translated by J. Bradford Anderson, Vera M. Kutzinski, and Anja Becker, vii–xxiv. Chicago: University of Chicago Press, 2011.

Lessing, Gotthold Ephraim. *Laokoon: oder über die Grenzen der Mahlerey und Poesie*. Volume 1. Berlin: Voss, 1766.

Lifschitz, Avi. *Language and Enlightenment: The Berlin Debates of the Eighteenth Century*. Oxford: Oxford University Press, 2012.

Lindstrom, Matthew, ed. *Encyclopedia of the U.S. Government and the Environment: History, Policy, and Politics*. Santa Barbara, CA: ABC-CLIO, 2011.

Makreel, Rudolf A. *Imagination and Interpretation in Kant*. Chicago: University of Chicago Press, 1990.

Markiewicz, Henryk, and Uliana Gabara, "Ut Pictura Poesis . . . A History of the Topos and the Problem." *New Literary History* 18.3 (1987): 535–58.

Martin, Alison. *Nature Translated: Alexander von Humboldt's Works in Nineteenth-Century Britain*. Edinburgh: Edinburgh University Press, 2018.

Matherne, Samantha. "Kant on Cognition by Analogy." Unpublished ms.

McLaughlin, Peter. *Kant's Critique of Teleological Biology*. Lewiston, NY: Edwin Mellen Press, 1990.

Meyer-Abich, Adolf. *Die Vollendung der Morphologie Goethes durch Alexander von Humboldt: Ein Beitrag zur Naturwissenschaft der Goethezeit*. Göttingen: Vandenhoeck und Ruprecht, 1970.

Millán, Elizabeth. "The Quest for the Seeds of Eternal Growth: Goethe and Humboldt's Presentation of Nature." *Goethe Yearbook* 18 (2011): 97–114.

Millán, Elizabeth. "Saving Nature from Vicious Empiricism." In *The New Light of German Romanticism*, edited by B. Frischmann and E. Millán-Zaibert. Paderborn: Schöningh, 2008.

Molnár, Géza von. "Goethes Studium der *Kritik der Urteilskraft*: Eine Zusammenstellung nach den Eintragungen in seinem Handexemplar." *Goethe Yearbook* 2 (1984): 137–222.

Morton, Timothy. *Ecology after Nature*. Cambridge, MA: Harvard University Press, 2007.

Mücke, Dorothea von. "Goethe's Metamorphosis: Changing Forms in Nature, the Life Sciences and Authorship." *Representations* 95.1 (2006): 27–53.
Müller, Günther. "Goethes Elegie die 'Metamorphose der Pflanzen.'" In *Morphologische Poetik*, edited by Elena Müller, 357–87. Tübingen: Max Niemeyer, 1974.
Müller, Günther. "Morphologische Poetik." In *Morphologische Poetik. Gesammelte Aufsätze*, edited by Elena Müller, 225–46. Tübingen: Max Niemeyer, 1974.
Muthu, Sankar. *Enlightenment against Empire*. Princeton, NJ: Princeton University Press, 2003.
Nassar, Dalia. "The Challenge of Plants: Goethe, Humboldt and the Question of 'Life.'" In *Nature and Naturalism in Classical German Philosophy*, edited by Johannes-Georg Schülein and Luca Corti. London: Routledge, forthcoming.
Nassar, Dalia. "Friedrich Schlegel, 1770–1829." In *Oxford Handbook of German Philosophy in the Nineteenth Century*, edited by Michael Forster and Kristin Gjesdal, 68–87. Oxford: Oxford University Press, 2015.
Nassar, Dalia. "Pure versus Empirical Forms of Thought: Schelling's Critique of Kant's Categories and the Beginnings of *Naturphilosophie*." *Journal of the History of Philosophy* 52.1 (2014): 113–34.
Nassar, Dalia. "Rational Empiricism?" In *"Dear Friend: You Must Change Your Life"—the Letters of Great Thinkers*, edited by Ada Bronowski, 91–98. New York: Bloomsbury, 2020.
Nassar, Dalia. *The Romantic Absolute: Being and Knowing in German Romantic Philosophy, 1795–1804*. Chicago: University of Chicago Press, 2014.
Nassar, Dalia. "Sensibility and Organic Unity: Kant, Goethe, and the Plasticity of Cognition." *Intellectual History Review* 25.3 (2015): 311–26.
Newton, Isaac. *Philosophical Writings*. Edited by Andrew Janiak. Cambridge: Cambridge University Press, 2005.
Nicholson, Daniel J. "The Return of the Organism as a Fundamental Explanatory Concept in Biology." *Philosophy Compass* 9.5 (2014): 347–59.
Nisbet, H. B. *Goethe and the Scientific Tradition*. London: Institute of German Studies, University of London, 1972.
Nisbet, H. B. *Herder and Scientific Thought*. Cambridge: Modern Humanities Research Association, 1970.
Nussbaum, Martha. *Frontiers of Justice: Disability, Nationality, Species Membership*. Cambridge: MA: Harvard University Press, 2006.
Paatz, Walter. *The Arts of the Italian Renaissance: Painting, Sculpture, Architecture*. Englewood Cliffs, NJ: Prentice Hall, 1974.
Pausas, Juli, and William Bond. "Humboldt and the Reinvention of Nature." *Journal of Ecology* 107 (2019): 1031–37.
Plumwood, Val. *Environmental Culture: The Ecological Crisis of Reason*. London: Routledge, 2002.
Plumwood, Val. "Toward a Progressive Naturalism." In *Recognizing the Autonomy of Nature*, edited by T. Heydt. New York: Columbia University Press, 2005.
Puig-Samper, Miguel Ángel. "Humboldt, un Prusiano en la Corte del Rey Carlos IV." *Revista de Indias* 59.216 (1999): 329–55.
Regan, Tom. *The Case for Animal Rights*. Berkeley: University of California Press, 1983.
Reill, Peter Hanns. *Vitalizing Nature in the Enlightenment*. Berkeley: University of California Press, 2002.
Richards, Robert J. "Kant and Blumenbach: A Historical Misunderstanding." *Studies in the History and Philosophy of Biology and the Biomedical Sciences* 31.1 (2000): 11–32.

Richards, Robert J. *The Romantic Conception of Life: Science and Philosophy in the Age of Goethe*. Chicago: University of Chicago Press, 2002.

Rigby, Kate. "Art, Nature, and the Poesy of Plants in the *Goethezeit*: A Biosemiotic Perspective." *Goethe Yearbook* 22 (2015): 23–44.

Rigby, Kate. "Earth's Poesy: Romantic Poetics, Natural Philosophy, and Biosemiotics." In *Handbook of Ecocriticism and Cultural Ecology*, edited by Hubert Zapf, 45–64. Berlin: de Gruyter, 2016.

Rigby, Kate. *Topographies of the Sacred: The Poetics of Place in European Romanticism*. Charlottesville: University of Virginia Press, 2004.

Rigby, Kate. "Writing after Nature." *Australian Humanities Review* 39–40 (2006), http://australianhumanitiesreview.org/2006/09/01/writing-after-nature/.

Riskin, Jessica. *Science in the Age of Sensibility: The Sentimental Empiricists of the French Enlightenment*. Chicago: University of Chicago Press, 2002.

Roe, Shirley. *Matter, Life, and Generation: Eighteenth-Century Embryology and the Haller-Wolff Debate*. Cambridge: Cambridge University Press, 1981.

Roger, Jacques. *Buffon: A Life in Natural History*. Translated by Sarah Lucille Bonnefoi. Ithaca, NY: Cornell University Press, 1997.

Romanowski, Sylvie. "Humboldt's Pictorial Science: An Analysis of the Tableau physique des Andes et pays voisins." In Alexander von Humboldt and Aimé Bonpland, *Essay on the Geography of Plants*, edited by Stephen T. Jackson and translated by Sylvie Romanowski, 157–98. Chicago: University of Chicago Press, 2009.

Rousseau, Jean-Jacques. *Oeuvres completes*. 5 volumes. Paris: Gallimard, 1958–96.

Routley, Richard. "Is There a Need for a New, an Environmental, Ethic?" *Proceedings of the XVth World Congress of Philosophy*, 205–10. Varna, Bulgaria: Sofia Press, 1973.

Sachers, Regina. *Goethe's Poetry and Philosophy of Nature*. London: Routledge, 2017.

Sachs, Aaron. *The Humboldt Current: Nineteenth-Century Exploration and the Roots of American Environmentalism*. New York: Viking, 2006.

Sauter, Eugen. *Herder und Buffon*. Rixheim: F. Sutter & Cie, 1910.

Schieren, Jost. *Anschauende Urteilskraft. Methodische und Philosophische Grundlagen von Goethes Naturwissenschaftlichem Erkennen*. Dusseldorf: Parerga, 1998.

Schiller, Friedrich. *Schillers Werke. Nationalausgabe*. Edited by Julius Petersen et al. 43 volumes. Weimar: Hermann Böhlaus Nachfolger, 1943–.

Schlegel, Friedrich. *Kritische Friedrich-Schlegel-Ausgabe*. Edited by E. Behler, J. J. Anstett, and H. Eichner. Paderborn: Schöningh, 1958–2006.

Seeley, T. D. "The Honey-Bee Colony as a Superorganism." *American Science* 77 (1989): 546–53.

Sepper, Dennis L. "Goethe against Newton: Towards Saving the Phenomena." In *Goethe and the Sciences: A Reappraisal*, edited by Frederick Amrine, Francis Zucker, and Harvey Wheeler, 175–94. Dordrecht: Reidel, 1987.

Sepper, Dennis L. *Goethe contra Newton*. Cambridge: Cambridge University Press, 1988.

Serje, Margarita. "The National Imagination in New Granada." In *Alexander von Humboldt: From the Americas to the Cosmos*. Coordinated by R. Erickson, M. A. Font, and B. Schwarts. New York: Bildner, 2005.

Singer, Peter. *Animal Liberation*. New York: Avon, 1975.

Sloan, Philip. "Buffon, German Biology, and the Historical Interpretation of Biological Species." *British Journal for the History of Science* 12 (1979): 109–53.

Sloan, Philip. "The Buffon-Linnaeus Controversy." *Isis* 67.3 (1976): 356–75.

Sloan, Philip. "The Idea of Racial Degeneracy in Buffon's *Histoire naturelle*." *Studies in Eighteenth-Century Culture* 3 (1973): 293–321.

Smith, Justin, ed. *The Problem of Animal Generation in Early Modern Philosophy.* Cambridge: Cambridge University Press, 2002.
Soper, Kate. *What Is Nature? Culture, Politics and the Non-human.* Oxford: Blackwell, 1995.
Staël-Holstein, Germaine de. *De L'allemagne.* 2nd ed. Reprint: Paris: H. Nicolle, 1813. Original: Paris: H. Nicolle, 1810.
Steigerwald, Joan. "The Cultural Enframing of Nature: Environmental Histories during the Early German Romantic Period." *Environment and History* 6.4 (2000): 451–96.
Stephenson, Roger. *Goethe's Conception of Knowledge and Science.* Edinburgh: Edinburgh University Press, 1995.
Stone, Christopher D. "Should Trees Have Standing?—Toward Legal Rights for Natural Objects." *Southern California Law Review* 45 (1972): 450–501.
Sultan, Sonia E. *Organism and Environment: Ecological Development, Niche Construction, and Adaptation.* Oxford: Oxford University Press, 2015.
Tang, Chenxi. *The Geographic Imagination of Modernity: Geography, Literature and Philosophy in German Romanticism.* Stanford, CA: Stanford University Press, 2008.
Tantillo, Astrida Orle. *The Will to Create: Goethe's Philosophy of Nature.* Pittsburgh, PA: University of Pittsburgh Press, 2002.
Troll, Carl. "Die tropischen Gebirge." In *Bonner Geographische Abhandlungen* 25. Bonn: Ferd. Immlers Verlag, 1959.
Tropp, Gabriel. "Poetry and Morphology: Goethe's 'Parabase' and the Intensification of the Morphological Gaze." *Monatshefte* 105.3 (2013): 389–406.
Uexküll, Jakob von. *A Foray into the World of Animals and Humans.* Translated by Joseph D. O'Neil. Minneapolis: University of Minnesota Press, 2010.
Waldow, Anik. *Experience Embodied: Early Modern Accounts of the Human Place in Nature.* New York: Oxford University Press, 2020.
Waldow, Anik, and Nigel De Souza, eds. *Herder: Philosophy and Anthropology.* New York: Oxford University Press, 2017.
Walls, Laura Dassow. *The Passage to "Cosmos": Alexander von Humboldt and the Shaping of America.* Chicago: University of Chicago Press, 2012.
Watkins, Eric. "The Antinomy of Teleological Judgment." *Kant Yearbook* 1 (2009): 197–222.
Wheeler, William Morton. "The Ant Colony as Organism." *Journal of Morphology* 22 (1911): 307–25.
Whyte, Kyle Powys, and Chris J. Cuomo. "Ethics of Caring in Environmental Ethics: Indigenous and Feminist Philosophies." In *The Oxford Handbook of Environmental Ethics*, edited by Stephen Gardiner and Allen Thompson, 234–47. Oxford: Oxford University Press, 2017.
Williams, Raymond. "Ideas of Nature." In *Problems of Materialism and Other Essays.* London: Verso, 1997.
Wolf, Norbert Christian. *Streitbare Ästhetik. Goethes kunst- und literaturtheoretische Schriften 1771–1789.* Tübingen: Niemeyer, 2001.
Wolfe, Charles T. "On the Role of Newtonian Analogies in Eighteenth-Century Life Science: Vitalism and Provisionally Inexplicable Explicative Devices." In *Newton and Empiricism*, edited by Zvi Biener and Eric Schliesser, 223–61. Oxford: Oxford University Press, 2014.
Wolff, Christian. *Vernünftige Gedancken von Gott, der Welt und der Seele des Menschen, auch allen Dingen überhaupt.* 9th ed. Halle: Renger, 1743.
Wulf, Andrea. *The Invention of Nature: Alexander von Humboldt's New World.* New York: Knopf, 2015.

Zammito, John. *The Genesis of Kant's "Critique of Judgment."* Chicago: University of Chicago Press, 1992.
Zammito, John. *The Gestation of German Biology: From Stahl to Schelling.* Chicago: University of Chicago Press, 2017.
Zammito, John. *Kant, Herder, and the Birth of Anthropology.* Chicago: University of Chicago Press, 2002.
Zammito, John. *A Nice Derangement of Epistemes: Post-positivism in the Study of Science from Quine to Latour.* Chicago: University of Chicago Press, 2004.
Ziguras, Jakob. "Archē as Urphänomen: A Goethean Interpretation of Aristotle's Theory of Scientific Knowledge." *Epoché: A Journal for the History of Philosophy* 18 (2013): 79–105.
Ziguras, Jakob. "Aristotle's Rational Empiricism: A Goethean Interpretation of Aristotle's Theory of Knowledge." PhD thesis, University of Sydney, 2010.
Zuckert, Rachel. "Herder and Philosophical Naturalism." *Herder Jahrbuch* 12.1 (2014): 125–44.
Zuckert, Rachel. *Herder's Naturalist Aesthetics.* Cambridge: Cambridge University Press, 2019.
Zuckert, Rachel. *Kant on Beauty and Biology: An Interpretation of the "Critique of Judgment."* Cambridge: Cambridge University Press, 2007.

Index

abstraction (critique of), 29–33, 55–56, 58, 59, 67–69, 83, 85, 95, 116, 141, 170, 195, 246–247, 264n17
active
  engagement of the knower, 95, 115–116, 124, 138, 168, 271n22
  forces (material bodies), 89–90
  living beings as, 60, 186–187, 191, 208, 210
  nature, 127, 242
  seeing, 137, 155, 268n1
aesthetic
  capacities, 11 (*see also* perceptual capacities)
  cognition, 154 (*see also* symbolic cognition)
  education, 5, 11, 106–107, 110–129, 145, 150, 154, 166, 212, 214, 247, 269n7
  encounter, 8
  experience, 1, 5, 8, 17, 106–107, 214–217, 237, 247
  feeling, 235, 238
  integrity, 144, 179
  judgment, 13–14, 23, 62, 278n27, 285n30
  means and methods, 6
  pleasure, 7
  science, 1, 4, 6, 12, 14, 28, 44, 169–171, 194, 212–215, 237–238, 285n31 (*see also* scientific works of art)
  sense, 212–213
  significance, 282n2
  value, 106
  works, 215
  See also artistic
aesthetics, 1, 5–11, 115, 167, 217, 244–245, 247, 262n4, 272n24
  and ecology, 178–179, 214–217, 237–240
  moral significance of, 241
  See also art; embodied aesthetics
Amrine, Frederick, 162
analogical cognition, 9, 77–84, 147, 259n40

analogical judgment, 8, 22–24, 33–34, 44, 50, 84, 88
analogical reflection, 24, 28, 43–44, 51–55, 84, 88, 91–95, 252n11, 258n32. *See also* teleological judgment
analogy, 16–19, 22–30, 43–51, 53, 74, 88, 251n1, 251n8, 252n9, 252n10, 252n21, 253n31, 253n35, 255n3
  the as-structure of, 76–83, 86, 92
  Buffon and, 28–29, 32–33
  Herder and, 54–55, 74, 81–82, 84–86, 88, 92–95
  inference by, 24, 30, 33–35, 46, 87–88, 146
  and intuitive understanding, 50–51
  Kant's critique of, 33–36, 54
  between nature and art, 8–9, 16–19, 22, 27, 44, 47–52, 53–54
  and reflecting judgment (*see* analogical judgment)
  in science, 32–33, 35, 44, 54–55, 86
  and teleological judgment, 22–25, 43–49, 51
apodictic certainty, 30, 37
approach (to the study of nature), 1–3, 5–6, 8, 10, 28, 32, 34, 52, 55, 59, 84–87, 102, 105, 127, 133, 146, 150–151, 155, 165, 168, 178–180, 182, 188, 196, 245–247, 250n7, 255n5, 261n10, 264n17, 270n11, 272n24, 272n27, 273n31, 277n21, 278n22, 283n7. *See also* hermeneutic/hermeneutics; method/methodology
archetypal phenomenon, 157–158, 161–162, 270n14. See also *Urphänomen*
archetype, 270n14. *See also* type (*Typus*)
Aristotle, 41, 63, 163, 212–213, 254n41, 272n31
art, 2, 4, 7–11, 16, 22, 27, 44, 47–52, 111–115, 125, 196, 214, 217, 221–226, 237, 251n1
  appreciation of, 150
  and education, 106 (*see also* aesthetic education)
  epistemic significance of, 110
  galleries, 110–111

art (*cont.*)
  history of, 217–219
  and knowledge, 217 (*see also* symbolic cognition)
  and morals, 22, 47
  nature and, 8–10, 16–19, 106, 187, 218
  practice of, 110
  and science, 1, 4, 6, 11, 12, 14, 28, 112–114, 126, 169, 212–218, 237–238, 285n31
  scientific works of, 12, 236
  as skill, 70–71
  and truth, 219, 283n7 (*see also* truth to nature)
  work/works of, 8, 16, 18, 21–22, 51, 60, 62, 64, 79, 82, 106, 112–113, 115, 125, 144, 150, 154, 179, 214–216, 237, 257n17, 278n27
artistic
  capacities, 9
  choices, 223
  cognition, 17
  depictions (of nature), 218–219 (*see also* living depictions)
  dilettante, 106, 115
  disposition, 218
  genres, 223
  medium, media, 179, 219, 224–225
  objects, 111
  practice, 106
  productivity, 17
  quality, 282n2
  skills, 126, 138, 218
  tools and methods, 214, 218
  view, 179, 219
  works, 108, 110, 113
artwork, 49, 110–111
  as composition, 18, 49, 113–114, 231
  composition of, 114, 154
Athenäum (journal), 4

Bacon, Francis, 272n31
Baumgarten, Alexander, 106, 262n4
beauty, 8, 23, 25, 251n8, 283n5
Beck, Hanno, 276n9, 281n42
Beiser, Frederick C. 250n12, 285n30
Bild (image, form), 55, 183. *See also* form
Bildung, 159, 188, 262n19. *See also* education; formation

Bildungstrieb (formative drive), 87, 90, 261n11
biological individuality, 281n44
biology, 8, 28, 89, 166, 258n33, 260n5, 270n14, 278n30, 279n31
Blumenbach, Johann Friedrich, 87, 90, 97, 99, 260n4, 260n9, 261n11, 261n14, 261n15, 270n16
Böhme, Gernot, 221, 272n24, 283n8
Böhme, Hartmut, 276n10, 285n31
Bonnet, Charles, 58
Bonpland, Aimé, 176, 220, 275n7, 285n31
botany, 109, 282n47, 110, 125–126, 141, 193, 275n7
bottom-up, 8. *See also* approach; method
Boyle, Nicholas, 96
Brady, Ronald, 265n21, 270n12
Braun, Alexander, 281n44
Breitenbach, Angela, 251n5, 254n47
Buffon, Georges-Louis Leclerc, Comte de, 1, 7–9, 11, 28, 30–33, 57, 131, 145, 177, 183, 184, 193, 210, 253n31, 255n3
  on analogy, 28–29, 32–33
  on climate, 59, 84, 86, 257n12
  critique of Linnaeus, 29, 109
  distinction between real and abstract truths, 29–33
  and Herder, 54–60, 85, 86, 256n11, 257n16
  and Humboldt, 220, 277n11, 282n1

Caldas, José, 210, 275n7
Celermajer, Danielle, 246, 272n28
Classicism (Weimar), 4, 249n3, 250n14
climate change, 246
Condillac, Étienne Bonnot de, 58, 69, 72, 83, 258n28
contingency
  in knowledge, 15, 49, 92, 102, 146, 164
  in nature, 3, 13, 19–21, 28, 36, 39, 48–50, 53, 102–103, 113–114, 245, 252n11, 253n36
convergent forms (convergent evolution), 281n42

Darwin, Erasmus, 264n20
Daston, Lorraine and Peter Galison, 270n11, 283n7

INDEX   301

denkende Betrachtung (thinking observation, thinking seeing), 176, 180, 194, 276n9, 276n10
DeSouza, Nigel, 261n10
Dettelbach, Michael, 217, 249n3, 282n3
Diderot, Denis, 1, 32–33, 54–55, 58, 253n31
Driesch, Hans, 260n5, 271n17

Eberhard, Johann August, 30
ecological
　community, 85
　consciousness, 175
　crisis, 179, 246
　factors, 276n7
　form (conception) of knowledge, 6, 148–149, 173
　insight, 178–179, 185, 209–211, 276n7
　investigation, 178
　observation, 176
　perspective, 183
　thinking, 2
　understanding of nature, 6, 55, 183–185
　value, 167
ecology, 2, 6, 175, 176, 179, 184, 246
　and aesthetics, 6, 179, 183–185, 209–211
　history of, 6, 85, 176, 274n1, 274n2
education, 5–6, 11, 103, 104–107, 110–111, 115, 126–127, 145, 150–151, 154–155, 166, 168, 173, 212–214, 247, 262n3, 262n5, 269n7, 269n10. *See also* aesthetic education; formation
efficient cause, 19–21, 36–38, 41–42, 73, 258n31, 258n32. *See also* mechanism
embodied aesthetics, 217, 233–235
　environmental significance of, 237–241
　moral significance of, 241–244
embodied cognition (knowledge), 12, 81, 212–217, 233–234, 286n31
empiricism, 1–2, 5–8, 146, 157, 163–165, 169, 179–180, 245, 250n15, 259n40, 269n6
Enlightenment, 3, 249n3, 249n7
environment, 6, 40, 70–74, 83, 93, 102, 148, 175, 192–197, 258n30
　as dynamic, 6, 60, 84–85, 145, 155, 159, 170, 176–178, 183, 185, 193, 196, 216, 226, 238, 247, 256n7, 257n26, 259n44, 260n10, 262n19, 277n11
　as expressive, 55, 76, 194, 196, 206, 216, 230, 242, 255n5, 261n17
　organism and, 177–179, 183–188, 192, 203–211, 235
environmental
　action, 286n34
　change, 207
　concerns, 217, 272n24
　conditions, 184
　crisis, 241, 245–247
　ethics, 149, 166–174, 246, 272n27, 274n38
　factors, 202
　movement, 274n1
　reductionism, 279n32
　thought and philosophy, 148, 245–247, 272n24, 273n35
environmentalism, 176, 274n1, 286n32
epigenesis, 90, 259n39, 260n8
epistemology and ethics, 6, 166–175, 181, 237–241, 243–244, 245–247
Ette, Ottmar, 231, 284–285n25
explanation
　and analogy, 92–93
　causal, 70, 73, 89, 90–91, 102, 190
　as derivation, 43, 46–47, 73, 88, 90, 169, 203, 261n11
　and description, 72–73, 84, 101, 153
　and inference, 88, 91
　and interpretation, 64, 92
　mechanical (*see* mechanical explanation)
　and necessary knowledge, 103
　the phenomenon as, 101–103, 153, 189–190, 195
　in science, 44, 46, 52, 236, 238
　and teleological judgment, 23, 46–47, 50
　and understanding, 52, 255n49
eye of the mind (*Auge des Geistes*), 129–130, 136. *See also* intuitive judgment; perceptual thinking

feeling, 12–13, 78, 115, 179, 217–235, 238, 242–243, 246. *See also* aesthetic; sense
final cause, 39, 41, 51, 102, 251n41, 254n42. *See also* teleological judgment; teleology

form, 9-11, 19, 34, 41-42, 48, 72, 80, 84, 85, 86-88, 91, 98-103, 108-110, 112-113, 118-128, 142, 154-155, 158-161, 176-185, 188-212, 225, 254n41, 256n8, 260n5, 261n10, 264n14, 266n36, 268n42, 270n11, 271n17, 271n22, 274n37, 278n22, 278n28, 279n32, 280n36, 280n38, 280n39, 281n41, 284n16. See also *Bild*; *Bildung*; Humboldt and plant form; living form; poetic form; static form; structure; transforming form
form drive (*Formtrieb*), 214
formal cause, 41, 51, 251n41, 254n42, 271n22
formation (biological and cultural), 10, 42, 80, 90, 104, 142, 159-160, 167, 233-235, 237, 247, 265n31, 270n11, 271n16, 285n26. See also *Bildung*; education; form
Förster, Eckart, 3, 49, 52, 148, 150, 166, 262n3, 265n31, 269n3, 269n4, 269n6
Forster, Georg, 276n7
Forster, Michael, 249n4, 250n13, 257n18, 258n34
Foucault, Michel, 279n31
Frank, Manfred, 250n12

Gemälde, 282n2. See also *Naturgemälde*
gentle empiricism (*zarte Empirie*), 273n31
Gjesdal, Kristin, 249n4, 257n17
Goethe, Johann Wolfgang von
  on abstraction, 116, 141, 163, 170, 264n17, 272n31, 273n34
  and anatomy, 10, 96-100, 114, 166, 181-182, 261n17, 263n2, 265n22
  on archetype, 100-101, 159, 262n19, 263n12, 270n14
  on art, 106-107, 110-115, 125-125, 144, 150, 154, 169, 187, 269n9, 278n27
  and Blumenbach, 270n16
  and botany, 109-110, 125-126, 141, 264n15
  and ecological model of knowledge, 6, 148-149, 173-176
  on education, 5, 6, 11, 103, 104-107, 110-116, 126-127, 145, 150-151, 154-155, 166, 168, 173 (*see also* aesthetic education)
  and empiricism, 130, 135-136, 146-147, 157, 163-166, 169, 269n6
  and environmental ethics, 149, 166-173, 272n27, 274n38
  and environmentalism, 272n24
  epistemology (theory of knowledge), 104-110, 130-136, 147-149, 150-154, 158 (*see also* epistemology and ethics; Goethe and ecological model of knowledge; Goethe on intuitive judgment)
  and Herder, 4-5, 55, 85, 86-89, 96, 100-103, 250n10, 260n5, 265n27, 271n17
  in (and on) the history of science, 95-100, 261n14, 261n15, 264n15, 264n19, 265n23, 270n14
  on human-animal continuity, 96-100
  and Humboldt (Alexander), 178-185, 187, 193, 195, 203, 209, 210, 212, 225, 240, 243, 247, 249n3, 249n7, 249n11, 261n11, 264n15, 276n10, 276n11, 277n13, 277n15, 277n21, 277n22
  and Humboldt (Wilhelm), 166, 180-181, 277n13
  on intuitive judgment, 10-12, 105, 117, 133, 148-169, 262n3, 269n4, 269n7, 270n12, 271n18, 276n10
  and Kant, 14, 52, 53, 100, 187-188, 190-192, 263n6, 265n26, 269n4, 269n6, 270n16, 278n26, 278n27, 278n31, 278n32
  and Linnaeus, 109, 154-155, 160, 270n11, 272n31
  on metamorphosis, 10, 110, 117-123, 127-129, 138, 142-144, 155, 162, 182-183, 188, 225, 270n11, 271n16, 278n22
  methodology, 91, 96, 99-102, 104-110, 115-118, 124-125, 130-132, 146-156, 163, 165-166, 168, 170, 174, 178, 189-190, 262n3
  and morphology, 6, 103, 113, 159, 189-190, 270n14, 271n17, 271n22
  and Newton, 272n31, 273n32, 273n33, 273n34
  and philosophy, 11, 116-117, 124, 130, 148, 163, 264n17

on plants, 10, 107–109, 112–116, 117–131, 136–144, 154–155, 158, 160, 162, 189–191, 225, 265n31, 271n22, 278n22 (see also *Urpflanze*; *Urphänomen*)
and poetry, 106, 136, 138–144, 262n5, 266n33, 266n36, 268n41, 268n42
and rational empiricism, 146, 163–166, 270n15
as romantic empiricist, 3–6, 9–12, 91, 146, 250n16
and Rome, 111, 263n9, 263n10
and Schiller, 11, 107, 115–118, 124, 127–130, 146–147, 154, 157, 163–166, 264n17, 270n15
and science, 95–100, 103, 105, 112–116, 126, 133, 145, 151, 154, 157–159, 166–171, 182, 261n14, 262n5, 264n19, 270n14, 271n22, 273n31, 273n36
on seeing, 11, 85, 129, 131, 194, 244 (*see also* eye of the mind; perceptual thinking)
and *sehen lernen*, 115
and Spinoza, 265n27, 269n3, 269n4, 269n6
on *Steigerung* (intensification), 120, 143, 263n13, 268n41
travels to and in Italy, 107–108, 110–114, 131, 189, 263n7, 263n9
on *Typus* (animal type), 98–103, 117, 134, 166, 181, 262n19, 263n12, 270n14 (*see also* archetype)
on *Urpflanze* (archetypal plant, primal plant, symbolic plant), 117, 162, 263n8, 265n31, 265n21, 271n19 (*see also* Goethe: on plants; metamorphosis)
Goldstein, Amanda Jo, 268n1
Goy, Ina, 271n19

Haeckel, Ernst, 176, 274n2
Haldane, J. S. 278n28
Haller, Albrecht von, 90, 260n8
Hamann, Johann Georg, 58, 96, 256n11
Hardenberg, Friedrich von (Novalis), 4, 250n12
harmony
between animals and their worlds, 259n43

in cognitive faculties, 25, 79
in nature, 213, 241
pre-established, 259
in self, 214
Heinz, Marion, 3, 259n40
Herder, Johann Gottfried
on animal languages, 67–77, 83
on animal worlds (animal circle), 6, 9, 60, 66, 70–75, 84, 92, 258n30, 277n11
and Buffon, 54–60, 84, 86, 256n11
critique of abstraction, 55–56, 58–59, 61, 69, 83, 85, 95, 246
and ecology, 6, 55, 85
and empiricism, 82, 259n40
and epistemology, 9, 55, 76–82
on force, 59, 87–89, 91, 102, 257n16, 258n36, 260n3, 260n5, 260n10
on form (versus force), 85, 86–88, 91, 98–103, 258n32 (see also *Hauptform*)
and geography, 6, 61, 257n16, 259n60
and Goethe (*see* Goethe and Herder)
and the *Hauptform,* 9, 85, 91–96, 98–103, 154, 194
and hermeneutics, 62–67, 256n5, 257n17, 257n18
on human languages, 66–76, 82–84, 258n27, 259n42, 261n10
and Humboldt (Alexander), 177, 183–184, 193–194, 207, 210, 242, 258n31, 276n11, 282n1
and Kant, 4, 9, 28–29, 33–36, 256n8, 259n39
methodology, 53–61, 70–72, 85, 86–89, 91, 255n5, 258n32, 260n10
and naturalism, 82–85, 256n8
on "nature" 55–56, 82–85
use of analogy, 54–55, 74, 76–88, 91–95
hermeneutic/hermeneutics, 5, 60, 84–85, 102, 255n5, 261n10. *See also* interpretation
Hindrichs, Gunnar, 153
Holdrege, Craig, 261n17
Die Horen (journal), 212, 261n11
Humboldt, Alexander von
on abstraction, 195
and aesthetic education, 212–214 (*see also* Humboldt and Schiller)
and art, 179, 196, 214–223, 285n31 (see also *Naturwahrheit*)

Humboldt, Alexander von (*cont.*)
  on botany, 193, 275n7, 282n47
  and Caldas, 210, 275n7
  on colonialism, 177, 239, 286n32
  and Creole scientists, 210, 275n7
  on description versus history of nature, 195, 279n34
  on destruction of nature and culture, 2, 177, 239–243, 286n32
  and ecology, 176, 178–179, 183–185, 209–211, 274n1, 274n2, 275n6, 276n7
  and empiricism, 179–180
  and geography, 183, 187, 194–195, 210, 213, 275n7, 280n34, 282n46, 282n47
  and Goethe (*see* Goethe and Humboldt)
  and Herder (*see* Herder and Humboldt)
  and history of art, 11, 217–223
  and history of science, 11, 217–218
  and indigenous cultures, 176, 231, 239
  and Kant, 177, 182, 183, 196, 204–206, 210, 218, 279n32, 283n5
  on landscape painting, 179, 183, 196–197, 210, 215, 219, 221–224, 227–230
  on literature, 179, 221–223, 224–225
  methodology, 179–180, 192, 195–197, 218, 276n9 (see also *denkende Betrachtung*)
  and morphology, 182, 209
  and *Naturgemälde*, 12, 215, 216, 224, 282n2
  on physiognomy (of nature and of plants), 6, 192–195, 197–198, 206–209, 277n11, 280n36
  on plant form (*Urformen*), 183–184, 192–210, 213, 225, 230, 278n22, 280n34, 280n35, 280n39, 281n41, 281n42
  on poetry versus painting, 227–230
  and rational empiricism, 180, 238, 276n9
  rationalism, critique of, 178–180
  as romantic empiricist, 3, 11–12
  and Schiller, 180, 212–216, 218, 223, 227–231, 237–238, 241, 242, 261n11, 276n7, 283n6
  and science, 194, 212–216, 217–218, 237–240, 278n22, 284n25, 285n31
Humboldt, Wilhelm von, 166, 180–181, 226–227, 277n13

Humboldtian science, 284n25
Humboldtian writing, 285n25

idealism, 1, 4, 150, 250n12, 262n3
imagination, 9, 12, 133, 215, 217, 223, 232, 244, 246–247, 253n31, 269n9
  engaging the reader through the, 118, 142, 215, 225, 233
  epistemic significance of, 110, 133, 142, 156, 183
  work with sensibility and reason, 25, 77, 81–82, 246–247
interpretation, 60, 62, 66, 95. *See also* hermeneutics
  of nature, 33, 54–55
intuitive judgment (*anschauende Urteilskraft*), 10–12, 105, 117–118, 133, 148–156, 158–160, 262n3, 269n6, 269n7, 270n12, 271n18, 276n10
intuitive understanding (*intuitiver Verstand*), 17, 49–52, 172, 269n3, 269n4, 269n6, 278n26
Irmscher, Hans-Dietrich, 250n10, 252n19

Kant, Immanuel
  on analogy, 23–28
  on analogy between art and nature, 8–19, 16–19, 22
  critique of analogy, 28, 33–36
  and Goethe (*see* Goethe and Kant)
  and Herder (*see* Herder and Kant)
  and Humboldt (*see* Humboldt and Kant)
  and intuitive understanding, 17, 49–52, 172, 269n3, 269n4, 269n6, 278n26
  on matter, 36–38, 90
  on organization in nature, 8–9, 13–14, 22, 27, 36–48, 51, 53–54
  as romantic empiricist, 3, 6–8, 13, 52
  and science, 28, 35–37, 43
  on symbolic (analogical) cognition, 22–28, 43, 251n6, 252n11
Klee, Paul, 284n17
knowledge
  and ethics, 6, 149, 167–168, 171, 174–175, 245–246, 272n27, 273n36, 274n38
  as responsive and situated, 6, 147–148, 173
  unity of (*see* unity)

Kohn, Eduardo, 286n34
Korsgaard, Christine, 274n37

Leibniz, Gottfried Wilhelm, 87, 259n40
Lessing, Gotthold Ephraim, 223–226, 284n15
life/living beings (biological), 37, 113, 117, 172, 174, 180, 183–188, 190–191, 196, 203–211, 225–226, 260n5, 261n17, 268n38, 271n17, 276n7, 278n24, 278n28, 279n32. *See also* organism
life force, 86–87, 261n11. *See also* *Bildungstrieb*
Lifschitz, Avi, 67, 257n24, 258n27
lived experience, 12, 179, 217, 222, 236, 239, 247, 284n10, 285n31
living depiction, 216, 219–220, 226, 232, 237
living form, 225, 271n17, 284n16. *See also* form; living depiction; poetic form
literary tools and methods, 54–55, 85, 215, 223–224. *See also* hermeneutics; interpretation

mechanism/mechanical (mechanical principles), 14, 19–21, 36–46, 48, 49–52, 53, 89, 110, 128, 168, 172, 186, 251n4, 251n5, 252n11, 253n36, 254n37, 254n40, 254n47
mechanical explanation, 45–47, 52, 89–90, 185, 255n50
mechanically inexplicable, 36, 42, 44, 48, 252n11, 254n43, 254n44
Mensch, Jennifer, 259n39
metamorphosis, 10, 110, 117–123, 127–129, 138, 142–144, 155, 162, 182–183, 188, 225, 270n11, 271n16, 278n22
method/methodology, 1, 3, 5–9, 11, 28, 32, 35, 52, 55, 57, 60, 70, 85, 86–89, 91, 95–96, 99–102, 104–110, 115–118, 124–125, 130–132, 146–156, 163, 165–166, 168, 170, 174, 178, 179–180, 189–190, 192, 195–197, 218, 250n12, 255n5, 260n10, 262n3, 276n9. *See also* approach
Millán, Elizabeth, 250n11
Molnár, Géza von, 278n26
mood, 12, 222, 227–230, 232, 234, 237, 283n8. *See also* feeling

morphological poetry, 262n5, 266n36, 268n42
Morton, Timothy, 246, 273n35
Muthu, Sankar, 2

national parks' movement, 275n6
Naturwahrheit, 219, 221, 283n7. *See also* truth to nature
necessity
  in knowledge, 14, 95–96, 99, 101–103, 116, 126, 146, 165, 253n36, 270n15
  in nature, 14, 18, 21, 39, 49–50, 86, 99, 101–103, 116, 125, 180, 245
  See also apodictic certainty; proper science
Newton, Isaac, 55, 87, 89–90, 169–170, 253n36, 260n4, 272n31, 273n32, 273n33, 273n34
Nisbet, H. B. 260n10, 269n6
Nussbaum, Martha, 273n37

objectivity, 179, 220
  in science, 237, 283n7
organism, 53, 79, 85–86, 93, 98, 113, 138, 148, 166, 176–195, 204–206, 252n11, 258n31, 258n33, 261n17, 277n22, 278n28, 278n30, 279n31, 282n44
  as cause and effect of itself, 39, 42–43, 186, 192, 204
  and environment, 85–86, 93, 98, 148, 166, 176–211, 277n22, 278n28, 278n30, 279n30, 279n31 (see also environment; Herder on animal worlds [animal circle])
  as expressive, 98, 194, 230, 261n17
  as theme in variation, 21, 121, 123, 129
  unity of, 39, 116, 144, 185, 268n42
  See also organization in nature
organization in nature, 8, 9, 13, 14, 27, 36, 41, 43, 51, 82, 168, 186, 188, 190, 193, 202–205, 260n6, 269n9, 278n30. *See also* life/living beings
organs of perception, 103, 105, 126, 162, 180, 185

passive, 73, 89–90, 137, 155, 170, 186–187, 191, 205, 210
perceptual capacities/organs, 11, 106, 111, 116, 258n30. *See also* organs of perception

perceptual thinking, 147, 156, 162, 180. *See also* eye of the mind; intuitive judgment
phenomenological, 102
phenomenon, phenomena, 2, 9, 11, 48, 53–54, 56, 60, 69, 73, 75–76, 84, 87–89, 91–92, 101–102, 105, 116, 130, 132–135, 141, 143, 146, 153, 155–158, 161–174, 179, 189–191, 195–196, 224, 227, 234–236, 247, 270n13, 270n14, 273n34, 286n31
physiognomy, 192, 194–195
  of nature, 6, 194, 198, 206, 207, 209
  of plants, 193, 195, 197–198, 207, 209, 277n11, 278n22, 280n36
play drive (*Spieltrieb*), 284n16
Plumwood, Val, 245, 246, 273n35
poetic form, 138, 142–145, 228, 262n5, 264n20
preformation, 90, 260n8
proper science (*eigentliche Wissenschaft*), 37, 95, 253n36, 255n50
purpose
  external, 40, 47–48, 187–190
  heuristic use of, 39–41
  as intention, 47–48
  internal, 48–49, 51, 188–190
  in machines, 47
  in nature, 16–18, 22, 252n11
  See also purposiveness
purposiveness
  external, 40, 42, 185–188, 190, 278n24
  and formal causality, 41, 254n41, 254n42
  Goethe's critique of, 188
  internal, 40–41, 48–49, 185–188, 190, 254n41, 254n42
  practical, 16, 17, 47

rational empiricism, 146, 163–165, 167n10, 180, 238, 270n15
rationalism, 5, 146, 163–165, 179, 245, 259n40, 269n6
receptive, receptivity, 113, 147, 155, 208, 242
reflecting (reflective) judgment, 8–9, 15–17, 21–23, 25–27, 44–45, 54, 152, 154, 187, 254n17, 255n1, 255n2
Regan, Tom, 272n27, 273n37

Reill, Peter Hans, 249n7, 255n3
reine Phänomen (pure phenomenon), 146, 156. See also *Urphänomen*
reiterating/repeating forms, 93–94, 98, 100, 194, 200–202, 229, 268n42, 281n42. *See also* form
remaining with the phenomena, 2, 54, 60, 88, 103, 156, 165, 169–170, 178–179, 189, 195, 243. *See also* abstraction (critique of)
responsibility (obligation)
  as emergent, 174
  in environmental ethics, 167–168
  epistemological, 171
  of the knower, 11, 55, 88, 138, 148, 162, 171, 174
  moral, 167–168, 171–174, 175
  of the reader, 138
  toward nature, 85, 148–149, 174–175
Richards, Robert J. 99, 250n9, 260n9, 261n15, 270n14
Rigby, Kate, 250n15, 256n5
Roe, Shirley, 260n8
romantic empiricism, 1–3, 5–8, 13–14, 98, 105, 146, 245, 250n14, 250n15
romantic imperative, 4–5
romanticism, 1, 3–4, 249n3, 249n7, 250n14, 250n15
Rousseau, Jean-Jacques, 67–69, 72, 83, 220, 257n22, 257n24, 258n27, 258n28, 286n32

Sachs, Aaron, 275n6
Schelling, Friedrich, 3, 4, 274n4
schematization, 22, 251n6. *See also* symbolic cognition
Schiller, Friedrich, 11, 107, 115–118, 124, 127–130, 146–147, 154, 157, 163–166, 180, 212–216, 218, 223, 225–231, 237–238, 241, 242, 261n11, 264n17, 270n15, 276n7, 283n6, 284n16, 285n29, 285n30
Schlegel, Friedrich, 3, 4–5, 250n12, 250n16
Schleiermacher, Friedrich, 4
science (*Wissenschaft*)
  and abstraction, 116 (see also abstraction [critique of])
  as active contemplation, 169

aesthetic, 1, 14, 212–214, 238, 285n31
    (*see also* aesthetic science)
  and analogy (*see* analogy)
  and art, 4, 12, 112, 114, 126, 145, 215
  Buffon's contributions to, 29, 32–33
  the English term for, 251n20
  and ethics, 105, 167, 171–174, 216, 273n36
  expansive approach to, 6, 212–214
  experimental, 32
  feminist philosophy of, 174
  Goethe's conception of, 52, 151, 154, 159, 166–170, 171–174, 262n5, 271n22, 273n31, 273n36, 278n22
  Goethe's contributions to, 4–5, 97–103, 113, 159, 261n14, 264n19, 270n14
  Herder's conception of, 52, 89, 91
  Herder's contributions to, 4–5
  Humboldt's conception of, 52, 176, 178–182, 192–194, 212, 217–218, 237–240, 276n54, 278n22, 285n31
  Humboldt's contributions to, 4–5, 11
  Kant's conception of, 35–37, 43–49, 52 (*see also* proper science)
  Kant's contributions to, 4–5
  and mathematics, 30–32, 37, 133–134, 170, 253n36, 265n28, 265n29
  See also proper science
scientific works of art, 12, 236. *See also* aesthetic science
sense, 12, 62, 78, 164, 212–215, 217, 228, 233–240, 246–247. *See also* aesthetic; feeling
sense drive (*Stofftrieb*), 214, 284n16
senses, the, 1, 70–71, 74–75, 78–81, 111, 131, 133–134, 146, 215, 217, 220, 262n4, 281n43
sensibility, 9, 12–13, 104, 130, 146, 168, 178, 244, 245–247
sensibly given, 130, 135, 154
Sepper, Dennis L. 273n32, 273n33, 273n36
Shakespeare, 62–65, 96
Singer, Peter, 273n37
South America, 176, 181, 184, 192, 199, 201, 214, 235, 239, 275n7, 283n9
Staël-Holstein, Germaine de, 250n14
static form, 10, 11, 31, 109, 114, 136, 158–159, 210, 216, 226, 262n9, 270n14, 271n17
Steigerwald, Joan, 278n22

Stone, Christopher D. 272n29
structure (*Bau, Bild, Bildung, Gestalt*), 7–8, 19–21, 25, 29, 36–43
  and symbolic cognition, 25–28
  See also form; transforming form
Sturm und Drang, 4, 96
subjective
  conditions of knowledge, 1
  experience, 218
  invention, 99
  versus objective, 12, 221
subjectivity, 179, 264n17
Sultan, Sonia, 178, 196
symbol, 17, 23–25, 215, 251n8, 252n9, 252n11, 278n26. *See also* Kant: symbolic (analogical) cognition
symbolic plant, 127, 265n21
system
  of experience, 17
  language as, 73
  Linnaeus', 29
  of nature, 8, 14–15, 32, 86, 94, 169, 186
  of philosophy, 28
systematic
  approach to nature, 1, 3, 33, 102, 169
  philosophy, 3, 58, 250n12
  unity, 32

teleological judgment
  and the analogy with art, 22, 44, 48–49, 50–51, 53
  antinomy of, 43–48, 50–53, 186, 254n46, 254n47
  as form of reflective judgment, 19, 22
  Goethe and, 188, 278n27
  as indispensable, 14, 19, 45
  and intuitive understanding, 49–51
  Kant's ambivalence toward, 52, 54, 186, 255n3, 260n6
  as non-explanatory, 23, 46–48, 52
  as problematic, 22–23, 46
  scientific status of, 14, 43, 44, 51–52
  structure of, 22–27, 43
  use/significance of, 36, 39, 46, 47–48, 51, 252n11
transforming form, 119, 121–122, 154, 161, 206. *See also* form; living form; metamorphosis

Troll, Carl, 281n42
truth to nature, 219–224, 232, 234, 237, 270n11. See also *Naturwahrheit*

Uexküll, Jakob von, 258n30
understanding, 1, 13, 17, 25, 40, 45–46, 49, 101, 110, 134, 152, 238. *See also* intuitive understanding
  categories of the, 13, 15–16, 26, 46, 49, 130, 154
  discursive, 17, 49, 51, 151–152, 255n49
  education of the, 175 (*see also* education)
  and explanation, 52, 91, 101–103
  and feeling, 12, 236, 238
  hermeneutic approach to, 54–55, 65–66, 133, 154, 257n17
  and imagination, 9, 25
  laws of, 15–16, 20, 43, 251n5
  as legislative, 13, 15
  and sensibility, 9, 13, 104, 244–247
unity
  abstract, 94
  in artwork, 49, 61–66, 126, 138, 231, 257n20, 264n17, 268n42, 285n31
  of cognitive faculties, 9, 12, 77–80, 82, 244, 247, 259n40 (*see also* harmony)
  in diversity, 5, 9, 16, 60, 108, 245
  hermeneutic, 54, 61–66
  integrated, 8, 21, 49, 53, 102, 191, 193, 205
  internally differentiated, 126, 155
  and intuitive judgment, 148
  of machine, 41, 47, 48, 50, 172, 254n43 (*see also* purposiveness)
  material, 37–39, 50
  moral, 214, 285n29 (*see also* harmony)
  in the multiplicity, 14, 57, 94, 116, 118, 161, 165, 176, 183, 185

  of nature, 9, 10, 16–19, 21, 32, 37, 50, 54, 60, 72, 79, 89, 100, 145, 158, 176, 183, 185
  as nonlinear/nonsequential, 10, 59, 60–66, 119, 134–136, 138, 257n20, 278n30
  of organism, 9, 39, 47, 50, 53, 98, 102, 109, 116, 127, 144, 186, 268n42 (*see also* form; organism; organization in nature; structure)
  and science, 57, 169
  of self, 238, 240–241, 244, 285n25
  systematic (*see* system/systematic)
  See also form; structure
Urphänomen, 105, 148, 154–166, 169, 174, 270n11

Valencia (Tacarigua), Lake, 176–177, 178, 209, 240, 275n6
vitalism, 249n7, 271n17

Walls, Laura Dassow, 274n1
Weimar, 107, 127, 182, 263n6, 277n15, 277n16
"whole as such" 49–51. *See also* unity of organism
Wolff, Caspar Friedrich, 90, 128–130, 155–160, 260n8, 261n11
Wolff, Christian, 30, 252n19
Wolffian, 30, 146
Wolzogen, Caroline von, 180, 212
Wulf, Andrea, 3

Zammito, John, 250n8, 251n19, 251n2, 252n12, 252n14, 255n4, 256n11, 260n5
Zuckert, Rachel, 250n18, 254n37, 254n44, 256n8

Printed in the USA
CPSIA information can be obtained
at www.ICGtesting.com
CBHW060832291124
18108CB00008B/25/J